After Auschwitz

JOHNS HOPKINS JEWISH STUDIES

Sander Gilman and Steven T. Katz, Series Editors

Books by Richard L. Rubenstein

After Auschwitz, First Edition
The Religious Imagination
Morality and Eros
My Brother Paul
Power Struggle
The Cunning of History
The Age of Triage
Approaches to Auschwitz (John K. Roth, co-author)

After Auschwitz

HISTORY, THEOLOGY, AND CONTEMPORARY JUDAISM

SECOND EDITION

Richard L. Rubenstein

THE JOHNS HOPKINS UNIVERSITY PRESS

Baltimore and London

The first edition was published, with the subtitle *Radical Theology and Contemporary Judaism,* by The Bobbs-Merrill Company, Inc., in 1966.

The Johns Hopkins University Press
2715 North Charles Street
Baltimore, Maryland 21218-4319
The Johns Hopkins Press Ltd., London

Library of Congress Cataloging-in-Publication Data

Rubenstein, Richard L.
   After Auschwitz : history, theology, and contemporary Judaism / Richard L. Rubenstein. — 2nd ed.
     p. cm. — (Johns Hopkins Jewish studies)
   Includes bibliographical references and index.
   ISBN 0-8018-4284-0 (hc). — ISBN 0-8018-4285-9 (pb)
    1. Judaism—Doctrines. 2. Judaism—20th century. 3. Holocaust (Jewish theology) 4. Holocaust, Jewish (1939-1945)—Influence.
5. Jewish-Arab relations—Religious aspects—Judaism. 6. Zionism and Judaism. I. Title. II. Series.
   BM601.R795 1992
   296.3—dc20   91-34956

A catalog record for this book is available from the British Library.

To John K. Roth
and
Michael G. Berenbaum

Contents

Preface

If I were to characterize the fundamental difference between the spirit infusing the original edition of *After Auschwitz* and that of the current edition, it would be the difference between the spirit of opposition and revolt, which was an almost inevitable consequence of my initial, essentially uncharted attempt to come to terms theologically with the greatest single trauma in all of Jewish history, and the spirit of synthesis and reconciliation which, I trust, can be discerned in the current edition. The fundamental insights of the original have been retained but with a greater degree of empathy for those who have reaffirmed traditional Jewish faith in the face of the Holocaust.

No person writing about the religious significance of contemporary history can rest content with what he or she has written at a particular moment in time. As history is an ongoing process, so too is theological writing concerning history. The first edition of *After Auschwitz* was published in 1966, twenty-one years after the end of World War II and a year before the fateful Six-Day War between Israel and its Arab neighbors. Much has happened within Judaism and to the Jewish people since 1966. For a long time friends and colleagues have urged me to consider revising the first edition. The present volume constitutes that revision.

The fundamental problem addressed in the first edition was that of defining and responding to the most severe crisis of disconfirmation faced by Jewish religious thought since the fall of Jerusalem in 70 C.E., namely, the systematic destruction of the Jews of Europe during World War II. In addition, I felt compelled to inquire into the theological significance of the reestablishment after two millennia of a sovereign Jewish state in the land of Israel and that state's never-ending war of survival against hostile neighbors. In reality, the two events are inextricably connected. Creation of the state was in fact the most important Jewish response to the Holocaust. Because the ultimate objective of Israel's neighbors remains the total destruction of the State of Israel and the elimination of its Jewish citizens as a demographic presence in the region, the Holocaust and Israel remain inextricably bound to each other.

My interpretation of the Holocaust and the return to Israel in the first edition of *After Auschwitz* was initially regarded as a distinctively Jewish expression of death-of-God theology. Indeed, I saw it as such myself. Understandably, it was the object of considerable controversy. The question of the meaning of the "death of God" remains a major issue in both editions, but over the years the first edition has come to be seen less as an expression of death-of-God theology than as the initial expression of contemporary Jewish Holocaust theology. The current edition emphasizes Holocaust theology to an even greater extent than did its predecessor.

Even in the first edition I carefully explained that the "death of God" was not an actual event that had happened to God. The language of religion was used more to make a statement about humanity and the secular culture of modernity than about God. That culture provided the moral preconditions for the implementation of the Holocaust. As my thinking developed, I came to view the Holocaust in its larger historical context. Consequently my interests tended to move back and forth between the study of the Holocaust and research into the kind of world in which such a state-sponsored program of mass extermination could take place. Sociology and political theory became as important as psychoanalysis for the understanding of historical events and religious phenomena. Already present in the first edition, these interests are more developed in the current edition.

The first edition was subtitled "Radical Theology and Contemporary Judaism"; the current edition's subtitle is "History, Theology, and Contemporary Judaism." The difference suggests a difference in emphasis. Consistent with its subtitle, the first edition was originally viewed as the most radical of all contemporary Jewish theological writings. Nevertheless there was a strongly conservative element in the book: unable to defend traditional religious *belief,* I attempted a functional defense of traditional religious *institutions and practices,* that is, a defense in terms of the human needs religion met. Men and women need *rites de passage* at such moments as the birth of a child, marriage, death, and the changing of the seasons. Other rituals also fulfill important functions. To dismiss such needs as a consequence of psychological regression or the acting out of obsessional neurosis is not a serious position. No two persons have the same ritual needs, nor does any person have the same ritual needs at every stage in the timetable of life. Still, the needs are there and have to be met whether or not a person finds traditional belief credible.

One of the most debatable aspects of the first edition was its affirmation of a form of Jewish paganism as an appropriate response to the Holocaust and the birth of Israel. Although this position is modified in the current edition, I continue to emphasize the immanence rather than the radical transcendence of God. Moreover, as a result of my study of and direct observation of both religious life and social reality in the lands of Confucian and Buddhist inheritance, especially Japan and Korea, the idea I expressed in the first edition, that God can best be spoken of as "the Holy Nothingness" has been strengthened. Paradoxically, my respect for the idea of the covenant and faith in the transcendence of God is deeper than it was in 1966. Events in Israel, both religious and political, have demonstrated that some forms of Jewish paganism, that is, the worship of the God or gods of place and space, are potentially disastrous for Judaism and the Jewish people. In contrast to apocalyptic Jewish messianism, which I view as a disguised form of Jewish earth paganism, I have stressed a form of nature religion in which *all men and women understand themselves as children of Earth.* The renewed contact of an important segment of the Jewish people with the land of Israel has contributed greatly to my appreciation of nature religion. Nevertheless, too rigid a commitment to *all of the land of Israel,* especially when combined with apocalyptic messianism, can lead the State of Israel into unnecessarily dangerous confrontations with its Arab neighbors and with international Islam.

When the first edition was published no post–World War II political leader had threatened to gas the Israelis with the German-made poison gas in his possession, as has Saddam Hussein of Iraq. There were, of course, threats to Israel's existence, but they have multiplied in seriousness since 1966. At that time, the State of Israel appeared to be the Jewish world's great consolation for the terrible losses incurred during World War II. Today Israel's neighbors are more likely to make threats of annihilation in Arabic than in English, but the unremitting threat ultimately to do away with Israel and the Israelis is greater and more dangerous than it was in 1966. Nor is it any consolation that a decisively defeated Israel would in all likelihood make its destroyers pay dearly. It is difficult to foresee a peaceful resolution of these ongoing conflicts.

While the writing of the current edition was in its final stages, the bloody Temple Mount clash of October 8, 1990, took place. That clash illuminated the nonnegotiable character of the ultimate, if not the immediate, conflict between Israel and its neighbors, as well as between Judaism and Islam. Contemporary Orthodox Jewish messianists are convinced they have an unconditional religious obligation to rebuild Judaism's Holy Temple on Jerusalem's Temple Mount. Of necessity, this activity would involve the destruction of the most sacred Islamic holy places, after Mecca and Medina, which were originally constructed by the tenth Caliph 'Abd al-Malik ibn Marwan. When he built the Dome of the Rock (688–91 c.e.) on what has traditionally been regarded by Jews as the site of the Temple's "holy of holies," he redefined in Islamic terms Jerusalem's sacred space and Islam's relation to Judaism. In spite of Islam's original seizure of the Temple site, no sane Israeli leader could today permit the destruction of the mosques. Nevertheless, the contradictory claims of Judaism and Islam concerning the Temple Mount and the City of Jerusalem symbolize the enduring conflict that bars the way to permanent peace. Thus, the image of the Holocaust continues to cast its dark shadow over Jewish thought and Jewish experience.

The first edition contained little, if anything, about the Palestinians or Islam. There is a great deal about these subjects in the current edition. Nine of the fifteen chapters in the first edition have been eliminated from the current edition, which has sixteen chapters, ten of them new to *After Auschwitz*.[1] The core material has been retained. In a few cases chapters were eliminated because they seemed dated. In most cases the new selection reflects issues within Jewish life which in my opinion are likely to be most enduring.

Major changes in my life and career have also affected the way *After Auschwitz* has been edited and modified. In 1966, although I was academically trained at the Jewish Theological Seminary and Harvard, my audience consisted primarily of members of the Jewish community. As a rabbi serving Jewish students at the University of Pittsburgh and Carnegie-Mellon University, I was also an active member of Pittsburgh's Jewish community, which was large enough to support a full complement of Jewish religious institutions for all three branches of American Judaism.

It is not without significance that the paperback of the first edition was published by the college division of Bobbs-Merrill rather than by the trade division. The publisher had determined that the primary market for the book was in college, university, and seminary courses, where Jewish readers are in a minority, rather than on the paperback racks of commercial booksellers, where intelligent Jewish laypersons were more likely to find the book. Thus, the original publisher anticipated that at least as many, if not more, non-Jews than Jews would read the book. Twenty-five years later the first edition remains in print, and, I believe, the publisher's marketing judgment has proven essentially correct.

As a result of the publication of both the first edition of *After Auschwitz* and *The Religious Imagination* (Bobbs-Merrill, 1968), I became virtually unemployable within the Jewish community or in any community where the Jewish community had substantial influence. Had I been a sociologist or a historian, the book might have had a less hostile reception. Fortunately, as I was being eased out of my Pittsburgh position, an academic career opened up for me. The Department of Religion at Florida State University in Tallahassee offered and I accepted the position of Professor of Religion. That has been the most fortunate career decision of my entire life. Because Tallahassee was far removed from any large center of Jewish life, it was possible for the university to hire me. Tallahassee offered me two things that were indispensable to further personal growth: a proper academic environment in which I could pursue my theological vocation, and a calm space in which I could study, think, and reflect without being drawn into unnecessary personal or religious controversy. In addition, in 1972 and 1975 the university sent me to its study center in Florence, Italy, for two six-month periods. Elected as a Fellow of the National Humanities Institute at Yale University for the academic year 1976–77, I was able to design a course on the Holocaust there which was later funded by the National Endowment for the Humanities as a model course to be taught at Florida State University. Because of the very small number of Jewish students at Florida State University I had not previously taught a course on the Holocaust, thinking there would be insufficient student interest. This was a mistake. Every year the Holocaust course is well attended by students who come predominantly from conservative southern Protestant homes.

John K. Roth of Claremont-McKenna College was also a fellow at the National Humanities Institute during 1976–77 and also designed a course on the Holocaust. We became and remain close friends. The work we did at Yale became the basis for *Approaches to Auschwitz* (John Knox Press, 1987), which we co-authored. This book is dedicated to John and to Dr. Michael Berenbaum, to whom I express my appreciation below.

In 1977 at the spring commencement, Florida State University conferred upon me its highest academic honor, Distinguished Professor of the Year. My rank became Distinguished Professor of Religion, a title that was subsequently changed to Robert O. Lawton Distinguished Professor of Religion. One of the benefits of the Robert O. Lawton Distinguished

Professorship is a greatly reduced teaching load. I have always enjoyed teaching and consider those former students who have remained in touch with me part of my extended family. Still, the enhanced opportunity the university has given me for research and study is the most priceless gift an academic institution can bestow upon members of its faculty. I am deeply grateful to the university for this gift, especially in connection with the current edition of *After Auschwitz*. The task of completing this volume was long and arduous. It would have been infinitely more so without the university's support.

Because of my persistent concern with the kind of world in which the Holocaust took place, I developed an ever stronger interest in public policy issues. In 1981 I became president of the Washington-based Washington Institute for Values in Public Policy, a position I held until 1991. Through the institute's many seminars, conferences, and lectures, as well as the direct contact it offered me with some of the country's political leaders and public policy experts, I became better acquainted with the complexity of the more difficult problems confronting the United States than would have been the case absent the Washington experience. This continuing learning experience has indeed been enlightening. For that opportunity I am indebted to Mr. Neil A. Salonen, Director of the Institute, and the institute's staff.

A principal, though by no means exclusive, focus of my work in Washington has been foreign affairs with special emphasis on the Pacific Rim. In the preface to the first edition of *After Auschwitz* I wrote of the influence of intellectual movements of European origins on my thought. That influence remains evident in the current edition. Nevertheless, in the past twelve years I have spent more time in Asia than in Europe, principally though not exclusively in Japan. My experience in Japan prodded me to reflect on the *functional truth* of the biblical idea of covenant. Unlike the United States with its biblical heritage, Japan has no way of incorporating the stranger within its midst. This attitude has roots in Shinto, Japan's indigenous religious tradition. Moreover, as former Prime Minister Yasuhiro Nakasone has indicated, the competition between Japan and the West has a religious as well as an economic dimension. Nakasone sees indigenous Japanese nature religion with its multitude of gods and its ancestor worship as superior to the biblical monotheism of the Judeo-Christian tradition.[2] I hope to write about this problem at greater length elsewhere.[3]

Today, much of the anger generated in the Jewish community by the first edition of *After Auschwitz* appears to have subsided. Although I have served as an academic teacher and researcher in a state university for the past twenty-one years, I have remained a member of the Rabbinical Assembly of America. Issues the book raised can now be discussed in a greater spirit of objectivity and reconciliation than was possible during the turbulent era of the late 1960s and early 1970s. For example, I was immensely gratified when the faculty of the Jewish Theological Seminary conferred upon me the degree of Doctor of Hebrew Letters, *honoris causa,* at the Seminary's Centennial Convocation on September 14, 1987. Both *After Auschwitz* and *The Religious Imagination* were explicitly mentioned in the degree citation. The event was gratifying and included the additional pleasure of the participation of my friend Harvey Cox, who has been supportive of my career at a number of critical junctures, as one of the convocation speakers.

Thanks are due to many people for making this volume possible. My deepest gratitude is for my wife, Dr. Betty Rogers Rubenstein, art historian and art critic. In addition to the companionship and profound emotional support she has given me throughout our marriage, she has used her very considerable literary and intellectual talents to help me to think through many of the issues that have been the subject matter of my scholarly and theological writings. Her help in criticizing and editing the entire manuscript of the current edition has been indispensable to the project.

I am also especially grateful to my former student and good friend of many years, Dr. Michael Berenbaum, Project Director of the United States Holocaust Memorial Museum, for encouraging me to take on this project. Without his persistent encouragement, it is doubtful that I would have done so. In addition to John K. Roth, this book is dedicated to him.

I wish to thank Dr. Alan Udoff of the Baltimore Hebrew University both for his encouragement and for introducing my work to the publisher, Johns Hopkins University Press.

I am indebted to my friend of long standing and colleague at Florida State, Professor Leo Sandon, Chairman of the Department of Religion, for his leadership of the department and his support of my work over the years. He has worked to create a harmonious atmosphere in which both good teaching and good research are constantly encouraged.

No one can work in a vacuum, and the fact that I have had good and helpful departmental colleagues has been indispensable to my research and writing. A special debt of thanks is due to the department secretary, Maureen Jackson, whose unfailing helpfulness has been a wonderful resource to me and to all the members of the department.

I wish to thank Eric Halpern, Editor-in-Chief of the Johns Hopkins University Press, for assuming the responsibility of guiding the current volume through production and for his helpful suggestions on what to include and exclude. I also wish to thank Carol Zimmerman and the staff of the press for its role in bringing the work of publication and distribution to fruition. A special word of thanks is due Terry Schutz for her thoughtful and careful copy editing of the manuscript. Finally, thanks are due to Professor Steven Katz, co-editor of the Johns Hopkins Jewish Series, and Professor Susannah Heschel for their support.

Preface to the First Edition

The Jewish community has experienced more monumental changes in the twentieth century than at any other time in its very long history. The uprooting involved in the emigration of millions of Jews from eastern Europe to the United States and Canada, the death camps, and the rebirth of Israel each represent enormous alterations. Any one of these by itself would have been enough to create extraordinary problems in Jewish life; their occurrence in relatively rapid succession has created religious and cultural problems of unparalleled magnitude. Furthermore, the upheavals must be seen in the context of a world radically in flux. The loss of the religious dimension in secular society, the rise of technopolis, the revolutions in mass media, and the loss of the remnants of a stable moral order after the wars of this century have all contributed to the unprecedented upheavals in Jewish life.

In the face of so radical a change, some men romantically turn to an irretrievable past, yearning for a restoration of its virtues. They see the terrible flaws of the present and are most persuasive in delineating them. Unfortunately it is easier to be aware of the evils of our time than it is to be quit of them. It is better to recognize the irretrievability of the past and to explore the potentialities inherent in the present, regardless of the radical hiatus with accepted traditions this may imply. I am convinced that this latter approach will be forced upon us if we do not accept it willingly. It would have been better had six million Jews not died, but they have. We cannot restore the religious world which preceded their demise nor can we ignore the fact that the catastrophe has had and will continue to have an extraordinary influence on Jewish life. Although Jewish history is replete with disaster, none has been so radical in its total import as the Holocaust. Our images of God, man, and the moral order have been permanently impaired. No Jewish theology will possess even a remote degree of relevance to contemporary Jewish life if it ignores the question of God and the death camps. That is *the question* for Jewish theology in our times. Regrettably most attempts at formulating a Jewish theology since World War II seem to have been written as if the two decisive events of our time for Jews, the death camps and the birth of Israel, had not taken place.

A religious community has some resemblance to a living organism. It is impossible savagely to rip out half of its substance without drastically affecting the surviving remnant. The first reaction to such a wounding must be shock and numbness. I do not believe the period of shock has entirely spent itself. It is only now that a tentative attempt can be made to assess the religious meaning of the events. This book represents one such attempt.

The time may come when the Jewish community can formulate its religious response as a community to what took place. That time remains a very distant prospect. For the foreseeable future, theological response will be private and subjective. Contemporary theology reveals less about God than it does about the kind of men we are. It is largely an anthropological discipline. Today's theologian, be he Jewish or Christian, has more in common with the poet and the creative artist than with the metaphysician and physical scientist. He communicates a very private subjectivity. Its relevance lies in the possibility that he may enable other men to gain insight and clarify their religious lives in the face of a common experience.

There are decided affinities between the theological insights expressed in this work and those of the contemporary Christian radical theologians. We have had some of the same teachers and we react to the same moment in history. Nevertheless, we react differently because our experience of the world has been so very different. I suspect that we part company most radically over what I regard as the Christian radical theologian's inability to take seriously the tragic vision. The tragic vision permeates these writings. How could it have been otherwise after Auschwitz?

The theologian writes out of his own experience and out of his own tradition. He addresses himself to all men. This work rests on the conviction that the experience of contemporary Jews has a relevance which exceeds the limits of the Jewish community. Many of the chapters in this book are the fruit of encounter and dialogue with Christians, both at home and overseas. I have been moved and altered by these encounters. It is my hope that what I have written will in some way contribute to the self-understanding of Christians as well as that of Jews in our times.

There was a time, not very long ago, when religious thinkers enjoyed the luxury of a stable institutional framework which allowed them to devote their time to research, study, and writing with few intrusions. Today's theologian enjoys no such calm. His ideas are as likely to be formulated while he is waiting for a jet as in the few moments he can spend undisturbed in his study. Although this work represents a relatively unified approach to the problems considered, it bears the marks of the highly mobile character of the theologian's vocation in contemporary America. The chapters in this book largely originated either as papers delivered at scholarly conferences, as university lectures, or as articles contributed to religious periodicals. I regard it as significant that they were written while I was a participant in the life of two secular universities, Harvard and the University of Pittsburgh.

I write as an American theologian, but Europe has had a very great impact on my thinking. This is evident in the very title I have chosen, *After Auschwitz*. It is also evident in the decisive influence upon my thinking of such intellectual movements of European origins as existentialism and psychoanalysis. During the time I was engaged in writing the papers in this book, I spent relatively long periods visiting France, Spain, Holland, and Germany. A brief visit to Poland had an overwhelming impact.

No man can write unaided. I have been helped, encouraged, and challenged by many good men and women. Above and beyond all other help I have received, that of my wife Betty was the indispensable ingredient for the completion of this task. My editor, Lawrence Grow of Bobbs-Merrill, guided this effort with a rare combination of theological insight and literary sensitivity. My secretary, Frances Hirsch, helped to type some of the manuscripts. The most important job she has done has been assisting me to meet my responsibilities in Pittsburgh over the last eight years.

I also want to acknowledge the encouragement, assistance, and influence of the following men and women: Rabbi Benjamin Kahn of the B'nai B'rith Hillel Foundations; Charles and Mary Merrill of Boston; Professor Rudolfo Cardona of the University of Pittsburgh; Henry Koerner of Pittsburgh; Doctor Ira Eisenstein of *The Reconstructionist*; Doctor Steven S. Schwarzschild of *Judaism*; Professor David Bakan of the University of

Chicago; Professor Harvey Cox of Harvard; Professor Thomas J. J. Altizer of Emory; Professor William Hamilton of Colgate-Rochester Theological Seminary; Professor Zalman Schacter of the University of Manitoba and the Advisory Board of the B'nai B'rith Hillel Foundation at the University of Pittsburgh.

Part I

THE ENCOUNTER OF
CHRISTIAN AND JEW

CHAPTER 1

The Dean and the Chosen People

In August 1961 I visited West Germany as the guest of the Bundes-presseamt, the Press and Information Office of the Federal Republic, to make a two-week survey of religious and cultural trends. It was my third visit in thirteen months. I was scheduled to arrive in Bonn by train from Amsterdam on Sunday, August 13. When I awoke that morning, I learned that the Communist East German government had suddenly closed the border between East and West Berlin. Because of the resulting interna-tional crisis, I delayed my journey for two days and then proceeded to Berlin to observe the events directly.

In Berlin the Bundespresseamt arranged a series of interviews for me with religious and cultural leaders. One encounter proved to be unfor-gettable, my interview with Probst (Dean) Heinrich Grüber of the Evan-gelical Church of East and West Berlin. No single encounter with another human being ever had so profound an effect upon my religious beliefs. In the apocalyptic atmosphere of Berlin at the moment of the initiation of the Berlin Wall, the Dean dramatized the consequences of accepting the normative Judeo-Christian theology of covenant and election in the light of the Holocaust. The interview pushed me to a theological point of no return: If I truly believed in God as the omnipotent author of the his-torical drama and in Israel as His Chosen People, I had no choice but to accept Dean Grüber's conclusion that Hitler unwittingly acted as God's agent in committing six million Jews to slaughter. I could not believe in such a God, nor could I believe in Israel as the Chosen People of God after Auschwitz.

As a matter of record, it is important to note that in the spring of 1965, Dean Grüber wrote to the American Protestant journal, *Christianity and Crisis,* denying the words I had ascribed to him. I replied that I did not bear the Dean any ill will or have any reason to falsify his words. The significance of the Dean's affirmation of God's lordship over the extermination camps is precisely that he was neither a Nazi nor an anti-Semite but a very decent human being who believed, without apparent reservation, in the traditional theological doctrines of the election of Israel and of God as the ultimate Author of the historical drama.

Before the Berlin visit I had spent the summer in Amsterdam with my family. I paid several visits to Amsterdam's Jewish Historical Museum, where I was especially impressed with an enlarged photograph of a Christmas party celebrated by the SS and their women. It was taken at Westerbroek Concentration Camp, where the Jews of Holland were collected before being shipped off to Auschwitz. The photograph epitomized much that Jews feel concerning Christianity's role in the Final Solution. Those responsible for the death of more than one hundred ten thousand Dutch Jews took time out of their grisly labors to celebrate the birth of their Jewish God in the very place where they were sealing the doom of every single Jew they could find. The plain fact is that those who murdered the Jews were, if not believing Christians, at least men and women whose only exposure to religion was derived from Christian sources. Furthermore, the people directly involved in the assembly-line extermination were not gutter riffraff. Very often, they had university or professional training. In some instances, former pastors were active leaders in the Nazi work of death.

Christian thinkers often point out that Nazism was an anti-Christian explosion that departed utterly from Christian morality. While this view is undeniably true, it glosses over the difference between anti-Christian motives that are rooted in a competing value system, such as Islam, and the anti-Christian explosion of Christians against their own value system. National Socialism was an anti-Christian movement. It was nevertheless dialectically related to Christianity. It was the *negation* of Christianity as *negation* was understood by Hegel and Freud. It could have as little existed without Christianity as the Black Mass of medieval satanism could have existed without the Mass of Roman Catholicism. The classic villains of Christianity, the Jews, became the prime objects of extermination of the anti-Christian Christians, the Nazis.

Studying the classical utterances of Christianity on Jews and Judaism, and at the same time reviewing the terrible history of the Nazi period, prompts one to ask whether there is something in the logic of

Christian theology that, *when pushed to an extreme,* justifies, if it does not incite to, the murder of Jews. Though there is pain in the exploration of this question, neither Christians nor Jews ought to avoid it.

In view of my questions concerning the relationship between Christianity and the Holocaust, I considered myself fortunate when the Bundespresseamt arranged an interview for me with Probst Grüber at his home in Berlin-Dahlem. Thousands of Germans could have testified against Adolf Eichmann, one of the leading SS officers assigned to the Final Solution, at his trial in Jerusalem in 1961. Dean Grüber was the only one who did. The Dean had a long and heroic record of opposition to the Nazis on Christian grounds as well as friendship and succor for Nazism's chief victims. In the end, his courage brought him to Dachau and near martyrdom.

After the war Dean Grüber devoted himself to the work of healing and reconciliation. He was instrumental in creating the Heinrich Grüber Haus in Berlin-Dahlem, an old-age residence for victims of the Nuremberg laws. These included Germans who had married Jews, Jews who had converted to Christianity, and a few old Jews who wanted to end their days in Berlin in spite of the fury that had disrupted their lives. With public and government support, a spacious and attractive home was built for these people, who were the very special concern of the Dean.

In addition to testifying at the Eichmann trial, Dean Grüber worked to foster reconciliation between Germany and Israel on the political level, and between German Christians and Jews at the religious level. Following his suggestion, on his seventieth birthday German friends and admirers contributed well over one hundred thousand marks for the planting of a forest in his honor in Israel. Rejecting all personal gifts, he insisted that the money be given to build Israel. He was also active in a German-Israeli organization devoted to the exchange of visits between the youth of the two countries, and he personally had visited Israel three times.

When I met the Dean he was past seventy, but a healthiness and a heartiness about his person was immediately noticeable. His home was attractive and spacious, a rarity in 1961 in West Berlin, where apartment living was all that most people could hope for. He met me at the door and took me to his study, which was lined with books and which contained a rather attractive oil copy of Rembrandt's *Flora* and all sorts of relics and souvenirs of a long and distinguished career. An impressive sculpture of the Dean's head stood in one corner.

After many sessions interviewing Germans in all walks of life, I had come to expect a respondent to need a warmup period before discarding initial reserve. In the case of Dean Grüber, this was unnecessary. There was an admirable bluntness and candor to his manner which revealed that the man meant exactly what he said. He was not given to allegorical interpretation. Like his spiritual master, Martin Luther, Grüber conducted himself in accordance with the belief that ". . . it is the prophetic—i.e. the literal—[sense] which is the foundation of all the others, their master and light and author and font and origin."[1] Both his literal consciousness and his thoroughgoing honesty were present to the point of pain throughout the interview. These were not qualities valued by the Nazis, who preferred clergymen who could somehow gloss over the contradiction between unconditional obedience to both the Führer and God.

The most obvious point of departure for our conversation was the trial of Adolf Eichmann. Grüber explained that he had gone to Jerusalem with the greatest reluctance, and only after his name had come up so frequently that he felt he had no decent alternative. He also said that he had gone as a German, a member of the people who had perpetrated the injustice, and as a member of the Christian Church, which had remained silent before it.

"Did testifying cause you any harm with your own people?" I asked.

He replied that it had not and went on to say that he did not really see much difference between himself and Eichmann, that he too was guilty, that, in fact, the guilt was to be shared by all peoples rather than by Eichmann alone.

"If there had only been a little more responsibility all around, things would have been different."

He complained bitterly that the governments of practically every civilized country had turned their backs on the Jews, making it impossible for them to leave Germany. He spoke of his own efforts to secure immigration visas and complained of how seldom he succeeded.

I asked him about the Heinrich Grüber Haus. He explained that he had helped hundreds of people, many of whom were victims of the Nuremberg laws, to leave Germany. In recent years some had wanted to return. Originally he had founded his home for twenty people, most of whom were Christians who had lost Jewish relatives during the persecutions. He felt that these people deserved a more comfortable life in their remaining years than most old people could expect. It was also extremely difficult to place them successfully in the average German old-age home because many German old people were still bitterly anti-Semitic and would have objected. To meet these problems, he had built, with much public support, a unique institution.

Without being asked, the Dean informed me that he had never converted Jews and did not want to do so now. On the contrary, he wanted Christians to become better Christians and Jews to become better Jews. I quickly learned that the Dean had very decided ideas on what Jews ought to be and how they ought to behave.

Again continuing without being questioned, the Dean informed me that Germany's Jews were in great danger, that once again Jews were influential in the banks, the press, and other areas of public interest. This surprised me, as I had been informed during my visit that only eight thousand Jews were employed or self-employed in what was then a nation of fifty million.

"The problem in Germany is that the Jews haven't learned anything from what happened to them," he declared. "I always tell my Jewish friends that they shouldn't put a hindrance in the way of our fight against anti-Semitism."

In view of his long-established friendship for the Jewish people, I asked him to clarify his statement. He replied that many of the brothels and risqué night clubs, for example, were in Jewish hands, especially those in close proximity to the army camps.

"For hundreds of years, there has been a virulent tradition of anti-Semitism among the Germans. Hitler exploited that tradition for his own ends. It is very difficult for us to wipe it out. After the Eichmann trial, this is one of my tasks. I am involved in one or two meetings a week to help end anti-Semitism, but it is very difficult because of the Jews in prominent positions and those who are engaged only in seeking money no matter what they do."

In reply, I told the Dean that Israelis had told me that one of the things they liked best about Israel is that could live and work there without relating their behavior or their lifestyles to the Jewish problem. I put the problem to him in terms of the freedom everyone has to make life choices and to pay the price for so doing.

"Look, I don't understand why you are so troubled about a pitifully small number of Jews in shady positions or interested in making money rather than following more edifying pursuits," I said. "It seems to me that every person pays a price for the kind of life he or she leads. Why should Germans be upset about a few such Jews unless they are overly involved in other people's lives? Must every Jew make himself so pale, so inconspicuous, even invisible, that he will give no offense to Germans? Is that the lesson Jews must learn from the death camps, that they must prove to the Germans their preeminent capacity for virtue? Wouldn't it be far better if the few remaining Jews left Germany and went where they could live as they pleased, without worrying about what the Germans thought or felt about them? After what has happened, why should any Jew remain and worry about German approval?"

The Dean was not prepared to let go. He was disturbed at the thought of the few remaining Jews leaving Germany. He felt that I was correct that Jews had as much right as Germans to be anything they pleased, but he also felt that, after what had happened, they ought not to do these things, as it made the work of ending anti-Semitism so much harder. It was evident that in his mind Jewish behavior and anti-Semitism were objectively related.

Having asserted that the Jews had as much right to produce scoundrels as any other people, the Dean quickly retracted. He spoke of the ancient covenant between God and Israel and how Israel as the Chosen People of God was under a very special obligation to behave in ways that are spiritually consistent with Divine ordinance.

"I don't say this about Israel; God says this in the Bible and I believe it!" he insisted with considerable emotion.

The Dean was not the first German clergyman who had spoken to me in this vein. I had previously met a number of clergymen in Berlin and Bonn. All insisted that God and Israel have a special, providential relationship, that the history of Israel is wholly in accord with God's will. This was true, they told me, in the time of the Bible. Moreover, the *Heilsgeschichte*, the "salvation history," of the Jewish people continues to unfold to this very day. In fairness, it must be said that the same belief has been shared by the vast majority of religious Jews throughout history. The theological significance of the Zionist movement and the establishment of the State of Israel lay largely in the rejection of *Heilsgeschichte* and in the assertion that Jewish misfortune had been made by men and could be undone by men. For the pastors the conviction remained—nay, it was strengthened—that nowhere in the world were the fruits of God's activity in history more evident than in the history of the Jewish people. Every time I heard this view, I quickly rejoined that such thinking had as its inescapable conclusion the conviction that the Nazi slaughter of the Jews was somehow God's will, that, for His own inscrutable reasons, God really wanted the Jewish people to be exterminated by Hitler. In every instance before meeting Dr. Grüber I was met by an embarrassed withdrawal.

Countess Dr. von Rittberg, the representative of the Evangelical Church to the Bonn government, a charming and learned lady, was one of the German religious leaders with whom I discussed this issue. She offered the customary interpretation that Israel's destiny is guided by a special Divine concern, but she partially withdrew it in the face of my objection.

"Theologically this may be true, but humanly speaking and in any terms that I can understand, I cannot believe that God wanted the Nazis to destroy the Jews," she said. Her reluctance to follow the logic of her theology to its hideous conclusion, which made the Nazis the accomplices of a righteous God, was understandable. I found a similar reluctance on the part of the other clergymen with whom I spoke. However, in view of the fact that I was a rabbi and the interviews had been arranged by the government press office, some of the clergymen may not have been entirely frank when the issue was raised. In all likelihood I did not get a random sampling of German theological opinion.

The same openness and lack of guile that Dean Grüber had shown from the moment I met him were again manifest in his reaction to my question concerning God's role in the death of six million Jews, a question that, I believe, is decisive for contemporary Jewish theology.

"Was it God's will that Hitler destroyed the Jews?" I repeated. "Is this what you believe concerning the events through which we have lived?"

Probst Grüber arose from his chair, dramatically removed a Bible from a bookcase, opened it, and read: "Um deine Willen werden wir getötet den ganzen Tag"—for Thy sake are we slaughtered every day" (Ps. 44:22).

"When God desires my death, I give it to him!" he continued. "When I started my work against the Nazis I knew that I would be killed or go to the concentration camp. Eichmann asked me, 'Why do you help these Jews? They will not thank you.' I had my family; there were my wife and three children. Yet I said, 'Your will be done even if You ask my death.' For some reason, it was part of God's plan that the Jews died. God demands our death daily. He is the Lord, He is the Master; all is in His keeping and ordering."

Listening to the Dean, I recalled Erich Fromm's descriptions of the authoritarian personality in *Escape from Freedom*.[2] All the German clergymen to whom I had spoken had asserted the absolute character of God's Lordship over humanity and of humanity's obligation to submit unquestioningly to that Lordship, but none had carried the theological logic this far.

The Dean's disturbing consistency had its special virtue. No consideration of personal safety could deter him from total obedience to his Heavenly Master. In this he contrasted starkly with all too many of his fellow countrymen, who gave lip service to a similar ideal but conveniently turned the other way in the crisis. Nevertheless, there was another side to this stance which was by no means as pleasant. Eichmann had also served his master with complete and unquestioning fidelity. Sixteen years after the close of hostilities, not only Eichmann, but apparently his defense counsel, seemed to feel that such servitude was self-justifying. Furthermore, in both the Dean and his demonic antagonist, obedience to the will of the master, in the one case God, in the other case Hitler, was unredeemed by any saving skepticism. Neither man could accept an inconsistency in logic rather than the consistency of accepting the gratuitous murder of six million Jews.

When Dean Grüber put down his Bible, it seemed as if, once having started, he could not stop himself. He looked at recent events from a thoroughly biblical perspective. In the past, the Jews had been smitten by Nebuchadnezzar and other "rods of God's anger." Hitler was simply another such rod. The incongruity of Hitler and Auschwitz as instruments of a righteous God never seemed to occur to him. Of course, he granted that what Hitler had done was immoral, and he insisted that Hitler's followers were now being punished by God.

"At different times," he said, "God uses different peoples as His whip against His own people, the Jews, but those whom He uses will be punished far worse than the people of the Lord. You see it today here in Berlin. We are now in the same situation as the Jews. My church is in the East Sector. Last Sunday (August 13, the day of the border closing) I preached on Hosea 6:1 ('Come, and let us return unto the Lord: For He hath torn, and He will heal us; He hath smitten, and He will bind us up.'). God has beaten us for our terrible sins; I told our people in East Berlin that they must not lose faith that He will reunify us."

I felt a chill at that instant. There was enormous irony in the Dean's assertion that the Germans had become like Jews. *I was listening to a German clergyman interpret German defeat as the rabbis had interpreted the Fall of Jerusalem almost two thousand years before.* For the rabbis, Jerusalem fell because of the sins of the Jewish people. For Dean Grüber, Berlin had fallen because of the sins of the German people. When he sought words of consolation with which to mollify the wounding of his imprisoned church, he turned to the very same verses from Hosea which had consoled countless generations of Israel.

He pursued the analogy between Germany and Israel: "I know that God is punishing us because we have been the whip against Israel. In 1938 we smashed the synagogues; in 1945 our churches were smashed by the bombs. From 1938 we sent the Jews out to be homeless; since 1945 fifteen million Germans have experienced homelessness."

The feeling of guilt was very apparent; so too was the fact that for him German suffering appeased and ameliorated this feeling. Everything he said reiterated his belief that God was ultimately responsible for the death of the Jews. It may have been a mystery to him, but it was nevertheless taken as unshakable fact.

The Dean had asserted that God had been instrumental in the Holocaust. He had not asserted the nature of the crime for which God was supposed to have smitten the Jews. During the Eichmann trial, Dr. Servatius, the defense counsel, had offered the suggestion that the death of the six million was part of a "higher purpose" and in recompense for an earlier and greater crime against God, thereby joining the modern trial in Jerusalem with one held twenty centuries before.

But my interview time was almost over and I had no opportunity to question Dean Grüber concerning the nature of the enormous crime for which six million Jews perished. Nevertheless, his thinking was so thoroughly imbued with New Testament and prophetic categories that there is little reason to think that he would have disagreed with Dr. Servatius. Stated with theological finesse it comes to pretty much the same thing as the vulgar thought that the Christ-killers got what was coming to them.

However, in the face of a crime so hideous as the Holocaust, decent men recoil and attempt to do what they can to root out the incitement to further evil. At a number of mainstream American Protestant seminaries, attempts have been made to tone down some of the more patently anti-Semitic teachings in religious textbooks and literature. Similar efforts are today being made within Catholicism. The declaration concerning the Jews of the Second Vatican Council is the outstanding example. Many thoughtful Christians assert that *all* people, insofar as they are sinners, killed Christ and that the blame must therefore not be placed on the Jews alone. These attempts have been rightly appreciated in Jewish circles. Nevertheless, after my meeting with Dean Grüber I asked myself whether such efforts have any efficacy. It seemed at the time that the fundamental issue transcended the question of whether today's Jews continue to be regarded as deicides. At the heart of the problem is the fact that it may be impossible for Christians to regard Jews in other than mythical, magical, and theological categories. Because of their kinship with Jesus and their inability to accept him as the Christ, Jews alone of all the world's peoples are regarded by Christianity as playing a very special role in the divine drama of sin and forgiveness, guilt and salvation, perdition and redemption. The Christian Church must insist on the separate and distinct character of the Jewish people because of its claim to be the new Israel superseding the old Israel, which has proven incapable, either through spiritual blindness or malice, of recognizing Jesus Christ as Lord. It is Christ who is regarded as the perfect fulfillment (*telos*) of the covenant made by God with Abraham and Moses, a covenant that the Israelites were incapable of understanding in its plenitude. Christianity must regard Jews as special and, at least in matters pertaining to God's salvation, apart from humanity in general. As such, they are destined to be the objects of both the abnormal demands and the obsessive hatreds of which the Dean spoke.

As long as there is Christianity, Jews will be the potential objects of a special and ultimately pernicious attention that can explode in violence in times of stress. Even if all the textbooks were "corrected," there would still be the Gospels, and they are enough to foster the threat of a murderous hatred of Jews by Christians. Even when Christians assert that all people are guilty of the death of the Christ, they are asserting a guilt more hideous than any known to any other religion: the murder of the human incarnation of the Lord of Heaven and Earth. On the Jewish side, we would say that not only are the Jews not guilty of deicide, but that no one is guilty because it never happened. Here again there is an unbridgeable gulf. The best that Christians can do for the Jews is to spread the guilt, while always reserving the possibility of retracting the amelioration and ascribing it entirely to the Jews. By contrast, Jews must insist that the guilt exists for no one in reality, although some among them might admit that it exists for every person in fantasy.

Apart from his unequivocal assertion that Hitler was God's agent at Auschwitz, what made the visit to Dean Grüber so memorable was the fact that here was a Christian who had almost died as a result of his efforts on behalf of Jews—the Nazis kicked out his teeth, and at one point he was left for dead in Dachau—yet he was incapable of seeing Jews simply as normal human beings with the same range of failings and virtues as any other people. It may be argued that the Dean's opinions prove nothing, that he exhibited a characteristic incapacity to submit a religiously legitimated ideology to the test of the concrete, empirical facts of day-to-day life. There is undoubtedly some truth in this. Nevertheless, the Dean's attitudes, especially in view of his genuine contributions to the work of reconciliation, intensify the question of the role of Christian theology in fostering a moral climate in which the extermination of the Jews could become an acceptable policy.

My visit did suggest one element of hope. In recent decades the mainstream Christian churches in the United States, both Protestant and Roman Catholic, have sought to balance their claims to exclusive truth with the imperatives of a pluralistic society in which no religious tradition can any longer claim or enforce a cognitive monopoly.[3] This was not the case with Dean Grüber, who viewed the world and especially the Jews through the prism of an exclusive theological system claiming the status of divine revelation. In fairness to the Dean, however, it must be recognized that his religious beliefs were the unconditional ground of his decision to oppose National Socialism and to help Jews. Moreover, there seems to be something in the German mentality which demands utter metaphysical consistency. This has often been productive of much good. It has resulted in some of the greatest and most imaginative uses of the human intellect. The system of Hegel comes to mind immediately. Nevertheless, when human relations are subordinated to the constraints of ideological consistency life may be lost and a dead, murdering logic may destroy what it cannot countenance.

I came away from the interview with an urgent question for the Jewish community: Can Jews really blame Christians for viewing us through the prism of an exclusivistic theology of history when we ourselves were the first to claim this history? *As long as we continue to hold to the doctrine of the election of Israel, we will leave ourselves open to the theology expressed not only by Dean Grüber but also by some of this century's leading Orthodox Jewish thinkers: because the Jews are God's Chosen People yet failed to keep God's Law, God sent Hitler to punish them.*[4]

There is a way out: religious uniqueness need not place us at the center of the divine drama of perdition, redemption, and salvation for mankind. All we need for a sane religious life is to recognize that we are, when given normal opportunities, neither more nor less than others, that we share the pain, the joy, and the fated destiny that Earth alone has meted out to all her children.

I began this chapter with a question: Does the Christian Church's attitude toward Jews and Judaism involve it in a process that, in times of stress, can lead to the murder of Jews? I must now append a further question: Does the way Jews regard themselves religiously contribute to the terrible process? The tendency of the Church to regard Jews in magical and theological terms encourages the view that the vicissitudes of Jewish history are God's will. If we accept his theological premises, there is no way of avoiding Dean Grüber's conclusion that God sent Hitler. But how can we ask Christians to give up these premises if we continue to regard ourselves as the Chosen People and as the special object of God's concern in history? No one can predict the way the matter will develop. There is, however, no doubt that the simple capacity of Jew and Christian to accept their own and each other's humanity lies at the core of any possibility of reconciliation between the two great faiths of the Western world.

CHAPTER 2

Person and Myth in the Judeo-Christian Encounter

From the time of the first Jewish settlement in Cologne in the year 70 C.E. to our own terrible and barbaric era, crucial portions of the drama of Jewish history have been played out on the German scene. For Jews Germany is a bitter but an inescapable reality. Many Jews are tempted to avoid all German contacts, even those that are sincerely offered in friendship. I can understand such an attitude but I cannot share it. We have been too directly and too violently involved in each other's destiny for either side to permit murder to be the last word, if we can help it. As a rabbi, I find myself inescapably drawn to the study of German history, philosophy, and contemporary politics. No other European country exhibits a comparable fascination, for no other European people has affected the life and death of my people as have the Germans. I try to understand Germany the better to understand myself.

I wish to explore the meaning of two related, tragic encounters, that of German and Jew and that of Christian and Jew. For almost two thousand years, an honest Judeo-Christian religious encounter was all but impossible in Europe. At best, the Jew was the dependent, threatened client of the Christian. The implicit threat of superior power and its entailments hung over such meetings. That is why they were almost always disputations, forced upon a beset and fearful Jewish community that could rarely, if ever, afford the luxury of candor. Jews knew that victories in such disputations were actually defeats, for such victories were bound to be followed by the punitive anger of their opponents. It is not surprising that, in the meetings of Jew and Christian, Jews were more concerned with avoiding affronts to Christian sensibilities than they were with genuine communication.

Only in modern times has a beginning been made toward real communication, toward the meeting of I and Thou between Jew and Christian of which Martin Buber has written so persuasively. Such a meeting requires equality. The fact that I am a foreigner helps to make it possible for me to speak to you as an equal. I am neither your dependent nor your client, as Jews have so frequently been in the past. By the same token, I hope that I am beyond *ressentiment*, which is the fantasy revenge of clients against their protectors and persecutors alike. In this encounter neither you nor I am doomed merely to behold our own mirror image. What we behold in the mirror may be familiar, but he who tells you only what you want or expect to hear, as well as he who sits in judgment, reduces you to an object of manipulation. Inequality not only precludes genuine encounter for the client; it also distorts and debases the protector as well. Had I been born in Germany I could today expect no more than a bestowed equality. The pariah status of the Jew would be too ingrown to erase even after the events of World War II.[1] As Søren Kierkegaard has suggested in his parable of the king who would bestow his love on a servant girl, memory makes a bestowed equality impossible. A tolerated Judaism can never achieve real encounter with Christianity. In order to meet you at all, I must do so as a foreigner and an equal.

No one chooses the community, the nation, or the tradition to which he is heir at birth. There is an absurd facticity, not only to our modes of finding ourselves in the world, but to the ways in which we are thrust into our respective religious situations. Neither Jew nor gentile is entirely free to confront God's mysterious singularity as if no one had preceded him. Jew and gentile alike are thrown into historically, culturally, psychologically, and religiously defined situations that are, in a certain sense, beyond choice. You had no choice about being born German; neither did I about being born an American Jew. We can choose the degree to which we commit ourselves to our inherited religious traditions. We can, if we want, deny them, but our denial is dialectically related to those very traditions. Our religious affirmations are largely the ratification of what is given and the making explicit of what is originally implicit in our situations. Nevertheless, the more serious we become about the domain identified by Paul Tillich as "ultimate concern," the more we are likely to use the sacred forms and traditions of the communities into which we were thrust at birth. After Kierkegaard, we know that Jew and Christian are separated more by conflicting spiritual wagers than by proven certainties in either the moral or the sacred domain. We are divided by the absurd "thrownness" (*Geworfenheit*) of our concrete, historically determined situations. There is no way the Christian can confront the holiness of God save through Jesus Christ and the paths of sanctity in which He is Lord. For the Jew, the most likely path is the Torah as its traditions have been inherited, reflected upon, and transmitted by Israel's rabbis and teachers. Only God knows who, if anyone, ultimately dwells in His Truth.

At the same time, both Jew and Christian are heir to and participant in a spiritual conflict that is no longer of either's making. If each is true to his inheritance, he is destined to reject much that the other holds to be central to his existence. While both Judaism and Christianity can ultimately dwell outside God's Truth, only one of the conflicting traditions can conceivably dwell within it, at least with regard to the question of Christ. We are heirs to conflicts we did not create, but we cannot with dignity or honor entirely avoid them.

Judaism and Christianity share a crucial area of common belief found in almost no other religious system. As Oscar Cullman has observed, both biblical traditions ascribe to time and history a decisive place in the divine economy which is foreign to nonbiblical religions.[2] Judaism and Christianity differ in their interpretation of history but not in their basic affirmation that God's relation to the world is primarily historical. Hans Joachim Schoeps would seem to be correct in maintaining that Paul the Apostle was acting largely as a Pharisee who was convinced that Jesus was in fact and in truth the Christ.[3] Neither Paul nor his rabbinic contemporaries differed in their faith that God would send a Messianic Deliverer. They differed radically in their assessment of the career of Jesus of Nazareth. Similarly, neither Rabban Johanan ben Zakkai nor Justin Martyr differed in their belief that God was omnipotently active in history and that the Roman destruction of Jerusalem had been in accordance with God's will. They differed in their assessment of the sins of Israel which prompted God so to act. Rabban Johanan ben Zakkai, moved by a strong sense of Jewish self-criticism, ascribed the Fall of Jerusalem largely to the failure of his community properly to fulfill the injunctions of the Torah, God's expressed will, as interpreted by the Pharisees.[4] Justin, seeing history through the prism of the Christ-event, concluded that Jerusalem had fallen because the Jewish people had failed to accept and had in fact betrayed God's most precious gift, the saving gift of the Christ.[5] What united Justin and Johanan also separated them. Both saw history as the unfolding of the divine drama of humanity's salvation, yet this was the cause of a deep and persistent division that has by no means ended in our own times.

If one accepts this shared view of divine providence, it is impossible to avoid the conclusion that the National Socialist extermination of the Jews during World War II was a fulfillment of God's purposes.[6] Indeed, the prophets of Israel, the Rabbis, and the Church Fathers all interpreted the major disasters of Jewish history in this manner, and if one believes in the biblical God of Judaism and Christianity, there is no reason to exclude twentieth-century Jewish history. Given the Judeo-Christian conception that God is the ultimate actor in the historical drama, no other theological interpretation of the death of six million Jews is tenable. There is only room for debate concerning the sins for which Israel was so sorely afflicted. Nevertheless, little, if anything, need be added today to what Rabban Johanan and Justin Martyr have said on the subject. If one views time and history through the perspective of the Christ, one would have to assert that God caused the Jews to be exterminated by the Nazis because of their continuing failure to confess and acknowledge the Christ. If one shares Rabban Johanan ben Zakkai's view, one would be drawn to assert that the Jews of Europe perished because they failed to obey the Lord's commandments. Of course, it would always remain a mystery why the Lord had suffered the relatively prosperous and religiously permissive American Jewish community to escape intact while consuming the Polish Jewish community, which included the greatest number of the most religiously compliant Jews.

Perhaps no twentieth-century figure has dealt so meaningfully or so feelingly with this problem in its universal form as the French thinker Albert Camus in *The Plague*. A plague of immense proportions breaks out in the city of Oran and very quickly begins to consume thousands of people in utter indifference to every human standard of virtue, vice, age, status, or social utility. The central issue of Camus's great work is the question of the meaning of the catastrophe. In terms of the normative Judeo-Christian interpretation of history, the plague can have only one meaning—it must represent the punitive anger of the Lord visited upon the sinful city. Camus illustrates this view in the character of Father Paneloux, the Jesuit priest who leaves the solitude of scholarship to preach repentance to the stricken community. In the presence of a large and anxious congregation gathered in the cathedral, the good father interprets the disaster that has overwhelmed his community in the very same way that Dean Heinrich Grüber explained the modern Jewish catastrophe to me in Berlin in August 1961 and Rabban Johanan ben Zakkai and Justin Martyr interpreted the Roman victory over Jerusalem in ancient times: The plague has been sent by a just and angry God to punish the sins of a wicked community. The plague would only be lifted when the community truly heeded its meaning and turned from its wickedness to the ways of the Lord. For Father Paneloux, human suffering could only be understood as retribution visited upon the sinner for rebellion against God. When Paneloux first preaches, it is as if the Book of Job had never been written. The tragedy of the victim is aggravated by the conviction that suffering is deserved divine punishment.

In the nineteenth century, the Russian novelist Fyodor Dostoevsky dealt with very much the same issue in *The Brothers Karamazov.* Ivan Karamazov, the atheist, rejects the normative Judeo-Christian interpretation of history. He refuses to justify the suffering of even one innocent child in terms of the big picture, namely, that the child's suffering is necessary for the ultimate happiness God will bestow upon humanity. Camus shares Ivan's refusal to justify the Lord in the face of innocent suffering.

Father Paneloux is capable of maintaining his harsh interpretation of the plague from the pulpit. Later, he is broken emotionally when he witnesses the excruciatingly painful death of a child. He is never again the same man. His life is too thoroughly committed to the theology of covenant and election for him to retract. Nevertheless, something in him has seen the limitations of that view. Camus wisely and compassionately describes the way in which the priest takes sick and dies, not because of the plague, but because his world has been shattered and he knows no way to reconstitute it. In Father Paneloux human solidarity finally triumphs over an interpretation of events which equates human suffering with divine retribution.

At every point of significance in Camus's own thinking, human solidarity is preferred to ideology. When we finish *The Plague,* we are aware of the fact that this solidarity is the deepest root of Camus's atheism. He refuses, as does Ivan Karamazov, to see man as inevitably and inescapably guilty before God. He accepts the tragedy, the inevitability, and the gratuitous absurdity of suffering, but he refuses to consent to its justice. He would rather live in an absurd, indifferent cosmos in which people suffer and die meaninglessly but still retain a measure of tragic integrity than see every last human event encased in a pitiless framework of meaning which deprives people of even the consolation that suffering, though inevitable, is not entirely merited or earned. We know that Camus reacted with deep sensitivity to World War II. The plague of which he writes was in reality the same plague that consumed Europe's millions. It was Camus's genius to be able to universalize the problem.

Camus's inability to accept the God of the Judeo-Christian tradition in the face of the suffering of the innocent and his choice of an absurd cosmos that at least preserves a measure of human solidarity and dignity is reminiscent of an earlier decision of the same sort taken by an apostate from Rabbinic Judaism in the first Christian century, Elisha ben Abuyah. He also elected an absurd and meaningless cosmos rather than interpret the suffering of the innocent as divinely inflicted retribution of sin. In the face of overwhelming Jewish suffering during the war between Rome and Judea of 131–35 C.E., he exclaimed *"Leth din v'leth dyan"*[7]—"There is neither judgment nor Judge." Anticipating Camus by almost two thousand years, he elected a world without meaning rather than accept the justice of human suffering.

We concur in this vision of an absurd and ultimately tragic cosmos.[8] We do so because we share with Camus a greater feeling for human solidarity than the Prophetic-Deuteronomic view of God and history can possibly allow. We part company only with Camus's atheism. *It is precisely because human existence is tragic, ultimately hopeless, and without meaning that we treasure our religious community. It is our community of ultimate concern.* In it we can and do share, in a depth and dimension no secular institution can match, the existence Camus has so well described. We have turned away from the God of History to share the tragic fatalities of the God of Nature. It is no accident that this turning is concurrent with the return of at least a portion of the children of Israel to the earth of Israel.[9]

Immigration to Israel was not accomplished by miracle, and statehood is maintained, not by transcendent events, but by a modern defense force. Similarly, the question of God arises when the question of the theological meaning of the Final Solution is raised. In reality, no meaningful contemporary Jewish theology can exclude the decisive question of God and the death camps. *All contemporary Jewish theology must be Holocaust theology.*[10] Jewish life in the twentieth century has known two moments of *kairos:* the death camps and the restoration of Zion, which took place because Israelis and other Jews deliberately turned their back on Rabban Johanan ben Zakkai's ideology. Though Jewish religious leaders may verbally reaffirm that ideology, their acts belie this posture. *The meaning of the restored Zion is that the normative theology of history traditionally identified with prophetic and Rabbinic Judaism has been effectively demythologized.*[11] This is an awesome and momentous change in Jewish religious sentiment after two thousand years. Its full meaning will be understood only by generations yet to come. The demythologizing fact has yet to appear in most contemporary expressions of Jewish theology. These hardly ever seem to be written in the twentieth century after the death camps and the restoration of Zion.[12] There is an understandable hiatus between religious ideology and explicit action where real Jewish interests are involved. I believe that what Jews have done since the war offers a better key to what they think than the continued reiteration of the older, discredited historical myth. It is very difficult for a people to surrender a myth that has infused its existence with meaning for over two thousand years until a way is found to incorporate the newer, demythologized *Weltanschauung* into its religious and institutional structure.

This demythologizing process is everywhere apparent in deed if not in explicit ideology. After the experiences of our times, we can neither affirm the myth of the omnipotent God of History nor can we maintain its corollary, the election of Israel. After the death camps, the doctrine of Israel's election is in any event a thoroughly distasteful pill to swallow.[13] Jews do not need these doctrines to remain a religious community.

After the death camps, life in and of itself, lived and enjoyed on its own terms without any superordinate values or special theological relationships, becomes important for Jews. One cannot go through the experience of having life called so devastatingly and radically into question without experiencing a heightened sense of its value, unrelated to any special categories of meaning which transcend its actual experience. This distrust of superordinate ideologies is increased immeasurably because of our knowledge of the role such ideologies played in the creation of the death camps. Life need have no metahistorical meanings to be worth living. In a world in which so much gratuitous insane fury has been expended upon the Jews, those Jews who have extricated themselves from this terminal threat have a duty at least to be sane about themselves, especially where others have lost that capacity.

Undoubtedly, this need for sanity within the community has been underscored by our rediscovery of Israel's earth and the lost divinities of that earth. Once again we have come in contact with those powers of life and death which engendered men's feelings about Baal, Astarte, and Anath. These powers have again become decisive in our religious life. When we use, as we must, traditional forms and rituals, it is to these powers that we are responding.

We cherish our hallowed, ancient traditions, not because they are better than other people's or because they are somehow more pleasing in God's sight: we cherish them simply because they are ours and we could not with dignity or honor exchange them for any other. By the same token, having lost the need to prove that what we are or have is better than what others are or have, we have gained a reverence for the sacred traditions of others. This is a corollary of our belief that these traditions are not matters of original choice but are part of the absurd givenness of every concrete, limited human perspective. As children of Earth, we are undeceived concerning our destiny. We have lost all hope, consolation, and illusion. We have also lost all *ressentiment*, that emblem of poverty of spirit, and we have found a renewed strength, dignity, and vitality. Jewish life must live beyond all ideology in the joy as well as the pain of the present, seeking no pathetic compensations in an imaginary future for a life unlived in the now. It is either this or a return to an ideology that must end by praising God for the death of six million Jews. This we will never do.[14]

We will never again regard ourselves in the old mythic perspectives.[15] Nevertheless, the doctrine of the election of Israel seems to be indispensable for Christianity. Unless Israel is the vessel of God's revelation to humanity, it is difficult to proclaim Christ as the fulfillment and climax of that revelation. While Jews can, and I believe must, demythologize their religious ideology, I see no way believing Christians can demythologize Israel's special relation to God without radically altering the meaning of Christian faith. Unfortunately, Christians will always encounter Jews as mythic figures rather than real persons unless some way can be found to demythologize the Christian conception of Israel. In this dilemma, the tragedy of the Judeo-Christian encounter becomes explicit.

It has been said that English literature has portrayed the Jew as the best of saints and the worst of sinners but never as a simple human being. This characterizes more than English literature; it characterizes the Christian view of Israel. Regrettably, the demonological interpretation of Israel is by far the more potent. Christian thought on Jews and Judaism extends from Jesus to Judas but knows no middle ground. After times of great hatred and slaughter, the Christian image of the Jew will stress the resemblance to Jesus, recalling Jewish virtues and contributions to humanity's spiritual treasury. This is inevitable in a time of reconciliation, but it may have about it more than a little of the fattening of the sacrificial lamb for another round of slaughter. In any event, *philo-Semitism is as unrealistic and as pernicious as anti-Semitism,* for it destroys our most precious attribute, our simple humanity. Jews are not, nor are they obliged to be, paragons of virtue or models of holiness. To expect us to be more than other men, to pay us the unwanted and unasked-for compliment of asserting that we are, is an unintended cruelty but a cruelty nonetheless. A superlative degree of virtue excludes from the human community at least as effectively as a superlative degree of vice. Furthermore, since people are more likely to be convinced of their sinfulness than of their virtue, they will have little reason to honor or admire those who either assert themselves or are condemned to be lauded by others for an inhuman virtue.

Sooner or later the image changes. Usually the Judas image comes to the fore when the Jews attain a certain numerical strength within a country and begin to compete effectively with a significant segment of the non-Jewish population. The image of the Jew as the giver of religion is superseded by another image, the image of Judas, who betrays his Lord by a loving kiss for thirty pieces of silver. Nothing so poisons Jewish-Christian relations as the Judas story. The moral of the tale is simple and direct: No Jew can be trusted. Even his seeming virtue is only a demonic disguise for the betrayer's role. He may seem like a good citizen, a valued intellect, an unselfish patriot, but one can never be sure whether behind these postures there lurks a betrayer. It is impossible to tell this story to children, to rehearse it in the Passion, to celebrate it in song, drama, and religious ritual without its casting a black cloud over Jewish-Christian relations.

Normally this image does its subtle work without becoming manifest. However, in time of stress, the power of the image is greatly enhanced. In place of rational, reality-oriented modes of relationship, men and communities tend to regress to irrational images in which people cease to be flesh-and-blood persons, mixtures of virtues and vice, and become unambiguous embodiments of principles that are never found in the real world in an undiluted state. In the language of psychoanalysis, there is a regression from the rational secondary-process to the irrational primary-process level of mental functioning.

When regression takes place under extreme conditions, one of the most important casualties is an individual's or a community's sense of responsibility for its own destiny. A search begins for a magical betrayer who has been guilty of the "stab in the back" and is responsible for every imaginable ill that has befallen the community, as happened in Germany after November 11, 1918.[16] Such accusations are always credible when directed against the Jews in Christian lands because they represent a contemporary restatement of the mythical drama. As Jesus was betrayed by Judas, so the Jew is regarded as betraying his Christian hosts. There is always a small element of truth in accusations leveled at the Jew, for he participates in the same spectrum of virtue and vice as does his neighbor. There is, however, a very different level of expectation in his case. Since he has been praised as like Jesus, his failure to measure up to this unattainable image makes the Judas accusation all the more plausible. When the image has been reiterated for millennia in every conceivable form of religious literature and ritual, it can offer a comforting, albeit unrealistic, key to understanding why the host nation has fared badly, why its armies were defeated, why depression and inflation have supplanted prosperity. Furthermore, in defeat one can always wound the Jew with the blows that are meant for the victor but that can never safely be directed against him.

The Jewish claim of divine election, that the Jews are or ought to be "a kingdom of priests and a holy people" (Exod. 19:6), as well as the perennial Christian association of the Jews with the life and death of Jesus of Nazareth, condemns Jews to dwell in the domain of the sacred. Unfortunately, it is often the destiny of sacred persons to die as a sacrificial offering. In ancient times, the final piety of the king-priest was to be offered up as a human sacrifice. In Christianity, Jesus, the King-Priest-Savior, redeems a sinful world through his atoning and sacrificial death. In sacrifice, the human predicament is dramatized most effectively. Men and women, who are unable either to abide the disciplines of society or to overthrow them, dramatize their ambivalence in this holy act. In a sense, sacrifice redeems and saves, because it contains homicidal aggressiveness within controlled limits. Furthermore, sacrifice dramatizes the most important fact about human beings. We would, if we could, become deicides. Had we but the power, we would murder God, for we will never cease to be tempted by Ivan Karamazov's demonic fantasy that if God were dead, all things would be permitted. It is impossible to avoid a sense of amazement at Christianity's marvelous mythical and psychological power, for in the crucifixion we behold the symbolic acting out of this deepest wish.

There is, however, a difference between the pagan priest lifting his sorrowful knife to offer up the innocent sacrificial victim and the Christian. The pagan priest knows that the guilt for the holy murder is his and that of the community he serves. He can perhaps justify his deed by insisting that, were he not to commit the limited act of religious violence, his community would soon disintegrate into a cannibal horde knowing no limits to its aggressive violence save those that nature herself finally imposes by sheer exhaustion. The Christian has a deeper insight into the meaning of the sacrifice. He intuits that it is God whom we would murder even in the moment of our most reverential homage. Unlike the pagan priest, he need not accept the guilt as his own. The actors in the mythical drama, the Incarnate God, His betrayer, and those who reject and crucify Him, all are Jews. One can hate God for the virtue He commands, yet displace one's murderous feelings onto the Jew as His murderer. Whether one sees the Jew as Jesus or Judas, it is all the same. He must ultimately be condemned to play his final role in the domain of the sacred, that of sacrificial victim.

Even when not destroyed physically, he who is condemned to the domain of the sacred is excluded from the community of men. This is perhaps a fate as bitter as actual death, for it is social death. Nor can we forget that the sacrificial victim is the scapegoat. As long as life is prosperous and undisturbed, people let things proceed on what we Americans call a "live-and-let-live" basis. Under stress, the humanity of the other disappears. At this point the ritual-murder aspect of sacrifice predominates. Its essence is the primordial hope that, in the suffering and death of the victim, the community will avoid or forestall its own injury or doom. The extermination camps were one huge act of ritual murder in which the perpetrators were convinced that only through the elimination of the Jews could Germany's safety be vouchsafed. The years since 1945 have demonstrated the extent to which the death of the Jews has contributed to the actual safety of the German people.

I want to stress that I draw this picture with no sense of blame or anger. Myths and religious traditions are not conscious inventions. As a Jew, I find myself in the peculiar situation of regarding myself as of absolutely no consequence or meaning beyond my own projects and those of my family and the larger community in which I am involved. I know, however, that, though I did not and would not have made the choice, I have an unwanted superordinate significance for others. My belief or unbelief figures in their understanding of the divine drama of salvation. I also recognize, to my very great sorrow, that I have this superordinate significance largely because non-Jews took my ancestors seriously when they claimed for themselves a special religious destiny. I desire no such destiny for myself or for my community. I have tried to demythologize my situation for myself and my community, but I can hardly blame Christians if they refuse to follow me. I know how difficult it is to persuade Jews to accept the demythologizing process with regard to their own status. It would be far more difficult to get others to do so.

The deepest tragedy in Jewish-Christian relations is that true dialogue, the genuine meeting of persons, is impossible so long as Jews and Christians are committed to the religiohistoric myths of their respective communities. For the Jew who holds firmly to the doctrine of the election of Israel and the Torah as the sole content of God's revelation to mankind, the Christian insistence upon the decisive character of the Christ-event in human history must be at best in error and at worst blasphemy. For the Christian who is convinced that the divine-human encounters recorded in Scripture find their true meaning and fulfillment in the Cross, Jews are at best the blind who cannot see and, at worst, demonic perverters, destroyers, and betrayers of humanity's true hope for salvation. Regrettably, these positions cannot be mediated or diluted if they are held to be absolutely and unquestionably true. Not only do the mythical contents of our religious faiths impede meaningful community; they absolutely preclude it.

Nevertheless, meaningful and friendly relations do exist between Jew and Christian. In spite of all the impediments that we know too well, Jews and Christians have frequently lived together in harmony and friendship. In my own country this is due to the fact that the religious factor, while undoubtedly a powerful influence, is by no means the predominating element in most human relations. The simple pragmatic concern to find a way to make a social situation work is extremely important. American society is neither ethnically nor religiously homogeneous. A multiplicity of elements enter into social relations, and the religious factor is by no means always predominant. To the extent that people are prepared to risk open encounter without preconceived ideological intrusions, meaningful relations between Jew and Christian are possible. Let us, however, recognize that a dilution of the mythical factor is involved. One partial solution to the problem of the meeting of persons would seem to be the pragmatic approach of allowing ideas and myths concerning Jew and Christian which are not necessarily consistent to coexist. This approach is probably the most realistic. It reflects the fact that people confront one another in a multiplicity of roles and relationships, that they are probably better off when they develop a tolerance for ambiguity, which allows them a freedom in encounter that unrelieved theological consistency would withhold. This may be the best that can be expected. It is limited by the fact that the mythical element can always overwhelm the pragmatic in times of stress.

Another possibility that has held a great attraction for many Jews has been the commitment to secular society devoid of any contact with religion. I am convinced that the root of Jewish atheism and secularism in modern times has been the insight that Jewish suffering could not be separated from the Judeo-Christian conflict. If only religion could be totally eliminated, some Jews have reasoned, no further problem of the alienation of brother from brother would exist.

I cannot share this view, no matter how much I may understand the underlying pathos that has motivated it. Because our religious myths preclude that genuine meeting of persons which is the essence of true community, it does not follow that we can place our hopes in a completely secularized society. Society will always exhibit characteristic flaws. In our times, the ever-widening extension of the domain of technical rationality in our secular society presents its own special threat to the genuine community of persons. With the growth of urban communities and their characteristic anonymity of persons, with the increased specialization of labor and with the proliferation of dehumanizing modes of competence in the management of human affairs, the religious factor tends to disappear. Here, however, the disappearance contributes to, rather than diminishes, the depersonalization and dehumanization of social encounter. The conflict between Christian and Jew seems to be minimized, because a society of myth is replaced by a society of calculation and manipulation. What is needed, however, is a society of persons.

The rational society of contract subjects personal relations to a very high degree of abstraction. In its terminal expression it is possible to forget that we dwell in a human world at all. The icy symmetry of the modern skyscraper harms no one, but it does express the distance we have come in one symbolic area from the world of Gothic architecture, whose genius it was to objectify the unconscious of humanity in stone. The worst expression of this world occurs when the vocabulary of mass murder is so sterilized by terms like *Lösungsmöglichkeit, Sonderbehandlung, Evakuierung,* and others that it is possible to ignore the fact that human beings are being annihilated. This is, however, the final manifestation of a dehumanizing process that is everywhere apparent in some measure throughout the Western world.

In its less pathological forms, such an abstract society runs counter to our earliest and most decisive experiences of social encounter, which are emotionally determined. Let us go further and agree with Freud that our earliest experiences are erotic in character. We never really forget this paradigmatic experience of the primacy of *eros* in social encounter. The impersonality of so much of adult economic and social organization is undoubtedly indispensable to the successful functioning of our highly complex civilization. Nevertheless, in a very deep sense, this complex world is experienced as an expulsion from Eden. In most situations normal men and women can accept the necessity of being treated abstractly and impersonally without so regarding themselves, for there is no way to turn back the clock to the experience of early childhood or to that of the earlier homogeneous ethnic communities that once predominated throughout Europe and America. The trend toward pluralism is irreversible.[17] Neither the abstractions of a depersonalized secular society nor the dehumanizing myths of a religious society are ultimately conducive to that community of persons which alone offers hope that the fragile human enterprise will not break asunder through its own inner failure. The tragic encounter between Christian and Jew has an importance that transcends itself. James Baldwin has commented that all that white men fear and distrust about themselves is reflected in their image of the Negro. The same can be said of the relation of Christian and Jew.

Our greatest need is the need to know who we are. Only a person who has gained such knowledge, who has come to terms with himself, can meet the other in openness and fellowship. It is here that a demythologized Judaism and Christianity together hold the contemporary world's best hope. If we concentrate less on what our religious inheritances promise and threaten and more on the human existence that we share through these traditions, we will achieve the superlative yet simple knowledge of who we truly are. Through our religious traditions we come to a knowledge deeper than words of our guilt, our alienation, and our pathetic finitude. Nothing so humbles and teaches us our true station as do our traditions. Here we see all human projects cast into their proper perspective. We intuit the insurmountable irony of existence. As we pass through life, each crisis of transition and each seasonal renewal is celebrated and marked within a meaningful community. We know where we are on life's road. When finally we return to the Holy Nothingness from which we have come forth, we do not leave our survivors so bereft of resources that our end denies them openness in the life that yet remains to them.

When I hear the *Agnus Dei* of the Mass, I am separated from my brother in his belief that the Christ is in truth and in fact the Lamb of God who takes away the sins of the world. I cannot join him in his faith.[18] I can, however, join him in common recognition that we are all guilty men, that we all yearn for that precious healing promised by Isaiah: "Though your sins be as scarlet, they shall be made as white as snow" (Isa. 1:18). Faith separates me from my brother. What faith points to unites me with him. This is even true of the person of the Christ. I cannot accept the historicity of the tradition. The historical Jesus remains for me a charismatic Jewish religious leader.[19] I can, however, share with my brother the complex intersection of promethean self-assertion and pious submission which all people feel before the incarnational reality of the Divine.

No such knowledge is possible in a purely secular society, for it lacks a sense of the tragic. It has yet to know what even the most archaic religions comprehended: that all human projects are destined to falter and fail. For technical society, failure is an incident to be overcome by further effort facilitated by the replacement of older units of manpower with newer units. For the human person, failure is of the very essence.

The whole weight of religious tradition, with its insistent and dramatic reiteration of God's holy majesty and the finitude and creatureliness of man, reminds me over and over again of who and what we are. Furthermore, it does more than teach us these lessons at the conscious, intellectual level. It allows us to share these truths in the multiple levels of emotion which religious ceremony at its best can elicit. We have been cast up absurdly and without reason into a world that knows no warmth, concern, care, fellowship, or love save that which we bestow upon one another. Our myths tell us of gifts that await us. We can be far more certain of the need that makes mythical promises alluring than of fulfillment of the promise. Since we cannot be brothers in promise, let us at least be brothers in need.

There are no innocent men. Freud's myth of the primal crime may tell us little concerning religious origins, but it can illumine our present predicament. Civilization begins, not with the recognition by brothers of their impeccable virtue, but with the first and awesome discovery of their ineradicable guilt. In the beginning was the deed—the guilty deed. The person who confesses his own potential for murder, and that of his religious tradition, is far more likely to master this potential than the one who refuses this terrible truth about himself. I do not love my sons the less because I am aware of the unconscious patricide dwelling in their psyches. When I see Christian *Heilsgeschichte* as leading potentially to murder, I do not forget its Jewish origin. I can sense the potential murderer in my brother only because I have intuited it in myself. As Christian and Jew we cannot be united in innocence. Let us at least be united in guilt, leaving it for God alone to weigh each person's measure thereof. If we fail to learn the simple lesson that community is possible only through the encounter of persons rather than of myths or abstractions, we will only doom future generations to repeat the horrible deeds of our times in ways that will arise out of their as yet unrevealed situations. But perhaps out of our tragic common past there can arise a deeper compassion, a deeper mutual involvement, and a deeper sense of the urgency and the perils of the human vocation.

CHAPTER 3

Religion and the Origins
of the Death Camps
A PSYCHOANALYTIC INTERPRETATION

For centuries men and women will try to understand why it happened. No two explanations will entirely coincide, and no single attempt, including this one, will be entirely adequate. We are now quite certain, however, about some aspects of the death camps. We all agree that commonsense explanations simply don't explain. None of the ordinary hypotheses of lawlessness, lust, the desire for personal gain, utility, or even simple hatred are really plausible. Nazi motivations largely defied normal expectations or predictions.

Considerations of usefulness did not deter the Nazis. Had their first priority been to win the war, they would never have made the extermination camps so central a concern. They would have used every available talent, Jewish or gentile, in the war effort. Toward the end of the war, the dazed and defeated Germans were assured that German science would produce a secret weapon capable of turning the tide. Not infrequently an atomic weapon was hinted at. Ironically, many of the scientists who helped the United States produce its first nuclear weapons were German-trained Jews who fled their native lands when anti-Semitism left them no alternative. The sheer need for a compliant labor force in wartime should have dictated an entirely different approach, not only to the Jews but to the subject nations as well. Had final victory really been the Nazi aim, their whole conduct of the war would have been different. For die-hard Nazis, as opposed to the average German, the war was not a means to victory. It was an end in itself wherein the Nazis permitted themselves to ignore behavioral constraints observed in peacetime. The

Nazis often seemed far more intent upon achieving irrational victories over defenseless Jews and Gypsies than a real victory over their military opponents. They won the war that really counted for them, the war against the Jews. Eichmann's alleged statement that, though all else fail, he would go to his grave content in the knowledge that he had helped to kill more than five million Jews is very much to the point.[1]

Absent normal motives and given the mystique and ritual of National Socialism, it is impossible to avoid the question of religious origins. *Although the Nazis have been called pagans, they were never genuine pagans like the ancient Greeks.* They were satanic anti-Christians, saying no to much that Christianity affirmed and saying yes to much that was absolutely forbidden in Christianity. There is a striking parallel between the die-hard Nazi and the medieval priest who celebrated a Black Mass. The satanic priest was never an atheist or a pagan. His problem lay in believing too much. He celebrated the Black Mass, not because of lack of belief, but because he hated God and wanted to invert normal religious standards. Had he really been an unbeliever, he would not have been so dependent upon religion to determine the character of his rebellion.[2] The Nazis were religious rebels rather than genuine unbelievers.

Ancient Judaism and Early Christianity

In one area the Nazis took Christianity very seriously. They did not invent a new villain, but took over the ancient Christian tradition of the Jew as villain and epitome of the darkest evil. Nor did the Nazis create a new hatred. Folk hatred of the Jews is at least as old as Christianity. Creating very little *de novo*, the Nazis intensified what they found. Nevertheless, in their intensification of old hatreds, they added a new and radical element which had never been present in Christianity. They transformed a theological conflict, normally limited in its overt destructiveness by religious and moral considerations, into a biological struggle in which only one conclusion was thinkable—the total extermination of every living Jew. Unlike Christian anti-Semites of an earlier time, Hitler had no interest in regarding the Jews as anything but objects to be exterminated. Nothing the Jews could do by way of conversion, submission, surrender, betrayal, or apostasy could have altered their destiny.

Although the roots of the death camps must be sought in the mythical structure of Christianity, this should not in any way be interpreted as an imputation of genocidal guilt against Christianity. The Nazis both used Christian tradition and rebelled against it. Religious rebels are far more demonic than simple pagans or genuine atheists, and the Nazis were no exception. However, myths concerning the satanic role of the Jews had been present in Christianity for centuries without creating so dire a result. In addition to the religious background, the peculiar ambivalence of an influential part of the German literary and intellectual community toward Christianity in the nineteenth and twentieth centuries, as well as the response of the German people to defeat after World War I, were necessary preconditions before the Nazis could use the religious myths with such explosive force.

The oldest origins of the death camps can be found in the extremely complicated relationships of ancient Judaism and primitive Christianity. The rival faiths have never been entirely distinct and independent religious movements. The Church has always regarded herself as the fulfillment and the true successor of the Synagogue. This is apparent in the writings of Paul of Tarsus, the apostle who carried the message of Christianity beyond the confines of the Jewish community. According to Paul, only a Christian could be a true Israelite. The Jews who rejected Christ, though Israelites by birth, could not be considered Israelites after the spirit. In making his point, Paul delighted in drawing a parallel between the rivalry of Christian and Jew in his day and the ancient sibling rivalry between Ishmael and Isaac. In Abraham's times, Paul argued, not all who were of the patriarch's flesh were heirs to his promise. For Paul, only those who have faith in Christ, as Abraham had faith in the Lord, would truly belong to the community of God's elect. Faith in Christ, not membership after the flesh in the community of Abraham's physical descendants, was for Paul the *conditio sine qua non* of participation in the New Israel.[3] Paul never doubted that the Church was the fulfillment of the old Jewish community, because he was convinced that the revelation incarnate in the Christ was the fruition of the revelation originally given to Moses. From its inception, Christianity considered itself the successor of Judaism rather than an entirely different religion.

The conception of the Church as the true Israel necessarily involved a negative evaluation of the old Israel. This is not fully explicit in Paul, who regarded the "unbelief" of the Jews as part of the divine plan whereby the gentiles were first to be brought to the Lord, after which he expected the Jews ultimately would accept Christ. Paul felt a real sense of kinship with those he regarded as his erring kinsmen.[4]

Nevertheless, within a hundred years, the split between Judaism and Christianity had become bitter and irrevocable. Historical events exacerbated theological differences. The Jews had fought two wars against the Romans in 66–70 and 131–35 C.E. As a result of the first war, the Jerusalem Temple, the center of Jewish religious life, was destroyed. The young Church took this as double confirmation of Christian truth. It was seen as confirmation of Paul's contention that Jewish Law was no longer binding on those who were "in Christ." It was also taken as unmistakable evidence of God's punishment of the Jews for their rejection of the Christ and complicity in his death.[5] During the Second Roman War (131–35), many Jews, including Rabbi Akiba, regarded Simeon Bar Kochba, the leader of the revolt, as Israel's true Messiah. The Christians, some of whom were still of Jewish extraction, naturally interpreted this as a compounding of Jewish vice. Not only had the Jews rejected Christ, the true Messiah, but they had gone astray after a false pretender. When the Romans defeated the Jews and inflicted their devastatingly cruel revenge upon the losers, the Christians took the event as further confirmation of God's rejection of Israel and the truth of Christianity.

The development of the bitter religious antagonisms is plainly visible in the writings of Justin Martyr (ca. 100–ca. 165 C.E.), a Palestinian Christian apologist who flourished in the second Christian century. Paul's mild doctrine of the Old and New Israel was altered by Justin into an extreme contrast between the Church as the New Israel and the Synagogue as the despised and rejected of the Lord. There is a remainder of compassion for Israel "after the flesh" in Paul which is absent from Justin. In Justin's writings an old Jewish idea—God's punishment of sinful Israel—has been combined with a new sin, the murder of the Christ. This murder was soon regarded as the murder of God. As we shall see, the Christian conception of the Jew as deicide is a most significant component of the religious origins of the death camps.

In his *Dialogue with Trypho,* Justin frequently expressed the conviction that Jewish disaster is nothing more than what the Jews deserve. A frequently quoted passage indicates how violent these feelings had become. Referring to circumcision, Justin declared that it "was given for a sign . . . that you alone suffer that which you now justly suffer; and that your land may be desolate, and your cities burned with fire; and that strangers may eat your fruit in your presence, and not one of you may go up to Jerusalem."[6]

This was the reaction of one of the earliest and most important Christian theologians concerning the fate of the Jews after their catastrophic defeat in the Judeo-Roman war of 131–35. *Justin understood that Judaism and Christianity are religions of history and that a principal validation of their claims must be the evidence of history.* This interpretation is as valid as we approach the twenty-first Christian century as it was in the first. Few events are as enthusiastically described by Justin as the catastrophic Jewish defeat at the hands of the Romans. For both Justin and his rabbinic opponents, the war was more than a military contest. The Romans were God's retributive instruments against a sinful Israel. They played the same role in Justin's interpretation of history as the Babylonians in the theology of the prophets.

In the extermination camps Jews were murdered, not for what they did, but for who they were. No possible alteration of Jewish behavior could have changed their fate; the "crime" was simply to be a Jew. Jewish existence and the tenacity of Jewish survival were in and of themselves an affront to the claims of the Church. Faced with this survival, the Church usually interpreted Jewish existence as did Justin, as filled with deserved sorrow, thus establishing the greatest possible credibility for the Christian claim to be the true Israel.

Teutonism and Volksreligion

In the nineteenth and twentieth centuries, the Church's claim to be the New Israel was better understood by Christianity's Teutonic enemies than by either Jews or Christians. Resentment against Christianity and its enforced displacement of the Teutonic gods has been a significant motif in German life and letters since the Napoleonic wars. This resentment had important roots in the peculiar historical and geographical situation of the Germans. One root can be found in the old tension between the Teutonic north and the Latin south, from which Catholic Christianity originated. Charlemagne's forced conversion of the Saxons and Luther's break with Rome were in part manifestations of this tension. Modern German nationalism was first aroused during the War of Liberation against the French, 1806–13. Many of the German writers of the day interpreted their war against the French as a continuation of the age-old struggle of Teuton against Latin.[7] Christianity, regarded as the product and imposition of a foreign Latin culture, was resented in influential German circles. Nazism grew in part out of this aspect of German cultural history. Although Hitler was willing to use the churches for his own purposes, he was committed to their ultimate elimination. Shortly after his assumption of power, he revealed his intentions to his associate, Hermann Rauschning: "Neither of the denominations—Catholic or Protestant, they are both the same—has any future left, at least not for the Germans. Fascism may perhaps make its peace with the Church in God's name. I will do it too. Why not? But that won't stop me stamping out Christianity in Germany, root and branch. *One is either a Christian or a German.* You can't be both" (italics added).[8]

The theme of Teutonic roots turns up in Hegel's early writings. Although by no means an anti-Semite, Hegel titled one of his earliest writings, "Is Judea Then the Fatherland of the Teutons?" Hegel complains that Christianity has emptied Valhalla of its gods and forced the German people to accept Jewish gods and fables in place of their own.[9] This observation presupposes the concept of *Volksreligion* in which the religion, mythology, and social organization of an ethnic community (*Volk*) are regarded as a single organic unity. When any element in the constitution of the *Volk* is displaced or discarded, the unity of the whole is broken. Such a breach in *Volk* unity occurred when the indigenous Teutonic gods were displaced by the foreign gods and myths of the Jews. For Hegel, the gods of a people are an objectification of the inner nature of that people. By rejecting their ancestral gods, the Germans were in the deepest sense rejecting themselves. The young Hegel did not carry his own logic to its ultimate conclusion in action. He was, however, followed by others, such as Erich Ludendorff and Alfred Rosenberg, who were more prepared than he to enter that realm. They concluded that German alienation and self-estrangement could be terminated only by an end to the Jewish gods of Christianity.

This hankering for the simplicities of an indigenous *Volk* community was to become part of the reaction against the distressing complexities of an evolving modern civilization with its confusing mixture of morals, faiths, and peoples. This yearning figured very largely in Nazi ideology. It received one of its simplest formulations in the watchword of Hitler's Reich, *Ein Volk! Ein Reich! Ein Führer!* In such a community there could be no room for the disturbing dissonances of the Jews or even of Jewish Christianity.

There is a double irony in the claim of the Church that it is the New Israel. Since the Teutonists could not uproot the powerful Christian Church, they turned their anger on the infinitely weaker Jews, thus providing themselves with a cheap victory. It would have been infinitely more difficult for the Nazis to uproot the hold of Christianity on the German people. That, however, was their ultimate intent.[10] The ancient Jewish-Christian quarrel over the true Israel led to the use of the original Israel as a surrogate victim for the presumed sins of the New Israel in effecting the alienation of the German people from their native traditions. There were times when the Nazis had a clearer image of what and why they were fighting than either Jews or Christians.

The Deicide Accusation

While these historical events and theological conflicts help to explain the origins of the conflict, they do not by any means explain the mur-

derous hatred felt by the anti-Semite for the Jew or why only extermination was regarded as the Final Solution. Such extreme violence can in
part be accounted for by the accusation that the Jews are deicides, the
murderers of God. The Christian religion, alone among the religions of
the world, begins with a murder—the murder of God. Its decisive symbol
is the cross, the instrument of execution by which the deicide was carried
out. In Christian thought the Jews play a twofold role: they provide *both*
the incarnate Deity *and* His murderers. The assertions that the Christian
Church is the true Israel and that the Jews have been rejected by God
are of a piece. Without the alleged special relationship between Israel and
God, with its implied magic potency, the Jews could never have been
identified with either God or His murderers. Furthermore, the Christian
claim to be the truly elect was enhanced by the accusation that the formerly chosen were deicides, thereby compelling the Father to seek a new
and truly beloved child.

The emotions undergirding the deicide accusation and the competing
claims of election resemble those of sibling rivalry. The terrible accusation, "You have murdered or wanted to murder the Father," implies,
"therefore you are wholly unfit to be his beloved child." Because Jesus
is God, the Son of God, in Christian theology, the violence done to his
person is equally violence against God the Father.

In *Moses and Monotheism* Sigmund Freud has suggested that envy of
the Jew as the chosen of the Lord is an important component in anti-
Semitism.[11] This envy would seem to be exemplified in the Church's
claim to be the true Israel. The Jews made an extraordinary claim about
themselves—that they were in a special and decisive way God's Chosen
People. Instead of ridiculing it, a very large portion of the non-Jewish
world took the claim seriously. Lacking power of their own, the Jews com-
pensated by magically claiming a preeminent portion of divine concern.
To their ultimate disaster, the claim was met with neither scorn nor rid-
icule. Once accepted, as it was in a paradoxical way by Christianity, it
aroused envy and the desire to displace the favored child.

Though the Jews were hated before Christianity, especially in Hel-
lenistic Egypt, the intense hatred for them under Christianity must be
seen as in part related to one of the oldest conflicts between Jew and
Christian—the question of who is truly the elect of the Lord. By insisting
that it was the New Israel, the Church made the claim that only its ad-
herents were truly Jews before the Lord. Those who prized this status
were necessarily threatened by the real Jews, who challenged the Christian claim simply by their continued existence. Apart from anything the
Jews said or did to appease their more powerful rivals, the very existence

of the Jews was a threat to the New Israel. Because Jews were at home in the language of the Bible, they could claim that their traditions gave them greater familiarity with the world that had given birth to Jesus. Even when the manifest dialogue between Jew and Christian was cordial, Christians could perceive that Jews regarded the Christ tradition as an embellished fantasy on the career of another Jew. Through no one's fault, the denial of Jesus by the Jews, whether spoken or unspoken, was a greater threat to the Christian belief system than the nonbelief of any other people.[12]

The entire system exaggerated the importance of the Jews out of all realistic proportions. They were not seen as the defeated and impotent people they were, lacking a normal political life of their own; instead, the very marginality of their existence elicited mythical interpretations. Those who were homeless (*heimatlos*) became uncanny (*unheimlich*), the decisive actors in the drama of God and the devil, sin and innocence, salvation and eternal damnation. They were regarded as possessing a terrible magic potency, both as the people in whose midst God-in-the-flesh had been born and as His murderers. This helps to explain the widespread credibility given to so patent a forgery as *The Protocols of the Elders of Zion,* in which the leaders of the Jewish community are depicted as secretly plotting world domination. This document has been used as a "warrant for genocide," fostering the belief that the Jews must be destroyed lest they destroy the non-Jewish world.[13] Moreover, the *Protocols* are once again being published in Russian with murderous intent, together with *Mein Kampf,* by a New York–based, ultra-right-wing Russian publishing house, Russian Call (*Russkii Klich*), for dissemination in the crisis-ridden former Soviet Union of the 1990s.[14]

The terrible significance of the deicide accusation cannot be overemphasized: *In this system if God is dead, the Jews are his murderers.* At the extremely important vulgar level, the cry of "Christ-killer" has, more often than not, accompanied the instigation of anti-Semitic violence. In one of the most searing scenes in André Schwarz-Bart's novel of the Holocaust, *The Last of the Just,* small German children anticipate the development of Nazism by almost murdering little Ernie Levy as a Christ-killer.[15] In our own times, the deicide theme has been examined by Freud, Dostoevsky, Sartre, and others who have understood that the murder or displacement of God is humanity's most demonic fantasy.

According to Freud, civilization and religion began with a "primal crime" in which the father of the original human horde was cannibalistically murdered by his sons in order to gain sexual possession of his females. The father proved more potent dead than alive. His son-murderers experienced intense regret at their terrible deed and attempted to suppress its memory. Nevertheless, the unconscious memory of the deed continued to agonize the sons and their progeny, thereby causing the murdered father to be imagined as the ever-living Heavenly Father. For Freud, *the supreme object of human worship is none other than the first object of human criminality.* Freud maintained that a great deal that is irrational and opaque in the ritual and myth of both Christianity and Judaism can be traced back to mankind's unconscious memory of its earliest patricide and to the contradictory feelings of guilt and Promethean self-assertion that the original deed engendered. In Jesus' sacrificial death Freud saw the "return of the repressed." Mankind was compelled to repeat, at least symbolically, its primal crime against God, while attempting to atone for the continuing feelings of guilt which that unconscious memory sustained.

We will never know whether Freud's etiological myth is historically grounded. It is, at any rate, psychologically illuminating that Christianity begins with such a crime. Freud also believed that the cannibalistic aspects of the primal crime are repeated in the Mass, which he regards as both a symbolic repetition of and a ritual catharsis for the original crime.

Freud's myth of the origins of religion is less important as actual history than in what it suggests concerning the agonizing conflicts that continue to beset humanity.[16] Control of one's instinctual life is the precondition of participation in the social order. Such control is not easily acquired. Every society hangs precariously over the precipice of humanity's conflicting feelings about its instinctual life. There is, according to Freud, something in all of us which would destroy the slender fabric of personal and social discipline that makes civilization possible. If Freud's myth of original patricide tells us little about human origins, it expresses a great deal concerning the awesome ambivalence felt by human beings toward those who symbolize authority and civilization. *The murder of God is an immensely potent symbol of mankind's primal desire to do away with all impediments to unrestrained instinctual gratification—in the language of Freud, the triumph of the id over ego and superego. The symbolism of the death of God thus has awesome potency.*

Well-meaning Christians often deny that they are taught that Jews are the Christ-killers. They claim they are taught that *all* men and women are responsible through their sins for the death of the Christ. Unfortunately, the attempt to share the blame is of doubtful efficacy. Though all may have been responsible from the religious point of view, the actual deed is irrevocably depicted in the Gospels as having been committed by members of an identifiable historical community. The New Testament is explicit in its identification of these men and women. It is equally explicit concerning the continuing involvement of their descendants in the affair. Pontius Pilate is depicted as offering the Jews the opportunity to choose Jesus or Barabbas for release from the death penalty. The Jews chose Barabbas. Pilate insists that he finds no fault with Jesus. He washes his hands of the affair and permits the execution. The onus of guilt is clearly placed upon the Jews. In Matthew the Jews are depicted as replying to Pilate's protestations of innocence: "His blood be upon us and on our children" (Matt. 27:25). The murder of God is thus depicted as a continuing source of guilt of the Jewish posterity.

The explosive significance of the crucifixion story as a myth of the death of God is illuminated by Ivan Karamazov's remark in Dostoevsky's *The Brothers Karamazov*, *"If God does not exist, all things are permitted."* In both Judaism and Christianity, all moral restraints are ultimately derivative from God's lordship over creation. The wish to murder God is the terminal mythical expression of humanity's ineradicable temptation to moral anarchy. Given the Judeo-Christian view of God as the ultimate source of moral legitimation, a world without God would be a world with no impediment to the gratification of desire, no matter how perverse or anarchic. The perversity of the human heart finds its ultimate expression in the myth of the murder of God.

The accusation that a people is deicidal implies that they are utterly beyond all law and moral restraint.[17] This may seem a strange accusation to make against the Jews, a people who were the creators of so vast a system of religious law. The seeming paradox did not escape Justin's attention. Unwittingly, this basically decent philosopher helped to create the demonological interpretation of the Jews which was to result in so much bloodshed throughout the centuries. Justin argued that only the excessive moral weakness of the Jews made it necessary for them to be placed under the discipline of the Law. He interprets their outward personal and moral conformity as the fruit of a terrible inner lawlessness. In a sense, Justin was an excellent intuitive psychologist. Unfortunately, he turned his intuition of a universal inner conflict into evidence of a distinctive Jewish proclivity for evil. This contrasted, according to Justin, with those who enjoy the freedom of Christ. They need none of the legal constraints of the Jews. Only the enormity of the deicidal people's temptations make the special restrictions and inhibitions of the Law necessary.[18]

The Devil and the Jews

A universal tendency toward moral anarchy was thus identified and displaced onto the Jews. During the Middle Ages, the identification of

Jews as moral anarchists was intensified by the further identification of the Jew with the Devil and the Antichrist. These identifications were already implicit in the crucifixion story and the rivalry between the two religious communities. The identification of the Jews with the Devil is explicit in the Fourth Gospel, in which Jesus is depicted as saying to those who reject his mission: "If God were your Father, you would love me, for I proceeded and came forth from God; I came not of my own accord, but he sent me. . . . You are of your father the devil, and your will is to do your father's desires. He was a murderer from the beginning, and has nothing to do with the truth, because there is no truth in him. . . . But because I tell the truth, you do not believe me"(John 8:42–45).

In medieval Europe, the Jews were the only people who openly and successfully resisted Christianity. The Saxons tried and failed. Since the Jews were the one people resident in Europe who had seen the Christ and beheld his passion, their stubborn refusal to acknowledge him was ascribed to the supernatural power of their satanic master. The only other group that continuously resisted Christianity was the witch cult. The Jews were thus depicted as openly worshiping the blackest of masters, whose non-Jewish devotees, by contrast, were depicted as at least having the decency to pay their homage in secrecy.[19]

The identification of the Jew with the Antichrist was implicit in the earliest Jewish rejection of Christ. In medieval popular mythology, the final return and triumph of Christ was to be preceded by a battle waged between the forces of Christ and the Antichrist. As Christ was the son of God, born of a Jewish virgin, the Antichrist would be born of the union of a Jewish whore and the Devil. He would be raised in Galilee and trained by sorcerers and witches in the black arts. At the age of thirty he would announce himself to the Jews in Jerusalem as their Messiah. His actual mission would last only three and a half years, the duration of Jesus' ministry. During this time he would unite all previous heresies, use the blackest of arts, and raise up a huge army to do his evil work. In some versions of the myth, the army of the Antichrist is to battle against the legions of the Christ in a final Armageddon in which Christ will ultimately be victorious. The myth was connected with the legend of the ten lost tribes of Israel, who were regarded as dwelling in prosperity in vast numbers somewhere in Asia. At the summons of the Antichrist, they would form a formidable host challenging the Lordship of the Christ over Christian Europe.[20] This is a medieval anticipation of the related myths of a Jewish world conspiracy and of "Jewish" Bolshevik hordes determined to destroy Christian Europe which the Nazis used so effectively. Such a notion was supported by the very realistic dangers that stemmed from invasions and threats of invasions that Europe faced from the Huns, Turks, Mongols, and Arabs. Fear of the Antichrist's legions was a reflex of the folk anti-Semitism of European culture. The Antichrist myths can also be seen as an expression of the retaliatory anxieties experienced by anti-Semites as a result of their hostile intentions toward Jews.

It is interesting to note in passing that the identification of the Devil with the Jews survived Hitler in the German theater. Gustof Gründgens plays Mephisto with distinctly Yiddish overtones in the postwar recording of Goethe's *Faust*, Part I, presented by the Düsseldorf Schauspielhaus and released by the Deutsche Grammophon Gesellschaft. Gründgens popularized this interpretation of the Devil under the Nazis and did not see fit to alter his Yiddish Mephisto after the war. Nor apparently did anyone strongly object in spite of the terrible history of our times.[21]

The Antichrist was the polar opposite of Christ. As the Devil's Messiah, he represented a demonic reversal of the value system normative in Christian Europe. Unfortunately, the Jewish response was hardly ever relevant. Faced with the Christ-killer accusation, Jews usually took the accusation seriously at the manifest level and protested their innocence. Seldom, if ever, did they understand that the accusation was an attempt by the accuser to deny his own lawless temptations by ascribing them to the Jews. The Jewish protestation of innocence only made matters worse. One of the worst aspects of the two-thousand-year-old Judeo-Christian encounter has been the mutual incapacity of either side to understand what was vital to the other. Apparently, neither the Jews nor the Christians could acknowledge the problem of overcoming inner lawlessness to be a universal one.

No motive other than indecent willfulness and dedication to the demonic was permitted as an explanation of the continuing Jewish inability to accept Christianity. Trachtenberg points out that the Jews were regarded as knowing the truth about the Christ but deliberately rejecting it. They were more often regarded by the Church as *heretics* than as *infidels*. No imagined crime was too heinous to be ascribed to them. As they had been guilty of the crucifixion, they were regarded as symbolically repeating the crime by the sacrificial murder of Christian victims, especially at Passover time.

The blood libel has persisted down to our own times and was used by the Nazis. In the light of what we know of religious sacrifice, the continued use of the ritual murder accusation against the Jews is by no means inexplicable. In part, religious sacrifice had its origins in the ritual murder of a human victim in order thereby to assure the community's continued well-being and prosperity. Vicarious atonement figures very largely in such practices. There seems to be something in most of us which, when sufficiently threatened, sees safety in the death of the other. "Let him die instead of me" is an age-old human cry.[22]

The doctrine that Christ's death atones vicariously for the sins of humankind represents the manifest expression of humanity's buried wish. In Biblical Judaism, atonement was effectuated by the scapegoat offering on the Day of Atonement. The animal's character as a surrogate for an original human victim now seems indisputable. At some time in the past, the community or communities that preceded Israel offered human victims to effectuate atonement and cleansing. When John the Baptist greets Jesus upon seeing him at the River Jordan, he is depicted as saying: "Behold the Lamb of God who taketh away the sins of the world" (John 1:29). John is depicted as identifying the intended human victim with the animal surrogate.[23] The circle was thus completed. Once again the death of a divine-human victim brought forgiveness and security. The promise Christianity offers its believers is that this once-and-for-all human sacrifice has the power to save humanity from its sins. Many of the psychodynamic elements of ritual murder are present and resolved through such Christian rituals as the Mass and the doctrine of vicarious atonement.

There are, however, important differences between the ritual aspects of the crucifixion and other sacrificial deaths. In pagan ritual murder, the community accepts its own guilt for participating in the sacred violence. No outsider is blamed for the deed, which is regarded as a sad and bloody necessity. The community must choose between two unpleasant alternatives: a limited act of violence in which one dies for all, or the very real danger that all will succumb as a result of the false mercy of omitting the sacrifice. Faced with these alternatives, the pagan accepted his own guilt and reluctantly committed the bloody deed.

In Christianity, the victim is no longer a mere human being but the Deity, who is at once both wholly divine and wholly human. Furthermore, the Church does not have to accept the guilt for the original deed. The guilt is ascribed to the Jews. The actual sacrificial death of Jesus occurred only once. Insofar as the need for a scapegoat remained, as it did especially in times of stress, the memory of the one sacrifice could not satisfy the hunger for a victim. The Jews could. There is real irony in the age-old, anti-Semitic accusation that Jews practice ritual murder. The radical anti-Semite lives in a world that remains endangered as long as Jewry survives. For the radical anti-Semite, there is only one solution—extermination of the Jews. This is ritual murder made morally acceptable to the perpetrator by the deicide accusation. The sins and the guilts that beset the anti-Semite's existence demand the death of the Jews. At one level, the Nazi Final Solution represented one vast explosion of all of the repressed forces that in earlier times paganism had channeled into the controlled and regulated slaughter of one victim at a time. When the anti-Semite accuses the Jew of ritual murder, he accuses him of the very crime that he himself intends to commit. At the same time, he fails to comprehend the inherent gratuity of the whole business. The death of the sacrificial victim solves no problem in the real world.

National Socialism: An Inversion of Judeo-Christian Values

As suggested above, although National Socialism has often been characterized as pagan by Jewish thinkers, the movement was never really pagan. *National Socialism was an inverted and demonic transformation of Jewish and Christian values combined with a romantic hankering after a paganism it never understood.* It needed the Judeo-Christian *yes* to assert the National Socialist *no*. The Greeks were pagan. For them the decisive misdeed was *hubris*, the taking upon oneself of more than one's allotted portion in the nature of things. Hubris, man's rebellion against his limits, was always a limited self-aggrandizement. It was exhibited in the folly of Oedipus, seeking to avoid a fate that came closer with every step he took to escape it; it was also manifest in the desire of Clytemnestra, whose adulterous passion irretrievably furthered the fated destruction of the house of Atreus. Hubris never signified complete and total lawlessness, such as is implied in the notion of deicide. It was followed, as night follows day, by inevitable nemesis, which righted the wrong and restored nature's disturbed equilibrium. Good and evil were rooted in the very nature of the cosmos itself. By disturbing nature's equilibrium, evil was in a sense unnatural; inevitably fate would overtake its perpetrators. All things were measured out, and even the gods could not trespass their assigned limits.[24]

National Socialism is the product of a negative reaction to and an inversion of the values of the Judeo-Christian world. As much as the nineteenth- and twentieth-century Teutonists wanted to rid themselves of Christianity, they were far more influenced by it than they imagined. In the end, the Nazis were able to negate Christianity and its values while using the Christian myth of Jewish villainy to their own purposes. They were never able to restore a genuine paganism. Perhaps Goethe foresaw the ironies of a German attempt to restore paganism when in *Faust*, Part II, he made the union of Faust, the German, and the Greek Helen of Troy result in the birth of Euphorion. Euphorion very quickly evaporates into nothingness. National Socialism is Judeo-Christian heresy, not paganism. It presupposes, though it overturns, both its *mythos* and its *ethos.*

The difference between the Judeo-Christian conception of *sin* and the Greek conception of *hubris* is of decisive importance. In the Judeo-Christian universe, good and evil are not rooted in the nature of things. The natural and the moral worlds are regarded as entirely dependent upon the omnipotent will of the Creator-God. He who created the natural world also created good and evil. *Sin,* in both Judaism and Christianity, is rebellion against the will of the Creator; righteousness is conformity to that will. This is succinctly stated by Father Mapple in his homily on Jonah in Herman Melville's *Moby Dick:* "As with all sinners among men, the sin of Jonah was his willful disobedience of the command of God, which he found a hard command. But if we obey God, we must disobey ourselves; and it is in this disobeying ourselves, wherein the hardness of obeying God consists."[25] In biblical religion, God's will is not subject to man's critical scrutiny. We are expected to comply because of the ultimate authority of the Source.

Only in the Judeo-Christian conception of a divinely created cosmos does deicide make sense as an anti-value explosion. It did not make sense in paganism, for the pagan believed that even the gods are governed by law and necessity. There could be no comparable deicidal myths in paganism because riddance of the gods could not effectuate a riddance from the norms to which even the pagan gods were said to be subject. There are dying gods aplenty in paganism, but no pagan could ever join Ivan Karamazov in declaring that if God did not exist, everything would be permitted.[26]

Only in biblical religion is there a meaningful motive for deicide as a human temptation, for only in biblical religion are all norms derived from the God who transcends them. *The wish to murder God makes sense only when all values derive from Him.* In such a system the deicidal act is an assertion of the will to total moral and religious license. This is the real meaning of the Christ-killer accusation repeated *ad nauseam* for almost two thousand years. In Confucianism, for example, the absence of a sovereign transcendent God does not entail moral or ethical nihilism. Although other political, social, and economic conditions were necessary before the Final Solution could become an acceptable program of government, only the terrible accusation, known and taught to every Christian in earliest childhood, that the Jews are the killers of Christ, can account for the depth and persistence of this supreme hatred.

In a sense, the death camps were the terminal expression of Christian anti-Semitism. Without Christianity, the Jews could never have become the central victims. Moreover, the hatred lives. Every swastika painted on a public place or Jewish establishment since the end of World War II is an expression of dark admiration for Auschwitz.[27]

The Aftermath of World War I

The darker aspects of the myth came to the fore, united with the Teuton's resentment of Jewish Christianity, when in the aftermath of World War I, the bloodiest war in history up to that time, Germany was beset by an ongoing series of crises involving the loss of millions of men in combat, military defeat, the collapse of the monarchy, partial foreign occupation, hyperinflation, and, finally, unprecedented mass unemployment in the Great Depression. The crises and the inability of the German people realistically to accept the fact that they had brought their predicament upon themselves created a witches' brew that ultimately spawned the death camps.

The very selection of Adolf Hitler by the German people and the demonic fascination he exerted upon them cannot be divorced from the radical rejection of normality and its restraints which took place under National Socialism. Hitler was the man from nowhere, possessed of an all-consuming fury, with nothing to lose. He convincingly defined a minuscule, helpless minority as the enemy *par excellence* of the German people, thereby legitimating any action, no matter how draconian, taken against them. At the appropriate moment, he offered the Germans the simplest method of dealing with their enemy—extermination. The relations between a leader and his community are in any event emotionally overdetermined, but never so completely as in the mysterious affair between Hitler and the Germans. He elicited from them something atavistic and demonic. The man, the people, and the hour were made for one another.

Contemporary social theory has devoted much reflection to the strains experienced by the average man and woman as a result of modern urban civilization with its pluralism of values, traditions, religions, moral standards, and ethnic inheritances. Older, more homogeneous ethnic communities have been able to maintain themselves primarily in the less urban areas of Europe and America. Linz, the town in which both Hitler and Eichmann grew up, was such a community. By contrast, few communities have ever been as cosmopolitan as the pre-World War I Vienna that nourished Freud, the theoretical master of the irrational, and whose large Jewish population angered Hitler, its practical master.[28] There is probably in most of us some yearning for the simplicity and security of the older, homogeneous folk culture. There is something disturbingly alienating, even for members of the dominant majority, about urban civilization, especially in very large cities. Human relationships become anonymous; values are challenged rather than confirmed; men become strangers in the world their families created many generations ago. When an ethnic minority reaches a certain critical mass in the nation's capital and its most important cities, the dominance of the majority group is subtly challenged. The bitter complaints voiced not only by the Nazis but by conservatives with an aversion to pluralism concerning the importance of Jews in the cultural life of Europe's capital cities reflected this phenomenon.

When the Germans invaded eastern Europe, the alien character of the Jews intensified their hazard. As was the case elsewhere, the large cities of eastern Europe were centers of trade, commerce, and finance. The prominent role of the Jews in business life intensified the hostility the majority felt toward them. The traditional elites had no interest in commercial risk taking. The indigenous bourgeoisie, often descendants of an older urban merchant class, rejected bourgeois values and adopted the noncompetitive values of the traditional elites, which were based upon inherited status. The preferred fields of activity of the traditional elites and their imitators were the bureaucracy and the armed forces, where status-honor could be preserved without commercial risk taking. Consequently, the commercial and entrepreneurial classes were recruited from persons of low status, whether native or immigrant. Germans, Armenians, and Greeks were among those recruited, but the majority were Jews. In countries like Hungary and Rumania commercial activity was largely in the hands of Jews, many of whom had emigrated from Galicia and the Pale of Settlement. They were regarded as permanently alien and unassimilable.[29]

The commercial function fulfilled by the alien bourgeoisie in eastern Europe was economically indispensable. It was also bitterly resented by the indigenous majority, few of whose members had or have any realistic understanding of business and finance. *Like the Devil, the Jews were associated with money.* The association with Judas discussed above further poisoned relations. Thus, the commercial life of the countries of eastern Europe was largely in the hands of a group perceived to be deceitful, unremittingly hostile to the dominant religion, and ultimately in league with the Devil. As is evident from the intractable ethnic conflicts that beset so many business minorities, even without negative religiomythic associations the Jewish situation was extremely precarious in the best of times.

Whether the modern experiment in urban pluralism can really work remains a question for the future. In times of radical stress, people tend to lose their tolerance for cultural ambiguity and seek to recapture lost simplicities. Where ties between group members are impersonal, rational, and contractual, as they tend to be in the contemporary urban environment, they also tend to be alienating, involving primarily the legal status of the person. In ethnic or folk culture, ties are more likely to be emotionally determined. Folk ties offer group members a sense of mutual involvement and kinship. Each social arrangement has its advantages and disadvantages. Lest we romanticize folk homogeneity, let us not forget the enormous gains in freedom, privacy, mobility, and the potentialities for personal growth modern civilization has made possible.[30] Whatever may have been the emotional advantages of folk culture, human inventiveness, especially in communications and transportation, has placed severe limitations on its viability. Nevertheless, in times of stress, groups are likely to opt for more primitive, though not necessarily more realistic, methods of coping. The shock of defeat in World War I eventually led the Germans to attempt to reorganize society along the lines of a homogeneous *Volk*-culture.[31] Insofar as modern civilization was regarded by the Germans as the product of European liberalism and the French Revolution, there were, as noted, important German advocates of a return to *Volk*-culture throughout the nineteenth century. The shock of national defeat and systemic crisis added immensely to their influence and created a desperate need for a leader to make sense of their disoriented world.

Hitler as Charismatic Leader and the German Moral Universe

In *Group Psychology and the Analysis of the Ego*, Sigmund Freud offered a prophetic analysis of the way individuals surrender their judgment and moral responsibility to an all-powerful leader in the process of group formation.[32] Put differently, Freud set forth a psychoanalytic interpretation of the relationship between the *charismatic leader* and his followers. According to Freud, people permit themselves cruelties and immoralities as members of cohesive groups which they would not otherwise permit themselves. He maintained that under the influence of an emotionally powerful leader the behavior of group members is characterized by *intensification of affect and diminution of intellectual functioning* as well as by *identification with and absolute submission to the will of the leader (Führer)*. Writing shortly before Hitler was to compose the murky pages of *Mein Kampf* in Landsberg Prison, Freud suggested that unquestioning loyalty to the leader and *identification of the individual's moral standards with the leader's will* are indispensable features of such group behavior. Freud maintained that group members identify the leader with their own *ego ideal*. Since the ego ideal is the mental faculty to which self-observation, moral conscience, and censorship are ascribed, identification of the ego ideal with the leader's will entails complete suspension of moral judgment as well as identification with the morals of the leader.

After the Nazis took power, all German officials were compelled to take an oath of allegiance to the person of Adolf Hitler rather than to the constitution. Every German was thereby bound by the closest of psychological ties to the Führer. The ties were reinforced every time two Germans greeted each other with *Heil Hitler!* One could not even use the telephone without experiencing the Führer's presence in the simple but demonically effective greeting. Elsewhere in Freud's writings, the ego ideal is more or less identified with the superego, the faculty of criticism and moral judgment which makes for moral compliance in the individual. According to Freud, the superego ultimately derives from the introjection of parental authority in the individual's psyche. For Freud, God is the projected superego of the community. By becoming the superego of a very significant part of the German people, Hitler acquired the God-like ability to determine right and wrong simply on the basis of his anarchic, archaic, and totally destructive will. The Germans were bound to Hitler by primal libidinous ties as members of a psychically, if not racially, homogeneous community. When Hitler took upon himself ultimate responsibility for the actions of those bound to him by solemn personal oath, he completed the transformation of the German moral system. Right and wrong were no longer defined by obedience to or rebellion against the will of the biblical God; they were defined solely in terms of obedience to or rebellion against the will of the Führer. Even the most casual remark of Hitler at the table could and did become the basis of a nonnegotiable *Führer-Befehl,* an order of the Leader. The theological significance of taking an unconditional oath of loyalty to Adolf Hitler was clearly understood by Karl Barth in 1934. Knowing that refusal would cost him his position at the University of Bonn, he declined to heed the advice of his illustrious colleague, Rudolf Bultmann, that he take the oath.[33]

Non-Germans have often been puzzled by the postwar disclaimers of responsibility put forth by German participants in some of the worst aspects of the Nazi crimes. Invariably, they claimed, "I acted under orders. I did my duty." Eichmann's defense was hardly atypical. Few of those involved in major crimes had the courage to declare: "I was a Nazi.

I still am. I'd do it all over again if I could." The Swedish film *Mein Kampf* (1961), which depicts Hitler's career, ends very strikingly. After rehearsing the enormity of the Nazi crimes, it shows scenes of Hitler's major subordinates all disclaiming responsibility. The last image is a brief glimpse of Hitler as the narrator asks: "Did he do it all himself?"

More than one student of World War II has expressed wonder at the seemingly charmed life Hitler led in spite of the fact that the German general staff was largely aware that he was bringing Germany to ruin.[34] Notwithstanding the obvious destructiveness and folly of Hitler's military leadership, especially after the failure of the 1944 *Putsch*, the generals were utterly incapable of bringing about his downfall. They later explained that they could not bring themselves to violate the oath of allegiance they had pledged to him. Honor had reduced itself to absolute fealty to the most dishonorable leader history has ever known. Although the Germans were willing to make and break promises at will in their dealings with others, very few could break their oath to Hitler, the leader of their *Volk* community, without feeling that their entire moral universe, primitive and atavistic as it was, would fall apart. He had become their source of moral judgment and their conscience. The burdensome pain of the inevitable loneliness and alienation of modern pluralistic society was at an end.

After the oath to Hitler had been taken and Hitler had accepted complete moral responsibility for the actions of those loyal to him, the Germans had arrived at the point of no return. No absolute monarch ever bound his people to himself more completely or with stronger emotional ties than did Adolf Hitler. Henceforth, there would be only one real crime: disobedience to the will of the Führer. It is not surprising that the system could not outlive its leader. His will had become the collective conscience of the German people in very much the same way that the will of the Lord was the standard of right and wrong for Jews and Christians. While Judeo-Christian submission was normally life enhancing, the new German submission became an instrument of mass murder and, ultimately, of national self-destruction.[35]

The incapacity of the Germans realistically to accept defeat and their subsequent transformation under Hitler into a primitive *Volk* community were accompanied by the need to find a magic enemy of omnipotent proportions to blame for the terrible happenings. Always strangers, the Jews now became enemies in German eyes. Once a consensus to form a *Volk* community was achieved, there was no longer a viable place for the Jews in German life. If nothing else, their international connections, their involuntary cosmopolitanism, and the never-to-be-forgotten fact that

Jewish emancipation had first been brought to Germany by Napoleon's foreign armies, all made Jewish participation in German life utterly untenable.

The untenability of the Jewish situation in Germany was already implicit in the sociological distinction Ferdinand Tönnies drew between *Gemeinschaft* and *Gesellschaft* (1887).[36] Tönnies regarded *Gemeinschaft* as an organic group that shared common origins, values, beliefs, traditions, and inherited institutions; *Gesellschaft* was regarded as the rational and contractual association of isolated, self-aggrandizing individuals bound by no such organic ties. *Gesellschaft* is typical of modern Western urban society. Even as important a Jewish thinker as Martin Buber compared *Gesellschaft* unfavorably to *Gemeinschaft*.[37] By hankering after a *Gemeinschaft*, German high scholarship contributed its sophistication, albeit not always with malicious intent, to the National Socialist movement, which used genocide as its primary means of creating a racially pure *Volksgemeinschaft*. Even without National Socialism, Germany's Jews would have had no place in a German *Gemeinschaft*. Hitler won his war against the Jews. Save for a very small remnant, no Jews remain in Germany. Hitler did not fail the Germans on the Jewish question. Perhaps it is no accident that the same Vienna that was so influential in the careers of Hitler and Freud also nurtured Theodor Herzl, the father of modern Zionism.[38] His vision of a reconstituted Israel was ultimately the result of a radical pessimism concerning the place of the Jews in modern Europe.

In the end, Germany required more of the Jews than expulsion or assimilation. An allegedly omnipotent enemy was needed to provide the raw material for what was to become history's greatest ritual murder. German popular culture had long ago designated the villain-enemy-victim. As we have seen, the myth of the Jew as Christ-killer, from which were derived the secondary myths of the Jew as Antichrist, Devil's spawn, Satan, sorcerer, magician, cannibal, and murderer, pointed to the existence of a demonic power equal to the task of sapping Germany's strength, of secretly causing her defeat, and of gloating in the triumph of the victors. The age-old Passion plays, such as the one still performed at Oberammergau, the liturgy of Holy Week, the religious instruction of little children, the habit of providing Mephistopheles with a Yiddish accent in the oft-repeated performances of Goethe's *Faust*, and even the turning of Hansel and Gretel's witch into a Jewish crone, all reinforced an anc.ent hatred in a time of modern anxiety and bitterness. Just as the "demonic" Jews of the Middle Ages had supposedly brought about the Black Death by their midnight arts and had allegedly sacrificed innocent Christian children in order to drink their blood at Passover, so they were now regarded as a prime cause of the Fatherland's defeat. Not the open power of the known enemy but the hidden power of the satanic magic enemy had brought about the "stab in the back." Again, the Judas myth.

The Kiss of Judas

The paranoid myth of the Jew as the magic betrayer sufficiently potent to destroy Germany from within, as he had once destroyed Christ, was vastly reinforced by the *kiss of Judas* tale. In the Gospels Judas betrays Jesus for thirty pieces of silver. Judas identifies the divine-human victim by *a loving kiss*. The moral of the story is obvious: one can never trust a Jew. Even the most seemingly outgoing offer of friendship and affection by a Jew can never conceal the betrayer's curse or the enemy's cunning. Furthermore, these stories are not told when the hearers are at an age at which they are capable of realistically evaluating their applicability to flesh-and-blood Jews. They are first heard as tales for little children who have yet to separate the worlds of fact and fantasy. In later life, they are most operative in periods of stress, when the individual is most likely to regress from his adult faculties of rationality and self-criticism to the infantile level at which the stories were first heard. In the German turn from *Gesellschaft* to National Socialist *Volksgemeinschaft*, we have a social analogue of this process.

Even without Hitler, the Judas story is destined to continue to contribute a measure of poison to Jewish-Christian relations. The Judas tale is part and parcel of the Passion drama, which is retold and relived by every Christian during Holy Week. From the cradle to the grave, few stereotypical images are as consistently reinforced in the most emotionally potent environments as these. The high point of the Christian religious calendar rehearses, amidst utterly magnificent music, frequently aesthetically overpowering architecture, and ceremonial grandeur, the terrible tale of the Jewish betrayal and the Jewish murder of the Jewish God!

Judas was not the only betrayer image with which Jews were identified. There was also Hagen in Wagnerian opera. Peter Viereck has pointed to the influence of Wagner on the development of neo-Teutonic ideology.[39] In the opera house it was possible to resurrect the old Teutonic gods and give a ritual setting to their *mythos* without the necessity of a frontal attack against Christianity. Viereck contends, with considerable justice, that the Germans saw themselves largely in Wagnerian terms as a nation of Siegfrieds, especially after the First World War defeat. Just as Siegfried had his Hagen, so the Germans had their Jews. As blond Siegfried was basely betrayed by Hagen, the Germans increasingly regarded the Jews as Hagen-like betrayers. The dramatics of Wagnerian opera became real as the Nazi leaders enacted their own *Götterdämmerung* with the collapse of the Third Reich. Nevertheless, the figure of Hagen as the betrayer is quite secondary and derivative. The Germans may have seen themselves as Siegfrieds, but they saw the Jews as Judases rather than Hagens. Surprisingly, Viereck never mentions the Judas myth, in which the betrayer is firmly and explicitly identified with the Jews. In any event, both images were available to feed the flames of German paranoia.

Nor was Germany the only modern country in which the Judas myth exhibited its power. When Captain Alfred Dreyfus, the only Jew on the French General Staff, was unjustly accused by his colleagues in 1894 of having betrayed France's military secrets to Germany, he was identified with Judas. Commenting on Dreyfus's public degradation on the Champs de Mars, the parade ground of Paris's Ecole Militaire, *La Croix*, the anti-Semitic newspaper of the Assumptionist Fathers, declared, "His cry of '*Vive la France!*' was the kiss of Judas Iscariot."[40] As Colonel Jean Sandherr, head of the Deuxième Bureau, the army's intelligence agency watched the degradation, he told a colleague, "That race has done . . . nothing but betray. Remember they betrayed Christ!"[41]

The Judas story created the psychological ground on which Germans could, under stress, believe that the Judas-Jews had betrayed their country, caused her defeat in World War I, and hence, were the omnipotent enemy to be destroyed at all costs. It was futile for Jewish defense and veterans' groups to point to Jewish sacrifices on behalf of the Fatherland during the war. After all, Judas had betrayed his Lord with a kiss. The appearance of loyalty in a Jew could not be credited, even when that appearance was purchased through death on the battlefield.

By accusing the Jews of demonic powers, fiendish temptations, and complete lack of trustworthiness, the Nazis were able to use the most demonic of instrumentalities against them. *The demonic was thus made licit for the Nazis.* Nazi literature emphasized *ad nauseam* the alleged immorality of the Jews and the danger they presented to civilization, though no one ever endangered civilization as much as the Nazis. Those who accused the Jews of demonic intent and power created the most demonic environment ever known to man, the death camp, an environment in which God is dead and all things are permissible to the masters. Some who called the Jews Christ-killers did so out of envy.[42]

Anus Mundi

Consistent with these demonic associations, the Nazis referred to Auschwitz as the *anus mundi*. Such associations are hardly ever gratuitous. Norman O. Brown has pointed to the significance of the anal characteristics of the Devil.[43] The sulfurous fumes associated with the Devil were in reality a fecal stench. His color, like that of the SS uniforms, was black. The Black Mass included scatological rites in which offal of the worst sort, including feces and menstrual blood, were kneaded on the buttocks of the Queen of the Sabbath as a sacred host. Brown also points to Hieronymus Bosch's painting in which Satan is enthroned on a privy, where souls pass out of his anus into the black pit of Hell. Luther's encounters with the Devil are shown by Brown to have been overdetermined by anal and fecal considerations. Brown emphasizes the importance of the Devil as the decisive opponent of the German reformer. He omits, however, the portentous fact that in German folk culture the Devil is either a Jew or the Lord of the Jews, both of whom are supposed to exude a fecal odor, the so-called *foetor judaicus*.[44]

The *anus mundi* was the habitat of the Devil. If ever such a habitat was successfully established on earth, it was at Auschwitz.

Only at the *anus mundi* could the Jew as deicide, betrayer, and incarnate Devil be turned into the feces of the world. Rudolph Hoess, the Nazi commandant at Auschwitz, was one of the many Nazis to note and complain of the hideous fecal stench of the camp.[45] In addition, the camps smelled of human decay. The SS immersed themselves in human stench to destroy what they regarded as the ultimate in human evil. As had so frequently occurred before, those who saw themselves as overwhelming a radical evil felt compelled to fight evil with evil. The Devil could be fought only with the Devil's weapons.

Along a similar line of inquiry, Adolph Leschnitzer has explored the role of witchcraft in determining the German attitude toward the Jews. In the treatment of the witch, no mercy was to be shown because of her demonic powers and those of her satanic master. The parallels between the ascription of the ills of German society to witches in the sixteenth and seventeenth centuries and the imputations against the Jews in the twentieth century are instructive. According to Leschnitzer, more than one million unfortunates, most of them women, were killed as witches between 1500 and 1700. The vast majority of the executions took place in the Germanic lands. The witches were regarded as an anti-Christian force within the community, an attribute they shared with the Jews. Like most Jewish victims in the extermination camps, their bodies were ultimately disposed of by burning.[46]

Fire consumed the bodies of both the Jews and the witches, but the Jews were first executed by an *insecticide*, Zyklon B. In both Eichmann's and Hoess's testimony, the use of Zyklon B was ascribed to the desire to find an efficient exterminant that would not have the debilitating effect on the personalities of the guards that outright shooting of the victims had produced. Zyklon B was chosen because it could kill large numbers quickly and efficiently. It was a variant of Zyklon A. Zyklon was an abbreviation of the gas's most important ingredients, cyanide, chloride, and nitrogen. Perhaps it was no accident that Hitler had already written in *Mein Kampf*, "If at the beginning of the War and during the War twelve or fifteen thousand of these Hebrew corrupters of the people had been held under poison gas, as happened to hundreds of thousands of our very best German workers in the field, the sacrifice of millions at the front would not have been in vain."[47] In our world, where the actual has far outdistanced the fantastic in its gruesomeness, it is likely that Hitler decided upon the Final Solution at Landsberg Prison in 1923, if not earlier, rather than in preparation for the Wannsee Conference on January 20, 1942, at which Reinhard Heydrich informed senior officials in the German government that the Führer had decided upon the Final Solution of the Jewish problem.[48]

In Nazi propaganda the Jews are identified with lice, vermin, and insects, the very organisms for which an insecticide like Zyklon B was most appropriate. These were also the organisms most intimately associated with the Devil in medieval demonology. These insects and detestable animals were also thought to be the brood of fecal dirt and to find their nourishment and habitat by wallowing in the same fecal dirt from which they were spawned.

We can even speculate that a basic strategy of the death camps was to turn the Jews into feces, the Devil's food, gold, and weapon. In his confessions, Hoess insists that those who died did so with a minimum of pain and that only under very special circumstances was death accompanied by involuntary defecation. His testimony has been contradicted by a more reliable witness, Dr. Miklós Nyiszli, the Jewish assistant to Auschwitz's infamous Dr. Joseph Mengele. Nyiszli's description of the way the bodies were found after the gas chambers were opened is instructive:

> The bodies were not lying here and there throughout the room, but piled in a mass to the ceiling. The reason for this was that the gas first inundated the lower layers of air and rose but slowly towards the ceiling. This forced the victims to trample one another in a frantic effort to escape the gas. . . .
> The Sonderkommando squad [Jewish prisoners assigned to this task], outfitted with large rubber boots, lined up around the hill of bodies and flooded it with powerful jets of water. *This was necessary as the*

final act of those who die by drowning or by gas is an involuntary defecation (italics added).[49]

No matter how efficient the crematoria were, there were always mounds of corpses waiting for final riddance. The pervasive smell of decay was always there. The destruction process in the camps has been identified as "excremental assault."[50] Apart from the smell of decay, the Germans severely limited the times and places camp prisoners could eliminate their waste. Toilet facilities were hopelessly inadequate. One camp section at Auschwitz had only a single latrine for more than thirty thousand female prisoners.[51] Moreover, the soup that was the prisoners' principal fare made many ill with diarrhea and dysentery. Unable to control their bowels, they were compelled to risk severe beatings or death by "illegally" going to the toilet. Alternatively, they evacuated in their own eating utensils or clothing. The "excremental assault" actually began when Jews were first herded like animals into cattle cars to be transported to the camps. Forced to stand during the seemingly endless journey, it was often impossible to avoid vomiting, urinating, or defecating on the spot. To this must be added the fact that those who were not gassed were most likely to perish because of diarrhea and dysentery. The prisoner-victims were condemned to perish in their own excrement.[52] Only in the camps was Dostoevsky's vision of a world without God nearly realized, a world in which any act could be allowed the perpetrators. This was truly hell on earth.

The aim of creating a world in which God is dead (or, more precisely, in which the Judeo-Christian God is *negated*) was at the heart of the Nazi program. That such a world would be dominated by a real devil like Hitler rather than a fantasied Devil followed quite necessarily. When in August 1961 I visited Marienfelde, the refugee reception center in West Berlin for East Germans, I could not avoid contrasting the fate of Germans in defeat with what would have been the fate of Germany's eastern enemies had the Nazis won. The plight of the East German refugees was unenviable, but at least they had their health and, by and large, their families were intact. Few left Marienfelde without the assurance of a decently paying job somewhere in prosperous West Germany. Had the Nazis won, in all likelihood their death machines would have been self-perpetuating. Having acquired the administrative and managerial skills necessary to eliminate a defeated enemy, the Germans probably would have expanded their extermination campaign against Russians, Poles, and other Slavs with the demise of the last Jew. The Soviet Union's treatment of East Germany was a paradise of magnanimity compared with the German occupation of Russia or Nazi Germany's postwar plans for the Slavic peoples. There is no more reason to doubt Hitler's promise to find greater *Lebensraum* for Germany by enslaving and exterminating Slavs than his promise to exterminate the Jews. In the long run, a Nazi world would have consisted of Nazified Germans and their Nazified clients. Even the German people would have provided their share of victims for the destructive projects of their Nazi masters, as the so-called Euthanasia project demonstrates. In the name of the health of the German people, thousands of physically and mentally impaired Germans were put to death during the war.[53]

The Search for Paradise Lost

The anal character of the camps was not a phenomenon isolated from the larger German society or from important aspects of Western civilization outside of Germany. The creation of the camps was a search for a paradise lost, for a time, remembered from infancy, when little or no restraint impeded human impulse. All of us are heir to such longings. They powerfully affect our psychic structures. We do not normally succumb because we are not prepared to jeopardize the gratifications of adult life for the sake of infantile yearnings. When the strains of the adult world are too severe or its disappointments too bitter, the constraints against infantile gratification tend to diminish. When infantile regression is validated by collective consent, there is little limit to what a group will permit itself.

The fantasy of a world without restraints, the world in which God is dead, can be imagined at many levels. It can be seen as a world without impediment to sexual or aggressive activity. However, sexual and aggressive permissiveness are by no means the only infantile freedoms we secretly yearn for. In the Witches' Sabbath scene of *Faust*, in which Goethe paints a picture of utter abandon, there is another freedom related to aggression, the freedom to soil, evacuate, and pass wind at will.

Anal freedom and its relationship to the Devil and the Jews may not seem very important at first glance. Nevertheless, toilet training is one of the earliest and most trying aspects of the socialization process. Only when the child achieves a certain retentive ability can he or she be permitted the first tentative ventures into the wider community. Any attempt to overcome social constraints is likely to carry with it the dimly remembered vision of the time in infancy when the child was closest to mother and soiling was permitted without limit or restraint. It is unlikely that Adolf Hitler ever forgot this time.

Goethe was too great a poet to distort the truth about limitless freedom. When he depicted the seductions with which Mephistopheles sought to tempt the German Faust, the vision of excremental freedom was an important component. Satan's promise of freedom carries with it the freedom to soil at will. In the death camps this dimly remembered infant freedom was combined with the terror of adult power, technical intelligence, and efficiency.

In *Life against Death*, Norman O. Brown writes about the obsession of German culture, at least since the time of Luther, with the problems of anality.[54] Robert G. L. Waite has observed that Hitler's frequent use of anal imagery in private conversation expressed an unconscious fixation on feces, filth, manure, and fecal odors. In his *Table Talk*, Hitler described the Jew as taking "treasures into his hand" and transforming them "into dirt and dung," a description reminiscent of the psychoanalytic view of money as an unconscious substitute for feces and the medieval view that gold as a gift of the Devil is transformed into dung in the hands of its possessor.[55] One of Hitler's favorite words in private conversation was *Scheisskerl* (sh--head), a word he applied to himself when comparing his achievements to those of Frederick the Great.[56]

Obsession with anality came to a head in the camps, which the Nazis, as noted, referred to as the *anus mundi*. Sometimes they left corpses in large numbers to deteriorate unburied. The smell of carrion is awful, but there is little to distinguish it from the strong smell of feces. While the Nazis could not without incontinence give free rein to their own anal obsessions, they could and did turn the Jews, whom their folk culture regarded as the satanic murderers of the dead God, into feces.

Sadism and anality are related. Since great pleasure is derived from excremental action, a pleasure preserved in off-color jokes, attempts to curb free evacuation, such as toilet training, may be bitterly resented by the child. Those who remember toilet training as having been harsh are likely to deal with their own offspring with a similar harshness, unconsciously resentful at having once been curbed and intuiting how deeply rebellious the child in training really is. Most Germans have always been exceptionally proud of their orderliness, cleanliness, and frugality, character traits identified by Freud as "anal."[57] Klara Hitler, Adolf's mother, had a reputation for having "the cleanest house in town" and keeping her children "absolutely spotless."[58] Her son was also obsessed with his own personal cleanliness and tidiness.[59]

The Germans have also been known to possess another anal character trait, obstinacy. According to Freud, "'Orderly' comprises both bodily cleanliness and reliability and conscientiousness in the performance of petty duties: the opposite of it would be 'untidy' and 'negligent.' 'Parsimony' may be exaggerated up to the point of avarice; and obstinacy may amount to defiance, with which irascibility and vindictiveness may easily be associated.[60] Such traits tend to reflect inward rebelliousness and resentment. Men and women possessed of such traits tend to make excellent disciplinarians. They do not want others to escape the bitter training that was inflicted on them, a discipline that, with all its self-perpetuating harshness, begins with toilet training. By opposing toilet training, the child expresses hostility to the restraining and law-giving adult world.

Judaism as a religion of law represented much that such outwardly disciplined, inwardly rebellious men and women resent most deeply. This resentment was enhanced by the Church's claim to have liberated people from the God of the Old Testament and His Law. One of the greatest ironies of Jewish-gentile relations has been the enormous resentment the Jewish stress on behavioral discipline has elicited among non-Jews. Hitler is reputed to have said that conscience is a blemish like circumcision and that both are Jewish blemishes.[61]

Children have an ambivalent attitude toward their own waste products, which are regarded as both beloved object (i.e., feces as gift) and hated object, the dirty leavings that are sadistically "pinched off" one's own body.[62] According to psychoanalyst Otto Fenichel, sadistic adults often treat others as they once treated their own feces. Furthermore, the feces are the first part of one's own body to become dead, foreign, dirty, and alien. Elimination is the first process in which something human is turned into a dead object.[63] The quantifying rationality of modern society affords us, as adults, many opportunities to treat others as if they were inanimate objects, and quantifying rationality, the indispensable precondition of the modern world, has been identified as at bottom an anal character trait.[64] The tendency to treat human beings as objects is unavoidable in a complex technological civilization. For most of us, it is regrettable but necessary. The Nazis carried the tendency to an extreme, treating targeted categories of human beings as inanimate objects. This characteristic was manifest in the camps in the stench of the corpses and in the use of people as raw material to be turned into feces, the chief product of the camp in spite of the hundreds of millions of dollars spent by I. G. Farben to construct a synthetic rubber factory at Auschwitz. There were, of course, subordinate industries, such as the turning of the fat from Jewish bodies into *reine Jüdische Seife*, "pure Jewish soap," their gold teeth into Reichsbank deposits, and occasionally, their skin into luminous lampshades. Even direct passionate sadism at the level of individual personal relations seems to have been exceptional though permitted. The whole enterprise was directed primarily to the manufacture of corpses. The people alleged to be of the Devil were turned into the ultimate element of the Devil.

Anal sadism constitutes one attempt to regain the lost paradise of early childhood. The quest for the millennium, of which Hitler's "Thousand-Year Reich" was a demonic example, is another. This quest can be one of humanity's darkest temptations.[65] It is not an attempt to achieve in the future what has not been realized in the past or present but an attempt to embody concretely the fantasied remembrance of paradise lost, the time in childhood before the restraints of the world and society were known to be necessary. Nazi millennialism aroused deeper fanaticism than its Bolshevik counterpart because the Nazis understood that the lost paradise promised more than economic and sociopolitical fulfillment.

Perhaps a decisive turning point on the road to the Final Solution came when the Germans refused to accept the reality of their defeat at the hands of the Western powers in World War I. On December 11, 1918, exactly one month to the day after the Armistice, the returning German soldiers marched in review at the Brandenburg Gate before Friedrich Ebert, president of the Provisional German Government, as if they were victors. Ebert greeted the defeated army with the words, "I salute you, who return unvanquished from the field of battle." As English historian J. W. Wheeler-Bennett has succinctly stated: "The legend of the 'stab in the back' had been born, the seeds of the Second World War already sown."[66]

Following the lead of Ebert and Von Hindenburg, the Germans denied the terrible reality they themselves had wrought. Incapable of assuming responsibility for their own deeds, they could not say to themselves as they did after World War II, "We are not invincible. We have been defeated and now our business is to cope with a world very different from the one for which we fought." In 1918 the Germans had lost much, but they retained a unitary state. They possessed a land area that today's reunified Germans can only regard with envy and regret. Instead of accepting a peace that was far less onerous than the one they were finally forced to accept in 1945, they allowed their leaders to convince them that they had not really lost the war, that they had been stabbed in the back, and that victory would finally be theirs when they destroyed their betrayers. Only time, and not much of that, was needed before the betrayer label was firmly placed upon those who had in any event borne the Judas label for almost two thousand years. As noted above, the myth of Jewish magic villainy provided the perfect object for this fantasy. In the language of Jean-Paul Sartre, the "stab-in-the-back" legend was an example of German *mauvaise foi*, that is, the inability to accept responsibility for acts they themselves had freely undertaken; in the language of psychology, it was a massive withdrawal from reality to fantasy. Unfortunately, the withdrawal had very real consequences. Under National Socialism the goal of German life became the violent restructuring of the world to conform to primitive German wish by means of propaganda, totalitarian terror, military aggression, mass enslavement of defeated populations, and, above all, the extermination camps. Such a goal would have driven the Germans, had they won, to make the camps into the authentic prototype of the Nazi state, that is, a society of total domination. Hannah Arendt was the first to see this in *The Origin of Totalitarianism.*[67] Insights available since the publication of her work have tended to underscore the significance of her conclusions.

Reality will always have the final say, if only in the grave. When the game was up, Hitler wanted all of Germany to perish with him. When victory became impossible, Hitler and Goebbels could only envisage Germany's total destruction. According to Sebastian Hafner, from February to April 1945 Hitler pursued "the total destruction of Germany" with "the same energy that he had devoted to the annihilation of the Jews."[68] Goebbels actually gloried in the thought of the total destruction of Germany and welcomed the Allied bombers as bringing a necessary catharsis that would ruin the old and create the eventual conditions of a purified, truly Nazi Germany. Goebbels declared, "Under the ruins of our devastated cities the last so-called achievements of the bourgeois nineteenth century have finally been buried. Together with the monuments of culture, the last obstacles to the fulfillment of our revolutionary task are likewise falling."[69] At no point did it occur to the most radical Nazis that there might be a way their country, if not their inner circle, could live in a world that was resistant to their claims. Of course, when the Nazis had passed the point of no return in what the victorious Allies would come to view as criminality, they had no alternative but to fight to the bitter end or to escape to a sympathetic country like Argentina.

When the Germans refused to follow Hitler's suicidal scorched earth policy, he complained bitterly that the German people, who had sacrificed so much in men, treasure, and honor to follow him, were unworthy of him.[70] In March 1945 Albert Speer reminded Hitler that in defeat it was the leader's duty to preserve the nation. Speer later summarized the gist of the dictator's response. Hitler declared, "If the war is lost, the people will be lost also. It is not necessary to worry about what the German people will need for elemental survival. On the contrary, *it is best for us to destroy these things.* For the nation has proved to be the weaker, and the future belongs to the stronger eastern nation. In any case, only those who are inferior will remain after this struggle, for the good have already been killed."[71]

The final irony of National Socialism was its self-destructiveness. The Nazi love affair with death far exceeded Nazi violence against the Jews. It was to be found in the silver death's-head signet ring worn by proven SS men; in the names that they gave some of their units, such as the *Totenkopfverbände*, the Death's Head concentration camp guard units; and, above all, in the *Götterdämmerung* ending of Hitler's Reich.

Ultimately, the total end to restraint has no other meaning than the end to existence itself, for, of necessity, to be something means to be something definite, concrete, and limited. Only death and nothingness are without limit. Scholars may debate the exact merits of William L. Shirer's *The Rise and Fall of the Third Reich.*[72] It has at least one superlative merit. The author makes it very clear that the *Götterdämmerung* ending was implicit in the enterprise from the very beginning. The Nazi adventure must be seen as a psychotic affair in the sense that psychotics abjure and reject reality for their preferred world of fantasy. Reviewing the dreary history of the Third Reich, one gets the feeling that one is reading a Greek tale in which almighty nemesis must pronounce the final judgment. Perhaps a similar feeling moved Wheeler-Bennett to entitle his magnificent history of the German army in politics from 1918 to 1945, *The Nemesis of Power.* When Adolf Hitler inevitably failed to make the real world conform to his archaic fantasies, he had no choice but to eliminate reality by eliminating himself. Having been responsible for the cremation of millions, he now provided for his own burning. In those flames, he finally returned to the peace he had sought ever since the cruel fates thrust him forth from the bliss of his mother's womb. He had revenged himself upon a world that had disturbed that peace and had finally returned to it.

Apart from the fact that self-destruction was the inevitable climax, the whole business of moral anarchy soon lost its charm. Goethe clearly understood the limitations of moral anarchy in the Witches' Sabbath scene of *Faust.* He depicts Faust as irresistibly drawn to a beautiful naked witch. At the instant Faust reaches out to kiss the seductress, a bloody mouse leaps out of her mouth at Faust. Goethe's point is that things seldom end as we anticipate. When, as in the world of the death of God, all things are permissible, they are by no means necessarily enjoyable. On the contrary, the whole Nazi venture soon became a very dirty, dull enterprise that had to be rationalized into a quasi-business venture to be bearable at all. Thus we find Himmler, in a moment of self-pity, commending the SS for having had to take part in the mess and "still remain good fellows."[73] God was dead, hell—the *anus mundi*—had been established on earth, and yet, even hell had lost its fine savor. All that remained, then as well as now, was an ineradicable stench.

Postscript

On November 9, 1989, while in Toledo, Spain, I watched both West and East German television by satellite as the Berlin Wall came down. I was moved by the event, especially in view of the fact that I arrived in Berlin for the first time on August 15, 1961, two days after the wall went up. With the end of the wall, German reunification became inevitable. Moreover, almost all informed authorities agree that reunified Germany will be Europe's strongest power economically and potentially its strongest power militarily. How different were the attempts to restore German power after World War I and World War II! After 1945 the West Germans set out to restore their country's economy, its manufacturing base, and the reputation of German products instead of blaming their defeat on some magic betrayer and seeking once again to restore German power by military aggression. This time it cannot be said that the restoration of German power was achieved by means that were other than fair or honorable.

Had the Germans taken a similar path after World War I, Germany would now be far larger territorially and stronger economically than even reunified Germany promises to be. The post–World War II German achievement further highlights how suicidal and self-destructive National Socialism was for the very country to which it promised world dominion.

CHAPTER 4

The Auschwitz Convent
Controversy

The painful controversy over the location of the Carmelite convent within a building a few yards from Auschwitz brought to the surface many of the persistent wounds of the still unmastered trauma of World War II. Some of the most difficult aspects of Jewish-Christian and Jewish-Polish relations were once again made manifest. Fortunately, communication did not break down and the dispute appears to have been resolved, albeit less than perfectly.

To deepen my understanding of the controversy, I visited the city of Kraków and the nearby sites of Auschwitz and Birkenau during the week of December 11, 1989. Although I understand and share the feelings that compelled leaders of the Jewish community to request that the convent be relocated, the visit convinced me that it would have been better had no such request been made in the first place. However, by the summer of 1989 emotions had become so inflamed that relocating the convent a short distance away from the main camp and establishing an interfaith center, in accordance with the February 22, 1987, agreement of European Catholic and Jewish leaders, became the only way to calm a situation that had gotten so badly out of hand as needlessly to jeopardize the very real progress made in Jewish-Catholic relations since Vatican II.

Jewish-Christian relations carry a special burden in the post-Holocaust era of instantaneous global communication. Both traditions make claims to exclusive knowledge of God's revealed will. Unfortunately, the claims are contradictory. Each tradition finds itself in the position of disconfirming that which the other takes to be decisive and nonnegotiable in the divine-human encounter. Moreover, because of Christianity's supersessionary claims concerning Judaism, far more is at stake in the differences between these two traditions than in those between either tradition and Hinduism, Buddhism, or Shintoism.[1] In the past, the Christian Church has used whatever strategies were necessary to maintain its cognitive monopoly within the territories in which it was dominant. To the extent that Jews were permitted domicile, it was only under conditions in which that cognitive monopoly was not seriously challenged. Very often negative images of the Jew, which were largely a consequence of Church teaching, and the relegation of Jews to occupations regarded as degraded in premodern societies, served to reinforce the monopoly.

Given the global proliferation of low-cost communications media, no institution, political or religious, can any longer maintain a cognitive monopoly, a lesson the communist leaders of eastern Europe learned to their very great distress. Moreover, in religiously and ethnically plural societies such as the United States, the mainstream religious institutions, Protestant, Catholic, and Jewish, have come to accept a measure of ecumenical accommodation and cooperation. Nevertheless, the tension between exclusive religious claims and the imperatives of pluralism has yet to disappear. In times of stress and conflict the forces making for dialogue can easily be overwhelmed. This possibility became manifest in the convent controversy.

At the height of the controversy, there was a marked difference between the positions taken and the words spoken by József Cardinal Glemp, the Primate of Poland, and such Western Catholic leaders as John Cardinal O'Connor of New York, Bernard Cardinal Law of Boston, Franz Cardinal Koenig, the former Archbishop of Vienna, and, finally, even Pope John Paul II himself. Cardinal Glemp oversees the Catholic Church in a country in which its religious monopoly is unchallenged and in which its principal ideological adversary, atheistic communism, has been thoroughly discredited in the eyes of almost all Poles. Apparently, Glemp saw far less reason than did his peers outside of Poland to balance the Church's exclusivistic and traditionally negative attitudes toward the Jews with the imperatives of ecumenical cooperation.

During the visit to Poland, I was questioned concerning my own views on the convent controversy. I also had the opportunity to discuss the dispute with a number of well-informed and well-intentioned Poles. Since Poles in large numbers perished at Auschwitz, they argued that Auschwitz is an appropriate location for the convent. Given the historic link between Polish national identity and Roman Catholicism, none of my Polish informants could understand why anyone would object to the nuns devoting their lives to reconciliation and prayer for those murdered at Auschwitz. No Pole with whom I spoke regarded the convent as an attempt to appropriate Auschwitz as a Polish and Christian rather than a Jewish site. Moreover, even those who believed it best for the sake of interreligious concord to relocate the convent saw nothing wrong with its present location.

The fundamental difference between the attitude of most Poles and that of Jews and even many Western European and American Christian leaders was epitomized by a question put to me on December 13 at the State Cultural Center in Kraków following my lecture, "Religion and Politics in the United States," which offered an overview of the political attitudes of America's many religious groups.

"Do you think it is a good thing that America has so many religions?" I was asked. Like most Poles the questioner was not used to religious pluralism. He was genuinely puzzled by America's ethnic and religious diversity and had difficulty in understanding how it could possibly work. He did not see how pluralism could be consistent with national identity. To be Polish meant to be Roman Catholic or, in the case of atheistic communists, to be the offspring of Polish Roman Catholics. In spite of forty-five years of Soviet-imposed communist rule, Polish society remains a sacralized society.

Although there was no hint of ill-will in the way the question was asked, its implications mirrored many crucial elements in the tragic history of Jewish-Polish relations. To the extent that the newly independent Poles were unable or unwilling to create a genuinely pluralistic state in 1918 after World War I, the presence of Europe's largest Jewish minority, 10 percent of Poland's population, was bound to be untenable. When after almost one hundred fifty years of foreign rule Poland regained its independence, one of the most important questions confronting the nation was whether it would be a pluralistic community consisting of a federation of eastern European peoples such as Belorussians, Ukrainians, Jews, ethnic Germans, and Lithuanians, albeit led by Poles, or a homogeneous religioethnic community. Marshall Józef Pilsudski's (1867–1935) vision was of a Polish-led multiethnic federation. Pilsudski was Poland's leader and "uncrowned king" from the end of World War I until his death. The vision of an ethnically and religiously homogeneous Poland was fostered by Roman Dmowski (1864–1939), the most important leader of the ultra-right-wing, anti-Semitic National Democratic Party, popularly known as the *Endecja*. To this day Endecja remains a powerful force in Polish life. According to Abraham Brumberg, a leading authority on contemporary Poland, Józef Cardinal Glemp has professed sympathy for

Endecja, a fact confirmed to me by responsible Polish observers on my recent trip.[2]

In the first decade of the twentieth century Dmowski reflected on the reasons why Poland had not regained its independence and sovereignty. According to Dmowski, Poland's ethnic pluralism and its religious toleration constituted the nation's fundamental flaw. Poland contained too many unassimilable minorities, the Jews being the most unassimilable. Dmowski argued that the Poles would only regain their independence when they no longer needed any help from the minorities. He called upon the offspring of Poland's gentry to abandon agriculture and to train as professionals, managers, and technicians in order to provide the nation with the cadres necessary for a modern industrial society. He was especially insistent that they displace the Jews as Poland's commercial and professional class.[3] In 1914 Dmowski wrote that the whole tradition of European Christian society was alien to "the Jew." Hence, he considered the Jew to be "the most dangerous enemy of Polish civilization, bent on destroying all vestiges of those institutions and ideals that a Pole would hold dear."[4]

Dmowski served as one of reborn Poland's delegates at the Paris Peace Conference of 1919. In the confusion following the Bolshevik Revolution and the German collapse, Polish forces occupied territory on practically all of Poland's borders containing large numbers of Germans, Jews, Belorussians, Ukrainians, and Lithuanians. Reports of pogroms and widespread terrorism against Jews in newly independent Poland aroused concern among the Allies. Stephen Bonsal, an American official, was assigned the task of sounding out Dmowski on the Jewish question. Dmowski told Bonsal that the Jews "constitute at least ten percent of our population, and in my judgment this is eight percent too much. . . . Unless restrictions are imposed upon them soon, all our lawyers, doctors and small merchants will be Jews."[5]

Dmowski's frankness did not help his cause. The Allies compelled Poland to sign a treaty guaranteeing equal rights for all of her minorities. Articles 10 and 11 of the Minorities Treaty specifically applied to Jewish religious and cultural autonomy. The treaty was signed on June 28, 1919, the very same day Poland signed the Treaty of Versailles guaranteeing her independence.[6]

From the start, Jews and Poles had fundamentally different perceptions of the Minorities Treaty. The Jews assumed that the rights specified in the treaty had the force of international law. By contrast, the Poles saw the treaty as an affront to their national honor and dignity imposed upon them by foreigners. When the Jews criticized the Polish government for not living up to the provisions of the treaty, they were bitterly resented, a resentment that was intensified when influential American Jews supported their coreligionists.

Caste also played an important part in Polish-Jewish relations. According to Max Weber, "A caste is . . . a closed status group."[7] The issue of Polish-Jewish caste relations has been discussed insightfully by sociologist Celia S. Heller. Heller writes that as a distinct caste in Poland, "The Jews were considered the outsiders, the strangers in their midst. They were also considered the epitome of inferiority."[8] Understandably, Jews were not prepared to identify with the Polish status hierarchy. However, the Poles, not the Jews, were able to enforce their definition of social reality because caste relations reflect power relations. No matter what constraints the Allies wrote into the Minorities Treaty, no consortium of foreign powers could compel the Poles to alter their status hierarchy. As Heller observes, violation of the Minorities Treaty was regarded as a defense of Polish honor rather than a breach of faith.[9]

Nevertheless, Marshall Pilsudski was strongly opposed to anti-Semitism. According to Richard M. Watt, Pilsudski apparently saw himself as the heir of Poland's kings in their role as protectors of the Jews. Although unofficial harassment of the Jews continued, the government of Prime Minister Kazimierz Bartel, Pilsudski's choice, acted to repeal many of the old czarist laws that had been enacted to harass Jews. For example, the government announced its opposition to the *numerus clausus*, which strictly limited the number of Jewish students at Polish universities, and the police and courts acted to protect Jews against physical assault.[10] Pilsudski was also strongly opposed to Endecja, and there was persistent hostility between him and Dmowski.

Some Jewish authorities argue that Pilsudski's opposition to anti-Semitism was more cosmetic than real.[11] For example, as long as Polish Galicia was a part of the Austro-Hungarian Empire, thousands of Jews worked in the state-owned railroads, post office, and other bureaus. After Poland gained independence, Pilsudski's position notwithstanding, Jews were barred from positions in all state bureaus and state-owned enterprises.[12] In any event, there was an immediate upsurge of anti-Jewish violence following Pilsudski's death in 1935. The government approved an economic boycott of Jewish merchants, and the police became permissive with regard to anti-Jewish violence. Prime Minister Felicjan Slawoj-Skladkowski announced his approval of "an economic fight for survival between Jews and Poles."[13] According to Emil Lengyel, sixty-nine Jews were killed and eight hundred wounded in Polish anti-Jewish violence during 1936.[14] The difference between the government's Jewish policy and that advocated by Endecja began to narrow. In a famous speech before parliament Boguslaw Miedzinski, the regime's leading parliamentarian, declared, "Personally, I love Danes very much, but if we had three million of them in Poland, I would implore God to take them away as soon as possible."[15]

The theme of the Jews as a surplus population that Poland wanted to eliminate was taken up by government leaders. It was set forth in the *Theses on the Jewish Question* formulated by OZON, the progovernment "Camp of National Unity."[16] The theses were subsequently elaborated upon by Miedzinski. According to Edward D. Wynot, Jr., with Miedzinski's elaboration the theses "constituted the official program of the Polish authorities on the Jewish question."[17] Miedzinski advocated "the removal of this alien body" from Poland. In July 1939, a little more than a month before the German invasion, the official government journal, *Gazeta Polska*, declared: "The fact that our relations with the Reich are worsening does not in the least deactivate our program on the Jewish question— there is not and cannot be any common ground between our internal Jewish problem and Poland's relations with the Hitlerite Reich."[18]

The government's anti-Jewish policies were supported by the Roman Catholic Church, which regarded the Jews as agents of secularization, liberalism, and Bolshevism. In 1936 August Cardinal Hlond, the Primate of Poland, openly supported the regime's anti-Jewish measures, although he declared his opposition to overt violence. In a pastoral letter read in most Polish churches, the cardinal declared: "A Jewish problem exists and will continue to exist as long as Jews remain Jews." The cardinal counseled the faithful: "One ought to fence oneself off against the harmful moral effects of Jewry, to separate oneself against its anti-Christian culture, and especially to boycott the Jewish press and the demoralizing Jewish publications."[19] According to Heller, Hlond was regarded as belonging to the moderate wing of the Church. However, although we read Hlond's letter in the light of subsequent events, we must remember that he wrote as he did before Vatican II and from the perspective of a prelate for whom the Church's cognitive monopoly in matters religious was nonnegotiable.

By the late 1930s, most Poles regarded the elimination of the Jews as an overwhelmingly important component of public policy. Nevertheless, unlike the Nazis, Poland's leaders, both religious and secular, had no workable plan to implement the removal other than harassment and discrimination. Their basic objective was to encourage Jewish emigration.

Emigration had, however, ceased to be an option for all but a tiny minority. The Jews of Poland were locked in a death trap from which there was to be no escape.

If the Poles did not know how to "solve" their Jewish problem, under Hitler the Germans did. In the late 1930s, the Jewish policy of both official Poland and National Socialist Germany shared a common objective, namely, the elimination of the Jews from their respective societies. They did, however, differ radically in the methods they were prepared to use. Whatever violence was inflicted by Poles, no official Polish institution had any plans to exterminate Jews. Although the Church was a principal force in the negative definition of the Jews, it set limits on what the Poles could do to them. When the invading Germans exterminated the Jews, they achieved the objective of Poland's Jewish policy, but they did so by means the Poles themselves had been unwilling to adopt. Moreover, some selfless and heroic Poles saved Jews at the risk of their own lives. Although many stories can be told, the story of Wladyslaw Bartoszewski, retired Professor of History at the Catholic University of Lublin, is especially moving. After having been imprisoned at Auschwitz, Bartoszewski was released in 1941 at the age of nineteen. He returned to Warsaw, where he found a nine-foot wall erected around the part of the city that had become the Warsaw ghetto. Bartoszewski became the liaison between the Polish underground and the Jewish leadership within the ghetto. At great personal risk he attempted to rescue some Jews and to make the world aware of what was taking place. When I met Bartoszewski in Poland in 1965, he showed me two documents, his Auschwitz identity photos and the testimonial certificate in his honor given to him by Jerusalem's Yad Vashem.[20] In spite of the efforts of people like Bartoszewski, the sober weight of historical scholarship compels one to suspect that the majority of the Poles regarded the Germans as having "solved" their Jewish problem for them.

Nor did the killing of Jews in Poland stop with the war's end. After the war there were pogroms in Kraków, Chelm, Rzeszow, Kielce, and elsewhere.[21] In 1946, on the basis of a false rumor that Jews had kidnapped a Christian boy and killed him in a ritual murder, Poles murdered seventy Holocaust survivors in Kielce. The Jews of Kielce turned to Bishop Stefan Wyszynski of Lublin with the request that he condemn the massacre in order to stem the violence. Although the facts concerning the Holocaust were well known by that time, the Bishop not only refused but added that he was not altogether convinced that Jews did not commit ritual murder! Shortly thereafter he became a cardinal and the Primate of Poland. Moreover, Józef Cardinal Glemp was Wyszynski's handpicked

successor as Primate. Glemp's homily dealing with Jewish-Christian relations delivered to pilgrims at Poland's national shrine of Our Lady of
Czestochowa on August 26, 1989, proved to be the most controversial
statement of any religious leader involved in the convent dispute.[22]

Government hostility to Jews, Judaism, and Zionism continued after
the war. In the countries of Soviet-dominated eastern Europe Stalinist
anti-Semitism sought the total obliteration of Jewish cultural life. After
the death of Stalin in 1953 and the rehabilitation of Wladyslaw Gomulka,
Poland's nationalistically inclined Communist leader from 1956 to 1970,
a modicum of Jewish cultural life was temporarily restored. This came to
an end with the Six-Day War of 1967. Minister of the Interior Mieczyslaw
Moczar used anti-Semitism as a means of displacing Gomulka. Not to be
outbid, Gomulka instituted his own anti-Semitic campaign in the press,
radio, and television. Moreover, in recent years Cardinal Glemp has accused Solidarity of having been infiltrated by "Trotskyites," a code word
for Jews, according to Abraham Brumberg.[23] Although there were fewer
than six thousand Jews in Poland in 1989, on August 17 of that year Anna
Husarska, an editor of *Gazeta Wyborcza*, Solidarity's daily newspaper,
wrote in the *Washington Post* of the "persistence of anti-Semitism in Poland." According to Husarska, "For the past 44 years Polish public opinion has been manipulated by the state-monopolized media. Until a few
years ago, most of the rare appearances of the word 'Jew' in official print
were more or less open insults." When Husarska wrote objectively about
the demonstration on July 14, 1989, at the site of the Auschwitz Carmelite
convent by Rabbi Avraham Weiss and six companions and the physical
and verbal violence inflicted upon the Jewish group by Polish construction workers, she received insulting responses from more than a hundred
readers, many of which used unprintable language. She has written that
any doubts she had about the persistence of anti-Semitism in Poland were
dispelled by these communications.[24]

Given the history of the Jews in Poland both before and after the war,
it is not difficult to understand why the placement of the convent at
Auschwitz would elicit an emotional response among Jews, especially
Holocaust survivors. In spite of the help and rescue extended to Jews by
some Christians during the Holocaust, it is impossible for Jews not to see
in the pre–Vatican II definition of the Jews as deicides the legitimating
ideology that cast the Jews wholly outside of any shared universe of
moral obligation with Christians and thereby made genocide morally
acceptable.

There was also a distinctively Jewish aspect to the issue of memory
in the convent controversy. No curse is more terrible for Jews than, *Y'mach*

sh'mo v'zichrono, (May his name and memory be blotted out). That curse
has been visited upon the millions of Jewish families who died and whose
remains were incinerated without a trace at Auschwitz. Even for the surviving community of Israel as a whole, fear remains of the appropriation
and obliteration of memory. Pro-Nazi Holocaust revisionists make just
such an attempt. Moreover, although Jews were killed simply because
they were Jews, at Auschwitz, Treblinka, Sobibor, Maidanek, Babi Yar,
and Mauthausen in Austria they are memorialized as Poles, Austrians,
Russians, Hungarians, and Germans. When alive they were regarded as
unwanted aliens. Only in death did countries like Poland, the USSR, and
Austria claim them as war victims.

Another aspect of the Jewish fear is the theological appropriation of
memory, an ancient issue between Judaism and Christianity. Christians
regard the books of the Hebrew Scripture as witnesses to Christ as Lord.
Paul of Tarsus explicitly denied that his Jewish contemporaries could
understand their own Scriptures: "We do not act as Moses did, who put
a veil over his face (so that the people of Israel could not perceive the
ultimate significance of that which was to be abolished). But their minds
became hardened (and that is why) the same veil remains drawn, even
today (in spite of everything) at the reading of the Old Covenant. But
until today, every time that Moses is read, a veil lies over their minds. It
cannot be removed because it is only through Christ that it can be abolished" (II Cor. 3:13–15).

After the fall of Jerusalem in 70 C.E. membership in the Jewish community was conditional upon acceptance of the rabbinic interpretation of
Scripture as authoritative, at least in matters of Halakha or Jewish religious law. Nevertheless, because of the overwhelming numerical and cultural predominance of Christianity as a world religion, the Christian
reading of Scripture came to carry far greater weight and influence. Under the circumstances, it is understandable that many Jews were fearful
that the presence of the convent and the twenty-four-foot cross at Auschwitz would initiate a process in which the distinctive Jewish content of
the Holocaust would be lost to memory and ultimately assimilated to a
Christian interpretation of the event.

Theological appropriation of the Holocaust can become a problem
even when the intention is to heal and to reconcile. On June 24, 1988,
Pope John Paul II visited the site of the Mauthausen Concentration Camp
in Austria, where tens of thousands of Jews were put to death. In his
remarks at the camp site he referred to four camp victims but made no
mention of Jewish victims. The pontiff's omission was criticized by Paul
Grosz, the president of the Austrian Jewish community. The next day

during a visit to Lorch, Austria, the pope told an audience of eighty thousand during a prayer service, "Not far from here is Mauthausen, where Christians, Jews, and others were persecuted for many reasons, including their religion. Their suffering was a gift to the world."[25]

The idea that the suffering of those who perished in the camps was a gift is consistent with the image of Christ offering himself as a sacrifice for the sins of the world. The pope understandably interpreted the sufferings of the camp victims in terms of the symbolism of his own tradition. But such symbolism remains altogether foreign to Jews, who cannot see the greatest catastrophe in their history as a gift of any sort whatsoever.

In his speech at Mauthausen the pope further stated, "It would be unjust and not truthful to charge Christianity with these unspeakable crimes."[26] The pope is undoubtedly correct. Nevertheless, he failed to address the question of whether the Christian identification of the Jews as deicides created a moral climate in which millions of Europeans could, at least during wartime, regard extermination of the Jews as a legitimate enterprise. Nor did he consider the fact that many of the major war criminals, such as Franz Stangl, the SS commandant at the Treblinka Death Camp, were assisted in their flight from justice by Vatican and other church officials.[27]

Apart from the issues involved in the appropriation of the Holocaust to Christian meanings and to Christian supersessionary claims, approximately 750,000 people visit Auschwitz every year, most during the summer months. These numbers entail many problems, such as the need to define behavioral decorum and appropriate dress at the site and to determine the character of the exhibits at the Auschwitz Historical Museum. A very real possibility exists that a few people may identify with the perpetrators and that Auschwitz could provide them with material for a unique pornography of violence and domination.[28]

At some level Jewish sensibilities were understood and appreciated by the Catholic leaders, including Franciszek Cardinal Macharski of Kraków, Albert Cardinal Decourtray of Lyons, Godfried Cardinal Daneels of Malines-Brussels, and Jean-Marie Cardinal Lustiger, who signed the original 1987 agreement to relocate the convent. Their sensibilities were also understood by the Polish Bishops' Commission for Dialogue with the Jews. On September 6, 1989, the commission urged the construction of the proposed new interfaith center near the Auschwitz camp after Franciszek Cardinal Macharski of Kraków changed his mind and ordered the interfaith center project suspended.

Nevertheless, as stated above, I believe it would have been better had there been no request to relocate in the first place because *the indispensable precondition of diaspora Jewish religious life has always been religious pluralism*. Roman Dmowski campaigned to eliminate Jews from Poland because he regarded religious and cultural pluralism as a fundamental cause of the political, moral, and cultural debilitation of the Polish people. By actively seeking to eliminate Jews from Poland, Dmowski was convinced he was acting for the good of his own people. If pluralism is rejected, one can only criticize the *methods* by which governments achieve religious, cultural, or ethnic homogeneity but not the objective itself.

In spite of the bitter history of Polish-Jewish relations, recognition of the imperatives of pluralism should have led the Jewish leaders to accept the fact that Poles wanted to render homage to the memory of their fellow countrymen and coreligionists at the place where they perished. The presence of the Carmelites at Auschwitz cannot in any way minimize the fact that Auschwitz was a place of utter extermination for Jews. While few Poles left Auschwitz alive during the war, the case of Wladyslaw Bartoszewski shows that it was possible for Poles to be released. By contrast, extermination was the fate awaiting all Jews without exception. This does not mean that Poles and other Roman Catholics ought not to be able to pray for their dead at Auschwitz. *Pluralism entails recognition of the religious requirements of diverse religious communities.*

Unfortunately, too many things went wrong after the signing of the 1987 agreement. Having been a signatory to the original agreement, Franciszek Cardinal Macharski of Kraków had an obligation to see that it was carried out, but he did not. When it became evident that the deadline would pass without implementation, the Jewish signatories should have been informed openly and frankly. Instead, there was no communication and a twenty-four-foot cross was placed in the yard adjacent to the convent. Absence of frank discussion could hardly inspire trust and, in fact, had the effect of awakening Jewish apprehensions. The situation grew worse on July 14, 1989, with the protest demonstration led by Rabbi Avraham Weiss at the site of the Auschwitz convent. The fact that the rabbi and his group were violently assaulted by Polish construction workers whose leader yelled "Heil Hitler" while a priest egged them on and the nuns stood by without protest further exacerbated the conflict.[29] Old memories of Polish anti-Jewish violence were inevitably reawakened.

The assault on the rabbi and his colleagues was inexcusable. Nevertheless, neither the rabbi nor anyone else had the right to enter the convent precinct, as he did, without permission. When Rabbi Weiss first appeared at the door of the convent, he announced that he had come in peace and that undoubtedly was his intention. He and his companions then put on prayer shawls and began to chant Hebrew prayers on the convent grounds. Unfortunately, if the Polish assault against the Jews triggered unpleasant Jewish memories, neither the rabbi nor the leaders of the world's major Jewish organizations took into account the primal associations the rabbi's actions triggered in Poles. Whatever positive associations prayer shawls, sacred books, and Hebrew chanting have for Jews, they have no such associations for Poles. In his description of the demonstration, the rabbi gives no indication that he had any understanding of the kind of fearful primal associations that could be triggered in the psyches of theologically unsophisticated Polish Catholics when uninvited males enter a domain reserved for women who have devoted their lives to chastity and prayer. At the most primitive level, the symbolism involved in the idea of male invasion of a precinct reserved for pious virgins carries with it the most unfortunate sexual associations. Let us remember that Polish society has no experience with American-style demonstrations. Clearly, there was a major communications problem.

Rabbi Weiss's demonstration and the Polish workers' violent response brought the controversy to a head. It was featured on page 1 of the *New York Times*. On August 10, 1989, Cardinal Macharski announced that he was abandoning plans to construct a center for Christian-Jewish dialogue adjacent to Auschwitz as per the 1987 agreement. The cardinal also declared that the timetable for removal of the nuns to another location was unrealistic. He accused "some Western Jewish centers" of staging a "violent campaign of accusations and slander, outrageous aggression." Referring to the demonstration at the convent, he said, "The nuns, their human and Christian dignity, were not respected. The peace to which they are entitled was disturbed. The Christian faith, as well as symbols and piety, were not respected."[30] The cardinal's statement put the blame for breaking the convent agreement on the Jewish side. There was, however, some suspicion that this was only a pretext and that the decision to break the agreement had been made before the February 1989 deadline for its implementation. Furthermore, at that point, save for Rabbi Weiss, none of the major Jewish groups had done anything more than seek implementation of the agreement, an altogether legitimate enterprise.

Rabbi Weiss's convent demonstration was another matter. The cardinal's statement stressed the fact that Rabbi Weiss had entered the convent grounds without authorization. The cardinal had no words of regret for the assault upon the rabbi. In his statement responding to the cardinal, Rabbi Weiss stressed the violence against the demonstrators and the cardinal's bad faith in breaking the agreement. The rabbi declared,

"Cardinal Macharski's statement is repugnant. In seeking to break the Jewish-Catholic accord of 1987 which he personally signed . . . the Cardinal has, in almost classical anti-Semitic terms, chosen to portray Jewish victims as aggressors. It was not we who beat Polish Catholics. It was Catholic Polish workers of the convent who assaulted us, as the nuns and the priests looked on in silence."[31] Just as the cardinal expressed no concern for the construction workers' assault, the rabbi apparently had no understanding of and made no mention of the profound symbolic offense committed by the demonstrators in entering the convent grounds. Insensitive to the other's symbols and memories, each side succeeded only in angering the other.

The conflict was further exacerbated by the seemingly unrelated remarks made by Pope John Paul II at his weekly general audience of August 2, 1989. The pope spoke after the demonstration at the convent but before Cardinal Macharski issued his statement. In his homily the pope declared that the Old Testament showed many instances of the Jewish people's "infidelity to God." He further declared that the Prophets were sent "to call the people to conversion, to warn them of their hardness of heart and foretell a new covenant still to come. The new covenant foretold by the Prophets was established through Christ's redemptive sacrifice and through the power of the Holy Spirit. . . . This 'perfect gift from above' descends to fill the hearts of all people and to gather them into the church constituting them the People of God of the new and everlasting covenant."[32]

The pope's remarks were an expression of the traditional Christian claim that the Church had superseded Israel as the People of God in the new covenant established by Jesus Christ. In weighing the claims of religious exclusivism against those of ecumenical pluralism, in this instance the pope tilted the balance in favor of exclusivism. The pope's remarks were immediately protested by Jewish religious leaders, who reminded the pope of an occasion on which he had tilted the balance the other way. In 1980 when the pope spoke to Jewish leaders in Mainz, Germany, he referred to the Jewish people as "the people of God, of the Old Covenant never revoked by God." All doubt as to the pope's present position was put to rest the following week when on August 9 he told visiting pilgrims that God had created a new covenant with his people through Christ because of Israel's "infidelity to its God." *Implicit in the pope's remarks was the view that simply by being loyal to the teachings of their rabbis Jews were unwittingly in rebellion against God and that only by accepting Christ as their Lord could Jews truly be reconciled to God.* Although it was never said, one could draw the further implication that there was only one proper way to memorialize the dead at Auschwitz, that is, in and through Christ. No room for pluralism here. Because of the great moral authority of the pope, his remarks aroused all of the Jewish fears that their tragedy was being assimilated to Christian meanings.

The controversy threatened to become a major crisis in interreligious relations following Józef Cardinal Glemp's homily at the Polish national shrine of Our Lady of Czechostowa on August 26 and his statements to the press on August 28. The Czechostowa homily attracted worldwide attention. As is their wont, the newspaper accounts emphasized the cardinal's most inflammatory statements, all of which appear in his concluding comments. The body of the homily was devoted to reflections on Polish-Jewish relations on the fiftieth anniversary of the start of World War II. Understandably, the cardinal was especially concerned with the question of why the convent controversy had arisen "40 years after the ovens of the crematoria were extinguished." While most Jews would take issue with the cardinal's analysis of the history of prewar Polish-Jewish relations, it can be characterized as the prelate's sincere attempt to give what he regarded as a balanced account.[33]

The same cannot be said of his concluding remarks beginning with the statement: "We have our faults regarding the Jews, but today I would like to say: Beloved Jews, do not converse with us from the position of a people raised above all others and do not dictate conditions that are impossible to fulfill."[34] Referring to the Carmelite sisters, he continued: "Do you not see, esteemed Jews, that intervention against them injures the feelings of all Poles and the sovereignty we gained with much difficulty? Your power is the mass media, which is at your disposal in many countries. Let them not serve to inflame anti-Polish sentiment."

He then turned to the subject of Rabbi Weiss's demonstration at the convent: "Recently a detachment of seven Jews from New York attacked the convent at Auschwitz. To be sure, because they were restrained, it did not result in the killing of the sisters or the destruction of the convent; but do not call the aggressors heroes. Let us preserve the level of civilization where we live." The cardinal also argued that the convent was appropriately located at a part of the huge Auschwitz complex where mostly Poles died: "Let us be able to distinguish Oswiecim-Auschwitz, where mostly Poles and other nations perished, from Brzezinka-Birkenau a few kilometers distant, where mostly Jews perished." He concluded his remarks addressed to Jews with counsel on how anti-Semitism might be diminished in Poland: "If there is no anti-Polish sentiment, there will be no anti-Semitism among us."

The cardinal added further heat to the controversy on September 2, when he termed the 1987 agreement on the convent "offensive." He also said, "I want this accord to be renegotiated. It has to be done by competent people and not just by any cardinal who doesn't understand these things."[35] This was, of course, a direct rebuke to his fellow cardinals who had negotiated the original agreement.

Criticism of the cardinal came swiftly from many quarters. *Gazeta Wyborcza*, the Solidarity daily newspaper, featured a front-page editorial denouncing the cardinal's remarks and declaring that they "caused real not artificial or paper pain."[36] John Cardinal O'Connor of New York said that he was shocked by Cardinal Glemp's remarks. He said, "Normal decent people could construe from such a statement that the blame be shifted to the Jews for demanding that a signed accord be carried out. I don't think that is right. I don't think that is charitable. And it certainly doesn't represent my opinion."[37]

Albert Cardinal Decourtray of Lyons, Jean-Marie Cardinal Lustiger of Paris, and Godfried Cardinal Daneels of Brussels, three of the four cardinals who had signed the accord, issued a statement that read: "Cardinal Glemp could only have been speaking for himself in talking of re-negotiating of the Geneva accords, particularly since until now he has always let it be known that Cardinal Macharski was solely responsible and that the Polish Conference of Bishops, on March 9, 1989, had committed itself in turn by giving its support to the realization of this accord."[38]

In the United States, Catholic religious and lay leaders urged that the nuns be relocated. The religious leaders included Bernard Cardinal Law of Boston, Archbishop Roger Mahony of Los Angeles, Edmund Cardinal Szoka of Detroit, and John Cardinal Krol, retired archbishop of Philadelphia. The latter two are of Polish descent. Among the prominent Catholic laypersons who urged that the accord be kept were William F. Buckley and Michael Novak. Among the few who defended Cardinal Glemp was Patrick Buchanan. He denounced the Jewish community's attitude and gave evidence of little interest in pluralism. Even in Poland there was support for relocation among Catholic religious leaders. On September 6, 1989, the Polish Bishops' Commission for Dialogue with the Jews indicated its support, but reminded Jews of the importance of supporting construction of the interfaith center, which had also been part of the agreement.

I was queried about Cardinal Glemp's statement when I lectured in Kraków. By that time the cardinal had reversed his position and I had no desire to stir up further controversy. I did, however, take issue with two of the cardinal's statements. As stated above, I believe that Rabbi Weiss's group was profoundly in error in having entered any part of the convent without permission. Nevertheless, the cardinal's statement that "seven Jews from New York attacked the convent" and his accusation that the nuns were not killed because Rabbi Weiss's group "was restrained" were inflammatory in extreme. Whatever may have been the prelate's intention, his words could only fan the flames of hatred. There is absolutely no evidence that Rabbi Weiss or any member of his group had any intention, in their ill-advised, insensitive, American-style demonstration, of harming the nuns. If the rabbi's behavior had unpleasant associations for Poles, the cardinal's wholly unfounded accusations could very easily have elicited associations with the age-old canard of ritual murder. Certainly, the Primate of Poland had an obligation to measure his words carefully when he spoke at Poland's most sacred shrine.

The cardinal gratuitously raised yet another false and inflammatory issue when he warned Jews not to use their alleged power in the mass media "to inflame anti-Polish sentiment." Poland's struggle to liberate itself from communism and to put its economic house in order has received considerable support from almost all American newspapers. When President Bush proposed giving Poland a minimum of financial support, he was widely criticized for being niggardly and ungenerous. If Jews have the media power Cardinal Glemp alleges they have, they have used it in support of contemporary, Solidarity-led Poland, rather than to arouse hostility against Poland.

Cardinal Glemp does not seem to have understood that responsible Jews have no interest in arousing anti-Polish sentiment. The history of the Jews in Poland will in all likelihood continue to be viewed differently by Jews and Poles. Nevertheless, Jews have absolutely no interest in hostility toward the present, Solidarity-led government. On the contrary, both in Israel and the Diaspora they have every reason to want it to succeed in liberating Poland from the moral, political, and economic legacy of communism. On the Polish side, Poland's real problems would appear to be overwhelming, but with fewer than six thousand Jews remaining in Poland, there is no rational reason for continued Polish-Jewish hostility. Whatever anti-Semitism exists in Poland is an obsession that can only divert attention away from the country's real problems.

The controversy was brought to closure on September 19, when the Vatican's Commission for Religious Relations with the Jews issued a statement signed by Johannes Cardinal Willebrands to the effect that the Holy See is "prepared to make its own financial contribution" to the construction of an interfaith center at Auschwitz as called for in the 1987 agreement to relocate the Carmelite sisters.[39] On September 23 the Discalced Carmelites' generalate in Rome issue a statement to the effect that the position of the general of the order had been all along "that agreements must be honored." Finally, on September 20 Cardinal Glemp sent a letter to Sir Sigmund Steinberg, chairman of the executive committee of the International Council of Christians and Jews, declaring, "It is my intention that the Geneva declaration of 1987 should be implemented." Of the well-known personalities who had spoken out on the issue, only Patrick Buchanan issued a dissent, and an angry one at that.[40]

Before Vatican II it would have been highly unlikely that Catholic leaders such as Cardinal O'Connor, Cardinal Law, and the signatories of the 1987 agreement would have publicly taken issue with Cardinal Glemp or even that the agreement would have been signed at all. What has changed is the way the Church has balanced the claims of pluralism with its own claims to exclusive truth. Put differently, those Catholic leaders who had taken issue with Cardinal Glemp had accepted the reality of pluralism to a far greater extent than he. No Catholic leader could really see anything wrong in and of itself in the location of the convent or in the erection of the twenty-four-foot cross. Only when Jewish sensibilities were weighed in the balance were Church leaders willing to consider relocating the convent. Given the Church's cognitive monopoly in religious matters in Poland, its unique role in preserving Polish cultural autonomy in the face of Soviet-imposed communism, as well as Poland's tragic history since 1939, it is easy to understand why Cardinal Glemp was less concerned with the imperatives of pluralism than were his colleagues in the West and even in the Vatican.

Nevertheless, as stated above, in an era of global electronic communications, none of the major religious traditions any longer enjoys a cognitive monopoly even in countries like Poland, where the Church continues to enjoy the loyalty of an overwhelming majority. When events like the end of the Berlin Wall are instantaneously visible to hundreds of millions throughout the world and distance is no longer a factor in the encounter of world religions, some degree of accommodation to pluralism is indispensable for all of them. This does not mean that they can or necessarily should give up their exclusive claims. Intelligent men and women can find ways to balance these claims with the imperatives of pluralism. With the Jewish community in Europe largely destroyed, some Church leaders there could have argued that the Church could easily reject Jewish demands that the agreement be kept. Such a posture might have worked for a time in Poland and elsewhere on the continent. It could not have worked in the United States, where Jews and Christians have important reasons for maintaining dialogue and encouraging interfaith cooperation. Even in Europe, the Vatican recognized that moving the nuns fifteen hundred feet was far better than a public breach, especially on an issue concerning how the dead at Auschwitz are to be remembered.

Part II

THE MEANING OF
THE HOLOCAUST

CHAPTER 5

The Unmastered Trauma

INTERPRETING THE HOLOCAUST

The destruction of the European Jews by the government that exercised sovereign power on behalf of the German people from 1933 to 1945 has yet to be comprehended fully by men and women whose values have been shaped by the religious and cultural heritage of Western civilization. Such comprehension may never be achieved. Moreover, it is by no means certain that we have even been successful in giving the event an appropriate name. When Raul Hilberg first published his magisterial study of the destruction of the European Jews in 1961, he did not use the term *Holocaust*.[1] The principal definition of *holocaust* in the *Oxford English Dictionary* is "a sacrifice wholly consumed by fire; a whole burnt offering." Use of the word to denote the destruction of Europe's Jews assimilates genocide to the world of religious faith and implies that the victims offered up their lives in the tradition of Israel's ancient martyrs *al kiddush ha-Shem* (for the sanctification of the divine Name). One of the most persistent questions elicited by the Holocaust has been whether the event could in any way be consistent with the Judeo-Christian faith. Debate on that issue remains open, even though the event has been assigned a name that implicitly reaffirms the relationship.

George Kren and Leon Rappoport of Kansas State University are partly correct when they argue that the Holocaust is one of those historical crises that "break the preexisting social consensus and shared values" given by culture.[2] However, I now question whether they are correct when they identify religion and law as major institutions of Western civilization that proved impotent when confronted by the arbitrary power and authority of the modern state to isolate and exterminate any group of its citizens or subject peoples apart from all considerations of justice. In the case of the Holocaust, it is not accurate to describe religion as "impotent" before the state's power to exterminate. This would mistakenly imply that the extermination project did not have the tacit consent of most of European Christendom's institutions. Nor did law as an institution prove impotent. On the contrary, the Nazis were careful to render the Jews outlaws, thereby excluding them from all legal protection, before proceeding against them. Having succeeded in defining the Jews as mortal enemies of the Reich and even of European civilization to the satisfaction of most Europeans, the Nazis depicted the destruction of the Jews as a legitimate act of self-defense in accordance with traditional just-war theory.[3] I nevertheless concur with Kren and Rappoport when they argue that a third institution, science, made the Holocaust technically and psychologically feasible. In their words: "It is quite obvious that the rational-abstract forms of conceptual thought required and promulgated by science provided the basis of systematic identification of people by race; transportation of large numbers to concentration points; killing; and disposal."[4]

If we have thus far failed fully to comprehend the Holocaust, the *theory of cognitive dissonance* put forth by social psychologists such as Leon Festinger, Henry W. Riecken, and Stanley Schachter may help us at least to enlarge our understanding of both the Holocaust and its antecedents.[5] In the words of Festinger, one of the original proponents of the theory, "This theory centers around the idea that if a person knows various things that are not psychologically consistent with each other, he will in a variety of ways try to make them consistent."[6]

Festinger defined a "dissonant relation" as one in which two items of information do not fit together psychologically. He held that these items of information "may be about behavior, feelings, opinions, things in the environment." According to Festinger, the word *cognitive* is employed to emphasize that "the theory deals with relations of information." A successful attempt to make dissonant items consistent with each other is called *dissonance reduction*. Festinger and his colleagues found that dissonance reduction resembles hunger in that it is "a motivating state of affairs." It is, however, unlike hunger in that it is usually possible to assuage hunger in our society by finding something to eat, whereas it is often difficult or impossible "to change behavior or opinions that are involved in dissonant relations."[7] According to Festinger, the reason why dissonance reduction is a "motivating state" is that, in the course of our lives, all of us come to expect that certain patterns of behavior, opinions, values, and feelings go together and others do not. The intensity of discomfort produced by cognitive dissonance depends upon our emotional investment in the feelings, values, or opinions we perceive to be threatened. For example, a child who has come to associate loving behavior with the presence of his or her mother is likely to experience a traumatic sense of disorientation if the mother suddenly and inexplicably becomes cruel and sadistic. Confronted by apparently inconsistent maternal behavior, the child may seek to interpret the mother's actions so that they appear consistent with earlier, more loving patterns. One way to reduce the dissonance between the mother's behavior and the child's expectations would be to deny that the mother had really been cruel and to explain her novel conduct as a response to some real or imagined misdeed on the part of the child. An important gain in such self-accusation is that the child is able to retain a sense of trust in the all-important maternal relationship. This strategy has often been employed by adults as well as children. A similar dissonance reduction strategy has been used frequently by groups that have experienced unanticipated, traumatic misfortune but who nevertheless believe an all-powerful, beneficent deity guides their destiny. *Self-accusation and introjected guilt can permit a group to retain a belief in the existence and goodness of its deity.*

Another way of expressing the theory of cognitive dissonance is in terms of group psychology. In that context, the theory posits that when (*a*) a group is strongly committed to a belief that is relevant to its actions, and (*b*) this belief is seriously challenged by disconfirming evidence that is recognized as such by the believers, then (*c*) the group will usually find some way to reaffirm its original belief, or, put differently, it will find some way to reduce the dissonance between its beliefs and the disconfirming evidence, no matter how convincing the evidence may appear to be.[8]

One of the most startling instances of dissonance reduction in the history of religion occurred in 1661 and the years immediately following. Millions of Jews had become convinced that a middle-aged mystic, Sabbatai Zvi from Smyrna, Turkey, was Israel's long-awaited Messiah. As the messianic good tidings spread throughout the Jewish world, men and women everywhere made enthusiastic preparation for imminent redemption. The messianic faith was, however, faced with a crisis of disconfirmation when the "messiah" was brought before the Sultan's privy council and given the choice of decapitation or immediate conversion to Islam. As a result of the "messiah's" apostasy, many abandoned their newly acquired faith and fell back on older religious attitudes. Nevertheless, a surprisingly large number continued to believe in the "messiah" and his redemptive powers. The "believers," as they were called, sought dissonance reduction strategies that would permit them to assimilate the "messiah's" apostasy to their previously held notions of messianic redemption. As is customary in religious movements, this task fell to the theologians of the Sabbatian movement, who used their very considerable intellectual abilities to demonstrate that the "messiah's" unexpected apostasy was fully consistent with his redemptive mission.[9]

On the basis of the theory of cognitive dissonance it is possible to identify an important function of theology in a culture with a religious foundation: *a crucial function of theology is to foster dissonance reduction where significant items of information are perceived as inconsistent with established beliefs, values, and collectively sanctioned modes of behavior.* This dissonance-reducing function can be especially important in cultures, such as our own, in which the dominant religious institutions affirm that God is both the Creator and the ultimate Actor in the drama of history. Such a faith is especially vulnerable to empirical disconfirmation by historical events regarded as inconsistent with traditional notions of justice and divine governance. It should, therefore, occasion no surprise that the Judeo-Christian West with its religions of history has produced so large a number of intellectual professionals skilled in the reduction of dissonance. We call these professionals theologians.[10]

The relevance of the theory of cognitive dissonance to the Holocaust should be obvious. If our knowledge of that event includes significant items of information which are inconsistent with accepted notions of law, morality, faith, and scientific knowledge, and if the Holocaust is perceived as having called into question the viability of some of our most hallowed institutions and values as defenses against unlimited human destructiveness, then intellectual professionals in theology, ethics, history, and social science are likely to attempt to reduce the dissonance between previously accepted notions and the novel evidence of recent history. That process is currently visible in the aforementioned disciplines and is likely to continue for a very long time.

It is my conviction that the underlying purpose of much of Holocaust scholarship is dissonance reduction. This is especially true of the discipline of theology. It is probably also true of those historical studies that offer an overview of the destruction process and attempt to locate the event within the larger framework of German or world history. *What is ultimately at issue is our understanding of the kind of civilization to which we are heir.* Such an enterprise has an especial urgency for Jewish scholars, for whom the Holocaust must always be seen as both a past calamity and a deeply threatening future possibility.

When the existence of the camps was first revealed toward the end of World War II, a wave of repulsion spread through the civilized world. As the facts became known, the quest for understanding inevitably involved a search for antecedents. Viewed from the perspective of the Holocaust, all manifestations of hostility toward Jews and Judaism were understandably seen in a new light. It was not difficult to identify the thread of continuity between the religious defamation of Judaism in the Christian tradition, the policies of the Church toward Jews in premodern times, the racist attacks on Jews in nineteenth- and twentieth-century Europe, and the Final Solution itself.[11] In fairness to the Church, it must be stated that its historic position toward the Jews has been ambivalent rather than unremittingly hostile. Ever mindful of its Jewish roots, the Church saw itself as the "true Israel" and confidently expected that the Jewish community, called by St. Paul "Israel after the flesh" in contrast to "Israel after the spirit," would ultimately see the light and confess the lordship of Christ. Nevertheless, the continuity between Christian anti-Judaism and National Socialist anti-Semitism had been proclaimed by such leading perpetrators of the Holocaust as Hitler, Himmler, and Streicher, all of whom insisted that in eliminating the Jews they were merely carrying to the appropriate practical conclusion attitudes and aspirations that had long been rooted in the very substance of Christian civilization.[12]

As is known, in the aftermath of the catastrophe a number of Christian and Jewish scholars came to the conclusion that the Nazi claim that their anti-Semitism was consistent with Christian anti-Semitism was not entirely mistaken.[13] Where the scholars took issue with the National Socialists was, of course, in their sense of horror and revulsion at the outcome. Undoubtedly, much of the rethinking of the attitude of the Christian churches toward Jews and Judaism since World War II has been motivated by this revulsion. As the genocidal potentiality of hatred of the Jews in Christian culture came to be recognized, there have been serious attempts on the part of some Christian leaders to moderate their rhetoric concerning Jews and Judaism even when they were dealing with issues of abiding interreligious conflict.

This post-Holocaust awareness of the genocidal potential of anti-Semitism has also affected historical investigation, often with distorting effects. Because of the objective innocence of the victims, Holocaust studies have tended to emphasize what was done to the Jews rather than those elements of conflict and competition between Jews and non-Jews that could have contributed to the tragedy. As noted, there has been a persistent tendency to treat hatred of Jews and Judaism as a form of moral and psychological pathology. This tendency is certainly understandable in view of such gross and obscene institutions as Auschwitz and Treblinka. Nevertheless, as understandable as the emphasis may be, it tends to neglect or minimize what ought to be a fundamental issue in studies on the origins of the Holocaust, namely, in what ways did the interactions of Jews and Christians intensify the hazard of the more vulnerable group? Regrettably, the interactions, economic, political, and social, between the two communities, as distinct from the actions against Jews by Christians, are seldom dealt with in retrospective inquiries into the evolution of anti-Jewish ideas and policies.

The tendency to ignore the interaction issue leads to the interpretation of anti-Semitism in isolation from the context of intergroup conflict and competition. This isolation is evident in such standard works on the Holocaust as those of Raul Hilberg, Lucy Dawidowicz, and Nora Levin.[14] Hilberg's magisterial study of the actual destruction process is preceded by an oft-quoted description of the evolution of anti-Jewish policies from religious hatred to racist-inspired genocide: "The missionaries of Christianity had said in effect: You have no right to live among us as Jews. The secular rulers who followed had proclaimed: You have no right to live among us. The German Nazis at last decreed: You have no right to live."[15] Note the force of Hilberg's emphasis: In each of the three stages, the Jews are depicted as the objects of the action of others rather than as parties to a conflict. Anti-Semitism is thus depicted as something that happens to Jews rather than an expression of a conflict between the Jews and their enemies. This interpretation is certainly understandable in view of the utter disparity between any conceivable Jewish failing and the fate visited upon almost every single Jewish man, woman, and child in wartime Europe. Nevertheless, it tends to obscure the elements of admittedly unequal conflict in the Judeo-Christian encounter.

A somewhat similar attitude is manifest in the work of Lucy Dawidowicz. Dawidowicz explores the rise of anti-Semitism in Germany in the first two chapters of her major work, *The War against the Jews*. Her first chapter is entitled, "The Jews in Hitler's Mental World." The title itself suggests a projective interpretation of anti-Semitism. The author depicts the Jews as if they were neutral objects of Hitler's projected pathology. She briefly catalogues some of Hitler's principal anti-Semitic vilifications as well as his plans for exterminating the Jews. At no point in the chapter does the author seriously inquire concerning Hitler's motives or those of the German people in following him. Yet at the conclusion of the chapter she raises rhetorically the crucial issue: "The question continues to oppress us: how could a man with this poor baggage of ideas become Chancellor of Germany?" Having raised the issue, she proceeds to evade it. Instead of an answer, she poses another question: "Was it because their (i.e., the German people's) moral sense, at least with regard to the Jews, had become atrophied under the effect of generations of virulent anti-Semitism?"[16] This leads to the first sentence of the second chapter, entitled "Anti-Semitism in Modern Germany," in which she asserts: "A line of anti-Semitic descent from Martin Luther to Adolf Hitler is easy to draw. Both Luther and Hitler were *obsessed* by a demonological universe inhabited by Jews" (italics added).[17] For Dawidowicz the story she has to tell is one of pathology made all the more hideous by its outcome. Since pathology involves deviation from an accepted norm, Dawidowicz spells out for her readers the norm in terms of which she judges the evolution of German attitudes toward the Jews during the nineteenth and twentieth centuries. Her standard is the extent to which Germans conformed to or rejected her conception of the ideals of the Enlightenment: "The Enlightenment represented the break with the medieval world and its concepts of man's innate sinfulness, whose only hope of salvation was through divine providence. For this view the Enlightenment substituted the idea of progress, of man's perfectibility through the attainment of knowledge, and the theory that the universe was governed by reason."[18] Dawidowicz maintained that these ideas took hold principally in England and France but were successfully aborted by "German backward-lookingness."

According to Dawidowicz, the Germans preferred to retain their loyalties to the past and resisted accommodation of their customs and folkways to the enormous changes of modernity. Since one of the principal sociopolitical changes introduced by the Enlightenment was Jewish emancipation, Dawidowicz characterizes German resistance to the emancipation as an expression of "reaction" and "repression." Dawidowicz does not omit good Germans from her story. They are the "liberals" who supported the Enlightenment and its goals. Unfortunately, they proved "too weak and too indecisive to withstand reaction." The final blow to the slender hope of the triumph of liberalism and modernity came with Germany's defeat in World War I. Dawidowicz describes the German world that arose out of the defeat in the twenties: "It was a world intoxicated with hate, driven by paranoia, enemies everywhere, the Jew lurking behind each one. The Germans were in search of a mysterious wholeness that would restore them to primeval happiness, destroying the hostile milieu of urban industrial civilization that the Jewish conspiracy had foisted upon them. . . . National Socialism was the consummation toward which the omnifarious anti-Semitic movements had striven for 150 years."[19] Again, we are offered images of pathology lacking any real interest in the obvious question of why the National Socialist program could have achieved so extraordinary a consensus among Germans of all walks of life and of every talent and achievement, especially in the late thirties and early forties. Dawidowicz rests content with the suggestion that the Germans attempted a collective regression to an archaic or mystic form of wholeness. I can sympathize with Dawidowicz's attempt to make sense out of the triumph of National Socialism in Germany as an example of a collective regression. In my earlier attempts to understand the Holocaust, I offered a somewhat similar interpretation.[20] Nevertheless, there are many grave problems with this interpretation, not the least of which is that contemporary research sees a dark and vicious side to the Enlightenment, which was itself in many ways a *conditio sine qua non* of the Holocaust and the other manifestations of genocide in modern times. I discuss this issue below.

It is my conviction that the Holocaust can be understood with least mystification if we do not ignore the abiding elements of conflict characterizing the relations between the Jews and their neighbors throughout the entire period of their domicile in the European-Christian world. This view involves issues that must be handled with the greatest delicacy. Let me, therefore, first state what I do not mean: I do not in any sense want to suggest that the Holocaust was a fate the victims deserved, however remotely. Moreover, I reject as both false and malicious the thesis put forward by some psycho-historians, all too often of Jewish background, that the Jews unconsciously elicited their terrible fate. Group conflicts, such as those between Jews and Christians, are more likely to be a matter of inheritance than choice. Normally, the weaker party has every reason to avoid exacerbating the conflict. Nevertheless, it is an unhappy fact that for almost two thousand years Jews and Christians have been involuntarily thrust into a situation in which by affirming their most sacred traditions each side negated the sacred traditions of the other.[21]

An overwhelmingly important expression of the conflict has been the persistence within Christianity of a tradition of virulent defamation of Jews and Judaism. Because the vilifications have been so extreme, often ascribing unremittingly satanic characteristics to Jews, and because the policies the vilifications have engendered have been so murderous, there has been a persistent tendency on the part of students of the Holocaust to interpret anti-Semitism as an expression of psychological disorder.[22] It has become almost a cliche to assert that the negative traits anti-Semites cast upon the Jew are precisely those they discern within and cast out of themselves. It should be obvious that both the pathological and the projective interpretations of anti-Semitism are alternative versions of the interpretation of Jews as neutral objects of the assaults of others rather than participants in a two-way conflict. In the case of the projective theory, the role ascribed to the Jews as objects of anti-Semitic projections may be likened to a Rorschach inkblot in a psychological test. Because of the ambiguous character of the inkblot, the subject's account of the associations it elicits can, with justice, be understood as projections of his or her own mental world.[23] But people are never neutral objects like Rorschach inkblots. Even when they confront each other in silence, their encounters involve some interchange. Even when Jews remained quiet before the calumny of their adversaries, it is hardly likely that they were devoid of emotionally potent response or that their response did not become an element in the ongoing intergroup encounter. Before historical investigation rests content with interpreting anti-Jewish sentiment as the product of pathological emotion, ought we not to search for more concrete interests as motives for the behavior under investigation?

For example, Lucy Dawidowicz argues that Himmler's wartime refusal to honor, save temporarily, requests to reprieve from "evacuation" skilled Jewish workers employed in war industries is evidence of the irrational character of the entire destruction process.[24] But what if Himmler gave a higher priority to eliminating Jews than to winning the war? One could hardly call his allocation of resources or his calculation of ends and means irrational. His organization did achieve most of the goals it set for itself. Would we not learn more about the Holocaust were we to investigate the concrete interests, both material and nonmaterial, that men like Himmler perceived themselves to be fostering by the pursuit of their goals than we learn by resting content with characterizing those goals as immoral or irrational? I have spent most of my career with a profound concern for the unspeakable immorality of the Holocaust. Nevertheless, the time has come to ask whether we would not learn more about the phenomenon of anti-Semitism were we to focus our attention on the interests, again both material and nonmaterial, that such behavior may serve, rather than on ahistorical moral or psychological categorization.

The theory of cognitive dissonance discussed above can, I believe, enlarge our understanding of the nonmaterial interests served by the traditional hostility of the Christian churches toward Jews and Judaism. I hasten to add a cautionary note: The theory of cognitive dissonance *enlarges* our understanding of the Holocaust—*it does not offer a total explanation.* If, however, as Festinger and his colleagues maintain, cognitive dissonance is a motivating state of affairs, would not a situation of potential cognitive dissonance arise from the presence within Christian Europe of a rival community of the same background as that of the historical figure whom the Christian churches assert to be humanity's sole hope for eternal salvation, a community that nevertheless flatly rejected Christian claims about the Savior? Would not the possibility that the rival community might possess greater familiarity with the locale and the circumstances of the Savior's career create a situation of potential cognitive dissonance? Would not that situation call forth dissonance reduction strategies on the part of Christians, and most especially Christian theologians? In this regard, let us keep in mind that one of the most important roles of theologians is dissonance reduction. Since dissonance occurs when two items of information are psychologically inconsistent with each other, could not the defamation of the Jews be seen as partly motivated by the desire to discredit a potentially disconfirming item of information by discrediting its source? Could not the violence of the defamations be seen as related to the degree to which the potentially disconfirming information was perceived as threatening a value or an institution of overwhelming importance? Would this not help to explain the violent anti-Jewish animus of some of Christianity's most saintly personalities? The same genius, energy, and imagination that led them to initiate a universal religious civilization also impelled them to attack and discredit those whom they perceived to be challenging, even by their silent unbelief, the very foundation on which Christian civilization was constructed, faith in Christ as the Savior of mankind.

Let us remember that both Judaism and Christianity are religions of history rather than myth. Hence, the items of historical information which form the ultimate basis upon which their respective civilizations have been built, such as the claim that God spoke to Moses at Sinai or that the historical personality known as Jesus of Nazareth was in fact the unique Savior of mankind, are infinitely more vulnerable to empirical disconfirmation than mythical assertions concerning the gods in the pagan traditions. Instead of subsuming the hostility of the Christian Church toward Jews and Judaism under the category of hatred or pathology, would we not learn far more about the phenomenon were we to regard it as in part a strategy of dissonance reduction? If nothing else, the hostility would then be seen as more purposeful and goal directed than when it is viewed primarily as an expression of gratuitous malice. Such a view would also raise some very serious questions about the potential for violence of any tradition with exclusivistic claims to possess divinely inspired historical truth.

Furthermore, the spread of Christianity posed a problem of cognitive dissonance of comparable seriousness for Jews. Jews, who believed that an all-powerful God had elected their nation, could not entirely avoid the question of why that God had caused Judaism's principal rival to prosper and the Synagogue to languish. To the extent that Jews were isolated from and avoided connubium with their neighbors, they were engaged in dissonance reduction. The dangers involved in overt attempts to discredit the rival tradition caused the Jews to moderate the rhetoric employed in their dissonance reduction strategies. Nevertheless, nothing could eliminate the necessity to discredit the disconfirming challenge of the universal spread of the Christian Church. A principal Jewish dissonance reduction strategy was to characterize Christian belief in the Incarnation as a form of either idolatry or superstition.[25] In effect, each party to the conflict was compelled to discredit the other. Moreover, each perceived the other as so doing, even though the Jews refrained from overt expression of their views.

Beyond the question of religious rivalry, the anti-Semitic program for the elimination of the Jews can also be seen as motivated by a desire to eliminate a group of culturally disconfirming others. Highly visible Jews like Marx, Freud, Einstein, and a host of secular Jewish intellectuals were seen as unattached to traditional European Christian values and, in fact, responsible for their dissolution.[26] Radical anti-Semites, including Hitler, were far more troubled by assimilated Jews and intermarriage than by the more obviously alien, separatist Orthodox Jews. Although this concern was couched in the language of blood "pollution" and "purity," the destabilizing element in the Jewish presence was the alternative perspective that secularized Jews brought to political, social, cultural, and economic issues by virtue of their distinctive history and social location. While any foreigner would have had an alternative cultural perspective, non-Jewish Europeans shared a common Christian tradition as well as common origins in feudal Europe. The Jews shared neither the religious traditions nor the memory of an established place, no matter how lowly, in premodern Europe. The role of the Jews in the arts, the media, and literature was especially resented. One observer has commented that modern anti-Semitism was born "not from the great difference between groups but rather from the threat of the absence of differences, the homogenization of Western society and the abolition of the ancient social and legal barriers between Jews and Christians."[27] I would add that the threat came from the absence of *clearly perceptible* differences. Memory and social location are indispensable components of identity. The Jews shared neither component with their non-Jewish counterparts.

When confronted with dissonant items of information, those who resort to verbal violence as a discrediting strategy may be tempted to

employ harsher measures. Total, physical elimination of the most significant source of potential disconfirmation has been a perennial temptation
in Christendom. A principal question to be addressed by Holocaust research is why that temptation did not become official policy until the infamous Wannsee Conference of January 20, 1942. I shall return to that
question.

The theory of cognitive dissonance also helps to explain why so
many of the men and women who created and sustained Christian civilization resorted to extreme verbal intemperance in their dealings with
Christendom's principal spiritual rival. Because of the revulsion the Holocaust inspires in us, we are, for example, inclined to treat the virulent
anti-Semitism of Martin Luther as a flaw in his otherwise extraordinary
capacities. The theory of cognitive dissonance helps us to see that the
same energy that enabled the reformer to become the initiator of a new
era in Christendom also impelled him to attack those whom he perceived
to be negating Christianity.[28]

In addition, dissonance reduction has the advantage of avoiding
oversimplified characterizations of anti-Semitism as an instance of xen-
ophobia. Had the Jews been completely alien to the Christian world, they
would have elicited a less violent dissonance reduction response because
their information would not so readily have been perceived as potentially
disconfirming. The presence of a tribe of Buddhist traders from China in
the heart of Europe during the Middle Ages would have elicited hostility
and suspicion, but it is highly unlikely that such a tribe would have been
perceived as the minions of the Antichrist devoted to the destruction of
Christendom, as were the Jews. In rejecting the Christian Savior, the
Chinese could not have claimed historical familiarity with Jesus of Nazareth, as did the Jews. No other rejection of Christian claims presented
as serious a challenge as did that of Judaism, and no other religion has
been as abused by the best rather than the worst exemplars of a rival
faith.

Total elimination of disconfirming others has always been an ultimate theological aim of the Christian Church. The humane method of
eliminating the disconfirming other is, of course, conversion. Over the
centuries the Christian Church has had an active worldwide missionary
program for precisely this purpose. Stated theologically, the ultimate goal
of the Church is that all human beings become one in Christ. From the
perspective of social psychology, the unity of all people in Christ symbolizes the cognitive conformity based upon shared religious faith that
will in a future era be the decisive test of membership in the human race.
In fairness to the Church, it must be stated that the Synagogue has an

analogous goal. Judaism looks forward to the day when all people will acknowledge and serve the God of Israel. Such a goal could, of course, only be realized were all men and women to abandon their own traditions and accept the faith of Israel. At present, the leading representatives of both Judaism and Christianity see the process whereby the truth of their faith will be universally affirmed as essentially peaceful. Nevertheless, there have been periods in which both traditions resorted to more forceful means of conversion, if not to outright violence, in order to eliminate disconfirming others, and it is impossible to say that there will never again be such a time.

Thus, by virtue of (*a*) the radical asymmetry between the Christian claim that Jesus is the Savior of humanity and the Jewish insistence on his fallible humanity and (*b*) the dissonance-reducing strategies employed by Christianity, the Jews were thrust into an extremely dangerous, enduring religious and cultural conflict with an infinitely more powerful rival. Nevertheless, the cognitive conflict was a necessary, but not a sufficient, condition for state-sponsored genocide. Such a draconian project required the modernization of Europe's economy and society and historical events such as World War I and the Russian Revolution, which that process engendered. I turn now to the question of modernization and its destabilizing consequences.

In premodern times the conflict between Judaism and Christianity was somewhat moderated by the fact that Jews played a well-defined, necessary, albeit resented and despised, role in the precapitalist economy of Europe. Put differently, in the premodern period, the Jews were an economically complementary, rather than a competitive, population.[29] Some sociologists would say that, like the ethnic Chinese of Southeast Asia, the Ibos of Nigeria, and the Armenians of the Ottoman Empire, the Jews were an "elite" or a "middleman" minority filling certain commercial and professional roles that were not filled by the dominant majority.[30]

With the rise of a modern, urbanized middle class among the members of the dominant majorities of almost every European nation, the Jews ceased to play a complementary role and became highly visible competitors of an infinitely more powerful group. In addition, barred from participation in such high-status institutions as the military, the state bureaucracy, and, to a large extent, the universities, educated, secularized Jews came to play an overly important role in those institutions that are both the originators and custodians of cultural life—the arts, the media, literature, and publishing. Hannah Arendt has succinctly described the process: "What the nation-state once feared so much, the birth of a Jewish intelligentsia, now proceeded at a fantastic pace. The crowding of

Jewish sons of well-to-do parents into the cultural occupations was especially marked in Germany and Austria, where a great proportion of cultural institutions, like newspapers, publishing, music and theater, became Jewish institutions."[31] Even in contemporary, multicultural, multiethnic America, conservative voices frequently complain of Jewish influence in cultural institutions and the media. Indeed, before World War II it was exceedingly difficult if not impossible for Jews to secure tenured faculty positions at America's most prestigious universities.[32] Nevertheless, it may be hard for Americans to understand how deeply threatening the presence of Jews in those institutions was felt to be in societies with little use for cultural pluralism. Moreover, in Europe the tendency toward cultural uniformity was strongly encouraged by the tendency toward political centralization and cultural homogenization inherent in the modernization process itself.

Before the onset of modernization, a small number of Jews engaged in agriculture in Christian Europe, especially in the early Middle Ages, and Jewish moneylenders occasionally gained possession of the real property of members of the nobility who defaulted on their debts. Nevertheless, Jews served primarily as agents of a money economy in a predominantly agrarian, subsistence economy. Whether Jews were merchants, traders, artisans, tax farmers, innkeepers, distillers of alcoholic spirits, or moneylenders, their occupations were oriented toward the marketplace at a time when most economic activity was directed toward subsistence. Of fateful importance was the fact that medieval and early modern Jewish economic activity did not include the establishment of any significant industrial production although the available supply of impoverished artisans in the ghettos could have served as a labor pool.[33] Jewish economic activity was aimed primarily at the exchange, rather than the production, of goods.

The situation of the Jews in western Europe tended to deteriorate as a bourgeois capitalist economy replaced the subsistence economy of the feudal period. In the feudal period money was borrowed primarily for the purpose of consumption rather than production. Since consumption did not create new wealth, lenders had to charge usurious interest rates to compensate for the risk. With the introduction of capitalist finance, money was more likely to be borrowed for production, that is, for the creation of new wealth, rather than for consumption, the expenditure of old wealth. Hence, the position of the creditor became less precarious. In addition, rents and other peasant obligations due the lord were progressively transformed from a share of the crop and personal services to money compensation. This in turn gave landowners access to their own source of funds and made them less dependent upon moneylenders. As an indigenous, non-Jewish commercial class capable of filling the roles previously filled by Jews arose, Jews were forced into marginal enterprises such as peddling secondhand goods and pawnbroking. Eventually, the majority of the Jews found themselves closed out entirely and forced, as often by financial compulsion as actual expulsion, to leave western Europe. From the beginning of the sixteenth century, there was a definite pattern of migration of Jews from western to eastern Europe. This was a movement from the regions of Europe that were more highly developed economically to the less developed regions. In the early Middle Ages, the majority of Europe's Jews lived in western and central Europe. For several centuries before World War II, the majority were domiciled in the economically backward regions of eastern Europe.[34] In 1825 it is estimated that there were 2,730,000 Jews in Europe, of whom 458,000 lived in western and central Europe, and 2,272,000 in eastern and southeastern Europe. In 1900, 1,328,500 Jews lived in western and central Europe, and 7,362,000 in eastern and southeastern Europe. The largest number of Jews in Europe lived in Poland, which had a Jewish population of approximately 3,250,000 immediately before World War 11.[35]

The eastward migration was largely economic in origin. As long as western Europe lacked an indigenous commercial class capable of filling the same functions as the Jews, the Jews had a viable economic role there. Eastern Europe served as a population magnet because it remained feudal and agrarian for several centuries longer than did the West. Eastern Europe offered Jews opportunities for earning a decent livelihood which they had lost in the West. Yet, implicit in the eastward population shift was the seed of its own destruction. Sooner or later, the economy of eastern Europe was to go through an economic development roughly comparable to that of the West, at least with regard to the shift from a subsistence to a money economy and the subsequent displacement of the Jews by the dominant majority. Unfortunately, the Jewish role in the economies of eastern Europe became precarious at a time of unprecedented increase in both the Jewish and the general population, for which the economies of the region were unable to provide adequate work opportunities.

The transformation of the economies of those eastern European countries controlled by Russia was accelerated by the land reforms beginning in Poland in 1846 and Russia in 1861.[36] A process was initiated by which the serfs, who numbered forty-eight million, were emancipated. The old bonds of mutual responsibility between peasant and lord were severed, and the relationship was placed on an impersonal, monetary basis. Most peasants were both illiterate and among the least competent agriculturalists in Europe. In the new economic environment some peasants prospered and enlarged their holdings; most were not so fortunate and were proletarianized in a society with large-scale unemployment.[37]

Even those peasant families in eastern Europe who retained their small holdings were subject to mounting pressures because of the growth of population. In the premodern period, the population was sufficiently stable so that adequate land could be found for the younger as well as the firstborn sons of the peasants. As the population began to explode, the old symmetry between population and land disappeared. At first thousands and then millions were threatened with the most disastrous form of economic and social degradation that could be visited on a peasant, loss of land. To avert this disaster, peasants in eastern Europe resorted to subdivision.

Subdivision only worsened the situation. It brought reliance on the potato as the principal crop with which a peasant family could feed itself. As in Ireland, no other source of food could offer as much nourishment from so small an area of farmland. Also as in Ireland, there was a tendency to raise grain as a cash crop to pay the land rent rather than for food.

Nevertheless, subdivision could not go on indefinitely. Agricultural units of ever-diminishing size could not meet the needs of an ever-increasing population. Unable to find work in the village, millions of landless peasants turned to the towns and cities in the hope of maintaining themselves. Some peasants found work, but the industrial base in eastern Europe was so meager that millions found themselves hopelessly without work in the ever-expanding urban centers.

While urbanization offered no solution to the problem of agrarian unemployment, it did offer a powerful impetus to the consolidation of small peasant landholdings. The cities created a vastly enlarged demand for agricultural products, which could not be met by small peasant holdings. In its overall outline, the story of the modernization of eastern European agriculture is very much the same as elsewhere in the world. There was the same tendency toward the elimination of small holdings which was manifest in the English enclosure movement and in Ireland as a result of the great famine of 1846–48. Small holdings remained in peasant hands in Poland longer than in the West, but the movement toward consolidation was irreversible. There was no other way in which the growing urban population could be fed. Still, while consolidation enriched the larger and more enterprising farmers, it further disrupted the ancient social ecology of village life and greatly enlarged the number of uprooted, landless peasants.

The destruction of the old economy had disastrous effects on Jewish life in the villages. The transition to a market economy replicated the conditions that had originally driven the Jews out of western Europe into eastern Europe. As the larger farmers prospered, they began to displace Jews from their traditional economic roles. Under the goad of necessity, still other non-Jews divested themselves of the traditional distaste for trade and commerce and became direct competitors of the Jews.[38] Only in the most economically retrograde regions of eastern Poland did the Jews continue to own the majority of village shops in the 1930s.[39] Nor were the petite bourgeoisie the only new competitors. As state policy and economic constraint forced the Jews out of the villages, millions of Jews became an urban proletarian mass for the first time in their history.[40] The Jews found themselves competing for scarce jobs with an equally desperate non-Jewish proletariat. At the same time, as noted above, the Jewish population was experiencing an unprecedented explosion. In 1816 Jews constituted 8.7 percent of the population of Poland. By 1865 the proportion had risen to 13.5 percent, and in 1897, in spite of massive emigration, 14 percent of the population was Jewish.[41]

Further deterioration of the Jewish situation, always exacerbated by religious conflict, was caused by the introduction of machinery into the processes of production. Jewish artisans were especially hard hit. In eastern Europe Jews traditionally worked as tailors, bookbinders, cigarmakers, watchsmiths, goldsmiths, and silversmiths. Before the coming of the machines these fields required little capital but some skill. With the introduction of machines, the need for skill diminished while the need for capital increased. Jewish employers often found that it made more economic sense to hire unskilled Polish workers rather than declassed Jewish artisans and petty merchants. Hopelessly undercapitalized, the majority of Jewish artisans and merchants became dependent upon wage labor, when they could find it, at a time when a Polish working class was available to perform the same tasks, often more economically.[42] Moreover, employment in heavy industry, one of the most promising sources of job creation, was largely barred to the Jews by state policy and worker resistance.[43]

Although it is always difficult to pinpoint a date as initiating a new historical trend, 1881 can be seen as the watershed year for the fate of the Jewish communities of the Russian-dominated areas of eastern Europe. Because of the long-range impact of the fate of eastern European Jews on the Jews of western Europe, 1881 can be seen as a watershed year for those in the West as well. On March 13, 1881 (new calendar), Czar Alexander II was assassinated by members of a revolutionary terrorist group, *Narodnaya Volya* (People's Will). One of the plotters, Gessia Gelfman, was of Jewish origin. Her presence among the terrorists was enough to trigger the release of a massive, popular anti-Semitic explosion. Anti-Semitism had already been stimulated by the unsatisfactory peace treaty imposed upon Russia at the Congress of Berlin after the Russo-Turkish War of 1877–78, in which Benjamin Disraeli played an important role in limiting Russian ambitions against Turkey. Anti-Semitism was also fostered by press defamation and the generally depressed economic conditions. The objective conditions making for an anti-Semitic outbreak were already present without the assassination and Gelfman. These were nothing more than matches applied to a waiting fuse.

The first pogrom took place in Elizavetgrad (now Kirovograd) in the Ukraine on April 27, 1881. The details of the pogroms are too well known to require repetition. By the end of 1881, some 215 communities in southern and southwestern Russia had been victimized; hundreds of Jews were killed, mutilated, and raped. More than twenty thousand Jews lost their homes and at least four hundred thousand their livelihood.[44] The violence continued until 1884, and there was another wave of pogroms between 1903 and 1906, including the vicious Kishinev massacres.[45]

In his authoritative analysis of the pogroms, Steven Berk points to the deteriorating condition of peasants and workers throughout the empire as a principal economic factor. By the end of the seventies, less than half of the peasants had plots sufficient to sustain their families. Millions of peasants attempted unsuccessfully to rent more land or to hire themselves out as farm laborers. Unfortunately, land rents increased more rapidly than wages or the price of wheat.

There was, however, a massive migration of peasants from the land to the cities. According to Berk, between 1860 and 1870 the government issued fewer than thirteen million internal passports; in the crucial decade of the seventies, it issued thirty-seven million.[46] Peasants from the northern and central regions of the empire migrated south in search of work. The railroads were able to engage some of these wanderers, but the vast majority were itinerants in search of any kind of work. The condition of the peasants was not unlike that of undocumented aliens in the United States today. With little or no bargaining power, the migratory workers, known as *bosiaki* (the barefoot brigade), were compelled to take whatever work was available, no matter how harsh the conditions.

The presence of so large a mass of bitter, desperate people also constituted a threat to the indigenous artisans, workers, and merchants of the south who were trying to cope with the effects of the Great Depression of 1873–79. Normal competition between Jews and non-Jews was thus envenomed by the instability, diminishing opportunities, and basic poverty of the region. Not surprisingly, both the migratory workers and the urban non-Jews saw the Jews as the cause of their misfortunes.

According to Berk, the pogroms were primarily a Ukrainian phenomenon that invariably began in the cities or large towns and thereafter spread to the countryside. Berk has characterized the core group of *pogromshchiki* as composed of "the *meshchanstvo* or petty bourgeoisie, including shopkeepers, butchers, clerks, joiners, tanners, carpenters, and artisan elements of all types."[47] Railroad workers were especially active both as participants in the pogroms and in spreading word about them, which stimulated further pogroms. According to Berk, *the peasants were not primarily responsible for the pogroms*, which, he asserts, were "in terms of origin and severity, primarily urban events." The pogroms began in the cities and only later spread to the villages. Learning that Jewish property was available for the taking, the peasants tended to enter the cities toward the end of the pogroms to gather up their share. Nor were the pogroms nearly as violent in the peasant villages as in the cities.[48] Although the pogroms located primarily in the south, there was a large Great Russian component among the *pogromshchiki*. Russians constituted a large proportion of the migratory workers, the *bosiaki*.

Berk's findings are important because they tend to confirm that a very large proportion of those who actively participated in the pogroms were persons rendered vocationally redundant by the modernization process. This in turn tends to confirm the view that modern anti-Semitism, as distinguished from traditional religious anti-Semitism, is a modernization phenomenon. As long as the Jews remained a complementary economic population fulfilling middleman-minority roles, the alien character of their religious and ethnic roots could in most cases be grudgingly tolerated. With the modernization and industrialization of the Russian Empire—let us remember that it had already entered "the takeoff period" of modernization and by the next decade would have the highest annual growth rate of any industrial power—the Russian government was confronted with millions of desperate citizens who were prepared wholly to displace the Jews. And the success of the Narodnaya Volya in assassinating not only the czar but other high officials with the sympathy of the educated classes was enough to convince high officials of the need to reconcile the "people" to the regime. Under the circumstances, the Jews, who were almost universally regarded as exploiters of the people, could easily be dispensed with. In January 1882 Count N. P.

Ignatiev, minister of the interior, repeated the words of the Kiev public prosecutor, who had attacked the Jews at a trial of a group of *pogrom-shchiki*, saying, "The western frontier is open to the Jews; why don't they cross it for their own good?"[49]

The question of the regime's complicity in the pogroms has never been completely resolved. Berk has concluded that the pogroms were spontaneous. They usually spread from a large city to the surrounding area, then, after a break of several days, another pogrom would start in another large town. In spite of the unwillingness of the police and military to stop the violence and even on occasion their willingness to join in, Berk argues that "not a single document has come to light" indicating official government instigation of the pogroms.[50]

The question of instigation is less important than the response of the Russian government and educated classes to the events, which was one of sympathy for the perpetrators and harsh contempt for the victims. There was general approval of the pogroms among educated Russians, the terrorist Narodnaya Volya, and the authorities. The czarist government regarded the pogroms as a useful outlet for the discontented masses and as a means of injuring a despised minority that it sought ultimately to eliminate. Narodnaya Volya welcomed the pogroms as a foretaste of the political awakening of the masses, which was expected eventually to lead to the overthrow of the czarist regime.[51]

To the extent that perpetrators were arrested and lightly punished, the regime's motive was distrust of both disorder and popular spontaneity rather than a desire to rectify an injustice. The most important government official responsible for containing the pogroms was Count Dmitri Tolstoi, who succeeded Ignatiev as minister of the interior. Ironically, opposition to the pogroms was most effective among ultraconservatives like Tolstoi, Konstantin Petrovich Pobedonostsev, who is discussed below, and M. K. Reutern, chairman of the Council of Ministers.[52]

An important aspect of any pogrom instigated or tolerated by the state is its calculated denial of the normal protection of the law to the target population. This denial transforms the target population into a collection of outlaws whom members of the dominant majority are free to injure or kill at will. Although pogroms involve emotionally laden mob violence, they serve a rational political purpose by putting the target population on notice that they are cast wholly outside the social contract. Even if the government limits the period of active violence for reasons of public order, it demonstrates its capacity to renew the violence at any time. Thus, the basic purpose of the pogrom, whether the Russian pogroms of 1881–82, the anti-Armenian attacks in the Ottoman Empire, or the Nazi *Kristallnacht*, is to provide the target group with the strongest possible motivation to emigrate.

The 1881–82 pogroms had the desired effect: 1881 marks the beginning of eastern European Jewry's mass emigration. Between 1871 and 1880 the average annual Jewish emigration from eastern Europe was eight to ten thousand; between 1881 and 1900 it was between fifty and sixty thousand a year.[53] Incidentally, a high proportion of modernized Jews were among the first emigrants.[54]

For those Jews who could not or would not interpret the pogroms correctly, the czarist government offered an even more explicit indication of its intentions in what came to be known as the May Laws, promulgated on May 13, 1882. The May Laws were designed both to injure and to insult the Jews and succeeded in doing both. They forbade Jews to settle in the rural villages and made it difficult for Jews living in the villages to remain there. Jews who left their village even for brief periods were prevented from returning. Itinerant Jews looking for work were expelled from the villages as new settlers. The laws also prevented Jews from inheriting family property in other villages; nor could a Jew help a family member who lived elsewhere to settle in his village. The number of Jews permitted to enter Russian universities was drastically reduced, as was the number of Jews permitted to enter professions such as law and medicine.

Stringent controls were placed on Jewish artisans. A Jew lost his status as an artisan if he used a machine in his craft. A pastry cook who served coffee with his pastry was reclassified as a merchant. Reclassification could be followed by expulsion from the village.[55] In 1887 Jews who had been living in the villages before 1882 were forbidden to move to another village.[56] The May Laws were made even more severe when provincial authorities widened their applicability by reclassifying larger towns as villages, and in 1891 the entire Jewish community of Moscow, numbering twenty thousand, was summarily expelled. The Jewish communities of St. Petersburg and Kharkov were also expelled. The effect of the May Laws was further to concentrate the Jews in the overcrowded and underemployed cities of what was known as the Pale of Settlement.[57]

Furthermore, the czarist government's anti-Jewish measures initiated in 1881 were closely related to the emancipation of the Polish and Russian serfs. By laying the groundwork for the capitalist transformation of eastern European agriculture, emancipation created the conditions for the beginnings of a small but growing indigenous middle class. As this class developed, the Russian government, which had traditionally been hostile to the Jews, had even less reason to tolerate a minority that was seen as foreign to the nation's ethnic and religious consensus.

The ultimate aim of Russian policy in the aftermath of the events of 1881 was the total elimination of the Jews. This was clearly understood by one of the leaders most responsible for the formulation of that policy, Konstantin Petrovich Pobedonostsev (1827–1904), a highly influential anti-Semitic bureaucrat who served as Supreme Procurator (*Ober-Prokuror*) of the Holy Synod of the Russian Orthodox Church from 1880 until his death. A fanatic believer in czarist absolutism, Pobedonostsev pursued a policy of unmitigated Russification of all non-Russian minorities.[58] Ever the man of law and order, Pobedonostsev expressed his opposition to the pogroms in June 1881 in a letter addressed to the new czar, Alexander III. Several months later in 1882 Pobedonostsev denounced the Ministry of the Interior, then headed by Ignatiev, for permitting the riots to take place. Pobedonostsev strongly supported the May Laws and all other measures designed to bring about the removal of the Jews from Russia. He was also hostile to the Armenians, who, although Christian, were not members of the Russian Orthodox Church.[59] Pobedonostsev favored the transformation of czarist Russia into a homogeneous, centralized theocracy in which non-Russian minorities would be integrated into a monolithic Russian Orthodox civilization. His program of homogenization and centralization arose from the same modernizing impulse as did that of the Young Turks who were responsible for the 1915 genocide of the Armenians.[60] Historian James Billington describes Pobedonostsev as a modernizing bureaucrat:

> Pobedonostsev . . . was a thoroughly prosaic lay figure, whose ideal was the gray efficiency and uniformity of the modern organization man. He was the prophet of duty, work, and order—shifting his bishops around periodically to prevent any distracting local attachments from impeding the smooth functioning of the ecclesiastical machine. He was unemotional, even cynical, about his methods. But they were generally effective and earn him a deserved place as one of the builders of the centralized bureaucratic state.[61]

As a figure of consequence in Jewish history, Pobedonostsev is perhaps best remembered for the "solution" of the Jewish problem he is reported to have offered a group of Jewish petitioners in 1898: "One third will die, one third will leave the country, and the last third will be completely assimilated within the surrounding population."[62] *Thus, decades before World War II Russian policymakers sought to achieve for their country the very same goal with respect to the Jews as did the National Socialists.* There was no difference concerning the end; there was, of course, an overwhelmingly important difference between the means even a modernizing bureaucrat like Pobedonostsev was prepared to employ before World War I and those the National Socialists would use during World War II. Admittedly there were countercurrents of liberalism in Russia toward the end of the nineteenth and the beginning of the twentieth century, but the liberals were never more than a minority voice.

Nevertheless, while the czarist program of pogroms and legal discrimination was neither as efficient nor as successful as Hitler's, it was one of the most effective state-sponsored programs of population elimination up to its time. It set in motion the mass emigration from eastern Europe of more than four million Jews between 1881 and 1930. With the possible exception of the aftermath of the Fall of Jerusalem to the Romans in 70 C.E., never before had so large a proportion of the Jewish people migrated from one country to another in so short a time. Undoubtedly economic hopelessness was as much a spur to emigration as state hostility. Nevertheless, the economic and political elements making for mass migration cannot be separated.

If we recognize that in fostering the departure of the Jews the leaders of czarist Russia were pursuing a sociopolitical objective that was essentially the same as that of the Third Reich, although it employed far less radical and systematic means, we will also recognize that what is normally called the Holocaust can better be understood as the culmination of a historic movement whose modern phase began in the last quarter of the nineteenth century and had as its objective the total elimination of the Jews from European civilization. With the recent breakdown of the Soviet Union that process is accelerating once again, albeit without resort to mass destructiveness as yet.

With whatever understanding hindsight can offer us, it would appear that the social, economic, and political forces set in motion by the accelerating process of modernization in Europe effectively sealed the fate of Europe's Jews several decades before the beginning of the twentieth century. At some level, this was understood intuitively by those emigrants who were fortunate enough to flee the oncoming peril before the final blow. For those Jews who remained in Europe, only the hour and the manner of their elimination remained uncertain.

There is, incidentally, an eerie parallel between the beginnings of the process that led to the destruction of the European Jews and the one leading to the destruction of another minority, the Armenians. The modern travail of the Armenians had its beginnings at almost the same moment as that of the Jews, namely, 1876, the year of the accession of Sultan

Abdul Hamid II to the throne of the Ottoman Empire. The climax of the Armenian travail came in 1915, far sooner than did that of the Jews. Unfortunately, few Jews in the period between World Wars I and II were able to discern the sociological parallels between their situation and that of the Armenians or to draw the grim but necessary political conclusions from those parallels.

In western Europe the late 1870s can be seen as the launching period of the same, ultimately genocidal movement. Bismarck's creation of a unified German empire in 1870 was followed by the stock market crash of 1873 and the economic depression of 1873–79. The financial disturbances created especially difficult conditions for the lower middle class. Unfortunately, even the resumption of an upward trend in the business cycle was of greater benefit to the owners, managers, and laborers in large-scale financial and industrial enterprises than to artisans, small retail merchants, or rural laborers. Artisans, petty merchants, and rural workers tended to identify the new industrial capitalism with the Jews and to be equally resentful of Jewish industrialists, department store owners, bankers, and peddlers, all of whom were perceived as threatening the small merchant.[63] It has been said that "anti-Semitism rose as the stock market fell."[64] In 1878 Germany's first overtly anti-Semitic political party, the lower-middle-class Christian Social party, was founded by Adolf Stöcker, Court Chaplain to the Kaiser.[65] In 1879 Heinrich von Treitschke, one of Germany's leading historians, called for the transformation of Germany into a Lutheran *Kultur-Staat* and the elimination of Jewish influence.[66]

In 1879 in Austria, Georg von Schönerer, the leader of the Pan-German movement, offered a political program with anti-Semitic elements, although he continued to work with Jews as late as 1882.[67] Schönerer worked closely with the anti-Semitic student fraternities at the University of Vienna.[68] One example of the growth of the anti-Semitic movement among students at the university was the memorial service for Richard Wagner on March 5, 1883, organized by the League of German Students. The anti-Semitic composer had died three weeks earlier. At the service Hermann Bahr, the chief delegate of Albia, Theodor Herzl's fraternity, gave so violent an anti-Semitic speech that the police disbanded the meeting. Although inactive, Herzl realized that his fraternity had turned anti-Semitic and resigned.[69] By 1885 the Pan-German societies had expelled their baptized Jewish members. They also saw their Jewish peers as potential competitors. The students had a modernizing bias toward homogenization and centralization which was evident in their contempt for the multinational Hapsburg Empire and their longing to unite German Austria with the rest of Germany in a single *Gross-deutschland*. While Jews tended mistakenly to identify rationality and modernity with pluralism, liberalism, and tolerance, by the beginning of the twentieth century their non-Jewish counterparts were increasingly identifying it with homogenization, standardization, and centralization. The leadership role of the universities in anti-Semitic activities continued in Europe in the between-the-wars period. In the Germany of the Weimar Republic and in Poland in the 1930s, a far larger proportion of university students participated in violently anti-Semitic activities than did the general population.[70]

As eastern European Jews settled in large numbers in cities like Berlin and Vienna, the demand arose to restrict Jewish immigration. The urbanization of eastern European Jews can be seen in the population figures of Vienna and Berlin. In 1846, 3,739 Jews lived in Vienna; fifty-four years later there were 176,000, most of whom were of eastern European origin.[71] In 1852, 11,840 Jews lived in Berlin; in 1890 there were 108,044 or 5.02 percent of the city's population.[72] Schönerer, then a Pan-German member of Parliament, took the Chinese Exclusion Act passed by the United States Congress in 1882 as the model for his proposed legislation restricting the immigration of Russian Jews.[73] In 1887 he proposed that Jews be confined to ghettos and restricted as to profession.[74]

Moreover, *while eastern European Jews were immigrating to Germany and Austria, Germany was experiencing the largest emigration in its history.* Between 1871 and 1885, 1,678,202 people, approximately 3.5 percent of the entire population, migrated to the United States. The peak emigration of 250,000 occurred in the crucial year of 1881–82. The majority of the emigrants were from the agrarian regions of northern and eastern Germany, regions that had experienced the greatest social destabilization as a result of the new industrial civilization.[75]

The *Auswanderung*, or emigration, in nineteenth-century Germany was largely a lower-middle-class movement. Unlike the Irish poor, the very poor in Germany did not normally emigrate. Those who risked the overseas journey were generally artisans, small farmers, and small businessmen who had some capital with which to begin a new life overseas. The emigrants saw their prospects diminishing in Germany. They feared proletarianization were they to remain in a rapidly industrializing Germany and thereby exhaust their resources.[76] Lower-middle-class Germans who did not emigrate constituted the class with most reason to be fearful of capitalism, with its inherent bias in favor of large-scale enterprise. They were also the group most likely to be confronted by Jewish competition for available small business and professional opportunities.

Barred from state employment, including the universities, the Jews had no alternative but to maximize their opportunities within the private sector.

Fear of socialism as well as proletarianization intensified lower-middle-class anti-Semitism, especially in the between-the-wars period. The antisocialist attitudes of the German and Austrian lower middle class were not without an element of paradox. In general, the lower middle class understood that big business, whether it was the large-scale manufacturing firm, the big bank, or the department store, tended to undermine their economic and social standing. For example, the under-capitalized watchmaker could not compete with the assembly-line man-ufacturer, nor could the owner of a small retail store compete with either the immigrant Jewish peddler or the department stores, most of which were owned by Jews. The department stores were an enduring object of lower-middle-class anger. In addition to promising to eliminate the Jews, before the seizure of power the National Socialists promised the lower middle class relief from the threat of large-scale enterprise; they were able to make good on their promise about the Jews but not the one about large-scale enterprise, which was indispensable to the power needs of a mod-ern state preparing for war. In the takeoff period of industrial capitalism, the small businessman or artisan was often forced to choose between abandoning the dignity of his self-employed status and witnessing the steady erosion of his standard of living as he attempted unsuccessfully to compete against larger and better-financed enterprises. There was thus an anticapitalist component in the perceptions of the lower middle class. However, it was impossible for the socialists to enlist their support, since Marxism could only promise the petite bourgeoisie the very fate they feared most, proletarianization.

Racial nationalism offered the lower middle class a political program that proved increasingly popular over the years. It legitimated hostility toward the hated Jewish competitor, while offering an ideological basis for community with the owners of large-scale enterprise and the man-agers of large-scale government, with whom they were inextricably re-lated in any event. The middle class rejected the internationalism of a Marxism that proclaimed the coming triumph of the proletariat, the one class into whose ranks they did not wish to enter. The Social Darwinism inherent in racial nationalism offered the promise of wars of conquest against inferior peoples in which the declining fortunes of the lower mid-dle class would be reversed as they shared in the spoils of a triumphant racial empire.

By contrast, if the petite bourgeoisie dreaded working-class affiliation, politically romantic sons and daughters of assimilated or assimilating members of the Jewish bourgeoisie saw such affiliation as offering both escape from Jewishness and entrance into the world of the indigenous majority. Finding it impossible to support established institutions in Germany, Austria, and, most especially, czarist Russia, the sons and daughters of the Jewish bourgeoisie often enlisted in the parties of the Left and revolutionary movements. Wealthy Jewish families could give their offspring superb educational and cultural opportunities, but they could not rescue them from pariah status. The situation was, of course, worst in eastern Europe, where the hostility of the government toward Jews was altogether undisguised. Older Jews withdrew into the consolations of private life. Others despaired of achieving any integration with the larger society and turned to Zionism. Young Jews who did not abandon hope of integration but despaired achieving it under current conditions tended to turn either to Jewish or to general socialist organizations. Moreover, the role of the Christian Church as the most important legitimating institution of the established order enhanced the attractiveness of anti-religious Marxism to those young Jews who saw religion as ultimately responsible for their pariah status. The adherence of a visible group of Jews to the cause of the Left intensified the anti-Semitism of lower-middle-class racial nationalists. Not only were Jews hated competitors whose business activities threatened the petite bourgeoisie with reduction to proletarian status, but their sons and daughters sought the same result with their revolutionary activities. Articulate, secularized Jews had little reason to defend a traditional society that offered them only the despised status of pariahs. In the aftermath of the Russian Revolution, a very sizable group of the non-Jewish bourgeoisie came to see the Jews as enemies who threatened the very foundations of Christian civilization with their radicalism.[77] The idealism of the Jewish radicals only intensified the resolve of important elements of non-Jewish society to get rid of them, yet when the Left finally triumphed in Europe, its leaders were as interested in eliminating the Jews, at least as a distinctive group, as the Right had been. Because of the unresolved conflicts of religious belief and the inexorable trajectory of modernization with its population dislocations and its economic competition, *the European Jewish situation was without hope of fortunate issue.*

It has been said that the one war in which the National Socialists were ultimately victorious was their war of extermination against the Jews. The program of genocide was implicit in one of the key terms they habitually used to express their ultimate political and social aspirations, *Volksgemeinschaft.* The term gave succinct expression to the National Socialist yearning to create an ethnically and culturally homogeneous community from which all dissonant others would be totally eliminated.

Ironically, while the emancipation of Europe's Jews appeared to offer them civic equality as individuals, as a leveling measure it did away with official recognition of very real differences in tradition, culture, and function between the Jews and other groups. It was only a question of time before voices were heard demanding the elimination of those whose differences could not be leveled. Moreover, in most countries it was only with the highly problematic triumph of bourgeois liberalism that Jewish emancipation was seriously considered. In the *Philosophy of Right*, G. W. F. Hegel identified the bourgeoisie or "civil society" (*bürgerliche Gesellschaft*) as "the achievement of the modern world" and the domain of universal egoism.[78] By this G. W. F. Hegel meant that "individuals in their capacity as burghers in this state are private persons whose end is their own interest."[79] Put differently, in bourgeois society the private, self-aggrandizing interests of the individual (or individual corporation) take precedence over the well-being of the commonwealth. Community is exploded and society consists of congeries of self-regarding atoms whose interest in others is purely instrumental. When command of money became more important than command of men and English landowners used the acts of enclosure to evict their peasant tenants and depopulate the rural villages, they were exemplifying Hegel's view of civil society as the domain of universal egoism. If Hegel's characterization has merit, it can be said that the emancipation of the Jews, as well as the emancipation of Europe's peasants, occurred at a time when the realm of universal egoism was in the process of displacing traditional bonds of mutual dependence and responsibility. Only when a condition of universal otherhood displaced a society with some measure of brotherhood, however tenuous, were Jews permitted a status approaching political equality in western Europe. As every man became a stranger, it became possible for the Jew to become a neighbor.

From this perspective National Socialism can be seen as a movement that promised to restore civic altruism, not on the basis of a religious or humanitarian ideal of human solidarity, but strictly on the basis of the myth of primal tribal unity. To shape its racial policies, the National Socialist program used elements of racism or neotribalism, *Lebensraum*, anti-Marxism, and genocide.

Nazi racism was an attempt to establish a basis for community on the foundation of shared archaic roots. The exclusion of the alien was intrinsic to its very nature. In spite of its appeal to primitive tribal emotions, racism can be seen as a thoroughly modern response to the phenomenon of population superfluity and the fragmented affiliations of atomized bourgeois society. Racism was also an expression of and a response to the trend toward homogenization, centralization, and leveling that is a feature of modern bureaucratized society. Racism sought to establish an ideological basis for affiliation and community after all of the lesser units of community, such as the village, the Church, and even the nation, had proven unable to meet the challenge. Its message was simple and brutal: Only those who share our roots can hunt with our pack. All the rest are prey—first the stranger within our midst and later on the others, for the world is neither big enough nor rich enough for all of us. Moreover, we know that our program requires the kind of political leadership that will not be deterred from doing what has to be done by legal and moral abstractions, such as law, common citizenship, or taboos against murder of the innocent.

The tribalism of National Socialism was the sociopolitical expression of its racism. It was, however, not a restoration of something old, save in the mythical imagination of some National Socialist ideologues. It was a neotribalism that could only arise in a modern, industrial mass society. Like most other large linguistic groups, the Germans had been a group of tribes often at war with each other. The National Socialists proposed to complete the work of tribal consolidation by creating a single Aryan neotribe. The National Socialist project was both elicited and made possible by such tools of modern technology as high finance, industry, bureaucracy, transportation, and wireless communication.

The call to a primal unity of origin and kinship was made all the more radical as a result of Germany's defeat in the most industrialized war in all history to date, World War I. Whatever divided the German tribes, they shared the experience of defeat. Two million lives had been lost on the battlefield and another million had been lost through home-front starvation caused by the postwar Allied blockade, but to no avail. It was widely felt that only the most thoroughgoing internal cohesion would enable the nation to reverse the results of the lost war. Neotribalism was seen as a crucially important means to that end.

Lebensraum was a decisive Nazi concept. In 1891, ten years after the beginning of the historically decisive Russian pogroms, Leo von Caprivi, the Chancellor of the German Reich, observed that "Germany must export goods or people."[80] He preferred to export the former. Caprivi understood the classic dilemma of production and consumption that besets every modern technological society. Germany's ability to produce exceeded her capacity to consume. Without foreign markets, Germany would be faced with an unacceptable level of mass unemployment at home. Caprivi saw that domestic unemployment would have a destabilizing effect on German society and that the effect would by no means be limited to the working class.

In Caprivi's time, emigration was considered the acceptable method of population elimination. It is estimated that 6,000,000 people emigrated from Germany in the nineteenth and early twentieth centuries.[81] For the period 1846–1932, 4,900,000 emigrated from Germany and 5,200,000 from Austria-Hungary.[82] Admittedly, the figure from Austria-Hungary includes a large number of non-Germans, among whom were Hungarian and Galician Jews. Nevertheless, it is clear that conditions propelled an extraordinarily large number of Europeans to uproot themselves willingly.

The phenomenon of German emigration elicited the keen interest of Adolf Hitler as a young man. According to historian Robert G. L. Waite, one of the books in Hitler's library whose marginal notes attest the young Hitler's strong interest was *Auswanderungs-Möglichkeiten in Argentinien* (Emigration Possibilities in Argentina).[83] In *Mein Kampf*, Hitler wrote of the need for land to the east to absorb Germany's population surplus.[84] He came to regard emigration to the New World as a poor solution to Germany's population problem, for such emigrants ceased to be a human resource for Germany. His program of seeking *Lebensraum* in the east was designed to solve that problem by providing an area adjacent to the Reich to which Germany's surplus population could migrate. The demographic strength of the migrants would thus be retained by their native land.

As a youthful reader of Karl May's German novels about the American Wild West, Hitler came to see the elimination of North America's native population by white European settlers as a model to be followed by Germany on the European continent. In his eyes the Slavs were destined to become Europe's Indians. They were to be uprooted, enslaved, and, if necessary, annihilated to make way for Germany's surplus population. In his wartime *Tischrede*, his table talk, Hitler referred to the Russians as "Indians" and advised German officers to read Karl May to learn how to deal with them.[85]

Many of the Nazi leaders, Hitler included, understood the urgency of the problem of population redundancy through their own personal experience. According to the German historian Karl Dietrich Bracher, before the seizure of power in 1933, most members of the Nazi inner circles had been "petite bourgeoisie who had been for some time already engaged in the futile pursuit of a career."[86] Nowhere is this more evident than in the career of Hitler himself. Had he not succeeded in making politics his career, he might have spent his life as a shiftless outsider untrained for any normal vocation. Having escaped redundancy by the success of their political movement, the National Socialist leaders were determined to bring the overseas *Auswanderung* to a halt and redirect the flow of people eastward.

We have already noted the hostile reaction of the lower middle class to Marxism, a political movement that promised them the very proletarian status they were trying desperately to avoid. There were also other reasons why middle-class anti-Marxism was an important element in the political success of National Socialism. The American view of private property outside of the rural South comes closer than the European view to the capitalist notion that land is an alienable commodity freely and impersonally available for purchase and sale. In parts of Europe, inherited real property still has something of an emotionally tinged, if not sacralized, aura about it. Socialist confiscation of property by the state is therefore felt to be profoundly offensive, not only because of human possessiveness but also because of the destruction of a family's link to its past and its ancestors.

The affront involved in Communist seizure of property was compounded by the fact that Marxism was seen by conservative Europeans as Jewish in origin and leadership, a view that was reinforced in Germany by the three successive left-wing regimes that succeeded the Bavarian royal house of Wittelsbach from November 7, 1918, to May 1, 1919, at the end of World War I. In Munich, the city that did more than any other to give birth to National Socialism, and in the era in which Hitler first joined the minuscule party, a series of politically naive, left-wing Jewish leaders attempted ineffectually to bring about an enduring socialist revolution in Catholic, conservative Bavaria.[87] This brief episode ended in a right-wing bloodbath. Its effects were unfortunately enduring. Munich was a principal gathering place for White Russian refugees, who brought with them *The Protocols of the Elders of Zion* and its myth of a Jewish conspiracy to rule the world. The book was speedily translated into German and English and then given worldwide dissemination.[88] When the White Russians depicted Bolshevism as an assault by alien Jews on the fabric of European Christian civilization and as the very conspiracy to which the *Protocols* referred, the high visibility of Jewish leadership in the short-lived Bavarian Republic and the even briefer Soviet Republics lent credibility to the accusations. Incidentally, Eugenio Cardinal Pacelli, who was to serve as Pope Pius XII during World War II, was the Papal Nuncio in Munich during this crucial period. He was harassed by troops of the Munich Soviet, and Munich's Michael Cardinal Faulhaber was detained by the leftist regime. One is tempted to speculate that Cardinal Pacelli's

Munich experience with the Left helped to shape his wartime view that National Socialist Germany was Europe's bulwark against godless Bolshevism.[89] His Munich experience may also help to explain his wartime silence on the extermination of Europe's Jews, a project concerning which the Pontiff had excellent information.

Identification of the Jews with Marxism did not prevent them from being accused by the National Socialists and other anti-Semites of being responsible for capitalism, a system that, as we have seen, the lower middle class had reason to fear and resent. At times, Jewish capitalists were depicted as being in league with Jewish communists to bring about world domination.[90] Such accusations, many of them from the same source, have been regarded by students of anti-Semitism as evidence of either irrationality or the manipulative insincerity of those who employed them. Undoubtedly, propagandists are more interested in manipulation than in truth, yet there remains the question of why the propaganda seemed credible to so many people. The historic association of the Jews with money and the marketplace, as well as the mythical association of both Jews and the Devil with money and each other, undoubtedly reinforced the view that the Jews were responsible for inflicting the heartless, depersonalized world of money and universal otherhood on Christian Europe. In reality, Christian Europe required no Jews to inflict this world on it; it was ready to do the job itself.

If we recognize that capitalism and communism are alternative expressions of the modernization process, the one using the marketplace while the other resorts to the state's power of coercion, the real intent of the anti-Jewish accusations becomes apparent: they reflect resentment against modernization by those who perceived themselves to be its victims and regarded the Jews as both its carriers and its principal beneficiaries. In reality, no group was to pay more dearly for the modernization of Europe's economy and society than the Jews.

As soon as wartime conditions gave the German government a free hand, genocide became the almost inevitable consequence of the National Socialist program of anti-Semitism, *Lebensraum*, and *Volksgemeinschaft*. The goal of *Lebensraum*, the creation of a vast German racial empire in the east, involved the merciless elimination of all indigenous population elements that could not be integrated into the new system. As we know, the harshest forms of elimination were reserved for the Jews.

The goal of creating a "racially pure" *Volksgemeinschaft* would have doomed the Jews even had there been no *Lebensraum* policy. When the Germans invaded eastern Europe, they had a simple and demonically successful way of creating their *Volksgemeinschaft*: namely, mass murder of Germany's Jews and those elements of the conquered Jewish population that might someday be tempted to migrate to Germany. We have already noted Schönerer's efforts to limit Jewish immigration to Austria. A similar concern was expressed by one of Germany's most important historians, Heinrich von Treitschke in 1879 and 1880. Treitschke published a series of articles in the *Preussische Jahrbücher* entitled, "Ein Wort über unser Judenthum," in which he complained that "year after year there pours in from the inexhaustible Polish reservoir a host of ambitious pants-selling youngsters whose children will some day control . . . the stock exchanges and the newspapers."[91] The quest for racial homogeneity at all costs may explain why Himmler insisted on exterminating even those skilled Jewish laborers whom the Wehrmacht sought to keep working in Polish war industries. Thus, even when the war was lost, it was possible to achieve at least one crucial objective of National Socialism, creation of the *Volksgemeinschaft*.

With the doleful wisdom of hindsight, it is possible to see the doom of Europe's Jews becoming ever more certain in the between-the-wars period even before the National Socialist seizure of power. In the aftermath of World War I, the Russian Revolution, and the Russian Civil War, traditional political and social orders were overthrown throughout eastern and central Europe. Undoubtedly, even without Jews modernization would have transformed these societies sooner or later, as happened in Japan. Nevertheless, without the catastrophe of war and revolution the pace of change might have been manageable. Long before the catastrophes of World War I and its aftermath, thinkers like Max Weber and Friedrich Nietzsche understood the inability of traditional European society to withstand the onslaughts of modernity. Nietzsche's proclamation of the death of God is based upon just such an insight. In spite of the inevitable dissolution of traditional culture, many powerful and influential Europeans saw its demise as a consequence of a Jewish political and cultural assault. As we have seen, because of both their religious inheritance and the tendency of Jewish intellectuals and artists to reject religion altogether, the Jews were perceived as the principal agents of dissolution. This perception was rendered especially credible by the highly visible role played by the Jewish Bolsheviks in the Russian Revolution and Europe's left-wing parties. Those Jews who had mastered the art of effectively communicating with the non-Jewish world—the intellectuals, artists, journalists, publishers, and musicians—opted for modernizing political and cultural movements which promised them release from pariah status. They were incapable of seeing through their own illusions. Although it claimed to defend the traditional order, National Socialism was a mod-

ernizing movement using thoroughly modern means to achieve its political and social objectives.

The growing problem of millions of men and women people rendered surplus by political events in their native land was another post-
1918 phenomenon. As a result of the war, the Russian Revolution, the
Spanish Civil War, and the tendency of modern regimes unilaterally to
denationalize troublesome members of dissident political or national
groups, millions of people had become *apatrides*, men and women without a country.[92] Industrial unemployment, a problem few modern societies have been able to cope with, also increased dramatically after 1929.
Anti-Semitism again rose as the stock market fell. In 1932, six million
people were unemployed in Germany alone.[93] In the United States,
which had absorbed so great a proportion of Europe's surplus people
before World War I, almost a quarter of the work force was out of work
in the worst years of the Great Depression. Unemployment in eastern
Europe was even worse than elsewhere. Because of her rearmament program, Germany solved her unemployment problem by 1938. During
World War II Germany experienced an acute labor shortage. Nevertheless, even when Jews ceased to be economically redundant, they remained superfluous because of the ideal of *Volksgemeinschaft*. In a period
of acute economic crisis, the 1930s, the number of European Jews seeking
to emigrate increased as the number of countries willing to receive them
declined to the vanishing point.

Already in the 1920s the flood of eastern European immigrants to the
United States, the most promising destination, produced an explicitly
anti-Jewish response in Congress. The report of the Congressional Committee on Immigration entitled, "Temporary Suspension of Immigration," dated December 6, 1920, is concerned almost exclusively with
bringing Jewish immigration to a halt. The report cites the published
statement of a commissioner of the Hebrew Sheltering and Aid Society
of America: "If there were in existence a ship that could hold 3,000,000
human beings, the 3,000,000 Jews of Poland would board it to escape to
America."[94] In 1924, the year the membership of the Ku Klux Klan
reached an all-time high, Congress passed the Johnson Act, which established an annual quota of 5,982 immigrants from Poland, 2,148 from
Russia, and 749 from Romania. The act did to Jewish immigration to the
United States in the between-the-wars period what the Chinese Exclusion Act of 1882 did to Chinese immigration in the nineteenth century.[95]

There may have been an element of hyperbole in the 1919 statement
that all three million Polish Jews would immigrate to America if they
could, but the vast majority desperately wanted to get out. Moreover,

both the political and economic situation of the Jews of Poland, the European country with the largest number of Jews in the between-the-wars period, grew progressively worse with every passing year. The restoration of Poland's independence in 1918 was accompanied by a violent wave of anti-Semitism. Although thousands of Jews had fought under Pilsudski for Polish independence, the Poles regarded the Jews as unassimilable foreigners. The situation was exacerbated by the fact that the Jewish population was overwhelmingly urban, giving Jews a visibly disproportionate representation in Poland's cities, whereas the Polish population was overwhelmingly rural. In addition to the miserable condition of Polish peasants noted above, between seven and eight million Poles were unemployed or woefully underemployed in a country of 32,500,000.[96]

The Polish government reacted to the economic predicament by enacting a series of ever more stringent measures designed to transfer available jobs and resources from Jewish to Polish hands. Jewish downward mobility was immediately evident in government service and state-owned enterprises. To illustrate, as long as Galicia was a part of the Austro-Hungarian Empire, thousands of Jews worked in the state-owned railroad, post office, and other bureaus. After Poland gained independence in 1918, Jews were barred from positions in all state bureaus and state-owned enterprises.[97]

In both the private and public sectors, the government acted to deprive Jews of their ability to earn a livelihood on the highly questionable assumption that what was loss to Jews was gain to Poles. At no time did the Polish government attempt effectively to expand the economy so that both Jews and Poles might be gainfully employed.

The anti-Jewish measures were actively supported by Poland's Roman Catholic Church, which regarded the Jews as agents of secularization, liberalism, and Bolshevism. Roman Catholic faith was regarded as an indispensable component of authentic Polish identity, and religious hatred of the Jews attained a virulence of far greater intensity in Poland than in any other European country, including Nazi Germany. As noted above, in 1936 the Primate of Poland, August Cardinal Hlond, openly supported the anti-Jewish measures.[98]

By 1939 the explicit, officially stated policy of the Polish government was to seek by all available means to compel the Jews to emigrate from Poland. As a successor to the czarist government, it pursued a Jewish policy identical in ultimate aim. The theme of Poland's "surplus" Jewish population was constantly reiterated in official statements by Poland's leaders throughout the late thirties.[99] Even the threat of German invasion made no difference. Poland's determination to be rid of the Jews was not deterred by the threat of invasion and war. Throughout the period immediately preceding the German invasion of Poland, official government sources insisted that Poland would under no circumstances alter its own anti-Jewish policies because of the military threat from Nazi Germany. There was to be no connection between Poland's relations with the Third Reich and Poland's "internal Jewish problem."[100]

By 1939 the Jews of eastern Europe were caged in a death trap from which there was to be no escape. Poland was determined to make life as miserable for them as possible as a way of inducing them to leave, while Germany was preparing to murder them. Emigration had ceased to be a possibility for the vast majority. Even Palestine was closed by the British White Paper of May 1939, which ended all Jewish immigration save for fifteen thousand a year to be admitted for the next five years.

Nevertheless, while the Polish and the National Socialist governments shared a common aim in their Jewish policy, few Poles seriously entertained the possibility of establishing a system of mass extermination camps in their country. An important reason for the Polish preference for old-fashioned methods of harassment was the complex attitude of the Roman Church. As we have seen, the Roman Catholic Church in Poland sought the ultimate elimination of the country's Jews, but the Church was limited in the methods it could actively foster by its traditional moral constraints. Although the Church defined the Jews as unwanted aliens, it was also influential in setting limits on what the Polish state could do to them. When the invading Germans exterminated the Jews, they achieved the objective of the Jewish policy of Poland's Church and state. The Germans did so, however, by resorting to measures the Poles themselves had been unwilling to adopt. Yet in spite of numerous instances of Poles saving Jewish lives at the risk of their own, the sober weight of historical scholarship points to the dreary but inescapable conclusion that the majority of the Poles regarded the Germans as doing Polish dirty work. Moreover, as noted above, when the war was over, the Poles took up the killing where the National Socialists left off by instigating pogroms in Kielce, Kraków, Chelm, Rzeszów, and elsewhere.[101]

The Poles were neither modern enough nor secular enough to plan and execute a systematic program of mass extermination. The Germans were. There is evidence that from the very beginning of his political career Adolf Hitler understood the difference between an old-fashioned program of Jew hatred and a modern program of legally sanctioned, bureaucratically administered mass murder. His earliest political writing characteristically deals with the question of the elimination of the Jews. Early in September 1919 Hitler was asked by Staff-Captain Karl Mayr, who had put him to work as an army propaganda officer, to formulate a statement on anti-Semitism. In a letter dated September 16, 1919, a few days before he joined what was to become the National Socialist party, Hitler outlined the difference between the "rational anti-Semitism" he advocated and "anti-Semitism on purely emotional grounds": "Anti-Semitism on purely emotional grounds will find its ultimate expression in the form of pogroms. The anti-Semitism of reason [rational anti-Semitism] however, must lead to a systematic and legal struggle against, and eradication of, what privileges the Jews now enjoy over other foreigners. . . . Its final objective, however, must be the total removal *[Entfernung]* of all Jews from our midst."[102] Thus, in his earliest political document Hitler revealed himself to be a thoroughly modern figure who had little faith in the efficacy of pogroms and looked forward to a deliberately calculated, systematic struggle against the Jews that would begin with legal measures and end with their "total removal."

The acceptability of the "rational" solution Hitler had in mind was undoubtedly facilitated for him as well as millions of others by their experience in World War I. Hitler reported that on October 29, 1914, in its first major clash, the battle of Ypres, his unit, the Bavarian List Regiment, lost seventeen hundred of its thirty-five hundred men. In spite of the extraordinary slaughter, or perhaps because of it, Hitler, like so many others of his generation, found in the war the only home that suited him.[103] But World War I was a different kind of war from any ever fought on the European continent. It was a war of mass death in which for fifteen hundred days massed men were fed to massed fire power so that more than six thousand corpses could be processed each day without letup.[104] When it was over, ten million soldiers and civilians had been killed and mass death had become an acceptable part of the experience and values of European civilization. Worse still, after the war Europe was filled with men who looked back nostalgically to their war experience as the only period of real living they had ever known.[105]

In Germany, there was regret, not so much that so many lives had been lost, but that the sacrifice had been in vain. No sooner had the guns fallen silent than influential groups resolved that, whatever the cost, the enormous blood sacrifice would be made good in the victorious war of the future. At this point, the inherent indifference to moral constraints of the value-free, calculating rationality of the post-Enlightenment world and the revisionist passions of the defeated Germans found their synthesis. Mass extermination had become an acceptable method of restructuring European civilization. The road to Auschwitz was still obscure, but the moral constraints standing in the path of those who traveled on that road were in the process of being cleared away. Within a few years the problem of Europe's "surplus" Jewish population would find its "Final Solution."

The fate of Europe's Jews points to some of the more gruesome consequences of the modernization process and the rise of capitalism, although it would be a mistake to assume that capitalism has a monopoly on programs of mass population elimination as a means of social reconstruction. As we have observed, few groups have been as drastically affected by modernization as were the Jews. The political, social, religious, economic, and perhaps psychological transformations experienced by Jews were far more radical than those experienced by any other European group. A greater proportion of their number changed their domicile and a far greater proportion were murdered by the state than any other group. By the beginning of the twentieth century an urbanized Jewish mass was to be found for the first time in the national centers of England, France, Germany, Austria, Hungary, Poland, and the United States. In Europe the cities where the Jews congregated became the breeding ground of the first anti-Semitic political parties. Modernization had brought forth mass production, mass migration, and mass politics. In due time it would bring forth mass murder.

The concentrated presence in the metropolitan centers of people whose cultural and religious traditions were alien to the national consensus became a source of social, cultural, political, economic, and religious conflict. The conflict was strongest and most dangerous where cultural life had previously possessed a strong degree of ethnic and religious homogeneity. Moreover, the Jewish situation did not automatically improve when Jews acquired the culture of their adopted land. As we have noted, hostility was often intensified when a generation of "assimilated," university-educated Jews came to maturity. Jews were more likely to be regarded as a destabilizing element in the national culture after they had acquired the skills of communicating effectively in the new language than when they exhibited easily identifiable signs of foreign origin. Of paramount importance is the fact I have emphasized throughout this chapter: the Jews had ceased to be an economically complementary group and were forced to become competitors of an endangered and insecure, indigenous middle class.

There was also a highly dangerous conflict of social and cultural values between the Jews and other migrants to the urban centers. Although both the Jews and the displaced peasants were victims of modernization, most of the Jewish migrants felt they had no alternative but to embrace the very process that had uprooted them as well as the nontraditional values it engendered. Modern secular society seemed to offer Jews their only hope of full membership in the larger community, since it alone seemed to be sufficiently pluralistic to allow Jews a measure of civic equality and vocational mobility. Unfortunately, what Jews took to be a pluralistic community, influential members of the dominant majority took to be no community at all, but a congery of atomized strangers. Consequently, they sought to restore older bonds of community based upon kinship and shared origins. Of necessity, there could be no place for Jews in such a community. Confronted by this development, many Jews attempted to create their own community based upon kinship and common origin in the face of a hostile and disintegrating world. Zionism and the State of Israel are the fruit of their efforts.

When it was undeceived, European political Zionism was rooted in the perception that religious, cultural, economic, and political motives for the elimination of the Jews from Europe were rapidly and effectively converging. On the question of the Jews, as we have stressed, the churches and the parties of the Right were divided only on the question of the means by which the Jews were to be eliminated. That debate was ended by National Socialism.

The elimination of the Jews was also a nonnegotiable aspect of the political program of the European Left. According to the Marxists, the Jews were not a distinctive religiocultural entity, but a petit bourgeois stratum of the larger society whose religion was the ideological super-structure mirroring the group's concrete social and economic relations.[106] The Marxists saw the petite bourgeoisie, whether Jewish or non-Jewish, as a doomed and superfluous class. In both capitalism and socialism, the rationalization of the economy would bring about their elimination. Those who were fit for membership in a socialist society would eventually divest themselves of their class origins and accept their place in the working class. Those who vainly attempted to maintain their petit bourgeois status would in any event be eliminated, as indeed happened to millions of kulaks in Russia between 1929 and 1932 and to the ethnic Chinese in Vietnam more recently. The Jews would either disappear into the working class or be eliminated altogether. When this happened, the Marxists confidently expected the ideological superstructure that had mirrored the precapitalist Jewish situation to disappear because of its ir-relevance. This would result in the "withering away" of the Jewish re-ligion and, with it, Jewish identity. Thus, in addition to the Christian Church, both the European Right and the Left expected and were pre-pared to implement the elimination of the Jews as a distinctive group. According to the Left, the Jews would not survive the full rationalization of the economy; according to the Right, if the rationalization of the economy was inevitable, it was not to be permitted to turn society into a marketplace to which any person, irrespective of background, could gain free access. Even the Zionists saw the elimination of the Jews from Europe as inevitable. Unwilling to abandon Jewish identity or to equate it with petit bourgeois status, they sought an alternative basis for maintaining themselves as a distinctive community by seizing a monopoly of force in the territory that, according to their mythical inheritance, was their place of ancestral origin. As of this writing, the ultimate success of their radical attempt to escape the fate modernization had apparently meted out to their people remains in doubt.

While no single cause can explain a historical phenomenon such as the rise of a modern, anti-Semitic movement and the successful program of genocide in the heart of Europe, the phenomenon can be related to several principal factors including the following: (1) the persistence through the ages of the religiocultural conflict between Judaism and Christianity; (2) the role of the Jew as the *disconfirming other par excellence* within Christian civilization and the strategies employed by Christianity to discredit the disconfirming other; (3) the intensification of religious conflict by economic conflict in the nineteenth and early twentieth centuries; (4) the growing insecurity or downward social mobility of the undercapitalized, non-Jewish, lower middle class in the takeoff period of large-scale industrial capitalism; (5) the sudden influx of large numbers of displaced Eastern European Jews in the urban centers of Germany and Austria in the aftermath of the events of 1881 in the czarist empire and the simultaneous mass emigration of Germans and Austrians from their native lands; (6) the triumph of value-neutral, functional rationality as the predominant mode of problem solving in advanced technological societies such as Germany; (7) the impulse to centralization, homogenization, and leveling that we find so frequently as a feature of modernization and bureaucratization; and (8) the violent response of the European Right to the "deconstructive" role of secularized Jews in European cultural and political life, including both the value-neutral rationality of the intellectuals and the political role of the Marxists.

CHAPTER 6

Modernization and the Politics of Extermination

GENOCIDE IN HISTORICAL CONTEXT

Although thousands of books have been written about the destruction of the European Jews, few have been devoted to the problem of genocide per se.[1] At the 1983 convention of the American Political Science Association, a session on genocide featuring papers by a number of leading authorities drew an audience of no more than ten. A leading sociologist has pointed to the overwhelming importance of the study of the Holocaust for an understanding of modernity and the modernization process and to the almost total avoidance of the subject by sociologists.[2] In 1990 a suggestion that participants in an international conference of world religious leaders include a visit to the conference city's Holocaust memorial was tabled by the planning committee. Genocide is a subject many intellectual and religious leaders prefer to avoid.

It has long been my thesis that the relative silence on the subject stems from the inability of scholars, religious leaders, and the general public to face the fact that, far from being a relapse into barbarism or an atypical "episode," *genocide is an intrinsic expression of modern civilization as we know it.*[3] Put differently, the genocidal destructiveness of our era can best be understood as an expression of some of its "most significant political, moral, religious and demographic tendencies."[4] If indeed genocide expresses some, though obviously not all, of the dominant trends in contemporary civilization, it would hardly be surprising that few researchers would want to spend much time on the night side of the world we have made for ourselves.

Recently, Professor Tony Barta of La Trobe University, Melbourne,

123

Australia, raised the issue of the connection between civilization and genocide most directly.[5] According to Barta, the basic fact of his nation's history has been the conquest of the country by one people and the dispossession "with ruthless destructiveness" of another people, the Aborigines, those who were there *ab origine*, "from the beginning." Barta argues that, although it was by no means the initial intention of the British government to destroy the Aborigines, Australia is nevertheless a "nation founded on genocide," for genocide was the inevitable, albeit unintended, consequence of the European colonization of the Australian continent.[6] Barta's thesis puts him somewhat at odds with scholars who insist that genocide is the intentional extermination of a target group. According to Barta, in order to comprehend genocide we need a conception that embraces unplanned destruction and deemphasizes the elements of policy and intention with which the term is normally associated. Barta argues that Australian history amply demonstrates that genocidal outcomes can arise without deliberate state planning. But far from being a consequence of the actions of isolated men acting out their aggressions on a lawless frontier distant from metropolitan centers, the destruction of Australia's Aboriginal population was, in my opinion, very largely the projected outcome of modernizing transformations in the mother country, the first European nation fully to enter the economically rationalized world of the modern era.

If we wish to comprehend the roots of genocide as a modern phenomenon, the beginnings of the modernization process in Great Britain provide an excellent point of departure.[7] Modernization in England began with the acts of enclosure, which transformed a premodern, subsistence economy into the money economy of our era. In the process, the customary rights to land usage of the economically unproductive English peasant class were abrogated and that class was largely transformed into a congery of individuals whose survival was entirely dependent upon their ability to find wage labor. Absent gainful employment, the dispossessed peasants could only turn to a harsh and punitively administered system of poor relief, vagabondage, or outright crime. A crucial social byproduct of England's economic rationalization was the creation of a large class of people who were superfluous to England's new economic system.

A class of more or less permanently superfluous people is in every age a potential source of acute social instability, as can be seen in the contemporary American underclass. Having little hope of receiving society's normal rewards, a redundant population has little incentive, save fear of punitive retaliation, to abide by society's customary behavioral constraints. Even if such a group is tied to the rest of the population by common ethnicity and religion, it is likely to be perceived and to perceive itself as having been cast outside of society's universe of moral obligation.[8] A measure of mutual trust will normally characterize the behavior of members of such a universe toward each other. At the very least, members will not normally regard their peers as potential sources of injury or even destruction. To the extent that trust is possible between human beings, the actors within such a community are more likely to trust each other than those they regard as alien. Such attitudes have less to do with human virtuousness than with the way social relations are structured. The enclosure laws had the effect of expelling England's displaced peasants from the only community they had ever known, that of the manor and the parish. This was clearly understood by English decision makers as early as the enactment of the Elizabethan poor laws, which were as much police measures aimed at controlling England's first redundant population as they were philanthropic efforts to supply that population's irreducible needs for survival.[9]

In the rationalization of English agriculture, arable land taken from the displaced peasants was devoted to raising sheep, a cash crop, and to large-scale cash farming. Out of the vast social dislocation engendered by the process, England was able to finance its first modern industry, textiles. However, the transformation of arable land to pasture seriously diminished England's ability to produce its own food supply. Moreover, by the early nineteenth century, the country was no longer able to produce all of the raw materials necessary for its burgeoning industry.

Some of the raw materials were produced by Australia. In the late eighteenth century Australia was an ideal land for sheep raising. It was also a convenient outlet for the elimination of a goodly portion of England's redundant population. As Barta points out, England's transportation of its convict population to Australia was not unrelated to its dispossession of its peasantry by the acts of enclosure. Many uprooted peasants turned to vagabondage and crime when they could find no other means of support. Transportation to Georgia and, after the American Revolution, to Australia became a preferred alternative to harsh imprisonment and even execution for petty crimes.[10] England also had large numbers of undercapitalized small holders and artisans who were faced with the prospect of downward economic mobility in an increasingly capital-intensive domestic economy. Many of the more enterprising small holders took their meager assets to Australia. They knew that an ever-increasing demand for both sheep's wool and sheep's flesh in the mother country, as well as the availability of cheap convict labor in Australia, presented the undercapitalized free colonizers with opportunities that could not be duplicated at home. Like North America, Australia served as a demographic safety valve for those segments of England's population made redundant by the progressive rationalization of her economy and society.

Neither North America nor Australia were unsettled territories when white settlers arrived. The Australian Aborigines had developed a viable human ecology as seminomadic hunter-gatherers that was altogether incomprehensible to the settlers, as indeed the ways of the settlers were incomprehensible to them. Moreover, sheep raising and the settlers' rationalized and desacralized agrarian economy were incompatible with Aboriginal land use. Since both sides were unconditionally dependent upon the land, albeit in radically different ways, loss of the land for either one necessarily entailed the complete destruction of a way of life. As Barta writes, coexistence was impossible.

The issue was decided, as it almost always is, by superior power and technology. With their survival at stake, the Aborigines had no choice but to resist. As in North America, the predictable response of the settlers was to root out the native menace to their way of life. There were a number of bloody massacres. There were also government-sponsored attempts to diminish settler violence. Nevertheless, even without direct violence the Aborigines were destined to perish. Deprived of a meaningful future, most of the surviving Aborigines "faded away." Barta writes that between 1839 and 1849 only twenty births were recorded among the seven aboriginal tribes around Melbourne. He concludes that, whatever the official British intent, the very nature of the encounter between the white settlers and the Blacks entailed genocide.

Barta distinguishes between a genocidal society and a genocidal state. National Socialist Germany was a genocidal state. Its genocidal project was deliberate. British Australia was a genocidal society. It had no genocidal project. Nevertheless, its very foundation had genocidal consequences. The basic pattern of the colonization of Australia was everywhere the same: white invasion, Black resistance, violent victory of the whites, and finally the mysterious disappearance of the Blacks.

If Australian society was built upon a genocidal relationship with the indigenous cultures, so too was American society. The basic colonizing pattern described by Barta, namely, white settlement, native resistance, violent settler victory, and, finally, the disappearance of most if not all of the natives, was played out in both North and South America.[11] There was a time not so long ago when it was taken for granted that "the only good Indian is a dead Indian."

Although Barta confines his description to Australia, the process he describes was repeated in other European colonial settlements. In his biography of Oliver Cromwell, the English historian Christopher Hill comments, "A great many civilized Englishmen of the propertied class in the seventeenth century spoke of Irishmen in tones not far removed from those which the Nazis used about the Slavs, or white South Africans use about the original inhabitants of their country. In each case the contempt rationalized a desire to exploit."[12]

Hill could have added that Cromwell was fully prepared to exterminate those Irish Catholics who resisted exploitation and refused to turn their lands over to Protestant colonizers. The towns of Drogheda and Wexford refused to surrender to Cromwell. They were sacked, and those inhabitants unable to flee were massacred. In the case of Wexford, after all the inhabitants had been killed, Cromwell reported that the town was available for colonization by English settlers. An English clergyman commended the place for settlement: "It is a fine spot for some godly congregation where house and land wait for inhabitants and occupiers."[13] Even in the seventeenth century, it was clear to England's leaders that the more Ireland was cleared of its original Catholic inhabitants the more available it would be for Protestant English settlement.

The extremes to which England was prepared to go to empty Ireland of its original inhabitants became clear during the famine of 1846–48. Figures show that within that period the population of Ireland was reduced by about 2,500,000 out of an estimated 1845 population of 9,000,000. Approximately 1,250,000 perished in the famine, and about the same number were compelled to emigrate in order to survive.[14]

Elsewhere, I have attempted to show that the famine relief given by the English government to the Irish, who were technically British subjects at the time, was deliberately kept at levels guaranteed to produce the demographic result it did and that the result was welcomed by leading members of England's society and government. The deaths by famine and the removal by emigration were seen as doing for Ireland what the enclosures had done for England, namely, clear the land of uneconomic subsistence producers and make it available for rationalized agricultural enterprise.[15] The candor of an 1853 editorial in the *Economist* on the benefits of Irish and Scottish emigration is instructive: "It is consequent on the breaking down of the system of society founded on small holdings and potato cultivation. . . . *The departure of the redundant part of the population of Ireland and Scotland is an indispensable preliminary to every kind of improvement*" (italics added).[16] Unfortunately, the "departure" welcomed by the *Economist* entailed mass death by famine and disease for a very large portion of Ireland's peasant class. In the eyes of the British decision making class of the period, Catholic Ireland was an inferior civilization.[17] A class that was indifferent to the fate of its own peasants was hardly likely to be concerned with that of the Irish.

The link between genocidal settler societies of the eighteenth and nineteenth centuries and twentieth century genocide can be discerned in Adolf Hitler's *Lebensraum* program. As we have seen, as a young man Hitler saw the settlement of the New World and the concomitant elimination of North America's Indian population by white European settlers as a model to be followed by Germany in eastern Europe. Hitler was determined that there would be no surplus German population even if a significant portion of Germany's Slavic neighbors had to be exterminated to provide "living space" for German settlers adjacent to the homeland. Hitler proposed to repeat in Europe, albeit with infinitely intensified viciousness, the exploitative colonialism practiced by other Europeans overseas. In Hitler's eyes the Slavs were destined to become Europe's "Indians." They were to be displaced, uprooted, enslaved, and, if necessary, annihilated to make way for Germany's surplus population. Unlike the earlier European colonizers, Hitler had no illusions concerning the genocidal nature of such an undertaking. He had the historical precedents of earlier European efforts at colonization and imperial domination. He regarded the defeat of native cultures by white settlers and colonists as evidence for his version of Social Darwinism, the belief that history is the theater in which the races enact their life and death struggle for survival and the superior races destroy their racial inferiors. As is well known, this same Social Darwinism became an important component in the legitimating ideology for the Holocaust. In Hitler's eyes, the Jews were the most contemptible of all inferior races and were destined by fate and German strength for destruction.

As noted above, Hitler's policies were intentional and deliberately formulated. If the destruction of the aboriginal cultures of Australia was an unintended consequence of state policy, the destruction, enslavement, and eventual extermination of Germany's neighbors to the east were fully intended by National Socialist Germany. Nevertheless, that difference should not obscure the facts that (*a*) both colonizing policies were intended to solve the same fundamental problem, namely, the relatively humane elimination by the mother country of a redundant or potentially redundant sector of its domestic population and (*b*) both could be successfully implemented only by the merciless elimination of the indigenous population of the colonized lands. Moreover, the very success of earlier colonization projects invited their repetition by Hitler, who believed his nation was faced with the same demographic problems. Neither Hitler nor leaders like him could pretend ignorance of the consequences of their policies. One of the differences between Hitler and his predecessors was his lack of hypocrisy and illusion concerning the extent to which his project entailed mass murder. Nevertheless, it is clear from the history of the English in Ireland and Australia as well as the Europeans in the New World that the destruction of the indigenous population never constituted a reason for calling colonization to a halt. There is thus an historical continuum between the unintended genocides of the period of Europe's demographic projection beyond its original territorial limits and that of the period of Europe's self-cannibalization in the twentieth century.

According to the above argument, genocide can be defined as *the most radical means of implementing a state-sponsored or communal program of population elimination.* It should be noted that this definition *(a)* does not raise the issue of intention and *(b)* grasps genocide conceptually within the wider context of programs of population elimination. It allows comprehension of the larger historical conditions under which a population is likely to be identified as redundant and targeted for one or another form of elimination. And it also helps to suggest the connections between modernization, population redundancy, emigration, expulsion, colonization, and genocide.

A fundamental issue in the decision to initiate a program of genocide can be discerned in the question, *Who is to have a voice in the political order?* The issue of a voice in the political order is in turn related to the question of the universe of moral obligation discussed above. In ancient Greece, members of the polis belonged to a common community. This was especially evident in war. Only those who shared common origins, belonged by *inherited right* to the same community, and saw themselves as partaking of a common fate could be trusted in a life-and-death struggle. Neither the slave nor the stranger could be so trusted. Hence, they were regarded as outside of the shared universe of obligation.

A grave problem arises when, for any reason, a community regards itself as having within its midst a subcommunity or a group of strangers who cannot be trusted. The problem is especially urgent in time of war. It is even more urgent when a community has experienced what it perceives to be humiliating national defeat. The perception of disloyalty may be mistaken, as was initially the case of the Armenians in Turkey during World War I and the Japanese-Americans during World War II. The fundamental reason for the mass incarceration of Japanese-Americans was the belief of most Americans that the majority of Japanese-Americans were loyal to the Emperor rather than to their adopted country. The actual feelings of the minority are less important than the perceptions of the majority.

Sometimes the question of a voice in the political community takes on a class rather than an ethnic dimension. When Kampuchea fell to the Pol Pot regime in 1975, the victors had a very clear idea of the kind of agrarian communist society they proposed to establish. Rightly or wrongly, they regarded Kampuchea's entire urban population as objectively hostile to the creation of the new political order. This perception was consistent with the Marxist idea that the bourgeois class is destined to disappear with the coming of socialism. Not content to let this process take its course nonviolently, the regime determined upon the immediate elimination through genocidal measures of all those who were regarded as either incapable of fitting into the new system or objectively committed to its destruction.[18] In the aftermath of the Russian Revolution, a very similar logic compelled the departure from the Soviet Union of millions of "objective enemies" of the new system. Similarly, the Cuban revolution resulted in the enforced emigration of more than a million Cubans who could not fit into Castro's system, primarily to the United States.

A related development is currently taking place in South Africa. Because of the overwhelming number of Blacks and their necessity to the the economic order, the Afrikaners cannot eliminate them. Indeed, save for some ultra-Rightist groups, there is no evidence of any Afrikaner interest in so doing. Nevertheless, until recently Afrikaners answered the question, Who shall have a voice in the political community? by excluding all nonwhites. Of crucial importance has been the consistent refusal of the Afrikaners to admit the Blacks to any meaningful kind of suffrage. Apartheid and the denial of electoral rights are attempts to limit membership in the political community without resorting to outright mass murder. Nevertheless, it is important to recognize that all of the policies cited above—segregation, concentration-camp incarceration, expulsion, and genocide—are attempts to deal with a common problem.

The question, Who is to have a voice in the political community? was absolutely decisive for National Socialism. The political emancipation of the Jews in Europe in the late eighteenth and nineteenth centuries bestowed upon the Jews a voice in the political communities in which they were domiciled. With the dour wisdom of historical hindsight, the extermination of the Jews can be seen as an unintended consequence of their emancipation. Emancipation made membership of the Jews in Europe's political communities a political issue for the first time. It was opposed by all who believed that such membership should be restricted to Christians. It was, as we know, also opposed by those who sought to restrict membership to those who regarded themselves as bound together by ties of blood. An important reason why so little was done to assist the Jews during World War II, both in Germany and throughout occupied Europe, was the almost universal European acceptance of the National Socialist objective of excluding the Jews from membership in the political communities in which they were domiciled. This was certainly true of the mainstream Protestant and Catholic churches, which everywhere saw the denial of political rights to the Jews as a beneficial step toward the creation of a Europe that was culturally, intellectually, socially, and politically Christian. The fundamental difference between Hitler and the churches was that Hitler had no illusions concerning the extreme measures necessary to implement such a program. The churches never faced frankly the question of implementation. Nevertheless, one must ask whether the silence of the overwhelming majority of Europe's church leaders during World War II concerning the Holocaust may have been at least partly due to the fact that they fully understood that extermination was the only viable means of eliminating the Jews. Having no direct responsibility for carrying out the process of elimination, they preferred to leave the question of implementation to the German government. In any event, it is now clear that the insistent calls for the elimination of the Jews from membership in the body politic of the European nations was in fact a demand for their extermination.

In discussions of the place of the Holocaust in the larger context of genocide, the question of uniqueness looms large. Surprisingly, few discussions of the question deal with one aspect of the Holocaust that was absolutely unique: in no other instance of twentieth-century genocide was the fate of the victims so profoundly linked to the religiomythic inheritance of the perpetrators.[19] In Christianity the Jews are not simply one of the many peoples of the world. They are the people in whose midst God himself deigned to be incarnated. According to the classic Christian account, instead of being the first to recognize this supreme act of divine graciousness, the Jews rejected God-in-the-flesh and were responsible for the viciously painful way in which he was removed from the human scene. Alone among the victims of genocide, the Jews are depicted as the God-bearing and the God-murdering people *par excellence*. No other religion is as horribly defamed in the classic literature of a rival tradition as is Judaism. Moreover, as we have seen, starting with the Fall of Jerusalem in 70 C.E., Christianity has taken the disasters of the Jewish people to be a principal historical confirmation of its own truth. These have been interpreted in the classic sources to be God's punishment of a sinful Israel for having rejected Christ. The practical consequences of *(a)* the ascription of a demonic identity to Jews and *(b)* the interpretation of their misfortunes as just chastisements of a righteous Lord was to cast them out of any common universe of moral obligation with the Christians among whom they were domiciled. In times of acute social stress, it had the practical effect of decriminalizing any assault visited upon them. In effect, the Jews became outlaws, as Hitler and the leading National Socialists fully understood. The implementation of the Holocaust was thus greatly facilitated by the deicidal and demonic interpretation of the Jewish people in the Christian religious imagination. If the Holocaust was to some extent a unique event, its religiomythic dimension constituted a significant component of that uniqueness.

In addition to the religious aspect of the Holocaust, there was a highly significant economic component. To a very large extent, the European Jews constituted a *middleman minority*. The question of the proneness of middleman minorities to genocidal assault has been raised by Walter P. Zenner and a number of other scholars.[20] Zenner points out that the Armenians were also a middleman minority targeted for extermination. He also points out that a third middleman minority, the Hoa or ethnic Chinese of Vietnam, were the object of a large-scale, state-sponsored program of population elimination.[21] Zenner argues that there is no necessary link between middleman-minority status and genocide. He does, however, concede that such a status can be a precondition for genocide if other factors are present. According to Zenner, middleman-minority theory has yet to face the question of why economically integrated nonwage labor groups are more likely to be victimized than nonindigenous wage laborers, the marginalized, and the poor. In actuality, middleman minorities are usually permitted domicile in a community in order to do work that, for some reason, is not being done by the indigenous population. Their presence as strangers is tolerated because they constitute an *economically or vocationally complementary* population. They are most likely to be targeted for elimination when their roles can be filled either by the state apparatus or privately by members of the indigenous population. When either development takes place, the minority members become competitors of the majority. Moreover, they are likely to compete against one of the most dangerous and potentially unstable groups within the larger population, the lower middle class. In the case of wage workers, the marginalized, or the poor, the same bitter rivalry with a dangerous class does not arise. Wherever political leaders perceive vocationally redundant members of the majority to be a source of social or political instability, they have tended to encourage emigration, as was the case in western and central Europe during much of the nineteenth century. Nevertheless, there is usually some residual sense that the marginalized or superfluous people remain part of the nation's shared universe of moral obligation. This is not the case with middleman minorities, especially when they are outside of the majority religious consensus. They are usually tolerated only as long as they are needed.

In premodern societies it was not socially or economically functional for middleman minorities to share a common religion with the majority. The impersonal, objective attitudes necessary for successful commerce were less likely to develop between people who considered themselves to be kin worshiping the same gods. The flow of commerce often depended upon an in-group/out-group double standard. It was only with the rise of Protestantism that the personalized ethics of tribal brotherhood gave way to universal otherhood and a depersonalized, universal money economy could come into being.[22]

As an economy modernizes, the situation of middleman minorities is likely to become increasingly precarious. This was the fate of the Jews in pre-World War II eastern and central Europe. In countries like Poland, Hungary, and Romania, both the peasants and the nobility were convinced that a disproportionate share of the nation's commerce was in the hands of strangers with an alien religion and alien values in spite of the fact that the majority population had little or no understanding of or taste for business, commerce, and finance. Many Jews did, but their business acumen made them the objects of extreme distrust and resentment.[23] The situation was exacerbated by the deicide accusation.

Few members of the indigenous majority were inclined to take the risks demanded of successful entrepreneurs. Impoverished members of the nobility and the gentry rejected business careers and turned to the military and the bureaucracy for the kind of employment that would permit them to perpetuate their traditional status and values. In England the younger sons of noble families often entered commerce, but in eastern Europe money making was looked upon with contempt by those who had the power to define social reality. The need to "catch up with the West" was recognized, but the indigenous non-Jewish middle class capable of fostering a modern economy was weak and lacking in social prestige.

Throughout eastern Europe the Jews constituted the most visible—and the most hated—entrepreneurial class. Barred from "honorable" vocations and stigmatized as of low status, entrepreneurial risk taking offered Jews one of the few escape routes from ghetto poverty. Insofar as they succeeded in fostering economic development, they were envied, despised, and hated. With anti-Semitism endemic throughout the region, when the Germans invaded eastern Europe and rounded up the Jews for extermination, few eastern Europeans were sorry to see them disappear.

Even before the between-the-wars period, the condition of the Jews was becoming progressively more hopeless as the economies of western and eastern Europe modernized.[24] During the second half of the nineteenth century, the agriculture of eastern Europe was progressively rationalized. As a result, large numbers of peasants were dispossessed of their holdings and forced to seek scarce wage labor in the towns and cities. The peasants' predicament was further aggravated by yet another aspect of modernization: improved medicine and hygiene, which yielded unprecedented population increases. Desperate for any kind of work under conditions of massive unemployment and underemployment, some members of the former peasant class began to compete with proletarianized Jews for wage labor and also for those middle-class slots that had previously been predominantly in Jewish hands. In seeking to displace the Jews, the dispossessed peasants and their urbanized offspring had the support of the czarist government that, after 1881, made the Jews of the czarist empire the targets of one of the most successful state-sponsored programs of population elimination short of genocide in all of history.[25]

In addition to serving as a method of radically redefining and restructuring society, genocide has since ancient times been the most unremitting kind of warfare. Elimination of a potential future threat served as a powerful motive for wars of genocide. Undoubtedly, the human cost to the perpetrator played an important role in determining when a war was carried to such an extreme. After total defeat, the cost to the victor of eliminating a future threat was minimal. Since the enemy was outside the victor's universe of moral obligation, defeat removed the only practical impediment to genocide. As long as an enemy retained the power to injure, a would-be perpetrator had to weigh the relative costs of a precarious peace against those involved in genocide. If neither side had the power to achieve a decisive victory, there could be no possibility of a Final Solution. In the case of the Holocaust, the Jews were perceived as a hopelessly defenseless enemy with no significant capacity to retaliate. The problems involved in their extermination were reduced to the bureaucratic management, transport, and elimination of the target population. A principal motive for the establishment of the State of Israel and its acquisition of advanced weaponry has been to escalate the cost of killing at least those Jews who are Israeli citizens. There is little doubt that the cost now includes fearsome nuclear retaliation.

Frequently, programs of genocide are initiated in the aftermath of military defeat, especially under the devastating conditions of modern warfare.[26] An important reason for the Young Turk regime's decision to initiate a program of extermination against the Armenian Christian minority was Turkey's defeat by Bulgaria in 1912. Similarly, Germany's defeat in World War I created the conditions in which a radically anti-Semitic, revolutionary, revisionist National Socialist movement could come to dominate German politics. In defeat, the fringe often becomes the center. In defeat, a defenseless minority can become a surrogate object of revenge against the victorious enemy. Military defeat can also intensify the urgency with which the question of membership in the community is posed. As noted above, a fundamental issue in genocide is the question of who can be trusted in a life-and-death struggle. All minorities suffer some discrimination and experience some degree of resentment and incomplete identification with the majority, a situation that is as obvious to the majority as to the minority. In normal times, such tensions can be held in check. In the aftermath of catastrophic military defeat, they can get out of hand. Aggressive energies can achieve cheap victories over a defenseless minority. The reality of defeat itself can be denied, and responsibility for the misfortunes of war ascribed to the minority's hidden "stab in the back." The accusation of secret treachery can legitimate genocide against the minority. If such a group is perceived as bringing about national catastrophe, *while appearing to be loyal*, it can become a matter of the greatest public urgency to eliminate it from the body politic.

Almost from the moment Germany lost World War I, the Jews were accused of bringing about her defeat through treachery, an accusation that appears ludicrous in view of the extremely high proportion of German Jews who had served as front-line soldiers and who had made the ultimate sacrifice for what they regarded as their Fatherland. As I have noted, the tradition of Judas betraying Jesus with a *token of love*, a kiss, provided an enormously powerful religiomythic identification of the Jew with betrayal in the minds of German Christians.[27] When Hitler and the German Right ascribed Germany's defeat to the Jews, they had working for them this immensely powerful, pretheoretical archetype. Here, too, we discern a unique religiomythic element of enormous power that sets the Holocaust apart from other instances of genocide in our times.

Given the presence of religiomythic elements in the Holocaust, it is not surprising that many scholars have argued that the Holocaust was irrational in its objective if not in its methods. That is a view I no longer hold.[28] I have for many years been convinced that genocide is a "rational instrument to achieve an end."[29] In contrast to spontaneous outbursts of intergroup hatred and violence, modern, systematic, bureaucratically administered genocide can be understood as a form of instrumentally rational (*zweckrational*) action in contrast to value-rational (*wertrational*) action. Max Weber, to whom we are indebted for this distinction, has observed that instrumental rationality refers to the choice of means whereas value rationality is a matter of ends.[30] *Above all, it is important not to confuse humane action and instrumentally rational action.* The experience of our era should leave no doubt concerning the enormous potential for inhumanity present in morally autonomous instrumental rationality. The perfection of this mode of political and social action is indeed one of the most problematic aspects of the modern era.

The idea that genocide could in any sense be regarded as rational has been rejected by Ronald Aronson. In *The Dialectics of Disaster*, Aronson argues that the Holocaust systematically outraged the norms of the "normal world."[31] He insists that the Holocaust was a product of madness, which he defines as a systematic derangement of perception, a seeing what is not there. The National Socialists saw the Jews as the source of Germany's problems and regarded their riddance as a major element in the solution. Aronson argues that when rulers organize a society against false enemies and falsely propagate the view that society is mortally threatened by them, we may speak of madness as much as when a paranoid person behaves in a similar delusionary manner. Aronson insists that the Nazi attempt wholly to eliminate the Jews as a demographic presence first in Germany and then in all of Europe was insane because the Jews in no way constituted the threat the National Socialists alleged them to be. Aronson's views are not unlike those I held when I wrote the first edition of *After Auschwitz*, which are expressed in chapter 3 of this book.

Nevertheless, Aronson's analogy between the individual and the group is questionable. Aronson fails to deal with the underlying reason why the question, Who shall have a voice in the community? is raised in the first place. As noted, genocide is a violent means of determining who is to have a voice in a community whose members may have to sacrifice their lives in a life-and-death struggle with external enemies in a crisis. When a group regards itself as secure, it can afford to take a relatively benign view of the presence of a limited number of strangers in its midst. However, in times of acute national stress, such as economic dislocation, modern warfare, or military defeat, insiders are likely to view outsiders with intensified suspicion and hostility. In the case of middleman-minority groups specializing in commerce, insiders may suspect that the outsiders' love of gain outweighs their loyalty to the homeland. In an extreme situation, they may decide upon the total elimination of the outsiders.

Contrary to Aronson, the issue of the patent untruth of National Socialist defamations is irrelevant to the critical fact that during the Hitler regime the overwhelming majority of Germans regarded even the most assimilated Jews as enemy aliens whose elimination would benefit the nation. The Germans were not duped by mendacious Nazi propaganda. They wanted the *volkisch* homogeneity Hitler promised them. When it was all over, some regretted the *method of implementation* employed by their government but not the fact that Europe was largely empty of Jews. Moreover, all current expressions of German regret concerning the Holocaust, whether voiced by politicians, theologians, academics, students, or ordinary citizens, must be understood in light of the fact that Jews are no longer a significant presence in Germany or the countries of eastern Europe other than the former Soviet Union. With the Jews gone, expressions of regret and even opposition to anti-Semitism come with far greater ease than when their presence was a source of bitter political controversy. By contrast, in crisis-ridden Russia more than one million Jews have applied for permission to emigrate rather than become targets of the postcommunist, state-sponsored programs of population elimination they fear may lie ahead.

Unfortunately, one cannot even say it is irrational to want an ethnically or religiously homogeneous community consisting of those with whom one shares a sense of common faith, kinship, and trust. In much of the urbanized contemporary world, pluralism is a given. Nevertheless, there is nothing irrational about the desire for a community of moral trust and mutual obligation. Recent historical scholarship has demonstrated that a singularly important political purpose of the biblical religions of covenant was to unite under a common God in a shared community of moral and religious obligation those whose diverse tribal membership precluded them from creating a community based on kinship.[32] This was as true of biblical Judaism as it was of early Christianity. Moreover, one of the reasons for the astonishing success of contemporary Japan is its religioethnic homogeneity. It is not the irrationality of nonpluralistic communities that is problematic, but the extreme cruelty and inhumanity that must be practiced by the modern state in order to transform a pluralistic, multiethnic or multireligious political entity into a homogeneous community. Neither Hitler's ends nor his methods were irrational. They were, however, obscenely cruel, and they graphically demonstrate what citizens of one of the world's most advanced civilizations were willing to do to other human beings for the sake of national homogeneity.

Finally, there is the issue of genocide and national sovereignty, an issue that has become ever more important with the end of political imperialism and the attainment of national sovereignty by so many of the world's peoples. It is a well-known fact that the United Nations has never detected a single instance of genocide by a member nation, and that includes the Pol Pot regime, which until recently was recognized by the United Nations as the legitimate government of Kampuchea! Elsewhere, I have argued that as a sovereign community National Socialist Germany probably committed no crime at Auschwitz.[33] It was under no circumstances my intention to minimize the inhumanity and the obscenity of what the Germans did, but I wanted to point to one of the most urgent moral dilemmas involved in the notion of political sovereignty in our era. *Crime is a violation of behavioral norms defined by political authority.* Homicide, for example, is only a crime when the victim is protected by the state's laws. Even in National Socialist Germany, a very small number of SS officers were punished for the *unauthorized* murder of Jews during World War II. The state determined when homicide was an offense against its law and when it constituted the implementation of that same law.

If it be argued that the National Socialist state was by its very nature a criminal state because it violated God's laws or the laws of nature, one must ask what practical difference such laws made to the perpetrators. As long as the leaders of National Socialist Germany were free to exercise sovereignty, no superordinate system of norms constituted any kind of restraint on their behavior. As is well known, neither the German churches nor the Vatican ever asserted that the genocidal program of the National Socialist state was a violation of God's law, although the program was well known. *In reality, without God there are no human rights; there are only political rights.* That is why the question, Who is to have a voice in the political community? is the fundamental human question in our era. Membership in a political community is no absolute guarantee of safety. Nevertheless, to the extent that men and women have any rights whatsoever, it is as members of a political community with the power to guarantee those rights. This was clearly evident in the fate of the Armenians in Turkey during World War I and the Jews of Europe during World War II. Genocide is the ultimate expression of absolute rightlessness.

While highlighting the extreme moral limitations of contemporary civilization, genocide is, as noted, an intrinsic expression of that civilization. Genocide is most likely to occur when men and women refuse to extend the benefits and protection of their societies to strangers whom they cannot or will not trust. Obviously, that perception is highly subjective and may very well be in error. Nevertheless, one of the privileges of power is the ability to define social reality within one's own community. The objective facts are of far less practical consequence than the subjective perceptions of the majority.

CHAPTER 7

Covenant, Holocaust, and Intifada

The Holocaust has rendered few, if any, affirmations of biblical religion as problematic as the covenant between God and Israel. Nevertheless, if we reflect upon the original achievement of the Sinai covenant, namely, the joining together of a "mixed multitude" of escaped fugitives lacking common roots or common faith into an enduring community of moral obligation, united in worship of a God hitherto unknown to the majority, a God who had redeemed them from Egypt, the Holocaust becomes an object lesson in the consequences of the absence of a binding covenant between peoples.[1] In the bitter conflict between Israeli and Palestinian, we also see the consequences of the absence of such a covenant.

Elsewhere in this work, I discuss the theologically problematic aspects of the idea of covenant, which encourage the tendency to interpret the Holocaust as divine punishment. In the first edition of *After Auschwitz*, I stressed both the punitive and the exclusivist aspects of the doctrine of covenant and election. However, over the years I have come to appreciate other aspects of the idea of the covenant. These include (*a*) the highly significant role of the idea of the covenant in forming the characteristic institutions and values of the modern, post-Enlightenment world, and (*b*) humanity's profound need for the covenant or its functional equivalent.

Modern biblical scholarship has given us a fairly accurate picture of the origins of the covenant form.[2] In ancient times, ca. 1300 B.C.E., there were two types of covenant, one between equals, which need not detain us, and the suzerainty type, which had long been in use in the ancient Near East in international relations, especially among the Hittites, to define the relationship between a suzerain and his vassal-kings. As a suzerainty treaty, the covenant was a pact imposed by a powerful suzerain upon a dependent client king, stipulating what the latter must do to receive the former's protection. These Hittite pacts were basically devices for securing binding agreements in international relations. While there were means of enforcing agreements, once made, within a nation, there was (and is) no effective, impartial institution capable of enforcing promises between sovereign states if one of the parties should conclude that the promise no longer serves its interest. In such a case, the injured party originally had no choice but to accept the breach of faith or resort to military enforcement of the pact.

The purpose of the Hittite covenant was to give international agreements a binding character. This was done by the suzerain binding the client king by an oath to meet the pact's obligations. An oath is a conditional self-curse, in which a person appeals to *his own God or gods* to punish him should he fail to keep his word. Originally, oaths were an effective means of guaranteeing that a promise would be kept. Later on, they lost their effectiveness. We can also say that a covenant was a means of achieving unity of purpose between peoples bound to each other neither by ties of kinship nor ancestral gods. It was this aspect of the covenant form that was to prove so important for biblical religion.

The covenant at Sinai met the need to unify diverse groups. As the story of the Exodus and the revelation at Mt. Sinai is told in Scripture, the "Hebrews" who were enslaved in Egypt appear to share common tribal and religious origins. In reality, Scripture offers ample hints that the group that escaped from Egypt with Moses did not possess a common religioethnic inheritance. Referring to Moses' wilderness band, Scripture states: "Now there was a mixed company of strangers who had joined the Israelites" (Num. 11:4).

For several centuries before the Exodus, people from Palestine and Syria had entered Egypt. Some came as hostages and prisoners of war; some as merchants; some had been forced to take up residence in Egypt after engaging in activities hostile to their Egyptian overlords. Most modern biblical scholars believe that the name "Hebrew" referred originally to a number of alien peoples who shared something of a common condition and common social location in Egypt but were of diverse religious and ethnic origin.[3] Whether or not they were originally brought to Egypt as slaves, their condition tended to deteriorate over time. In some respects the situation of the "Hebrews" in Egyptian captivity was similar to that of citizens of a modern multiethnic city in which diverse groups share common problems in the present but remain distinct because of differences in origin, religion, and culture.

When the time came to depart from Egypt, the "Hebrews" shared a common yearning for liberation and, perhaps, a common hatred of their overlords, but little else. What they shared sufficed to unify them for a successful escape, but in the wilderness they required a compelling basis for continued unity beyond shared antipathy and a desire to flee. Otherwise, the band of fugitives would have been in danger from the natural and human hazards confronting them. Fortunately, the escape provided a further common, unforgettable experience, the Exodus itself.

In the ancient Near East, the distinction between group membership and religion was unknown. Since the "Hebrews" shared a common historical experience rather than kinship, ancestral gods were an impediment to unity. Neither the god-king of Egypt nor their diverse ancestral gods could unify them. Hence, the diverse groups could only become one people if they were united by a common God who was seen as the author of their shared experience.

According to George Mendenhall, an important authority on the subject, the Hittite covenants had an elaborate form that was later used in the biblical covenant.[4] Among the elements of interest to us are the following: (a) a preamble identifying the king who was the author of the covenant; (b) a review by the king, speaking in the first person, of the past benefits he had bestowed upon the vassal, as well as an assertion that these benefits were the basis for the vassal's future obligations to the suzerain (both in the Hittite documents and the biblical covenant, historical events rather than the magical qualities of the lord were the basis of obligation; since history is the record of the ways in which people have used power that are considered worthy of memory, it was the more powerful monarch's possession of and past use of power that constituted the basis of obligation); (c) a statement of the precise nature of the obligations incumbent upon the vassal-king. Moreover, in the Hittite treaties the vassal was explicitly excluded from entering into relationship with any other suzerain, just as in the biblical covenant Israel is excluded from having any God other than Yahweh.

Yet another resemblance between the Hittite treaties and the biblical covenant was the formula of blessings rewarding obedience and curses punishing disobedience.[5] While a breach of the Hittite covenant could lead to military action against the vassal, the sanctions explicitly provided for in the Bible were religious. The covenantal blessings and curses, such as those found in Deuteronomy 28, were thought to be God's response to the vassal's behavior in either keeping or breaking an oath.

It is impossible fully to reconstruct the events surrounding the giving of the covenant at Sinai, but there is no reason to doubt that Moses had a revelatory experience at a sacred desert mountain which became the basis for the covenant between the new God and the escapees. It is also reasonable to assume that there must have been an enormous sense of wonder and triumph among the "Hebrews" after their escape. It was natural for them to believe that whoever was responsible for their revelation was a divinity greater than the god-king who sat on Egypt's throne. There may have been some temptation to regard Moses in that light, but Scripture insists that Moses made no such claim on his own behalf. Moses is always depicted as acting on behalf of and in obedience to a power greater than himself. Moses mediates between the new God and His people, but he always does so as a human being. Neither Moses nor any Hebrew experiences a direct, immediate, visible manifestation of the God who was the author of their liberation.

The novelty of the encounter with the new God can also be expressed sociologically: Before Sinai there had been high gods, nature gods, ancestral gods, and gods of the polis, but there had never been a high God of escaped slaves and declassed fugitives. Moreover, by His election of the outcasts as His people, His "peculiar treasure," He had overturned all existing social hierarchies, in principle if not yet in fact. This was something utterly novel in human history and was to have revolutionary consequences. As we have noted, in the ancient world, and perhaps also in the modern, to be an outsider to all political structures can involve being deprived of all meaningful human status while possessing the full range of human capabilities and sensibilities. It was precisely such a band of outsiders who entered the covenant at Sinai.

The escapees had witnessed the dark side of Egyptian sacral kingship. They had good reason to reject its ethical and political values. Scripture assigns a number of traditions to the covenant at Sinai, but Mendenhall appears to be correct when he asserts that the new religion's values subordinated the power of the sovereign to the ethical concerns of human beings.[6] I would add that human status was no longer a function of membership in a political community in the new religion but derived from the God of the covenant. This was not explicitly stated at Sinai, but it was a corollary of that event, as later religious figures in Israel understood. In Egypt the ruler was a divinity and the interests of the state had a claim that transcended any possible claim of its subjects. There was, of course, a strong note of social protest in the new religion of the covenant. Escaped slaves, who had been the object of abusive power, were far less likely to give priority to the state's monopoly of coercive power than were members of the ruling class. Nor is it surprising that throughout history oppressed classes have tended to identify themselves with Israel in Egypt and at Sinai. In place of the kingdom of Pharaoh, there was to be a very different kind of a God, the God who had brought the slaves forth from Egypt.

Like the Hittite treaties, the Sinai covenant has a prologue in which Yahweh, the divine Author, identifies himself and states his past benefits to those with whom he is to enter a covenant. "I am Yahweh your God who has brought you out of the land of Egypt, out of the land of slavery" (Exod. 20:2) identifies the Author of the covenant and states the basis of obligation. Just as in the Hittite documents, the memory of concrete historical events is the basis of the vassal's obligation. Similarly, just as the vassal is prohibited from fealty to more than one lord, so the Hebrews are excluded from loyalty to any other god. "You shall have no other gods to set against me . . . for I am Yahweh, your God, a jealous God" (Exod. 20:3–5). Yahweh's insistence on exclusive worship had both political and religious import. It united those who accepted the covenant into a community and effectively barred them from giving their loyalty to any of the sacralized kingships of the ancient Near East or to their ancestral gods. *After* they had been unified under the God of Sinai, it was natural for the diverse peoples to claim that they had been kin all along and to read back elements of continuity between their common God and their ancestral gods. This is evident in Scripture as, for example, when God speaks to Moses: "I am Yahweh. And I appeared unto Abraham, Isaac and Jacob as El Shaddai, but by my name Yahweh, I was not known to them" (Exod. 6:2,3).

When, as in ancient Egypt or modern Japan before 1945, the ruler is declared to be a god, the state and its institutions are thought of as self-legitimating, a view vehemently rejected by Scripture. Where such is the case, whether in ancient sacralized kingdoms or modern states, there is no theoretical limit to the actions that can be committed and legitimated by those who command the political institutions and the state's monopoly of power. This does not mean that those in command will invariably abuse their power. Nevertheless, when political power is self-legitimating, there is in principle no effective check on those in command. Israel's ancient covenant was an attempt to create a viable alternative to the state's claim to ultimacy. By positing a God who possessed neither human image nor human incarnation as the power to whom the community owed its fundamental fidelity, the covenant had the effect of rejecting both the doctrine and the institutions that affirmed the ultimacy of the political order. Moreover, by insisting on the primacy of the ethical over the political in the new community's obligations to its God under the covenant, it set forth a principle that imposed unconditional standards on the behavior of men and nations alike. In addition, there was a harsh corollary to the idea that the community's obligations to its God were based on the fact that He had redeemed them from Egypt and had constituted them a nation. It followed that if ever the new community failed to meet the ethical and religious obligations of the covenant, their God could withdraw His protection from them and they might then be destroyed as a nation. In contrast to the sacralized kingdoms of both ancient and modern times whose religious traditions assured them that their community's security and stability is cosmically grounded, Israel's existence as a nation was seen as tentative and conditional on her keeping the covenant.

In the Sinai covenant, we can discern many of the most significant features of Israel's later religious life. By subordinating the political order to the obligations of the covenant, the Sinai covenant laid the foundation of the prophetic protest against the ethical and religious abuses of the period of the monarchy as well as the prophetic idea that men and nations alike stand under the judgment of the God of the covenant. Over and over again, Israel's prophets reiterated their warnings that the very survival of the nation depended upon keeping the covenant.[7] Perhaps of greatest long-range significance was the fact that the covenant provided the basis for Israel's extraordinary ability to maintain its religious and communal integrity in the face of repeated military and political catastrophes. Since the political order had been denied ultimacy from the very beginning, it was possible for the community to survive the destruction of the Judean state as well as to interpret its misfortunes as evidence of the uniqueness and majesty of its God.

Nor did this community of faith and value come to an end with the close of the biblical period. The rabbis were very much within the covenant tradition when they refused to accept the Roman destruction of Jerusalem as involving the end of Israel's communal existence or its distinctive relationship with its God.[8] As much as we may admire the men and women of Masada, their response was less in keeping with the covenant tradition. Given the biblical-rabbinic understanding of the subordination of the political order to the sovereignty of God, the rabbis were able to educate their community in a mode of life that permitted it to endure for almost two thousand years. Nor has that way of life yet lost its significance in our time. Although ritual was not stressed in the original Sinai covenant, the memory of the historic basis of obligation under the covenant was reinforced daily in the formula that the fulfillment of the commandments was a "remembrance of the going out of Egypt."

The covenant had yet other world-historical consequences, the most important and paradoxical being the fact that its distinctive conception of the ultimate source of power and obligation eventually became the basis for the creation of the modern secular world. At first glance, the idea that the wilderness experience of a group of declassed, escaped slaves could produce the modern secular world seems farfetched, yet that conclusion has been increasingly persuasive in the analysis of modernity since the time of Hegel.

Let us recall that the covenant's insistence that Yahweh alone is the God of Israel constituted a radical desacralization of the political institutions of the ancient Near East. For those who pledged themselves to the new God, both Pharaoh and the gods of Egypt were effectively dethroned. The gods of Canaan, as well as their sacralized political and social institutions, were similarly dethroned. The long-term effects of the covenant are everywhere the same: whereas sacral kingships see continuity between the human and the divine orders, the covenant unconditionally distinguishes between them. It took a long time before the full implications of the original desacralization became manifest. Nevertheless, after the covenant had rejected the sacrality of the political institutions of the ancient Near East, it was only a matter of time before *all* human institutions were denied any intrinsic sacrality.[9] The cultural process whereby both the natural and the human worlds came to be regarded as devoid of any inherent sacrality has been identified as *Entzauberung der Welt*, the "disenchantment of the world." According to Max Weber, where such disenchantment occurs, "there are in principle no mysterious forces that come into play, but rather one can, in principle, master all things by calculation."[10] As we know, it is the aspiration of the modern world to "master all things by calculation."

It is sometimes thought that the process of disenchantment is the result of modern rationalism or intellectual skepticism. In reality, it is unlikely that modern secularism could have achieved its mass appeal on the basis of intellectual criticism alone. Only a religious faith radically opposed to the forces of magic and to belief in the indwelling spirits could have initiated the profound cultural, psychological, and spiritual revolution that was necessary before entire civilizations could reject the gods and the spirits men had revered as sacred from time immemorial. Without faith in a new God, it would have been impossible to dethrone the old gods. *Only a God can overturn the gods.* Only those who believed in their God's exclusive sovereignty had the emotional and intellectual resources with which to abandon belief in magic, spirits, and sacralized institutions. Thus, *secularization is, paradoxically, the unintended consequence of a very distinctive kind of religious faith.* If one wishes to find the origins of the modern secular world, one must look for its beginnings at Sinai.

Yet there is irony in such a paradoxical cultural achievement. Once the process of *Entzauberung der Welt* is initiated, it is difficult to halt until the limit of radical atheism has been reached. The same dissolving skepticism that the original believers applied to the sacred claims of the Egyptian monarch was eventually applied to the heavenly Author of the covenant! In place of a world in which all values are ultimately a function of the state's requirements for self-maintenance, we finally arrive at a world in which *values no longer have any ground whatsoever.* Instead of a world in which only the outlaw, the man or woman who belongs to no political community, is treated with amoral calculation, kept alive and accorded decent treatment only if he or she is perceived to be useful, we arrive at a world in which all relationships are expressions of calculations of utility and no other standard need determine the relations between human beings. Put differently, we arrive at a world in which everyone is potentially an outlaw, the world of the death of God. Although the covenant originally attempted to solve one kind of abuse of power, it had as its paradoxical and unintended consequence the creation of another set of problems of comparable gravity.

Nevertheless, as long as faith in the Author of the covenant remained credible, the covenant did partly solve one very important problem. A primary social function of religions originating in a radical break with the past, such as Judaism, Christianity, and Islam, is to create a community for those who have none or whose inherited community has lost its relevance for their life situation.[11] The religion of the Sinai covenant is a supreme example of this phenomenon. We have seen how it enabled men and women of diverse tribal, religious, and cultural backgrounds to unite and create an enduring community. Christianity and Islam did the same. In the case of Christianity, Jesus Christ became the basis of unity for peoples dwelling in close proximity to each other in the cities of the Roman Empire who had hitherto been strangers. This has been given expression in the letters of Paul: "There is no such thing as Jew and Greek, slave and freeman, male and female; for you are all one person in Christ Jesus." (Gal. 3:28)

Before the development of covenantal treaties, kinship had been the primary principle of community organization. Today, racism, a contemporary expression of kinship, remains a defining principle in many communities. *Covenant and racism are diametrically opposed ways of organizing communities.* Covenant can unite diverse peoples under a common God or a shared body of law. Racism proclaims shared roots and kinship as the only viable basis for community. Merciless exclusion of the stranger is intrinsic to its very nature. A covenantal relationship serves little purpose among members of a closed kinship group such as the Japanese, who constitute one of the most self-consciously homogeneous nations in the world today. That may be one of the reasons why the Japanese are so resistant to biblical religion. In no other country have so many Christian missionaries labored with so little success as in Japan. Less than 1 percent of the population is Christian, and the numbers are declining.[12] By contrast, a covenantal bond tends to be necessary wherever diverse religious and ethnic groups must live together in a common community. The American Constitution can be seen as a secularized covenant that is peculiarly suited to an "invented" nation like the United States with its biblical religious heritage and its pluralistic population. In the United States, the religious roots of American civilization are normally identified as "Judeo-Christian" rather than simply Christian. This identification serves to include rather than exclude Jews from the American covenant.[13] Given the realities of modern communication, transportation, trade, and worldwide migration patterns, most of the world desperately needs ways to define community that transcend older boundaries of kinship obligation. The need is especially evident in eastern Europe and the former Soviet Union with the collapse of communism as a binding political ideology. Undoubtedly, the need has been felt in ever-widening circles from ancient times. When tribal groups and villages had little contact with each other, natural forms of religiopolitical affiliation sufficed. As human beings increased in number and as members of diverse groups were united in larger political entities, such as the kingdoms of the ancient Near East and the Roman Empire, kinship could no longer suffice as a basis for community.

In ancient times, and, as we shall see, still today, where no covenant exists between conflicting collectivities, there are few, if any, moral impediments to wars of enslavement and extermination. Thucydides describes the fate of the defeated Melians during the Peloponnesian War. The Melians had rejected the Athenian demand that they surrender and become tributary to Athens. In their dialogue with the Melians, the Athenians observed that "the strong do what they can and the weak suffer what they must." When Melos finally collapsed under siege, the fate of the Melians was sealed. Thucydides tells the terrible story: "The Melians surrendered unconditionally to the Athenians, who put to death all the men of military age whom they took, and sold the women and children for slaves."[14]

The treatment of the Melians had its parallel in the injunctions concerning the vanquished enemy in Deuteronomy: "When you approach a city to make war on it, you shall offer it peace. . . . If it does not make peace with you, but wages war against you, then you shall besiege it, and Yahweh your God will deliver it into your hands. You shall kill all the males with the sword. But the women and the children . . . you shall seize for yourself. You may consume the spoils of your enemies which the Lord your God gives you (Deut. 20:10–15)."[15]

Want of a covenant or its functional equivalent has been a moral precondition for genocide in both ancient and modern times. Long before Hitler, the Jews were regarded as largely outside of the German universe of moral obligation. By defining the Jews as collectively and for all generations murderers of God, the Christian Church had already prepared the way. By identifying the Jews as polluting vermin and bacilli, the National Socialists completed the work. We need not again recall the almost total indifference to the fate of the victims on the part of the predominant religious and political institutions of the Christian West before and during World War II. For our purposes, it is sufficient to note once again that the ascription of a deicidal or polluting identity to the Jews legitimated any act of violence and destruction, no matter how obscene, against them.

Nor were the Jews the only group cast out of any shared communal obligation by the Germans. By identifying the Slavs as *Untermenschen* and fighting a racial war of enslavement and extermination against them, the Germans made it abundantly clear that they regarded their eastern neighbors as without the slightest moral claim. In the past, even war did not completely cancel out a sense of moral responsibility between combatants. Between the nations of Christendom, there used to be religiously legitimated sanctions against wars of extermination. Moreover, the warring powers understood that, in spite of the killing, peace would some day come and former enemies would once again have to live with each other. There was a consensus concerning the treatment of prisoners of war and conquered populations. When, for example, Czar Peter the Great learned that his soldiers had killed King Charles XII of Sweden in battle (1721), the czar, who had spent twenty-one years in war against the Swedish monarch, was reduced to tears and ordered his court into mourning for a week.[16] During World War II to a certain extent Germany fought the older kind of war in the West. It was never Hitler's intention to fight a traditional war in the East.

Nor were the Jews the only people characterized as vermin during World War II. In confidential reports on the American political and social mood during the war, the British Embassy staff took note of widespread exterminationist sentiment against the Japanese and the popular view that the Japanese were "a nameless mass of vermin."[17] In March 1945, *Leatherneck*, the U.S. Marine monthly, carried a cartoon depicting the *"Louseous Japanicas."* The cure was, "The origin of the plague, the breeding grounds around the Tokyo area, must be completely annihilated."[18] In *War without Mercy*, John Dower graphically describes the prevalence of exterminationist sentiment toward the enemy in both Japan and the United States during the war in the Pacific.[19] Between 1941 and 1945 the United States and Japan fought a racial war with no quarter given or mercy extended. Admiral William D. Leahy, President Roosevelt's Chief of Staff, described Japan as "our Carthage" and advocated a Carthaginian peace in a conversation with Vice President Henry Wallace in September 1942.[20] Lacking the memory of a shared religious past, the United States and Japan were without even a minimal basis for a common morality. Calculations of power alone determined their relations. Unfortunately, that sorry condition continues to beset U.S.-Japanese relations.

The Japanese have been described as a "people with an isolationist soul and an internationalist economy, an insular clannishness and a worldwide impact."[21] The contradiction may yet prove explosive for the world. To this day Japanese society is based upon the belief that the Japanese are one extended family founded thousands of years ago and radically different from the rest of the world. Isaiah Ben-Dasan, a Japanese nationalist intellectual who wrote a book entitled, *The Japanese and the Jews*, under an Israeli pseudonym, argues that the real religion of Japan is "Japonism." Ben Dassan points out that there is an unbroken, organic relationship between Japan's archaic religious and cultural roots and its contemporary religion. He contrasts biblical religion with "Japonism." A natural, organic relationship is said to exist between the Japanese and their gods. The gods of Japan are like natural parents who set no conditions for their love. By contrast, the God of Israel is depicted as an adoptive parent who strictly stipulates the conditions under which He will bestow protection on Israel, His adopted child. Citing Deuteronomy 28 and other biblical texts, Ben-Dasan notes the conditional character of God's covenantal relationship to Israel. According to Ben-Dasan, such a relationship is absolutely unthinkable to the Japanese.[22]

There is, however, an important reason why biblical religion is both conditional and nonorganic. There is no way that a non-Japanese person can be fully embraced within Japan's sanctified community of moral obligation. To this day, the term *gaijin* or foreigner has the negative overtones of enemy as well as alien. A very large percentage of Japanese regard all *gaijin* as belonging to other, inferior species, if not as less than human altogether.[23] The sense of the foreigner's otherness is so strong that Japanese executives and students sent abroad are suspected of having been contaminated by alien contact when they return home. The non-reciprocal character of Japanese trade relations is but the tip of the iceberg, and the problems involved in Japan's sense of uniqueness are bound to grow as Japan's position in the international economy becomes ever more powerful.

The tragic encounter between Israelis and Palestinians, most recently expressed in the Intifada and Palestinian expressions of joy at Iraq's missile attacks against civilian targets in Israel, is yet another example of the absence of a covenant. The refusal of the Arab states, save for Egypt, to recognize the State of Israel and their persistent threats, muted in Western languages but altogether explicit in Arabic, ultimately to push the Israelis into the sea have convinced most Israelis that they are confronted by an uncompromising, mortal foe. After the Holocaust, the promise of extermination is not one that Jews take lightly.

Since the Six-Day War of 1967 critics of the State of Israel have complained of its failure to grant full political rights to its Arab citizens and its refusal to grant the right of self-determination to Palestinians in the occupied territories. Under Israeli rule no Palestinian can entirely escape being a political pariah.[24] Regrettably, such criticisms fail to consider the fundamental reason for this condition: *Citizenship is more than the abstract right to participate in elections or to claim equality of opportunity. Citizenship rests upon the unconditional obligation of the citizen to risk his or her life in defense of the community.* This is especially true of a small state in which a single military defeat could easily spell the end of the community. Palestinians cannot be faulted for their unwillingness to make a commitment to defend the State of Israel, but neither can the state be faulted for viewing every Palestinian as a potential security threat who would destroy the state if he or she could. Nor is there anything the Israelis could do to alter the texture of loyalties rooted in kinship, culture, and religion which bind the Palestinians to their fellow Arabs.

The real danger is that the conflict between the Israelis and the Palestinians will descend into a merciless, uncompromising war to the death. The enthusiastic identification of the Palestinian community with the cause of Saddam Hussein, the stoning of Israeli worshipers at the Western Wall of the Temple Mount on October 8, 1990, and the killing of between seventeen and twenty-one Palestinians by Israeli police on the same day have all made the war-unto-death scenario considerably more plausible. The fundamental issue at stake is whether a self-governing Palestinian community can coexist peacefully with an independent Israel. If the warring parties can find no credible solution, they will be compelled eventually to seek to drive each other out of the land each claims as its historic inheritance. Already young Arabs taunt Israeli soldiers with the challenge, "Kill us all or get out!" And they do not mean just out of the occupied territories. If the conflict intensifies, more and more Israelis, perceiving a threat to their very existence, may find reasonable the radical demand that all Arabs be removed from the occupied territories. The overwhelming Palestinian support for Saddam Hussein, the first national leader since Adolf Hitler to threaten Jews with extermination by poison gas, has widened the gulf between the two communities almost beyond any hope of repair.

As I reflect on the conflict between Israelis and Palestinians, I am struck by its partial analogy with that between the Texans and the Comanche Indians in the middle decades of the nineteenth century. Viewing the white settlers as a mortal threat to their territory, the Comanches used all available means to terrorize and drive them out. When the armed superiority of the whites was finally assured, the Comanches were stripped of most of their territory and confined to reservations. No other solution was possible given the understandable determination of the Comanches to resist the alien intruders. The analogy cannot be carried too far because of the presence of Muslim coreligionists in every state bordering on Israel. Nevertheless, there is some danger that the Israelis will come to see the Palestinians as contemporary Comanches and act accordingly.

To this scenario we must add the stark reality of Israel's nuclear arsenal, whose magnitude has recently been confirmed by the Mordecai Vanunu affair.[25] The fact that Israel may possess as many as two hundred hydrogen bombs cannot be separated from the experience of the Holocaust and Israel's perception that she is surrounded by mortal enemies. Having been taught by the Holocaust of the real value of international guarantees, it is hardly surprising that the Israelis have stockpiled an enormous number of nuclear weapons. The capacity grievously to damage or wholly to destroy an adversary is, at present, Israel's most credible guarantee of survival. Nor is it likely that, faced with defeat in a war of extermination, the Israelis would go quietly into the dust.

Obviously, no person with any concern for the future of humanity can rest content with such scenarios. What is needed today is an institution similar to that which enabled the Hebrews to unite under God at Sinai, a binding basis for community between men and women who share little but mutual distrust and fear. Unfortunately, it is easier to point to the need than to meet it. The need was partly met in three different historical eras by the rise of Judaism, Christianity, and Islam. With the globalization of civilization and the perfection of long-range weapons of extermination, the need has returned with greater urgency than ever before.

At this point, we have reached the limits of analysis. Perhaps American peace efforts, if genuinely even-handed, might help to avert the worst. However, if the past is any guide, the need for a new and broader basis for community is likely to be met, if at all, by religiously inspired men and women who have yet to be identified. Nor can we know whether a more inclusive covenant would avert or follow upon a large-scale, humanly produced demographic catastrophe. Nevertheless, we need to place the problematic theological aspects of the biblical covenant in the broader context of the perennial human needs the older covenants were able to meet, at least for a time. The negative aspects of the biblical covenant are far less important than the example it offered of a way out of unremitting mistrust and destructiveness.

Part III

THEOLOGY AND CONTEMPORARY JUDAISM

CHAPTER 8

Covenant and Divinity

THE HOLOCAUST AND THE PROBLEMATICS
OF RELIGIOUS FAITH, PART 1

In the aftermath of the *Shoah*, the question whether God, as traditionally understood in biblical and rabbinic Judaism, was the ultimate Actor in the catastrophic events is inescapable for religious Jews. From the perspective of biblical and rabbinic Judaism, neither the justice nor the power of God can ever be denied. Within Judaism God has been traditionally understood to be the infinitely righteous, radically transcendent, and absolutely omnipotent Creator of all things. At a very early stage in its development Judaism rejected moral and theological dualism as a way of solving the problem of theodicy. Deutero-Isaiah rejected the Persian idea that there are two equally potent divine powers in the cosmos, insisting that God alone is the creator of both good and evil.[1] Insofar as God is regarded as uniquely involved in the history and destiny of Israel, as indeed He is in Scripture and rabbinic literature, there is absolutely no way of avoiding the exceedingly painful conclusion that He is the ultimate Author of all that has happened to the people of Israel, including the Holocaust. Before such a God humanity must forever be in the wrong.

Nevertheless, men and women have found it difficult to accept so harsh and uncompromising a view of the divine-human relationship. One of the most influential philosophical attempts to resolve the apparent contradiction between the justice and the power of Divinity has been to interpret particular suffering as indispensable to the fulfillment of universal ends. In Hegelian terms, particular evil can be said to be overcome in the life of the Absolute. In contemplating the course of world history, with its record of crime, suffering, and slaughter, Hegel was able to write in utter calm and philosophical detachment: "In order to justify the course of history, we must try to understand the role of evil in the light of the absolute sovereignty of reason. We are dealing here with the category of the negative . . . and we cannot fail to notice how all that is finest and noblest in history is immolated on its altar. Reason cannot stop to consider the injuries sustained by *single individuals, for particular ends are submerged in the universal ends*" (italics added).[2]

For Hegel individual injury is overcome in universal ends. However, Hegel never faced a situation of universal injury, such as the Holocaust, or the threat of universal extinction in a nuclear Holocaust. When the universal order is itself threatened with extinction, the idea that a particular misfortune can be overcome in the universal loses its credibility. There is a profound difference between a situation in which some persons suffer and perish unjustly but the group survives and one in which an entire group or even all of humanity is obliterated.

The inappropriateness of the Hegelian reconciliation to the human condition after Auschwitz has been expressed by another philosopher, Theodor Adorno:

> We cannot say any more that the immutable is truth, and that the mobile, transitory in appearance. The mutual indifference of temporality and eternal ideas is no longer tenable even with the bold Hegelian explanation that temporal existence, by virtue of the destruction inherent in its concept, serves the eternal represented by the eternity of destruction. . . . After Auschwitz . . . events make a mockery of the construction of immanence as endowed with a meaning radiated by an affirmatively posited transcendence. . . . The administrative murder of millions made of death a thing one never had to fear in just this fashion. There is no chance any more for death to come into the individual's empirical life as somehow conformable with the course of that life. The last, the poorest possession of the individual is appropriated. That in the concentration camps it was no longer an individual who dies, but a specimen—this is a fact bound to affect the dying of those who escaped the administrative measure.[3]

Some modern philosophers have regarded the *Shoah* as presenting a problem unworthy of their reflection. For example, although François Fedier, a French disciple of Martin Heidegger, has characterized Victor Farias's book, *Heidegger et le nazisme,* as "a big media attack," Fedier did not regard Auschwitz as important enough to discuss with Heidegger. Fedier has been quoted as saying, "I never thought of posing questions except those about philosophy."[4] Nor did Heidegger believe that the Holocaust merited reflection or explanation. In response to a letter from his former student, Herbert Marcuse, asking why he had remained silent concerning the extermination of six million Jews, Heidegger equated postwar Soviet treatment of East Germans with the Nazi treatment of the Jews. Heidegger implied that the Soviet treatment was worse since it was done openly, whereas "the bloody terror of the Nazis was in fact kept secret from the German people."[5]

Traditional Religious Thought and the Holocaust

The question of God and the Holocaust has been of far greater interest to religious thinkers than to philosophers. Elsewhere I have argued that a principal function of theology is to foster dissonance reduction where significant items of information are perceived to be inconsistent with established beliefs, values, and collectively sanctioned modes of behavior.[6] At first glance, the Holocaust would appear to be such an item of information and one that would naturally concern religious thinkers. Nevertheless, as we shall see, many important Jewish religious authorities have emphatically rejected the idea that the occurrence of the Holocaust is in any way inconsistent with the traditional Jewish conception of divinity. In spite of the fact that the *Shoah* has been characterized by Rabbi Yitzhak (Irving) Greenberg, a leading Jewish Holocaust theologian, as "the most radical countertestimony to religious faith, both Jewish and Christian," some of the most faithful and observant Jewish religious leaders have offered a contrary opinion.[7] These leaders have asserted that their faith in God has been confirmed by the catastrophe. The views of Rabbi Elchonon Wassermann of Baranovitch (1875–1941) are representative of Orthodox Jewish thought during the Holocaust years.[8] Writing between *Kristallnacht* and the beginning of the war, Wassermann interpreted the Nazi onslaught as due to three Jewish "evils": secular nationalism; assimilation, especially through Reform Judaism; and the alleged contempt for the Torah in the scientific study of Judaism. For Wassermann, the Nazi assault was ultimately God's appropriate response against those who had proven unfaithful to His Torah. Wassermann also saw the promise of redemption in the misfortunes. Indeed, he argued that the more intense the suffering of the people, the closer the advent of the Messiah, a theme that has been taken up once again in contemporary Israel.[9]

Wassermann's life was fully consistent with his faith. When taken to be killed by four Latvian murderers in July 1941, he spoke of his own death, as well as the death of others like him, as a *korban*, a sacrificial offering, for the Jewish people: "Let us go with raised heads. God forbid that any thought should enter the mind of anybody to make the sacrifice (*korban*) unfit. We now carry out the greatest Mitzvah, *Kiddush Hashem* (sanctification of God's name). The fire which will burn our bodies is the fire which will resurrect the Jewish people."[10] Wassermann's response to the Holocaust was typical of that of the Orthodox rabbinate of the period in both eastern Europe and North America. Far from being a "radical countertestimony to religious faith," the events were widely regarded as confirming the tradition and the fulfillment of God's plan.

The opinions of Rabbi Joseph Isaac Schneersohn, the late Luba-vitcher Rebbe, were another example of the same tendency. According to Schneersohn, Hitler is but God's instrument for chastising the Jews, who had abandoned the ways of Torah; Nazism is divine punishment visited upon the Jews for rejecting the Torah and choosing assimilation.[11]

The Orthodox interpretation of the Holocaust as divinely inflicted punishment or the sacrificial precondition for the coming of the Messiah rests upon the biblical doctrines of covenant and election. As we have noted, whenever Israel experienced *radical communal misfortune*, her religious teachers almost always interpreted the event as did Wassermann and Schneersohn, that is, as divine punishment. This was the case in 586 B.C.E., when Jeremiah prophesied concerning the impending fate of Jerusalem, which was then threatened by Nebuchadnezzar, King of Babylon:

> These are the words of the Lord to Jeremiah: I am the Lord, the God of all flesh; is anything impossible for me? Therefore these are the words of the Lord: I will deliver this city into the hands of the Chaldeans and of Nebuchadnezzar king of Babylon, and he shall take it. The Chaldeans who are fighting against this city will enter it, set it on fire and burn it down, with the houses on whose roofs sacrifices have been burnt to Baal and drink-offerings poured out to the other gods, by which I was pro-voked to anger. From their earliest days Israel and Judah have been doing what is wrong in my eyes, provoking me to anger by their actions, says the Lord (Jer. 32:26–30).

Given Jeremiah's belief in the election of Israel, it was impossible for him to view the Fall of Jerusalem as an event devoid of profound religious significance. The prophet understood that divine election placed an awesome responsibility on Israel. Undoubtedly, he was mindful of the terrible warning the prophet Amos had pronounced upon his own people: "Listen, Israelites, to these words that the Lord addresses to you, to the nation that he brought up from Egypt: *For you alone have I cared among all the nations of the world; therefore will I punish you for all your iniquities"* (Amos 3:1–2, italics added).

Jerusalem fell yet again at the end of the Judeo-Roman War of 66–70 C.E. At the time, the rabbis, who had succeeded the prophets and the priests as the religious authorities within Judaism, interpreted their people's misfortunes as had their predecessors. A characteristic example of the rabbinic response is to be found in the liturgy for the Holy Days and Festivals still used by traditional Jews: "Thou hast chosen us from among all peoples; thou hast loved us and taken pleasure in us, and hast exalted us above all tongues; thou hast hallowed us by thy commandments, and brought us near unto thy service, O our King, and thou hast called us by thy great and holy Name. . . . *But on account of our sins we were exiled from our land and removed far from our country."*[12]

To the extent that Judaism and Christianity affirm the election of Israel, both traditions must consider the Holocaust as more than a random occurrence. Indeed, contemporary Orthodox Jews in Israel affiliated with Gush Emunim (the Bloc of the Faithful) consider the Holocaust to be an indispensable event in God's redemptive plan for human history. Unable to accept the Holocaust as a purely punitive event, they tend to interpret it as the catastrophic precondition for the final messianic redemption of Jewish and world history, the "birth pangs of the Messiah." For almost two thousand years traditional Judaism sought to restrain the messianic impulse within the Jewish people. In the aftermath of the Holocaust and the wars of the State of Israel, a highly influential segment of contemporary Orthodoxy has become overtly messianic.[13]

Historians have long debated the question of the uniqueness of the Holocaust. They have noted similarities between it and the massacre of the Armenians in World War I, Stalin's mass destruction of classes and groups he regarded as objectively antagonistic, and the Pol Pot regime's genocide of Kampuchea's urban population.[14] As noted above, there is one aspect of the Holocaust which is absolutely different from all other programs of extermination and mass destruction in the modern period: *The fate of the Jews is a matter of decisive religiomythic significance in both Judaism and Christianity.* No example of mass murder other than the Holocaust has raised so directly or so insistently the question of whether it was an expression of *Heilsgeschichte,* that is, God's providential involvement in history.

An important example of the mythic importance of Jewish misfortune, in this case as proof of Christian truth, is to be found in Martin Luther's "On the Jews and Their Lies": "Well, let the Jews regard our Lord Jesus as they will. We behold the fulfillment of the words spoken by him in Luke 21:20,22f.: 'But when you see Jerusalem surrounded by armies, then know that its desolation has come near . . . for these are days of vengeance. For great distress shall be upon the earth and wrath upon this people.'[15]

I have also noted that R. Johanan ben Zakkai also regarded the Fall of Jerusalem as a consequence of God's chastisement of a sinful Israel.[16] The terrible curses enunciated in Deuteronomy are part of the theological and religious basis for R. Johanan's interpretation of Jewish suffering. I cannot cite the entire text in this context; nevertheless, the following verses capture its spirit and intent: "If you do not observe and fulfil all the law written down in this book . . . then the Lord will strike you and your descendants with unimaginable plagues, malignant and persistent. . . . Just as the Lord took delight in you . . . so now it will be his delight to destroy and exterminate you. . . . The Lord will scatter you among all peoples from one end of the earth to the other" (Deut. 28:58–64).[17]

As noted, Jewish and Christian authorities had no disagreement concerning the belief that God is the ultimate Author of Israel's misfortunes. They disagreed only in identifying the nature of Israel's sin.

Given the classical theological positions of both Judaism and Christianity, the fundamental question posed by the Holocaust is not whether the existence of a just, omnipotent God can be reconciled with radical evil. That is a philosophical question. The religious question is the following:

> *Did God use Adolf Hitler and the Nazis as his agents to inflict terrible sufferings and death upon six million Jews, including more than one million children?*

Even if God is seen as the ultimate Author of the death camps, it does not follow that His actions at Auschwitz were necessarily punitive. Both Judaism and Christianity allow for the possibility that the innocent may be called upon to suffer sacrificially for the guilty. Neither the Hebrew Bible nor the Christian Scriptures interpret *every* misfortune as divine punishment. For example, in the Book of Job the protagonist is depicted as having experienced the worst misfortunes without having offended God. Similarly, the "Suffering Servant" of Isaiah 53 appears to have been an innocent victim. As we shall see, an important theological interpretation of the Holocaust depicts the victims as sacrificial offerings. As we have noted, the Holocaust has also been interpreted as the "birth pangs of the Messiah."

Nevertheless, until the 1967 war, whenever Israel experienced *radical communal misfortune,* her traditional religious teachers almost always interpreted the event as divine punishment. Of all the misfortunes experienced by the Jewish people, only three can be reckoned as major communal disasters that irrevocably altered the character of the Jewish world: Nebuchadnezzar's defeat of Judea in 586 B.C.E., the Fall of Jerusalem to the Romans in 70 C.E., and the *Shoah*. Not since 70 C.E. had world Jewry experienced a catastrophe remotely like what was endured between 1939 and 1945. In reality, never before in history had Jews experienced so overwhelming a disaster.

Nontraditional Interpretation of the Holocaust: Ignaz Maybaum

Two radical theological interpretations of the Holocaust were among the first to appear. They were *The Face of God after Auschwitz* by Ignaz Maybaum (b. 1897) and the first edition of *After Auschwitz*.[18] Both appeared in 1966. Maybaum was a Viennese-born Reform rabbi who emigrated to England in 1937 and served in that country for many years. Although written in English, Maybaum's book was published in the Netherlands. For many years it was almost totally unknown in the United States. The first edition of *After Auschwitz* received far more attention from both scholars and the media. No two works of Holocaust theology are in such total disagreement. However, their disagreements illumine many of the crucial issues confronting Jewish religious faith after Auschwitz.

In *The Face of God after Auschwitz* Maybaum affirmed the continuing validity of God's covenant with Israel. He insisted without qualification that God continues to intervene in history, especially in the history of His Chosen People, the Holocaust being one of His most important interventions. Maybaum also held that Israel has a divinely ordained mission to bring knowledge of the true God and His Law to the nations of the world. This idea was strongly affirmed in the nineteenth century by Reform Jewish thinkers in both Germany and the United States and is crucial to Maybaum's interpretation of the Holocaust. It met with little favor among traditional Jews or Zionists.

Although Maybaum saw the Holocaust as God's deliberate intervention, he categorically rejected the idea that it was in any sense divine punishment. Having rejected the punitive interpretation, Maybaum offered a sacrificial interpretation of the *Shoah*, using the Crucifixion as his model. Maybaum asserted that, just as Jesus was the innocent victim whose death made possible the salvation of humanity, so too the millions of Holocaust victims must be seen as divinely chosen sacrificial offerings.

The use of the Crucifixion as a theological model by a rabbi may seem

strange, perhaps even bizarre, but Maybaum argued that God's purposes can only be understood if God addresses the nations of the world
in the kind of language they understand. Maybaum contended that the
nations of the world can only hear and respond to God's call when that
call is expressed in the language of death and destruction. Hence, the
use of the Crucifixion, which is the only model by which the Christian
world can comprehend God's activity. According to Maybaum, it was the
awesome fate of six million Jews, *precisely because they were God's Chosen
People*, to become sacrificial victims at Auschwitz and the other camps so
that God's purposes for the modern world might be understood and fulfilled: "The Golgotha of modern mankind is Auschwitz. The cross, the
Roman gallows, was replaced by the gas chamber."[19]

Maybaum concurred in the view that the Jewish world has experienced three decisive communal disasters in its long history. He referred
to each disaster as a *Churban*, an event of utter destruction which, according to Maybaum, is world-historical in its scope and significance.
Each *Churban* is a divine intervention whose purpose is a decisive alteration of the course of history. Nevertheless, there is a creative element
in the destruction. A *Churban* marks the end of one era and the beginning
of a new and better one, both for the Jews and the world as a whole.
However, the new era can only come into being if the old is destroyed.

Maybaum held that the destruction of Jerusalem in 586 B.C.E., which
initiated the Diaspora of the Jews, was the first *Churban*. In keeping with
the Reform Jewish idea of "the mission of Israel," Maybaum argued that
the first *Churban* had the fortunate consequence of enabling the Jews to
bring knowledge of the true God and his Law to the pagan nations
beyond Judea's borders. Had not Israel suffered the pain of exile, knowledge of God's word might have remained confined to one small community. Thus, the first *Churban* was an example of God's "creative
destructiveness."

Maybaum also saw the second *Churban*, the Roman destruction of
Judea and Jerusalem, as yet another example of God's creative destruction. He regarded the shift of religious emphasis from animal sacrifice to
prayer and study as a spiritual improvement and held that only by means
of the destruction of the older, more "primitive" religious life could the
newer, more "spiritual" type come to predominate.[20] Maybaum also saw
the dispersion of the Jews among the nations of the Roman world as progress. Although the Jews lost their political independence, they were, in
Maybaum's view, enabled to fulfill their mission by spreading knowledge
of God throughout the Roman Empire. By contrast, traditional Judaism

has never regarded the Diaspora as a *felix culpa*, a fortunate fall, through which God in His mercy bestowed a messianic Redeemer.[21]

Maybaum argued that the third *Churban*, or the Holocaust, was yet another example of God's use of the Jewish people as sacrificial victims in an act of creative destruction. According to Maybaum, God used the *Shoah* to accomplish the final overcoming of the Middle Ages and the full transition of the peoples of the world into the modern world. Humanity's "sin," for which the Jews are alleged to have had to perish, was the retention in Europe of old remnants of the medieval feudal world in an age in which these structures were no longer appropriate. It was Maybaum's view that after World War I the West could have brought "freedom, land reform and the blessings of the industrial revolution to the East European countries."[22] Instead, they did nothing. As a result, the slaughter of that war was in vain and Hitler was sent by God to do what "the progressives" should have done but failed to do. This meant that the work of creative destruction had to be carried out at an infinitely greater cost in human suffering.

Maybaum regarded the Holocaust as God's terrible means of bringing the world fully into the modern age. He argued that this transition could not have occurred without the destruction of all that was medieval in Europe. Maybaum pointed out that the vast majority of Jewish victims were eastern Europeans who, he argued, still lived in a medieval, feudal way, more or less as their ancestors had, ritually and culturally isolated from their neighbors. In spite of the fact that it took a Hitler to destroy this allegedly outmoded way of life, Maybaum interpreted the extermination of eastern European Jews as an ultimately beneficent act of creative destruction. Unfortunately, so too did the National Socialists, though for very different reasons. With the passing of the eastern European Jewish community, which had been the most faithful to the ancient beliefs and traditions of rabbinic Judaism, the world's Jews were concentrated in countries such as the United, States, western Europe, Russia, and Israel, in which they were free to participate fully in an era of enlightenment, progress, rationality, and modernity.

It would appear that Maybaum was surprisingly uninformed concerning the actual character of the eastern European Jewish community in the period immediately preceding World War II. While it is true that many of eastern Europe's Jews lived self-contained, ghettoized lives, Maybaum ignores the fact that a very large proportion of the Jews of Poland, Lithuania, and Romania had fully entered the modern world, as indeed had many Orthodox Jews.[23] Maybaum naively equated religious traditionalism with medievalism. If that identification were valid, we would have to regard millions of Orthodox Jews, conservative Christians, and Muslims as somehow not a part of the modern world. In reality, there have been many legitimate ways of responding to modernity, among which participation in or return to traditional religion is by no means the least important. There is also reason for astonishment at Maybaum's inclusion of Stalinist Russia among the countries in which Jews were free to participate fully in an era of enlightenment, progress, rationality, and modernity.

Maybaum also expressed a quasi-messianic enthusiasm for the place and role of the Jews in the post–Holocaust world. Maybaum's enthusiasm for the destruction of the allegedly medieval elements in Jewish life was such that he equated the modernized, post–Holocaust Judaism of the "enlightened" Western world with the "first fruits" of redemption: "The Jewish people is, here and now, mankind at its goal. We have arrived. We are the first fruits of God's harvest."[24] As we shall see in a subsequent chapter, the messianic theme has a powerful hold over many Orthodox Jews in contemporary Israel, especially among those who have settled on the West Bank.[25]

Nor did Maybaum flinch from carrying his theological argument to its shocking but logical conclusion: When Nebuchadnezzar sought to destroy Jerusalem, Jeremiah referred to him as "my servant Nebuchadnezzar King of Babylon" (Jer. 27:6). In a deliberate allusion to Jeremiah, Maybaum depicted God as declaring, "Hitler, My Servant!"[26] Insisting that Hitler was God's instrument, Maybaum continues: "God used this instrument to cleanse, to purify, to punish a sinful world; the six million Jews, they died an innocent death; they died because of the sins of others."[27]

It should be obvious that there are enormous problems with Maybaum's defense of the biblical God of history and the election of Israel. No matter what "higher" purposes were, in Maybaum's view, served by the Holocaust, Maybaum's image of God was of one who was quite willing to subject millions of innocent people to the most degrading and obscene suffering and death ever experienced by a human collectivity. Moreover, there is the question of whether the "higher purpose," namely, the definitive onset of modernity, for which the victims were alleged to have sacrificed their lives, was worth even a single life. In the nineteenth century, German and American Reform Jews greeted the onset of the modern world, with its removal of ghetto restrictions, as a divinely bestowed, protomessianic redemption. It is not difficult to understand why those who for centuries had been restricted to a ghettoized existence were filled with enthusiasm for the Enlightenment and its promise of civil emancipation. It is, however, difficult to understand how an historically informed thinker can retain that kind of optimism now that the night side of modernity stands fully revealed. This is not the occasion to detail the horrors the world has experienced precisely because we have entered into the modern age. Nor do I suggest that modernity could or should be abandoned. Nevertheless, when we turn to the problems of environmental pollution, the threat of nuclear annihilation, the worldwide phenomenon of technologically induced mass unemployment and poverty, we see that there is reason for skepticism concerning Maybaum's unreserved, messianic enthusiasm for modernity.

Nor can the Crucifixion be used as an appropriate model for the Holocaust. In the Crucifixion, God is depicted as descending to the world, taking human form, and voluntarily giving up his human life to save a world of undeserving sinners. In the Crucifixion, God causes himself to suffer for the sake of others. In Maybaum's version of the Holocaust, God inflicts hideous involuntary suffering upon millions of frail, frightened, and undeserving human beings.

In fairness to Maybaum it must be stated that his interpretation of the Holocaust is motivated by a desire to defend the doctrine of covenant and election as that doctrine was understood in classical Reform Judaism. Maybaum understood the nature of the theological vocation and was prepared to fulfill it on behalf of his community. He grasped the logical entailments of the faith he defended. Most non-Orthodox religious thinkers affirm the God-who-acts-in-history but deny that he acted in history at Auschwitz. By asserting that God's ways are "mysterious," such thinkers seek to affirm traditional faith while evading the negative consequences of so doing. *What distinguished thinkers like Bernard Wasserman, Joseph Schneersohn, and Ignaz Maybaum was their refusal to take the easy escape route of liberal evasion.* They understood that, absent the affirmation of some version of the traditional biblical view of God, Torah, and covenant, Judaism becomes a socially constructed ethnic religion. Such a faith cannot fulfill one of religion's most important functions, the defense of men and women against anomy.[28] That which is recognized as humanly produced can be humanly altered to suit whim or impulse. For Judaism, the religious defense against anomy requires the grounding of beliefs, values, and norms in Torah as divine revelation and Israel's history as the theater of purposeful divine action. Regrettably, the defense against anomy is not easily purchased.

If is not surprising that many religious thinkers prefer to gloss over or ignore this issue. Life must go on. Members of any community minimally require life-cycle rituals consistent with their historic identity, even when they are skeptical about the literal meaning of the words of the liturgy. Civil ceremonies are a poor and unsatisfying substitute for religious rituals. There are some very good reasons for not pushing agonizing theological questions too far.

It is to Maybaum's credit that he confronted the theological question of God and the Holocaust forthrightly. At the very least, his position indicates the kind of affirmations that are logically entailed in the theological defense of the biblical image of God in the light of that event. This does not mean that Maybaum has provided the only logical defense. Maybaum has, however, shown that it is impossible to affirm the existence of the biblical God of covenant and election without also affirming some sort of purposeful divine involvement at Auschwitz. Usually, such a position involves affirming God's omnipotence at the cost of denying his justice, love, and mercy. Maybaum attempts to avoid this split by insisting that Auschwitz does not constitute evidence of the absence of God's love and mercy since (*a*) two-thirds of the world's Jews survived; (*b*) the Holocaust was of brief duration; and (*c*) it was followed by the "promised land" of the fully realized modern age. Maybaum cites the prophet Isaiah to make his point.

> For a small moment have I forsaken thee,
> But with great compassion will I gather thee,
> In a little wrath I hid my face from thee for a moment,
> But with everlasting kindness will I have compassion on thee,
> Saith the Lord, thy Redeemer (Isa. 54:7,8).

It is doubtful that many will concur in Maybaum's implicit characterization of the events of 1933–45 as "a small moment" or of the contemporary world as an example of God's "everlasting kindness." Many students of the Holocaust regard the catastrophe as a consequence rather than a cause of the modernization of Europe's economy and society.[29] In contrast to Maybaum, who interprets the Holocaust as the last gasp of medievalism, they maintain that the *Shoah* was a thoroughly modern, albeit demonic, enterprise in both spirit and method. One can credit Maybaum with courage for following his theological position to its logical conclusion without finding his position credible.

Non-Orthodox Interpretation of the Holocaust: The First Edition of After Auschwitz

I did not hear of Maybaum until many years after the 1966 publication of the first edition of *After Auschwitz*. Had I read Maybaum before writing the first edition, I would certainly have referred to him in explaining my reasons for rejecting the traditional biblical theology of covenant and election. Such a theologically controversial position was not initially triggered by intellectual speculation but by a crucial encounter with Dean Heinrich Grüber in Berlin on August 17, 1961, as I explain elsewhere in this volume.[30]

As we have seen, Grüber was also convinced that the Holocaust was God's work. However, where Maybaum likened Hitler to Nebuchadnezzar as God's "servant," Grüber likened Hitler to Nebuchadnezzar as the "rod of God's anger." In effect, Grüber asserted that God sent Hitler to punish the Jews at Auschwitz *because Israel, God's chosen people, had sinned and nothing can happen to the Jews save that which God intended.* As stated above, Grüber had no doubt that Hitler would be punished and that his actions, humanly speaking, were immoral. He also had no doubt that those actions ceased to be immoral when God was the ultimate perpetrator. Although Grüber did not identify the offense for which Israel had been punished, there is little reason to doubt that he regarded Jewish misfortune as Christian thinkers have throughout most of history. In fact, Grüber's colleagues in the German Evangelical Church meeting in Darmstadt in 1948, three years after the *Shoah*, asserted that the Holocaust was a divine punishment visited upon the Jews and, in a spirit of brotherhood, called upon the Jews to cease their rejection and continuing crucifixion of Jesus Christ.[31] In effect, the leaders of the Evangelical Church were telling the Jews that their only hope was to cease to be Jews and become Christians. While some of the document's signatories may have been motivated by malice, it is very likely that others were genuinely moved by the Jewish tragedy. Given their view of the role of the Jews in *Heilsgeschichte*, they were incapable of seeing any other way for Jews to escape the continuing wrath of Divinity.

Since the extraordinary encounter with Dean Grüber, I have often asked myself whether my views on God and the Holocaust would have changed as radically if Grüber had not been German and if he had offered his opinion in a less crisis-laden historical moment and a less apocalyptic setting than the former capital of the Third Reich during the week the Berlin Wall was erected. The dramatic encounter with Grüber strongly influenced the change in my views. Above all, the Berlin setting dramatized the fact that *the question of Holocaust and Divinity transcends academic speculation and is fraught with consequences in people's lives.* This is certainly the case in contemporary Israel, where radical messianists see the Holocaust as a divinely ordained prelude to the settlement of the whole land of Israel, the destruction of the mosques on the Temple

Mount, the rebuilding of the Holy Temple, and the climax of Jewish and world history with the coming of the Messiah.[32]

I have never had any doubt that Grüber was a man with an uncompromising sense of religious vocation. When his theological colleagues met at Darmstadt in 1948, some may have been motivated by anti-Jewish hostility and residual sympathy for National Socialism. That was not the case with Grüber. Like Maybaum, Grüber took his faith in the God-who-acts-in-history with the utmost seriousness, knowing full well what such a faith entailed. He did not attempt to avoid its painful, logical consequences. If God acts in history, it was clear to Grüber that He alone was the ultimate Author of the Holocaust. Grüber had the courage of his convictions, whether he was expressing his opposition to National Socialism during the Third Reich or affirming his belief in the God of the Bible.

There was, however, an important difference between Grüber and Maybaum. Ironically, the rabbi had used the Crucifixion as his model for interpreting the Holocaust, whereas Grüber had based his interpretation on the theology of covenant and election. Grüber saw the Jews as guilty offenders against God's Law. In fairness to the Dean, he had a similar view of his own people. By contrast, Maybaum could neither challenge God's sovereignty nor imagine any crime that would justify extermination at the hands of the Nazis. He had no doubt about the innocence of the victims. This compelled him to turn either to the model of the Suffering Servant or to the Crucifixion. Given his commitment to faith in the God of covenant and election, Maybaum had no option save to regard the Jews as innocent sacrificial victims.

When I left Grüber's home, something within me had changed irrevocably. Undoubtedly, the change had been gestating for a very long time. As a doctoral candidate at Harvard, I had attended Paul Tillich's illuminating lectures on classical German philosophy and I had been reading Freud, Hegel, Nietzsche, Alexandre Kojève, Sartre, and Camus, in addition to the Aggadic literature that was to become the subject matter of *The Religious Imagination*.[33] Nevertheless, the encounter with Grüber convinced me that I could no longer avoid the issue of God and the Holocaust. There was little Grüber had said about Jewish misfortune that had not been spoken by the prophets and rabbis in the past. Grüber was a man of courage who, because of his beliefs, could not have offered any other opinion. Since Grüber's position was essentially in harmony with Scripture, I finally acknowledged that an inescapable difficulty was involved in the position of both Grüber and traditional Judaism. I expressed these new convictions in March 1966 in the symposium, "The State of

Jewish Belief," published in *Commentary* and included them in the first edition of *After Auschwitz*:

> I believe the greatest single challenge to modern Judaism arises out of the question of God and the death camps. I am amazed at the silence of contemporary Jewish theologians on this most crucial and agonizing of all Jewish issues. How can Jews believe in an omnipotent, beneficent God after Auschwitz? Traditional Jewish theology maintains that God is the ultimate, omnipotent actor in the historical drama. It has interpreted every major catastrophe in Jewish history as God's punishment of a sinful Israel. I fail to see how this position can be maintained without regarding Hitler and the SS as instruments of God's will. The agony of European Jewry cannot be likened to the testing of Job. To see any purpose in the death camps, the traditional believer is forced to regard the most demonic, antihuman explosion of all history as a meaningful expression of God's purposes.[34]

This statement has been interpreted as an expression of atheism. On the contrary, it contains no denial of the existence of God, although it rejects the biblical image of the God who elected Israel. After my encounter with Dean Grüber, I became convinced that Jews were confronted by an inescapable either/or: *One can either affirm the innocence of Israel or the justice of God at Auschwitz.*

Today, I understand that there can be other alternatives. We can, for example, say with Maybaum that the Holocaust victims died a sacrificial death for the sake of the coming of the messianic era *precisely because they were innocent.* We can affirm with Jewish messianists that the Holocaust was an indispensable aspect of the "birthpangs of the Messiah"; we can also affirm with American premillennial dispensationalists that the Holocaust was part of the divine timetable leading up to Christ's Second Coming, the Rapture, Armageddon, and the Millennium. Nevertheless, Jewish messianists must face the fact that millions of innocent victims died horribly for the sake of the Lord's plan. For Christian dispensationalists there is no problem of the victims' innocence since those who perished were not faithful Christians. Apart from the question of whether any utopia is worth the bloody price of a Holocaust, the messianic views justify the real death of millions for the sake of an imaginary glorious future.

Those of us who prefer to wait until the arrival of the glorious messianic future before taking it into account have yet to find a credible alternative to the dilemma mentioned above: we can either affirm the innocence of Israel or the justice of God but not both. If the innocence of

Israel at Auschwitz is affirmed, whatever God may be, He/She is not distinctively and uniquely the sovereign Lord of covenant and election. If one wishes to avoid any suggestion, however remote, that at Auschwitz Israel was with justice the object of divine punishment, one must reject any view of God to which such an idea can plausibly be ascribed. Although not an atheist, I did assert that "we live in the time of the death of God." The meaning of that statement is summarized in the following passage:

> No man can really say that God is dead. How can we know that? Nevertheless, I am compelled to say that we live in the time of the "death of God." *This is more a statement about man and his culture than about God.* The death of God is a cultural fact. . . . Buber felt this. He spoke of the eclipse of God. I can understand his reluctance to use the more explicitly Christian terminology. I am compelled to use it because of my conviction that the time which Nietzsche's madman said was too far off has come upon us. There is no way around Nietzsche. Had I lived in another time or another culture, I might have found some other vocabulary to express my meanings. . . . When I say we live in the time of the death of God, I mean that the thread uniting God and man, heaven and earth, has been broken. We stand in a cold, silent, unfeeling cosmos, unaided by any purposeful power beyond our own resources. After Auschwitz, what else can a Jew say about God? (Italics added.)[35]

Today, I no longer regard the cosmos as "cold, silent, unfeeling." At the very least, insofar as man is a part of the cosmos and is capable of love as well as hate, the cosmos cannot be said to be entirely cold and silent. My earlier position can be seen as the expression of an assimilated Jew who had returned to Judaism because of the *Shoah*, devoted a quarter of a century to Jewish learning, committed himself to the defense of his people and its inherited religious traditions, and then found that he could no longer believe in the God of that tradition or in the crucial doctrines of covenant and election *without regarding Auschwitz as divine punishment.* Given both the loss of faith this entailed and the events of World War II which brought it about, my view of the divine-human relationship was, at the time, understandably bleak. Today, I would balance the elements of creation and love in the cosmos more evenly with those of destruction and hate than was possible in 1966. What has not changed is a view of God quite different from the biblical and rabbinic mainstream, as well as an unqualified rejection of the notion that the Jews are in any sense a people either chosen or rejected by God. On the contrary, Jews are a people like any other whose religion and culture were shaped so as to make it possible for them to cope with their very distinctive history and location among the peoples of the world. Put differently, I have consistently rejected the idea that the existence of the Jewish people has any superordinate significance whatsoever.

Rejection of the biblical God and the doctrine of the Chosen People was a step of extraordinary seriousness for a rabbi and Jewish theologian. These views understandably elicited the question whether anyone who accepted such views had any reason for remaining Jewish. For millennia the literature and the liturgy of normative Judaism have been saturated with the idea that God had chosen Israel and that the obligation to obey the laws and traditions of the Torah was divinely legitimated. Why, it was asked, should anyone keep the Sabbath, circumcise male offspring, marry within the Jewish community, or obey the dietary laws if the God of the Bible did not exist?

From one point of view there is considerable merit to these questions. From another there is none. Without a credible affirmation of the existence of the God of the prophets and the rabbis, Judaism becomes a matter of personal preference, a preference some may be tempted to abandon. Immediately after World War II the argument was advanced that racism prevents any escape from Jewish identity. In reality, intermarriage provides an escape route for the grandchildren, if not the children, of mixed marriages. Those who desire to abandon Jewish identity can begin the process even if they cannot complete it. Nevertheless, a knowledge of the negative consequences of unbelief does nothing to enhance the credibility of a belief system.

In the 1960s and 1970s, I responded to the question of whether Judaism can be maintained without traditional faith by arguing that the demise of theological legitimations did not entail an end to the psychological or sociological functions fulfilled by Judaism. Save for the case of conversion, entrance into Judaism is a matter of birth rather than choice. Even conversion to Christianity does not entirely cancel Jewish identity. There is an ethnic component to Jewish identity, intensified by recent historical experience, which persists long after the loss of faith. Every Jew says of the *Shoah*, "It happened to us." For non-Jews, the *Shoah* is something that happened to another people. Just as no Armenian can ever forget the Armenian genocide during World War I, Holocaust consciousness has become an ineradicable component of the Jewish psyche.[36] Religion is more than a system of beliefs; it is also a system of shared rituals, customs, and historical memories by which members of a community cope with or celebrate the moments of crisis in their own lives and the life of their inherited community.

Religion is not so much dependent upon belief as upon practices related to the life cycle and a sense of shared historical experience. No matter how tenuous the faith of average Jews or Christians, they normally find their inherited tradition the most suitable vehicle for consecrating such events as the birth of a child or a marriage. In a crisis such as the death of a parent or child, the need to turn to the rituals of an inherited tradition is even more urgent.

Although in 1966 I had become convinced that there is a void where once God's presence had been experienced, it did not follow that Judaism had lost its meaning or power or that a theistic God of covenant and election is necessary for Jewish religious life, at least for the first and second post-Holocaust generations. Dietrich Bonhoeffer had written that our problem is how to speak of God in an age of no religion. I saw the problem as how to speak of religion in an age of the absence of God. Judaism can be understood as the way Jews share the decisive times and crises of life through the traditions of their inherited community. The need for that sharing is not diminished in the time of the death of God. If it is no longer possible to believe in the God who has the power to annul the tragedies of existence, the need religiously to share that existence remains. In place of the biblical image of God as transcending the world he has created, I came to believe that a view of God which gives priority to immanence may be more credible in our era. I discuss this issue in a subsequent chapter.[37]

In mysticism and dialectic pantheism I found a view of God I could affirm after Auschwitz. Ironically, by virtue of His, or perhaps Its, all-encompassing nature, the God who is the Source and Ground of Being is as much a God-who-acts-in-history as the transcendent Creator God of the Bible, as any reader of Hegel would understand. What the dialectical-mystical interpretation excludes is the distinctive ascription of guilt to Israel and the category of divinely inflicted punishment to the Holocaust. *Creative destruction and even destruction transcending the categories of good and evil may be inherent in the life of Divinity, but not punitive destruction.*

The dialectical-mystical elements in my thinking have endured; the pagan element has proven less durable. In the aftermath of the *Shoah*, with the rebirth of an independent Jewish state for the first time since the Judeo-Roman wars, there was a certain plausibility to the argument that a people that is at home lives a very different kind of life than a band of wandering strangers. During the whole period of their wanderings, the vast majority of the Jewish people prayed that they might be restored to the land of their origin. Wherever they dwelt in the Diaspora their lives and their safety were wholly dependent upon the tolerance of others. During the two thousand years of the Diaspora, Jewish history always had a goal, namely, return to the homeland. That goal was given expression in prayers originally written in the aftermath of the Judeo-Roman Wars and still recited three times daily in the traditional liturgy.[38]

With his nineteenth-century Reform Jewish ideas about the "mission of Israel," Maybaum rejected the spirit of these prayers, arguing that the Diaspora was "progress" and an integral part of God's plan for humanity. By contrast, I identified the Diaspora as a form of communal alienation and further argued that the Holocaust had demonstrated how hazardous it is for any people to be utterly dependent for their security on a majority that regarded them as religiously and culturally alien, especially in times of acute political, social, or economic stress.

If Jewish history had as its goal return to the land of Israel, Jewish history appeared to have, at least in principle, come to an end when that goal was attained in 1948 with the establishment of the State of Israel. It may have made sense to worship a God of history while Jewish history was unfulfilled, that is, while Jews still envisioned the goal of their history as a return to Israel in the distant future. The Jewish situation changed radically when that goal appeared to have been attained. Not only did Jewish history seem to have come to an end, but after Auschwitz the God of History was no longer credible. In the biblical period, whenever the people had felt at home in the land, they turned to the earth gods of Canaan. Biblical monotheism had effectively defeated polytheism but not necessarily nature paganism. After Auschwitz and the return to Israel, the God of Nature, or more precisely the God who manifests Himself, so to speak, in and through nature was the God to whom the Jews would turn in place of the God of History, especially in Israel. This is consistent with the view that religion is essentially the way we share the crisis moments, that is, the turning points, of both the life cycle and the calendar. My rejection of the biblical God of History led me to a modified form of nature paganism.

With the passing of time, however, the pagan spirit that predominated in *After Auschwitz* receded into the background. That paganism was inextricably linked to the idea that a significant portion of the Jewish people was "at home" in the land of Israel. However, most of the world's Jews were not "at home" in Israel. Even those domiciled within its borders were ever mindful that the fragile state and its people could be annihilated were Israel's neighbors ever to win a single decisive military victory. Moreover, the majority of the Jews of the Diaspora had no desire to settle there. Clearly, the "goal" of Jewish history had not been reached and Jewish history was not at an end. On the contrary, having returned, the people of Israel may be faced with the prospect of an unending, non-negotiable life-and-death struggle against an implacable league of enemies. There may be intermittent periods of relative peace, but the historical model governing the Arab view of Israel remains that of the Crusades.

CHAPTER 9

Covenant and Divinity

THE HOLOCAUST AND THE PROBLEMATICS
OF RELIGIOUS FAITH, PART 2

Emil L. Fackenheim

The first theological response to the Holocaust that was received with widespread favor within the Jewish community was that of Emil L. Fackenheim (b. 1918), a Reform Rabbi and a distinguished philosopher who left his native Germany in 1939 and spent the major portion of his career teaching philosophy at the University of Toronto.

Fackenheim's thinking about God and the Holocaust must be seen against the background of his fundamental religious position. Fackenheim believes that both Judaism and Christianity affirm an "actual Divine Presence" that can and does manifest itself in the real world. This Presence is neither an intellectual hypothesis about God nor a mere subjective feeling on the part of the believer. It is the Presence *par excellence,* a Presence that is revealed in Scripture but hardly confined to it. Fackenheim has written that "in a genuine divine-human encounter—if and when it occurs—Divinity is immediately present to the believer."[1] Fackenheim explicitly denies that the social sciences have any constructive role in comprehending the Presence. The Presence is a real, not an imaginary or projected, datum of the believer. The Presence can be met; it cannot be argued into or out of existence. Fackenheim's religious thought, including his reflections on the Holocaust, can thus be seen as an attempt to spell out the consequences for contemporary religious faith of the experience of the Divine Presence.

It is, however, important to keep in mind that Fackenheim's position has evolved considerably as his own reflections about and knowledge of the Holocaust have deepened. Fackenheim has written that for more than twenty years he was convinced that the Holocaust was not a theological problem for Judaism. Judaism, he argued, was subject to no historical refutation until the time of the Messiah.[2] In the late sixties, he changed his mind: "Doubtless the greatest doctrinal change in my whole career came with the view that at least *Jewish* faith is, after all, *not absolutely immune to all* empirical events" (italics added).[3]

Recently, Fackenheim has elaborated on that change, expressing agreement with Rabbi Yitzhak (Irving) Greenberg's observation, cited in the previous chapter, that "the Holocaust poses the most radical counter-testimony to both Judaism and Christianity. . . . The cruelty and the killing raise the question whether even those who believe after such an event dare to talk about a God who loves and cares without making a mockery of those who suffered."[4] Fackenheim's view of revelation is quite different from the traditional view.[5] Fackenheim emphatically rejects the idea that the Holocaust was divine punishment. Moreover, he is no more able to accept the doctrine of covenant and election *as understood by Orthodox Jews or Christian fundamentalists* than I. Fackenheim's idea of the Divine Presence is by no means identical with the traditional biblical-rabbinic God, who rewards obedience to his commandments and punishes disobedience. Fackenheim also rejects Maybaum's idea that the victims were in any sense sacrificial offerings.

As early as 1951 Fackenheim distinguished the *presence* of Divinity from the explicit *content* of the covenant:

> Revelation thus remains a mystery even while it is being revealed; and every single word spoken by any prophet is inexorably shot through with human interpretation. Franz Rosenzweig observed: "Revelation is not identical with legislation; it is, in itself, nothing but the act of revelation itself; properly speaking, it is completed with the word *vayyered* ('and He descended'); even *vayyadaber* ('and He spoke') is already human interpretation." . . . Orthodoxy identifies the human—if ancient—interpretation of revelation with revelation itself. . . . All interpretation of revelation is human.[6]

The above passage points to a fundamental difference between my position and Fackenheim's. I am a native-born American who has been more deeply and persistently influenced by conservative American Protestantism than Fackenheim. While in no sense rejecting the idea that the text of Scripture requires interpretation, *I am convinced that when one is confronted with doctrinal issues as fundamental as God's relation to Israel, the "plain meaning of Scripture" must be taken very seriously.* If Scripture depicts

God as demanding Israel's obedience on pain of dire punishment for disobedience, we cannot soften the intent of the text because we are embarrassed by its modern application, namely, that Hitler is to be seen as
a modern Nebuchadnezzar. On the contrary, we are faced with a choice
that can neither be evaded nor glossed over: *either Scripture's account of
the covenant is credible, or, however we understand God, Divinity is not the
biblical God-who-acts-in-history-and-chooses-Israel.* My Berlin meeting with
Dean Grüber was decisive because both of us took the plain meaning of
Scripture seriously. Grüber accepted its meaning. I had too much respect
for the integrity of the text to water down its meaning. Since I could not
accept Hitler as a modern "rod of God's anger," there was no alternative
save rejection of the biblical doctrine of covenant and election.

In reality, Fackenheim also rejects the *literal* biblical doctrine, although he continues to employ Scriptural imagery *as if* he affirmed the
old tradition. This is neither dishonesty nor evasion. It represents an honorable and creative but very different approach to religious faith, an approach that holds that all revelation is mediated by believers who stand
in a particular historical context and who reflect that context in the way
they understand and testify to their encounter with Divinity. As we shall
see, for Fackenheim the context in which the Jewish people experience
the Divine Presence after Auschwitz is radically different than it was
before.

In his early writings Fackenheim expressed no doubt that God was
present at the Holocaust, as indeed He had been encountered in all of
the decisive moments of Israel's history. According to Fackenheim, God
has revealed Himself in Jewish history through a series of "root experiences," events of such decisive character that they influenced all subsequent periods of Jewish life. These "root experiences" include the
Exodus from Egypt and the giving of the Torah at Sinai. Both at the Red
Sea and at Sinai, Israel experienced the saving activity of God, which
shaped her character ever after. At Sinai the saving God was also experienced as a commanding God. Moreover, in every age Israel has recol-
lected these "root experiences" not as events of a long-vanished past but
as present assurances that "the saving God of the past saves still."[7]

In addition to "root experiences," Fackenheim held that Israel experienced "epoch-making events" that have tested and challenged the
"root experiences" with new and terrible situations. The destruction of
Jerusalem, first by the Babylonians and then by the Romans, constituted
such epoch-making events. In both cases, the test was met. In spite of
the overwhelming nature of the tragedies, first the prophets and then the
rabbis taught their community to hold fast to their faith in God's presence

in history and to their hope that God would redeem Israel in the future as he had in the past. These were by no means the only epoch-making events. Throughout the long night of the Diaspora, Israel's "root experiences" were tested over and over again. In every instance, Israel reaffirmed its commitment to the "saving and commanding" God of the Exodus and Sinai.

According to Fackenheim, the Holocaust was the most radically disorienting "epoch-making event" in all of Jewish history. Insisting that the Jewish people must respond to this shattering challenge with a reaffirmation of God's presence in history, Fackenheim acknowledged that it is impossible to affirm God's *saving* presence at Auschwitz. Nevertheless, he insisted that while no "redeeming Voice" was heard at Auschwitz, a "commanding Voice" was heard and that the "commanding Voice" enunciated a "614th commandment."[8] The new commandment is said to be that "the authentic Jew of today is forbidden to hand Hitler yet another victory."[9] Fackenheim has spelled out the content of the 614th commandment:

> We are, first, commanded to survive as Jews, lest the people of Israel perish. We are commanded, second, to remember in our guts and bones the martyrs of the Holocaust, lest their memory perish. We are forbidden, thirdly, to deny or despair of God, however much we may have to contend with Him or with belief in Him, lest Judaism perish. We are forbidden, finally, to despair of the world as the place which is to become the kingdom of God lest we help make it a meaningless place in which God is dead or irrelevant and everything is permitted. To abandon any of these imperatives, in response to Hitler's victory at Auschwitz, would be to hand him yet other posthumous victories.[10]

Probably no passage written by a contemporary Jewish religious thinker has become as well known as this. It struck a deep chord in Jews of every social level and religious commitment. Most of Fackenheim's writing is on a philosophic and theological level that is beyond the competence of the ordinary layman. Not so this passage, which is largely responsible for the fact that Fackenheim's interpretation of the Holocaust has become so influential within the Jewish community. A people that has endured catastrophic defeat is likely to see the survival of their community and its traditions as a supreme priority. Fackenheim gave this aspiration the status of a divine command. Instead of questioning whether the traditional Jewish understanding of God could be maintained after Auschwitz, Fackenheim insisted that God's Presence to Israel, *even in the death camps,* was not to be challenged on pain of being considered a posthumous accomplice of the worst destroyer the Jews have ever known. The passion and the psychological power of this position is undeniable. There were, however, unfortunate consequences. Those Jews "who denied or despaired" of the Scriptural God were cast in the role of accomplices of Hitler. Given the influence of Fackenheim's ideas within the Jewish community, that was a matter of considerable seriousness. Moreover, Fackenheim went so far as to suggest that those who did not hear the "commanding Voice" at Auschwitz were *willfully* rejecting God: "In my view, nothing less will do than to say that a commanding Voice speaks from Auschwitz, and that there are Jews who hear it and Jews who *stop their ears* (italics added)."[11]

Fackenheim excluded or ignored the possibility that some Jews might honestly be unable to believe that God was in any way present at Auschwitz, no matter how metaphorically the idea is presented. To stop one's ears is, after all, a deliberate act. The practical consequence of Fackenheim's insistence that the "commanding Voice" prohibited Jews to deny or despair of God has been to limit meaningful theological debate on the Holocaust within the Jewish community to those who could affirm, as did Fackenheim, that the God of Israel was somehow present at Auschwitz. Instead of seeing the Holocaust as the shared trauma that had shaken every Jew, and certainly every Jewish theologian, to the core of his or her being, following Fackenheim's lead the community has tended to treat theological dissenters as if they had handed Hitler "yet other posthumous victories." I do not regard Fackenheim as responsible for this development. Nevertheless, his description of the commanding Voice at Auschwitz gave expression to a deep-seated Jewish response to the Holocaust and defined the limits beyond which the community was apparently unwilling to tolerate theological debate.

In spite of its power, Fackenheim's position was not without difficulty even for the tradition he sought to defend. Given his conviction that revelation was inseparable from interpretation, it is not clear whether the "commanding Voice" was a real or a metaphorical event. There is now reason to believe that Fackenheim would reject both alternatives and would hold that the commandment would have been unreal without an affirmative Jewish response. One could, however, ask those who took it as a real event whether they or anyone else had actually heard the commanding Voice enunciate the 614th commandment during the Holocaust years. If language is to have any reliable meaning, *something* resembling the content described by Fackenheim had to be communicated to somebody who thereafter testified to his or her experience. Taken literally, it did not appear that anybody heard the 614th commandment, as indeed Fackenheim's recent description of how he came to write the passage would indicate. In *To Mend the World* (1982), Fackenheim told his readers that after he had come to the conclusion that the Holocaust was a radical challenge to Jewish faith, "My first response was to formulate the 614th commandment."[12]

Still, Fackenheim's language appeared to convey the idea that a precise content had been conveyed at Auschwitz by a real commanding Voice. Moreover, Fackenheim seemed to have overlooked the fact that in Judaism only God or a prophet acting as God's agent can formulate a divine imperative.

Fackenheim's critics also found considerable difficulty with his assertion that the commanding Voice had enjoined Jews to "survive as Jews." In the case of traditional Jews, no such commandment was necessary. They have always believed that Jewish religious survival was a divine imperative and had no need of an Auschwitz to receive such an injunction. In the case of secularized Jews, the "614th commandment" appeared to be a case of pedagogic overkill. It hardly seemed likely that even a jealous God would require the annihilation of six million Jews as the occasion for a commandment forbidding Jews to permit the demise of their tradition.

Perhaps the most questionable aspect of the "614th commandment" was the injunction not to deny or despair of God lest Hitler be given "yet other posthumous victories." Here Fackenheim confronted the fundamental issue of Holocaust theology, but whereas other theologians attempted, each in his own way, to offer a view of God that was not at odds with the empirical evidence of history, Fackenheim told his readers what God was alleged to have commanded.

Does that mean that Fackenheim had perpetrated a fiction in order to maintain the theological integrity of his reading of Judaism? I do not regard this as worthy of consideration. Given Fackenheim's faith in the Divine Presence, there was simply no way he could have thought of God as absent from Auschwitz. It was impossible to speak of a saving Presence at Auschwitz. Yet, utter defeat and annihilation could not be the last word. A way out of the ashes had to be found. The "614th commandment" expressed what most religious Jews regard as their sacred obligation in response to the Holocaust. In the language of Jewish faith, that response could most appropriately be communicated in the imagery of the commandments. As we have observed, the "614th commandment" is religiously and existentially problematic. That, however, is beside the point. *It is perhaps best to see Fackenheim's 614th commandment as a cri de coeur transmuted into the language of the sacred.* That would at least help to explain why it has touched so many Jews so deeply.

In *To Mend the World* Fackenheim returned to the problem of the Holocaust as a radical "countertestimony" to religious faith. Although he did not reject the notion of a commanding Voice at Auschwitz, his response to the Holocaust had lost the dogmatic edge it seemed to have a decade earlier. More than ever he emphasized the fact that the Holocaust was not a "relapse into barbarism" but "a total rupture" with the previously accepted values of Judaism, Christianity, and Western philosophy. His view is largely in accord with that of George Kern and Leon Rappoport, who have written that the Holocaust is a crisis in human behavior of such dimensions that all of the guidance mechanisms of Western society, "institutions of law, religion and obligation," proved impotent in meeting it.[13] According to Fackenheim, not only did these institutions fail to respond to the crisis, but in the ensuing years they have largely taken the path of escapism in treating the Holocaust as if it were an unfortunate incident that requires neither self-examination nor serious inquiry into how to prevent its repetition. Fackenheim insists that there can be no mending of the rupture unless the full measure of the catastrophe is understood.

Regrettably, I have come to the conclusion that the Holocaust was not the complete rupture with the values of Western religion and philosophy depicted by Fackenheim. On the contrary, given the radical demonization of the Jews in traditional Christian thought and the just-war tradition that legitimates whatever measures are necessary to combat a mortal enemy, once the Nazis succeeded in convincing a majority of Europeans that the Jews were a mortal threat to Christian civilization, it became morally acceptable for normal men and women to participate in the project of mass extermination *with a good conscience* and for the churches to remain silent and, in some cases, even to aid the perpetrators to escape after the war.[14]

Nevertheless, for Fackenheim the rupture was real, and he then asked how the mending and healing process could begin, using a term taken from Jewish mysticism, *tikkun,* to mend or restore, to denote the process. In *To Mend the World,* Fackenheim stated the nature of his quest: "But if the Holocaust is a unique and radical 'countertestimony' to Judaism and Christianity . . . how can there be a 'commandment' to resist its destructive implications, to say nothing of the will and the power to obey it?"[15]

According to Fackenheim, in no case could the mending take place solely in the "sphere of thought." The rupture had taken place in the sphere of life, and it is in that sphere that *Tikkun* must also take place. Fackenheim did not regard thought and life as opposing categories. He did, however, regard life as the prior category in the present crisis. The creation of the State of Israel "on the heels of the Holocaust" was the most authentic Jewish response to the National Socialist "logic of destruction," which had come to full expression in the Holocaust. That "logic of destruction" was totally different from all previous attempts of one people to exterminate another. Following Hitler's lead, the National Socialists regarded the Jews as vermin and bacilli rather than human beings and were determined to murder them, wherever in the world they were to be found. They were not, however, content with murder. They created a "logic of destruction" in which technical intelligence, planning, and rationality were employed in the death camp universe to bring about, first, the most extreme form of Jewish self-loathing and, then, mass Jewish *self-destruction*.

As we have noted, Terence Des Pres has identified this process as "excremental assault."[16] Des Pres and others have pointed out that the whole system had the deliberate purpose of filling prisoners with such deep self-contempt that they no longer had any wish to survive. Many of the victims were transformed into a new kind of being, the *Muselmänner*. Fackenheim cites Primo Levi's terrible description of the process of turning human beings into *Muselmänner*:

> On their entry into the camp, through basic incapacity, or by misfortune, or through some banal incident, they are overcome before they can adapt themselves; they are beaten by time, they do not begin to learn German, to disentangle the infernal knot of laws and prohibitions until their body is ready to decay, and nothing can save them from selection or from death by exhaustion. Their life is short, but their number is endless; they, the *Muselmänner*, the drowned, form the backbone of the camp, an enormous mass, continuously renewed and always identical, of non-men who march and labour in silence, the divine spark dead within them, already too empty really to suffer. One hesitates to call them the living; one hesitates to call their death death.[17]

According to Fackenheim, the most original and characteristic product of the Third Reich was the *Muselmann*, the person who is dead while alive and whose death is no longer a human death. The "destructive logic" of the system operated inexorably to mass produce those whom the Germans worked to death, transforming them into *Muselmänner* before they expired. Moreover, the power equation was such that no victim stood any chance of successfully resisting the National Socialist machine, which aimed to rule the world and did in fact rule Europe during the war.

Amazingly, there was resistance and in that resistance Fackenheim finds both the Jewish religious response to Auschwitz and the beginning of the Jewish *Tikkun*. The first response occurred when some camp inmates resisted the "logic of destruction" and prevented themselves from becoming *Muselmänner*. Resistance also took the form of pregnant mothers in the camps refusing to abort their pregnancies, hoping against hope that their children would survive and frustrate the National Socialist plan to eradicate every last Jew. It took other forms as well: Jewish partisans took to the woods to fight the Nazis in spite of the fact that Polish partisans were often as determined to destroy them as were the Germans; Hasidic Jews prayed when forbidden to pray; young Jews who could have fled to the woods elected instead to remain in the ghettos with their families in the hope of giving them some protection.

Fackenheim acknowledges that, when measured against the success of the destruction process, the number who resisted was small. That, however, was not the fundamental issue. What was decisive was that some did resist against hopeless odds. By their acts they demonstrated that the "logic of destruction" could be overcome.

Fackenheim insists that it is not enough to grasp the Holocaust universe conceptually. As a trained philosopher, he understands that when thought completes the work of philosophic comprehension, the thinker is left with a peculiar sense of tranquillity not unlike that felt by an audience after witnessing a Greek tragedy. For example, after contemplating the whole course of human history, with its record of crime, slaughter, and horror, Hegel was able to write in utter calm and philosophical detachment: "The wounds of the spirit heal and leave no scars behind."[18]

Contemplation of the Holocaust leaves us with no comparable tranquillity. The Holocaust cannot be transcended in thought. A universe that systematically aims to create *Muselmänner* is radically different from that of the tragic hero. Fackenheim therefore insists that it is not enough to understand the Holocaust intellectually, theologically, philosophically, or historically. Instead, the Holocaust universe must be *resisted* in "flesh-and-blood action and life." Moreover, once an enterprise like the Holocaust has proven its success, everything that follows is changed. State power becomes infinitely more threatening. Anti-Semitism takes on a permanently genocidal character. Civilization itself now includes death camps and *Muselmänner* among its material and spiritual products.

Those who understand something of what took place in the Holocaust can no longer view European civilization without seeing rationally organized, systematized "excremental assault" as one of its components.[19] It is, for example, difficult for a knowledgeable visitor to look at the handsome uniform of a Paris policeman without recalling that it was men wearing the same uniform, not the SS, who rounded up Paris's Jews for the cattle car trip to Auschwitz, which started on the French National Railroads. Nor can one forget that scientific papers on sadistically abusive experiments on death camp victims were read without protest at meetings of German medical societies during the war. The Holocaust has revealed new dimensions in the practice of medicine. As a result, resistance to the Holocaust universe and *Tikkun* become never-ending imperatives. It is in that sense that Fackenheim can still speak of a commanding Voice at Auschwitz.

Fackenheim stresses that it is only as a consequence of the *deed* of resistance that *resisting thought* can come to have any meaning. Such practical resistance is an "ontological category." The Holocaust, he argues, was both an ordered and a disordering universe designed to leave its victims with no possibility of reorientation so that they might escape the fate of becoming *Muselmänner* and passing from the world of the living dead to death itself. The first act of resistance was the simple decision, against all odds, to survive and, if the worst came, die the death of a human being. The second was to grasp the nature of the "logic of destruction." This is a difficult enterprise because there is always the danger, as we have seen with Hegel, that what is understood will be accepted, at least in thought. Fackenheim therefore insists that such thought must be accompanied by active resistance.

Thought and action were intertwined in those victims who found the courage to resist. Referring to these victims, Fackenheim has observed, "Their recognition of the Nazi logic of destruction helped produce resistance to it—a life-and-death struggle that went on day and night."[20] Furthermore, more was involved than mere self-protection. As the Holocaust was a *novum* in human history, this resistance was also a *novum*. It was both a way of being and a way of thought. During the Holocaust, Fackenheim asserts, authentic thought was not to be found in the greatest of philosophers such as Heidegger, who neither understood Nazism nor were troubled by the death camps, or within the circles of Europe's religious leaders. Authentic thought existed only among the resisting victims.

One of those resisting victims was a Polish Catholic noblewoman, Pelagia Lewinska, who was an Auschwitz inmate. Fackenheim cites her memoir, in which she told of her resistance:

> At the outset the living places, the ditches, the mud, the piles of excrement behind the blocks, had appalled me with their horrible filth. . . .
> And then I saw the light! I saw that it was not a question of disorder or lack of organization but that, on the contrary, a very thoroughly conscious idea was in the back of the camp's existence. They had con-

demned us to die in our own filth, to drown in mud, in our own excrement. They wished to abase us, to destroy our human dignity, to efface every vestige of humanity, to return us to the level of wild animals, to fill us with contempt toward ourselves and our fellows. But from the instant I grasped the motivating principle . . . it was as if I had awakened from a dream. I felt under orders to live. . . . And if I died at Auschwitz it would be as a human being. I was not going to become the contemptible, disgusting brute my enemy wished me to be.[21]

Lewinska's testimony is of great importance to Fackenheim. She felt under orders to resist and to survive. Fackenheim interprets her experience as evidence of the ontological dimension of resistance and of the "commanding Voice." He acknowledges that Lewinska does not tell us who gave her the orders. He does, however, tell of other victims, religious Jews, who felt they were under the same orders and had no doubt that the orders came from God.

According to Fackenheim, Lewinska's testimony represents a new kind of sanctification. In previous eras, the ultimate testimony of Jewish fidelity was *kiddush ha-shem*, the sanctification of God's Holy Name. Such fidelity was expressed when a Jew voluntarily accepted martyrdom rather than betray his or her religion. According to Fackenheim, such martyrdom no longer made sense in or after the Holocaust. There was no sanctification in the pathetic death of *Muselmänner*. Moreover, to die under any circumstance was to give the German death machine what it sought of all Jews. Thus, resistance embodied a new kind of sanctification, *kiddush ha-hayyim*, the sanctification of life. Any refusal to die and thus to outlive the infernal process became holy, not only for individual survivors but for the religious tradition National Socialism sought to destroy.

We can now understand Fackenheim's answer to the question, "Who heard the commanding Voice at Auschwitz?" It is: All who felt "under orders" to survive, resist, and overcome the "logic of destruction." Nevertheless, in *To Mend the World*, he does not seek to defend the traditional Judaism of covenant and election, reward and punishment. He is no longer interested in reducing the dissonance between the "countertestimony" of the Holocaust and the teachings of Judaism, as was, for example, Ignaz Maybaum. On the contrary, he emphasizes the rupture between the pre-Holocaust and the post-Holocaust worlds. He insists that the Holocaust is not a "relapse into barbarism" but a "total rupture." Citing Elie Wiesel, Fackenheim frankly acknowledges that in the aftermath of the Holocaust "our estrangement from God has become so 'cruel' that even if He were to speak to us, we have no way of understanding how to 'recognize' Him."[22]

Among the examples of the rupture cited by Fackenheim are the indifference of Martin Heidegger to the Holocaust and the failure of Pope Pius XII to condemn the destruction process. According to Fackenheim, even after abandoning his earlier enthusiasm for National Socialism, the greatest philosopher of the twentieth century, Martin Heidegger, was unable to be seriously concerned with the fact that his nation had introduced such prototypically modern phenomena as the death camps and the *Muselmänner* into the heart of Europe. Similarly, although the Vatican was undoubtedly one of the world's best informed institutions during World War II, the pope was unable to utter a single word *explicitly* condemning the Final Solution or warning Catholics of the danger to their souls of participation in it.

Nevertheless, Fackenheim argues that the rupture cannot, must not, be the last word. What has been broken must be mended by acts of *Tikkun*. In the past Jewish mysticism audaciously described the disasters experienced by the Jewish people as catastrophes within the very substance of Divinity. Thus, when the Jewish people were driven into exile in consequence of the Judeo-Roman Wars of ancient times, the kabbalistic tradition described God's Holy Presence, *Shekhinah*, as also going into exile. The seventeenth-century mystic, R. Isaac Luria, described the creation of the universe as a consequence of a cosmic rupture in the Divine Ground, which he called the "breaking of the vessels." This was a kabbalistic metaphor for the Jewish experience of being out of place and homeless at a particularly dark hour in Israel's history.

The mystics sought to mend both the earthly rupture, which had rendered the Jew homeless, and the heavenly rupture, which, so to speak, had made God a stranger to himself, by special prayers and rituals. They regarded these as mystical acts of *Tikkun*. Today, Fackenheim argues, new acts of *Tikkun* are required to mend the ruptured world. Such acts may prove impossible. Under the best of circumstances, they are likely to be only fragmentary. Still, we have reason to hope in their partial success because contemporary acts of *Tikkun* were already accomplished during the Holocaust years. Fackenheim cites the example of Dr. Kurt Huber, the Munich professor of philosophy, who publicly protested the acts of the National Socialist regime and, as a result, was sentenced to death on April 19, 1943, by the court of Roland Freisler, Germany's most notorious Nazi judge. Huber could easily have enjoyed the relatively comfortable life of a philosophy professor. All he had to do was to keep his opinions to himself. Instead, invoking the ideals of Kant and Fichte, he willingly took upon himself the role of philosophic martyr. Huber refused to restrict his opposition to the realm of thought. He chose to unite thought and action. While Martin Heidegger was Germany's greatest "thinker," Huber took the path of Socrates and became a martyr.

Fackenheim cites another act of *Tikkun*, that of Canon Bernard Lichtenberg of Berlin's St. Hedwig's Cathedral. On November 10, 1938, the day of *Kristallnacht*, Canon Lichtenberg beheld the monumental pogrom initiated by the Nazis and went to his church and prayed publicly for the Jews and concentration camp prisoners. He continued to do so daily until he was arrested on October 21, 1941. When brought to trial, he testified that he was scandalized by the vandalism in an ordered state and felt that the only thing he could do to help was to pray for the Jews. He said that, if freed, he would continue to do so. While in prison, he resolved to join Berlin's Jews, who had been shipped to the Polish city of Lodz, upon release. He never got the chance. He died on the way to Dachau.

Fackenheim compares the public prayer and martyrdom of Canon Lichtenberg with the silence of Pope Pius XII. He sees Lichtenberg's martyrdom as an act of *Tikkun*. As with Huber, all that Lichtenberg required for safety was silence. In both instances the "logic of destruction" was resisted not by theory but by utterly selfless action.

As noted, the first Jewish acts of *Tikkun* were the astonishing acts of resistance to total excremental assault during the Holocaust. The most profound response to the Holocaust was the collective decision of the survivors to make their way from the graveyard of Europe to the one place where Jews could be at home. He sees the establishment of the state of Israel as the fundamental Jewish act of *Tikkun*. It is, he admits, an incomplete and endangered *Tikkun*. Nevertheless, it constitutes a profound attempt to overcome the Holocaust, not in theory or by a return to the grudging sufferance of the Christian world, but by the creation of conditions in which, for the first time in two thousand years, Jews have assumed responsibility for their own future, both biologically and spiritually. Moreover, Fackenheim argues, the emergence of the State of Israel is the indispensable precondition of a "post-Holocaust *Tikkun* of Jewish-Gentile relations."[23]

During the Holocaust Jewish powerlessness was such that the survival of the Jews was wholly dependent upon non-Jews. According to Fackenheim, "After the Holocaust, Jewish people owe the whole world the duty of not encouraging its vices—in the case of the wicked, murderous instincts, in the case of the good people, indifference mixed with hypocrisy—by continuing to tolerate powerlessness."[24]

Implicit in Fackenheim's conception of the post-Holocaust Jewish *Tikkun* is a rejection of the Judaism of the Diaspora, if for no other reason than the fact that in the Diaspora Jews remain dependent upon others for their survival. Only in Israel are they in control of a state possessed of the weapons with which they can defend themselves. Mindful of the total character of the rupture created by the Holocaust, Fackenheim declares that, although Jews continue to live in the *Galut*, the Diaspora, *Galut* Judaism was probably destroyed by the Holocaust, an opinion that I share to a certain extent. I also partly concur in Fackenheim's view that, if the broken threads of Judaism are to be mended, the mending is likely to take place in Israel. Moreover, this *Tikkun* will involve both religious and secular Jews, who are bound togther by a common inheritance that includes not only the Holocaust but the Bible. Neither the secular nor the religious Jew would have found a home in Israel were it not for the Bible. The Holocaust may have driven them to the eastern shores of the Mediterranean. Only the Bible has the power to keep them there. Thus, in Israel and probably in Israel alone is there hope for the beginnings of a Jewish *Tikkun*.

It is noteworthy that the subtitle of *To Mend the World* is *Foundations of Future Jewish Thought*. Fackenheim does not offer a complete theological response to the Holocaust or a new dogmatic foundation for post-Holocaust Judaism. He merely points the way and suggests the dimensions of the task. Fackenheim's religious journey has thus taken him from his personal encounter with the National Socialist "logic of destruction" in the land of his birth, including his own incarceration in Sachsenhausen, to a period in which he reacted to the total rupture of his world by attempting to find security in a posture of dogmatic and fideistic neo-Orthodoxy, and now to a position of openness, tentativeness, and awareness of how profound the rupture has been and how fragile and beset are our post-Holocaust resources for *Tikkun*.

There was a time when my own theological position was profoundly at odds with Fackenheim's, especially with regard to his conceptions of the Divine Presence, the commanding Voice at Auschwitz, and the "614th commandment." As the dogmatic elements in his thinking have been modified, I have come to recognize him as a contemporary in the deepest sense, that is, a thinker who has shared the same time and the same spiritual agonies. When I write of the world of the "death of God" after Auschwitz, I believe I am pointing to the same reality characterized by Fackenheim as the total rupture created by the Holocaust.

A final word is in order concerning the richness of Fackenheim's thought, which encompasses, among other disciplines, an authoritative knowledge of Western philosophy, especially German philosophy in the modern period, Jewish religious thought and philosophy, and modern European history. His knowledge has enabled him to examine with great lucidity the profound character of the modern crisis. Above all, it has enabled him to move reflection concerning the Holocaust and its aftermath beyond the parochial and to demonstrate its universal significance.

Arthur A. Cohen

The late Arthur A. Cohen is another Jewish thinker who has reflected on the silence of God during and after Auschwitz. Cohen was one of the first Jewish thinkers of the post–World War II generation to publish a major theological work, *The Natural and the Supernatural Jew*.[25] Like Fackenheim, Cohen was initially silent on the problem of God and the Holocaust. He did not address that problem in a book-length publication until the 1981 appearance of *The Tremendum*, in which he explained his silence. He wrote that, like many of his peers, he "had no language with which to speak of evil (other than by exhibition and denunciation)." This left him deeply moved by the Holocaust but unable to speak of it. Cohen admitted he "had constructed a modern theology without dealing with evil, either in itself or in its horrific manifestation as *tremendum*."[26]

In the first edition of *After Auschwitz*, I criticized Cohen for writing a Jewish theology without confronting the question of God and the death camps.[27] Nevertheless, I recognized that in the aftermath of a trauma as radical as the Holocaust, it was not surprising that Jewish thinkers waited a whole generation before turning to the question. The shock was simply too great.

In *The Tremendum* Cohen took the unusual step of acknowledging the criticism expressed in *After Auschwitz*: "Richard Rubenstein was right. I had ignored Auschwitz, imagining that somehow I had escaped. But he was not right in that imputation. I did not imagine that I had escaped (or that any Jew of the non-European diaspora had escaped). But I was struck dumb and turned aside . . . and that amounts to the same thing: avoidance. The *tremendum* cannot be avoided."[28]

In writing about the Holocaust Cohen created a neologism, the *tremendum*, to denote the event. He has written that he was mindful of Rudolf Otto's characterization of God's holiness as *mysterium tremendum* when he chose his term. According to Cohen, both *mysterium tremendum* and *tremendum* convey "the aspect of vastness" and "the resonance of terror."[29] Nevertheless, the two terms refer to utterly disparate realities. In contrast to God's awesome holiness, Cohen saw the Holocast as "the human *tremendum*, the enormity of an infinitized man, who no longer seems to fear death or, perhaps more to the point, fears it so completely, denies death so mightily, that the only patent of his refutation and denial is to build a mountain of corpses to the divinity of the dead, to placate death by the magic of endless murder."[30]

Cohen offered a further explanation of his use of *tremendum* in connection with the Holocaust: "I call the death camp the *tremendum*, for it is the monument of meaningless inversion of life to an orgiastic celebration of death, to a psychosexual and pathological degeneracy unparalleled and unfathomable to any bonded to life."[31]

An important reason for Cohen's use of *tremendum* is that, like Otto's *mysterium tremendum*, it conveys the sense of unfathomable mystery. Cohen wrote of the "palpable irrationality" of the Holocaust, an event he regarded as surpassing all others in its extremity and its uniqueness. Cohen ruled out the possibility that the intellectual tools used by historians and political and social scientists to comprehend war, religious and social conflict, and mass slaughter are appropriate to an understanding of the Holocaust. This is a position with which I disagree most emphatically.[32] The uniqueness of the Holocaust does not make it opaque to historical and scientific research.

Like Fackenheim, Cohen eventually came to see that the Holocaust had rendered problematic faith in the biblical God of covenant and election. Nevertheless, Cohen was more explicit in addressing the difficulties the Holocaust poses for *philosophical theism* than for the normative biblical-rabbinic view of God's relation to Israel. (Let us recall that the philosophical problem is the perennial question of the contradiction between an omnipotent and omnibenevolent God and the existence of even a single case of innocent suffering.) Cohen argued that a constructive theology after the Holocaust must have at least three characteristics:

1. God must abide in a universe in which neither evil nor God's presence is accounted unreal.
2. The relation of God to *all* of creation, including demonic elements and events, must be seen as meaningful and valuable.
3. The reality of God can no longer be isolated from God's real involvement in the life of creation.

Cohen asserted that, if any of the three characteristics is without foundation, God ceases to be anything other than a "metaphor for the inexplicable."

Like most of the other Holocaust theologians, Cohen leaned heavily on the kabbalistic theology of Isaac Luria (1534–72), as mediated by the scholarship of Gershom Scholem. In attempting to satisfy these criteria, Cohen also acknowledged his indebtedness to an existentialist tradition appropriated for Jewish thought by the German-Jewish thinker Franz Rosenzweig (1886–1929). This tradition was spelled out most completely by Hegel's contemporary, the German philosopher Friedrich Wilhelm Joseph von Schelling (1775–1854). Schelling in turn was strongly indebted to the medieval Rhineland mystic Jakob Boehme (1575–1624) and to the first words of the Fourth Gospel, "In the beginning was the Word."

The idea of human freedom is crucial to Cohen's Holocaust theodicy. Relying heavily on the aforementioned sources, Cohen held that in the beginning the divine *Urgrund* (Primal Ground of all reality) overflowed its original and absolute self-containment in a movement of love. As long as God was all-in-all and nothing existed, so to speak, beside Him, there could be no manifestation of divine love or divine personality, both of which require a nondivine otherness, such as a created world and creatures capable of responding to God. The world is thus for Cohen, as for his theological predecessors, God's created other lovingly formed by the divine Word. However, without the presence of man, the world would be devoid of freedom and incapable of responding to God's love or to His personality. It is man who, partaking of God's speech and His freedom, is alone capable of responding to God. According to Cohen, freedom was originally intended by God to be tempered by reason, thereby preventing it from becoming willful caprice. Unfortunately, this did not happen, and man's freedom, without which he could not be human or respond to God, eventually became the willful caprice of the Holocaust.

Cohen was especially concerned with responding to those who complain of the silence of God during the Holocaust. He argued that this complaint is in reality a mistaken yearning for a nonexistent, interruptive God, who is expected magically to intervene in human affairs. According to Cohen, if there were such a God and if He were capable of interfering in history, creation would be an extension of God rather than an independent domain brought into being by God's creative love. Freedom, the essence of man, would be nonexistent, and human beings would be mere automatons. Put differently, if man is free, God cannot intervene in human affairs, no matter how depraved human beings become.

Cohen's position is summarized in the following statement:

> What is taken as God's speech is really always man's hearing. . . . God is not the strategist of our particularities or of our historical condition, but rather *the mystery of our futurity,* always our *posse,* not our acts. If we can begin to see God less as the interferer whose insertion is welcome (when it accords with our needs) and more as the immensity whose reality is our prefiguration, . . . whose plenitude and unfolding are the *hope of our futurity,* we shall have won a sense of God whom we may love

and honor, but whom we no longer fear and from whom we no longer demand (italics added).[33]

Clearly, Cohen did not see God as having a concrete role in history. He thus rejected the idea that God was ultimately responsible for the Holocaust. Instead, he relegated God's active role in history to the future, a theological strategy not unlike that of the German theologian Jürgen Moltmann. It is, however, subject to much the same criticism: *by denying God's role in contemporary history and by relegating His decisive activity to the future, Cohen, like Fackenheim in his earlier period, consigned God's activity to a domain wholly inaccessible to empirical confirmation and hence subject to every conceivable flight of fancy.* One can say almost anything about God's future activity because there are no hard facts against which such claims can be measured. Although powerfully evocative, one wonders what actual content can legitimately be assigned to words such as "the hope of our futurity."

Nevertheless, Cohen did not see God's presence in history as limited to the indefinite future. Cohen described the divine life as "a filament within the historical but never the filament that we can identify and ignite according to our requirements."[34] Cohen held that man has the power to "obscure, eclipse, burn out the divine filament," but it is not in God's power to limit human freedom. Insofar as God takes an active role in human affairs, it is as Teacher *par excellence.* The speech of God offers humanity a teaching with which to limit the destructive and capricious elements in human freedom. According to Cohen, that teaching is to be found in the *Halakha,* the corpus of rabbinic law. Moreover, beyond the role of Teacher, God exercises no direct interference with human freedom.

There is, of course, a very powerful reason why Cohen refrained from seeing God as playing a greater part in history than that of "divine filament." Had Cohen done so, he would have been confronted with all of the difficulties that flow from seeing God as the ultimate Author of the Holocaust. Nevertheless, one can ask whether the problem of God and the Holocaust has been solved by limiting God's role to that of "divine filament" and Teacher of essentially free agents. *By such a limitation, Cohen may have portrayed God as functionally irrelevant.* A human being prepared to accept the consequences of his or her actions will have no reason to take God-as-filament into account. As long as such a person is prepared to accept the costs as well as the benefits of his or her deeds, there will be no reason to be concerned with a God who places no restraint on human freedom.

Cohen thus stressed the impotence of God before human freedom, a position not unlike that of the Orthodox Jewish thinker Eliezer Berkovits.[35] According to Berkovits, God created free men, not automatons. This has had the paradoxical consequence that "while He [God] shows forbearance with the wicked, He must turn a deaf ear to the anguished cries of the violated."[36] Both Cohen and Berkovits insist that the Holocaust was not the work of a punishing God but of men who obscenely used their freedom for mass destruction.

The election of Israel is another traditional doctrine Cohen sought to defend. Cohen argued: "The death camps ended forever one argument of history—whether the Jews are a chosen people. They are chosen, unmistakably, extremely, utterly."[37]

Cohen's defense of Israel's chosenness is less than persuasive. One must ask whether he has confused being targeted for annihilation by men with being chosen by God. Unless one sees the Holocaust as either divine punishment or some sort of vicarious sacrifice, as does Maybaum, it is more likely to raise doubts about rather than serve as proof of Israel's election. In and of itself the Holocaust simply reveals the obvious fact that Europe's Jews were successfully targeted for annihilation. The fate of the victims demonstrates, if any demonstration be needed, that in times of acute stress Jews are in danger of becoming the target *par excellence* of the nations of the world. This is hardly identical with being chosen by God.

Like Fackenheim, Cohen recognized that the Holocaust has resulted in a Jewish return to history, by which he means a return to a situation in which, at least in the State of Israel, Jews are dependent upon themselves rather than host peoples for their survival. As noted, Fackenheim regards the return as the beginning of a Jewish *Tikkun*. Cohen's assessment was less positive. He opined that the return to history may prove "more threatening even than genocide has been, for in no way is the Jew allowed any longer . . . to repeat his exile amid the nations, to disperse himself in order to survive."[38] In a similar vein Cohen commented that immersion in a history without transcendent meaning may lead to a modern form of paganism: "History without a capstone, time without eternity, the present moment without the inbreeding of the *eschaton* leaves us, as Jews, with little more than the chthonic vitalities of our blood as shield and buckler."[39]

The Greek word *chthonos* means "earth." Cohen thus concluded that absent faith in some version of the God of History the Jewish return to history is likely to be a return to a modernized version of a very ancient earth paganism. I had come to a similar conclusion two decades earlier, although there is far more evidence today of the revival of traditional Judaism and apocalyptic messianism than of earth paganism in contemporary Israel.

Cohen was unwilling to rest content with a Jewish people enmeshed in the powers of earth. Having failed to find a "beyond" for the individual Jew, he refused to abandon hope in the immortality of the Jewish people as a sacred collectivity. In the light of this hope, he saw the State of Israel as a far less significant response to the Holocaust than do the other Holocaust theologians. According to Cohen, a Jewish state is no exception to the rule that political states are part of the incessant rhythm of history's rise and fall. Hence, the eternity of the Jewish people cannot take a political form. Cohen wrote that he stands outside the wall of the Jewish state as well as any other state. Nevertheless, he does not stand outside of the Jewish people, which, he asserted, constitutes "the eternal speaking of revelation to the Jew of history." In view of the twentieth-century experience of the Jews, Cohen understood his position to be problematic, for *if the Holocaust has a single overriding lesson, it is that there is no limit to the obscenities a determined and powerful aggressor can freely visit upon stateless, powerless victims.* In the aftermath of the Holocaust, the survivors could no longer trust their safety to anyone save themselves. They risked their lives to create a Jewish state in the full knowledge that it might be destroyed by its enemies. If the state survived, they would enjoy a measure of normal human dignity; if it perished, they would at least die honorably defending themselves rather than as pathetically impotent victims of some future excremental assault.

Cohen's critics have found much to praise in *The Tremendum*. They have, however, tended to find his attempt at a constructive Holocaust theology the weakest part of the book. Nevertheless, if Cohen failed to offer a credible post-Holocaust theodicy, his failure probably tells us more about the inevitable difficulties confronting Jewish theology after Auschwitz than about any lack of ability or brilliance on his part. Put simply, it may be impossible to affirm the traditional Jewish God without also affirming ideas every post-Holocaust Jewish thinker, save Maybaum, has rejected, namely, that the Holocaust was either divine punishment or some kind of mass sacrificial offering for the sake of messianic redemption. Cohen himself apparently recognized the limitations inherent in any attempt to write Jewish theology after the Holocaust. He writes: "I have promised only to cross the abyss. I have not promised to explain it. I would not dare."[40] Yet, if Cohen has failed to offer a credible post-Holocaust theology, his failure can, with justice, be described as tragic rather than personal. Let us recall that tragedy is not so much the story of human error or folly as it is the inexorable unfolding of a destiny wholly resistant to human intention. When Oedipus learned that he was destined to kill his father and marry his mother, he did everything he could to evade that destiny. Nevertheless, every evasive measure only brought him closer to the fated denouement. For the best and certainly the most understandable of motives, Cohen may simply have attempted the impossible.

The Survival of Faith in the Traditional God

Does that mean that the ancient and hallowed faith in the biblical God of covenant and election has no future among religious Jews? On the contrary, it is probably the one theological option most likely to have a future. Whatever doubts secularized Jews may currently entertain, that belief has been the hallowed, authoritative faith of the community of Israel from time immemorial until the modern period. It has given the Jewish people the supremely important gifts of meaning and hope. Instead of viewing their experiences as a series of unfortunate and essentially meaningless happenings, biblical-rabbinic faith has enabled the Jewish people to see their history as a meaningful expression of their relations with God. Moreover, no matter how desperate their situation became, their faith enabled them to hope that, sooner or later, "Those who sow in tears will reap in joy." The old biblical-rabbinic view that God is the ultimate Actor in history and that the Jewish people are bound to him by an eternal covenant remains the most coherent, logically consistent way of understanding Jewish experience and history which is acceptable to the Jewish people. In my own theological writings I have pointed out the bitter, yet inescapable, consequences of affirming that faith after Auschwitz. Nevertheless, no credible theological alternative has emerged which does not deny the very foundations of normative Judaism.

I have also become convinced that most religious Jews will eventually affirm faith in the God of covenant and election, even if such an affirmation entails regarding Auschwitz as divine punishment. Faith in covenant and election appear to be indispensable to the Jewish religious mainstream. One does not have to be a Jew to be a monotheist. What distinguishes Judaism is the faith that God has chosen the Jewish people to serve and obey Him by fulfilling his commandments as revealed in Scripture and authoritatively interpreted by the rabbis. Only a Judaism that is firmly rooted in the divine revelation at Sinai can defend the community from anomy. The liberal compromises that have flourished since the Enlightenment detach Jewish life and practice from all intellectual and theological moorings. In the long run, the liberal compromises offer little more than institutionalized alienation in which functional legitimations, supported by nostalgia and the guilt the living feel toward the dead, act as surrogates for lost theological legitimations.

In the past, traditional Judaism enabled most Jews to cope with their very difficult life situation as strangers in the Christian and Moslem worlds. However, the world's largest Jewish community, the American Jewish community, is diminishing in numbers as a result of an historically unprecedented intermarriage rate. One can ask whether large-scale intermarriage may be a delayed demographic response to the Holocaust on the part of those who no longer believe, as Jews once did, that Judaism is worth dying for. If this is the case, it is very likely that outside of Israel the Jewish religious mainstream will eventually consist primarily of a relatively small remnant who continue to affirm faith in the God of history and the election of Israel. Without traditional faith, there may simply be no reason for Jews to remain eternal strangers in a predominantly Christian world.[41]

Moreover, most Christian religious authorities expect Jews either to affirm faith in the biblical God of covenant and election or to accept Christ as their Savior. From an evangelical perspective, the Jews are the chosen people to whom God sent His Son as humanity's Redeemer. In the Christian view, the Jews have, of course, failed to recognize the true nature of Jesus Christ. Hence, God's election passed from the Israel "according to the flesh" to the Israel "according to the spirit," which consists of all those who have recognized Christ's true nature. Nevertheless, believing Christians have no doubt that, sooner or later, at least a "saving remnant" of Israel will finally see the light.[42] Like Judaism, Christianity cannot abandon the doctrines of covenant and election.

Moreover, Christian influence on Jews and Judaism is far greater than is often recognized, especially in the United States. By virtue of the fact that both Christians and Jews regard the Bible as of divine inspiration, Christians give Jews a context of plausibility for their most deeply held beliefs. If Jews lived in a culture in which the majority accorded the Bible no greater respect than the Greek myths, Jews might still hold fast to their beliefs, but they would receive no cognitive reinforcement. Even the fact that Jews and Christians disagree about the true nature of Jesus reinforces the context of plausibility, for the disagreement is about the true meaning of the Book both regard as divinely inspired.

The profound influence of American Christianity on American Judaism, even Orthodox Judaism, ought not to be underestimated. The world's largest Jewish community lives in and is ultimately dependent for its security and the security of the State of Israel on the world's largest Christian community. The State of Israel's strongest American Christian supporters are Fundamentalists, especially Protestant premillennial dispensationalists, who believe in the inerrancy of Scriptural revelation and who also believe that the return of the Children of Israel to the Promised Land is an indispensable element in God's plan for humanity's salvation in Christ. As conservative Christian influence continues to grow within the United States, it will encourage Jews to affirm a faith rooted in biblical revelation.

Thus, both external and internal influences foster a renewed Jewish affirmation of covenant and election. Even those Jews whose reasons for remaining in the Synagogue are primarily ethnic rather than religious are likely to convince themselves that the principal beliefs of the Jewish mainstream are true. To do otherwise would be to create too great a dissonance between belief and practice. If the survival of the Jews as a group outside of Israel is perceived to depend upon religious affiliation and some measure of Jewish religious practice, which in turn are thought to be legitimated by faith in the God of covenant and election, even those whose basic commitment is ethnic are likely to find some way to affirm *the only system of religious belief that legitimates Jewish survival.* The alternative is to abandon Jewish identification altogether. That alternative is actually being taken by the unprecedented number of young Jews who marry non-Jews and whose children or grandchildren are raised as Christian. While this is not the context in which to discuss the widespread phenomenon of intermarriage among contemporary Jews, that phenomenon must be seen as a powerful response to the Holocaust on the part of those Jews who have asked themselves Fackenheim's question concerning the morality of exposing distant descendants to anti-Semitic indignities by bringing children up as Jews. Those Jews who believe that in preserving Judaism they are fulfilling God's will have no difficulty in exposing their descendants to the potential hazards of a future catastrophe. Those who have lost that faith have no reason for so exposing their descendants. Religious belief and practice will remain in tension as long as the traditional legitimations of Jewish religious practice cannot be affirmed. Traditionally, the entire body of Jewish religious practice was founded upon the belief in God's revelations to Moses, the patriarchs, and prophets. As long as this fundamental belief is not affirmed, there will be a painful dissonance between Jewish religious practice and belief. As the horror of the Holocaust recedes in time, religious Jews, although greatly diminished in number, may once again find themselves reducing the dissonance by declaring with the traditional Prayer Book that "because of our sins all this has come upon us." That time has not yet come, but it may very well be on its way.

Of necessity, those Jews will reject the interpretation of Divinity I have set forth in these pages. That is to be expected. It is by no means certain that Judaism can survive without faith in the God of Israel as traditionally understood. I can only hope that those who affirm the traditional interpretation of God are motivated by honest belief rather than the conviction that, true or false, such a credo must be given verbal assent for the sake of Jewish survival, often hoping that their children will be able to believe what they cannot. A proud and glorious tradition deserves more than a self-deceiving exercise in bad faith.

For those of us who lived through the terrible years, whether in safety or as victims, the *Shoah* conditions the way we encounter all things sacred and profane. Nothing in our experience is untouched by that absolutely decisive event. Because of the *Shoah*, some of us enter the synagogue to partake of our sacred times and seasons with those to whom we are bound in shared memory, pain, fate, and hope; yet, once inside, we are struck dumb by words we can no longer honestly utter. All that we can offer is our reverent and attentive silence before the Divine.

CHAPTER 10

The Rebirth of Israel in
Contemporary Jewish Theology

The meaning of God in human experience is a variable that is inevitably altered by radical changes in that experience. Scientific arguments for or against the existence of God are far less significant than the life situation out of which such affirmations or denials flow. The possibilities of renewal which the Zionist movement has made available to the Jewish people are evident in the life and culture of both Israel and the Diaspora. Less evident but no less real is the influence Zionism is destined to have on the religion and theology of the Jewish people as well. It is not likely that the Jewish life situation could change so decisively without a concomitant change in Jewish religious sentiment. We see the negative side of the change in the rejection of traditional Jewish forms by most Israelis; the full significance of the positive side has yet to come to expression.

One of the most important but least noticed aspects of Zionism is the extent to which it represents a Jewish expression of the twentieth century's urge to return to primal origins. This is evident in many cultural endeavors of our times. In philosophy, Martin Heidegger has characterized his thought as an attempt to get behind more than two thousand years of European philosophy's estrangement from "being." In psychoanalysis there are similar trends. The concept of genitality as a key to the mature functioning of an adult personality casts a negative evaluation on all of the roles, status attainments, and cultural substitutions that people so frequently use as self-measures. The simple functioning of human sexuality—an act little affected by either cultural or historical variation—achieves an importance possessed by no aspect of "civilized" strivings.

Moreover, the attempt to get at the hidden and the decisive in the early life of the individual has been paralleled by an attempt to restore to consciousness the hidden and decisive in the early life of mankind. The Freudians have pursued this theme in the myth of the primal crime; the Jungians have sought to restore to mankind a life lived in harmony with primal archetypes, which our urbanization has almost destroyed. Zionism has pursued its return by making of Diaspora Judaism an episode and writing a Jewish ending to a struggle that the Roman Emperor Hadrian had seemed to terminate in a vastly different way almost two thousand years ago by rebuilding Jerusalem as the pagan Roman city of Aelia Capitolina.

Zionism is part and parcel of the twentieth century's recognition that much of the progress of mankind has been objectified self-falsification rather than progressive distillation of the best in the human spirit. The significance of Zionism does not lie in the fact that a pathetic human refuse has at last found a haven. Its real significance lies in the fact that nineteen centuries of self-distortion, self-estrangement, and self-blame have ended for a people that is now free to live its own life in its own land at every level of emotional and cultural experience.

Such a renewal cannot but affect every aspect of Jewish experience. For those who believe that religion is the quintessential expression of man's ultimate meanings, Zionism must result in a renewal of Jewish religious sentiment rather than in its ending. Perhaps, just as it took forty years for the Jewish people to lose its slave mentality and enter the earth-reality of the Promised Land at the first redemption, so the new redemption will require time before the old-new divinities can emerge.

Zionism has frequently been referred to disparagingly as a messianic movement. There is much truth in this identification but little justification for the attendant disparagement. In the more obvious sense, without messianism as an integral component of traditional religious sentiment, it is unlikely that Herzl's call would have had the enormous impact on the Jewish psyche it did. Unfortunately, the hideous character of the German and Russian experiments in political messianism under National Socialism and Bolshevism has led to a negative evaluation of all messianic movements in our time. Properly understood, messianism is essentially an attitude toward time and history rather than a strictly political movement. Its most characteristic feature is its fervid desire to bring time and history to an ending. Thus the study of messianism is called eschatology—"the word concerning the end." *The goal of messianism is neither the end of man nor the end of civilization; its real goal is the end of historical man.* In a very real sense, all of the twentieth century's attempts to return to primal origins, including Zionism, are attempts to make a circle out of a process that previous generations regarded as linear and progressively developmental. The goal of much of the twentieth century's cataclysmic strivings has been to put an end to the development of historical man.

In the deepest spiritual sense, Zionism is and must be antihistorical. Zionism, the Jewish people's yearning to return to its ancient homeland and to find there a creative union with earth and earth's powers, begins with the alienation of that people from its soil. For almost two thousand years Jewish history has been the history of Jewish alienation. Hegel, perhaps the world's most sensitive critic of the ontological foundations of culture, intuited in the Jewish people the elements of estrangement and negativity.[1] Understandably, he assumed that the slave loved his chains. Actually, the yearning of the Jewish people for an end to the very negativities of its existence, which Hegel so tellingly described, constituted its deepest eschatological hope. With the destruction of Jerusalem and Judea, two forces converged to create guilt and self-blame as the dominant psychological motifs throughout two millennia of dispersion. The stronger element was Jewish self-blame, which saw in every misfortune the hand of an angry and punitive God; the lesser element was the Christian theological tradition, already explicit in Justin Martyr, that the Jewish people's alienation from their soil and homeland was God's retaliation against a deicidal community.

In both traditions, the history of Jewish dispersion is equated with the history of Jewish guilt and punishment. An end to Jewish guilt would bring about an end to Jewish alienation. For the Christian this could come about only through submission to Christ; for the traditional Jew it could be the result only of a Jewish piety of such perfection that its realization still lay in the very distant future. For Herzlean Zionism the ending came neither through Christ nor through Jewish piety; it came through action that broke with the idea that Diaspora Jewish history was a woeful tale of Israel's sin and God's punishment. Zionism thereby demonstrated that we are prisoners of the past only as long as we permit ourselves to be. By breaking the chain of sin and punishment—a self-imposed chain in large measure—Zionism was able to bring to fruition the *telos* that was the goal of Jewish history by any reading, traditional or secular, the end of the alienation of the Jewish people from its ancestral homeland.[2]

One of the reasons that Zionism is frequently misunderstood is that an end to history is taken to mean the necessary end to suffering or tragedy. Frequently messianism has been dismissed with the empirical argument that an end to tears, suffering, and death is not visibly at hand. Similarly Zionism is often thought to be discredited by the discovery that the same human weaknesses are alive in Israel as elsewhere. This completely misses the real point. Messianism's real meaning is the proclamation of the end of history, which is characterized by the return to nature and its vicissitudes rather than the abolition of nature's tragic and inevitable necessities. History does not conclude with the abolition but with the restoration of *ananke* (necessity). Now nature's inevitabilities are seen as part of the tragic course of existence itself rather than as God's chastisement for human sinfulness.

Historical man, with his Lord of history and his estrangement from nature, saw suffering primarily as the payment of a debt exacted by an angry Master. Even nature itself was interpreted as punishment, born not of necessity but of wrath. Death, for example, came to be seen as the "wages of sin" rather than the natural termination of organic existence. To the necessary and ineradicable anxieties of natural existence were added the unnecessary fears, anxieties, and estrangements that characterize contemporary culture. For many, the Freudian couch is a cultural necessity, a last resort after the violation of nature's necessity. The tallest skyscraper is small consolation for failure to achieve the permissible and essential joys of the body. Art fails deeply to satisfy when it substitutes for rather than celebrates and affirms life. The dehumanization of the human spirit is the final term in historical man's self-estrangement. The death camps of the twentieth century may yet prove to be no aberrant accident representing a soon-to-be-forgotten fortuity. They may prove to be the terminal expression of man's historical existence. Unless humanity overcomes its history, the camps may truly prove to be the foretaste and substance of things to come.

The people who, in their estrangement, gave historical religion to mankind and who have suffered most bitterly from it are today the first to put an end to history and begin posthistorical existence.[3] The return to Israel's earth is more than a mere real estate transaction or some American's act of charity toward a poor relative. The result of the attainment of the goal of Jewish history must inevitably be that the people of Israel will cease to see gratification as a future hope and will learn to live their lives so that each generation takes its fair share of life's joys and sorrows, knowing that it will be succeeded by other generations who will repeat the cycle rather than improve upon it.[4] Nor does Zionism mean an end to life's inevitable insecurities. It merely means an end to the interpretation of insecurity as guilt, with its psychic impediments to those joys that are realistically available. Sooner or later Israel's Jews will come to understand that they have no need of distant utopias or far-off lands, that their task is to enjoy the fullness of being in the present. This is, in principle, a decisive turning of world-historical significance. The deliberate turning of the people of the religion of history to the religion of nature is a moment of *kairos* fully in keeping with the twentieth century's return to primal origins and primal circularities.

Increasingly, Israel's return to the earth elicits a return to the archaic earth religion of ancient Palestine. This does not mean that tomorrow the worship of Baal, Asherah, Astarte, and Anath will supplant the worship of the God of Abraham, Isaac, and Jacob; it does mean that earth's fruitfulness, its vicissitudes, and its engendering power will once again become central spiritual realities of Jewish life, at least in Israel.[5]

In the religion of history, only man and God are alive. Nature serves only as the material of tool-making man's obsessive projects. Nature does not exist to be enjoyed and communed with; it exists to be manipulated and subordinated to man's wants—the fulfillment of which brings neither happiness nor satisfaction. In the religion of nature, ahistorical, cyclical religion, man is once more at home with nature and its divinities, sharing their life, their limits, and their joys. The devitalization of nature, no matter how imposing, has as its inevitable concomitant the dehumanization of man and the loss of *eros*. Herbert Marcuse states the issue extremely well when he writes of the subordination of the logic of gratification to the logic of domination. Only in man at one with nature is *eros* rather than eroticism possible.[6] The return to the soil of Israel promises a people bereft of art, nature, and expansive passion a return to *eros* and the ethos of *eros*. In place of the Lord of history, punishing man for attempting to be what he was created to be, the divinities of nature will celebrate with humanity their "bacchanalian revel of spirits in whom no member is not drunk."[7]

In the religion of history every generation is different from previous generations. In addition to its own burden of guilt, it must bear the guilts of all who have preceded. The effect is darkly cumulative. In the religion of nature, all generations are essentially the same; they grow, they unfold in ecstatic creativity, they ripen, and finally they return, becoming the substance of other individuations that repeat the cycle. Nature and humanity are one; nature is humanity's true being and strength; humanity is nature's self-reflective expression. Fertility, fecundity, and joy are nature's piety rather than God's sins. Only *hubris* is humanity's real sin, and *hubris*, humanity's sin against its limits, characterizes its refusal of the ecstasy and passion of existence as well as its insistence on too great an aggrandizement of them. *Hubris* characterizes humanity's refusal of its limits. When all sins have been reduced to their final term, humanity's greatest sin will be understood to be its sin against its own being.

Enthusiasm for nature must, however, be tempered by an understanding of the indispensability of the historical period. The return
reveals the dialectic quality of reality, in which existent beings, as distinguished from Being Itself, are fulcra, balancing life and death, individuality and universality, love and hate, growth and decay.[8] Only the dead
are without contradictory tensions. The return to earth does not cancel
out history's gains. It assures that the fruits of that period will be properly
enjoyed. Unending greed, acquisition, and repression are key motifs of
the historical period. There is, however, a profound difference between
possession and inner gratification. The historical period has provided the
fruits that call for its own abolition.

Nowhere is the ironic character of possession, the fruit of history, as
visible as in half-assimilated Diaspora Jewry. The problem is not to do
away with possession but to acquire the capacity to enjoy what one possesses and to seek to possess no more than what one can enjoy. Only an
end to alienating guilts and their history can create the ground of such
enjoyment.

Hegel saw the end of history as producing, as one of its fruits, the
healing of the wounds of history and the spirit so that they reveal no
scar. It is too early, and Jewry's wounds too deep, for that moment to
have come to Israel, yet a beginning has been made. A break with history
means a break with history's hurts. Others may want to perpetuate the
memory of Israel's injuries and a relation of resentment to those responsible for it; but Nietzsche taught us that resentment is the slave's aggression. Free people living in the present deal realistically with it in terms
of its promise and its necessities. This does not mean that the past is to
be forgotten or ignored. One can learn from the past; one must never be
enslaved to it.

The return to Israel has been characterized by a major break with
membership in a middleman-minority as the characteristic form of Jewish
economic and social existence.[9] Middleman-minority existence was the
externally imposed lot of an otherwise unemployable people. It often
brought wealth but hardly ever honorable status. Here again the ironies
of possession and enjoyment are relevant. A religion that proclaimed its
relevance and universality for all people was, in large measure, the possession of a very limited segment of the middle class. That there is a
connection between traditional Jewish values and the requirements of a
pariah commercial class has frequently been understood and commented
upon. One of the great weaknesses of Diaspora Judaism has been its
inability to transcend middle-class forms and sentiments. In the West this
has been achieved most successfully by the Roman Catholic Church.

In Israel the growth of the *kibbutz*, the compulsory military service of women, and the simple national need of a laboring class represent a decisive break with the predominance of middle-class forms as the root expression of Jewish existence.[10] This does not mean that middle-class life deserves its frequent caricatures, or that any other form of social existence is necessarily better or more humanly satisfying. It does mean that the life and experience available to Jews who wish to continue to be religiously identified now include a wider range of vocational options than was possible when the synagogue was a predominantly middle-class institution.

Above all, an old-new understanding of God is almost inevitable in our times. With the end of man's estrangement from nature, it is very likely that there will come an end to God's estrangement from nature as well. No more will God be seen as the transcendent Lord of Nature, controlling it as if it were a marionette at the end of a string. God will be seen as the source and life of nature, the Being of the beings that ephemerally and epiphenomenally are nature's self-expression.

There are parallel developments elsewhere. Paul Tillich has proclaimed the death of the God of theism, the Lord of History. He has also called for the expression of religion and life's meanings in the idiom of art, and has understood God as the Ground of Being of which all identifiable individualities are but partial and epiphenomenal expressions.[11] Tillich believed that an end to man's estrangement is implicit in Christ; we see an end to estrangement implicit in the return to Israel's earth and to the divinities at the source of that earth.

The dark wisdom of Heraclitus proclaimed that all things are alive with gods. In the return to the earth of Israel we become aware of the fact that we, too, are alive with and are the expressions of the powers and divinities of that earth. Only historical man in his alienation sees nature as devoid of the divine.[12] Humanity at home with itself sees the cosmos as alive with the very same life that infuses its own being. That is why the ancients depicted their gods as suffering, mating, dying, and being revived. Humanity in its at-one-ness with the gods did not deny or annul passion or tragedy; it celebrated them as divinity's very life, without which divinity itself would be an empty abstraction. No return, however, can deny the intermediate negativities. As Hegel understood, they are taken up (*aufgehoben*), sublimated, in the final reconciliation. For Israel the return to nature will not mean a return to polytheism, though such a step has its real attractiveness. The unity of God will continue to be maintained, for the Lord of History has given us insight into the partial and tentative character of all polytheistic representations of the life and source of the cosmos. God will be seen as one, but He will be understood to participate in nature's vicissitudes and necessities rather than to create them outside of His solitary, transcendent perfection.

A new understanding of God arising out of the return to earth and nature must inevitably confront the issue of the dark side of divinity. The archaic ancients knew that the word holy—*kadosh-sacer*—contained a hidden awesomeness that transcends all categories of goodness, virtue, and morality. For the Lord of History there can be no such issue, for all guilt and darkness rests on man's side. Not so, in the religion of nature. Insofar as there is a sense of mankind's unity with nature and nature's source, a demonic aspect to reality and divinity must be accepted as an inescapable concomitant of life and existence. To say that God and nature are at one with each other, that they are alive and life engendering, is to affirm the demonic side not alone in us but in divinity as well. The tragedies, ironies, and ambiguities of existence cease to reflect historical man's willful rebellion; they become internalized in the self-unfolding of divinity. Virtue ceases to be a choice of discrete alternatives and becomes an overcoming. The contradictory character of existence makes goodness and virtue an overcoming in us as well as in divinity. The very character of life makes the divine source a ceaseless self-striving in which the unending negativities and affirmations of existence follow one another and in which individual forms of life are expressions of the self-construction and self-separation of divinity. Life on life is thrust forward in divinity's ceaseless project to enjoy its hour and then to become the consumed substance of other life. Such a view of divinity makes tragedy and destruction inescapable and ineradicable. Paradoxically, though it ascribes an ontic quality to evil, it possesses far more compassion than the terrible view that makes of evil a free act of will. In place of a moral philistinism that draws small comfort from the knowledge that others are more guilty, it affirms, but also endows with proportion and measure, both the loving and the demonic in man.

History comes to a stop religiously as it will politically.[13] Religiously it achieves an ending in the recognition that there is absolutely no way out of the incessant self-strife of *eros* and *thanatos*, of individuation and group formation, of affirmation and negation, which is the very life of the cosmos and its divine Source. The circle can be ended only by universal cosmic death through the implosion of the entire universe to its original state before the "Big Bang"; however, the Greeks enjoyed a wisdom that taught that even the return of all things to their cosmic starting point may be infinitely repeatable. The existence of the present universe hints at the possibility that Nothingness cannot tolerate its own solitude and that, were the present cosmic era to end, there would be other cosmic ecstasies of Nothingness.

I therefore conclude that Zionism can be far more than the provincial strivings of the Jewish people. In Israel the Jewish people are in the process of completing what they and fate had long ago begun.[14] Spirit has in principle returned from its estrangement; and history, man's inescapable negativity, has returned to the nature that gave it birth. Some will maintain that a theological interpretation of Zionism is irrelevant, that it is a movement lacking both old and new gods. Yet long ago the Romans argued that the Jews, worshiping an invisible God, were atheists. The past two millennia have demonstrated that the assertion reflected insensitivity to a power the Romans could neither understand nor cope with. Today the world's largest shrine to that invisible God stands, as visible proof of Rome's turning, in the city of Rome itself. It may be that the resurrection of the divinities of Israel's earth again looks like atheism to those who only know or deny the Lord of History. For the Lord of History any recognition of the earth gods is a blasphemy; these divinities may, however, be very real and very potent expressions of contemporary Israel's inner vitality. Atheism is, in any event, a term of limited utility. Denials are frequently pregnant with new religious affirmations.

With the closing of the circle of exile and return, religious Jews need no longer be strangers to art and creative passion. Hopefully old guilts and resentments will dissolve in the fullness of an existence devoid of "unlived lives," for the first time in many millennia. Perhaps in the place of apologetic literature elaborating upon Jewish "contributions" to civilization and morality, a dubious gift at best by any reflective standard, there may arise, not in books but in life, a new Jewish contribution, the example of self-liberation and self-discovery, of humanity restored to its only true hearth—the bosom of Mother Earth. Such a return could also be part of humanity's slow recognition of its links to nature in which the heedless pollution of the planet is finally reversed and all peoples once again render homage to the "gods" of earth, air, fire, and water.

CHAPTER 11

War, Zionism, and Sacred Space

In the first edition of *After Auschwitz*, I detailed my conviction that, with the return of the Jewish people to their ancient land, the maternal and matriarchal aspects of deity, often denied in normative rabbinic Judaism, would again come to the fore. Earth is, after all, both a nurturing and a cannibalistic mother from whom we have come and to whom we must inevitably return. The powers of earth and the divinities of the earth, I thought, might "again become decisive in our religious life."[1]

These views appear to have been disconfirmed by the course of events. In the early years of the State of Israel, a Canaanite movement among a small group of writers and intellectuals attempted to deny all connection between life in Israel and the religion and culture of Judaism in the Diaspora, but this essentially literary movement had little lasting influence.[2] On the contrary, neither the Canaanite movement nor liberal Judaism but Orthodox Judaism has manifested the greatest vitality in *Eretz Israel* (the Land of Israel) and the Diaspora. What greater proof could there be that the return to Eretz Israel entailed no revival of the ancient earth deities, however understood?

Or so I thought for many years—but no longer. A new Orthodoxy has appeared, so passionately attached to both the territorial dimension of Judaism and the imminent messianic climax of Jewish history that it is willing to endanger the security of the state to gain its objectives. Its drive to bring about messianic redemption through settlement of the whole Land of Israel expresses the same attachment to sacred space and, unwittingly, to the earth deities as was felt in Palestine before the emergence of biblical Judaism.

This new orthodoxy is radically different from Orthodox Judaism before the 1967 Six-Day War. Before that war, Diaspora Orthodoxy was politically quiescent, concentrating its energies on creating new centers of religious life and learning to replace the great centers destroyed in eastern Europe. In Israel, the Orthodox were involved in coalition politics with the secular Labor-Zionists to guarantee rabbinic control of marriage, divorce, and adoption laws plus adequate state financing for a separate system of Orthodox schools and yeshivas.

After the 1967 war, under the influence of the teachings of Rabbi Abraham Isaac Kook (1865–1935) and his son Rabbi Tzvi Yehuda Kook (1891–1982), the most activist wing of Israeli Orthodoxy became messianic and identified settlement of the whole of *Eretz Israel*, including Judea and Samaria, as a fundamental religious obligation of all Jews and an indispensable prelude to the climax of Israel's redemptive history. The elder Kook was the Chief Rabbi of the Ashkenazic community of Palestine under the British mandate from 1921 to 1935. Almost all of Kook's Orthodox rabbinic contemporaries had been opposed to the Zionist movement and immigration to Palestine, which was being settled primarily by secular Jews. Unlike his peers, Kook interpreted the return to Zion in messianic terms and taught that secular Jews were unwittingly playing a role in Israel's redemptive history. According to Kook, by settling in *Eretz Israel*, and working its soil, secular Zionists were fulfilling the divine plan for the coming of the Messiah and Israel's redemption. Eventually, Kook believed, secular Zionists would come to understand the redemptive significance of their achievements and would return to authentic Judaism.[3]

Both the father and the son believed that the return was *athalta de geulah*, the beginning of the messianic redemption. The father, who died in 1935, before the Holocaust, had avoided linking concrete events too closely with the actual hour of redemption. Not so the younger Kook. Even though Tzvi Yehuda had lived in Eretz Israel during World War II, he was nevertheless deeply affected by the catastrophic destruction. He taught that, with the establishment of the State of Israel, final redemption is imminent and all Jews are obliged to further the process of redemption by extending Jewish sovereignty over the whole land of Israel.[4]

Although he did not publish as much as his father, Tzvi Kook had a more direct impact on contemporary Israel. Perhaps the most important event in his career took place on the eve of Israel Independence Day in May 1967, three weeks before the Six-Day War. Kook gave a commemorative sermon in which he told his disciples of his unhappiness on the occasion of the founding of the State of Israel when he learned of the decision of the United Nations to partition Palestine into two states, one Jewish, the other Arab: "I sat alone—quiet and depressed. In those very first hours I was not able to accept what had been done, that terrible news. . . . Yes, where is our Hebron—have we forgotten it? And where is our Schechem, and our Jericho, where—will we forget them?! And all of Transjordan—it is all ours, every single clod of earth, each little bit, every part of the land is part of the land of God—is it in our power to surrender even one millimeter of it?"[5]

Kook was then asked by his disciples whether it was permitted to view the military parade scheduled for the following day in Jerusalem. He is reported to have replied, *"Of course, know that this is the army of Israel that will liberate the land of Israel."*[6] When, three weeks later, his disciples found themselves citizens of an Israel that included Hebron, Shechem, and Jericho, they were convinced that God had indeed manifested his redemptive power and that their rabbi had been blessed with the spirit of prophecy. Kook's prestige was enormously enhanced.

When, as a result of the war, Jews regained control of all of Jerusalem for the first time in nineteen hundred years, most Jews were surprised to discover how much *sacred space* meant to them, in particular, the site of the ancient Jerusalem Temple. I shall never forget my own unexpectedly strong feelings in the summer of 1967 as I stood at the Western Wall, popularly known as the Wailing Wall, for the first time on the evening of Tishe B'Ab, the fast day that commemorates the destruction of the Temple by Nebuchadnezzar in 586 B.C.E. and by Titus in 70 C.E. Nevertheless, the rediscovery of sacred space—an ongoing phenomenon throughout the whole of the return to Zion culminating in the capture of the Temple Mount—was not without vexing problems. Although the Israeli government was committed to religious freedom for all groups, Orthodox Jews began to consider the question of the restoration of the Temple, the quintessential expression of Israel's sacred space. One group of Hasidic Jews in Jerusalem are today actually weaving the vestments that they expect will be worn by the priests when the Temple is rebuilt.[7]

Until the Six-Day War Israel's Orthodox Jews were content to wait passively for redemption, leaving the restoration of the Temple to God. The situation began to change after the war and changed radically when the apocalyptic messianic movement, Gush Emunim (the "bloc of the faithful"), came into being shortly after the 1973 Yom Kippur War. *Gush Emunim's stated purpose was to advance "the Zionism of Redemption."*[8] According to Gush Emunim, the Zionist movement, the Holocaust, the establishment of the State of Israel, and occupation and settlement of all the land of Israel, including Gaza and the West Bank, are divinely ordained redemptive preludes to the messianic climax of Jewish *and* world history. That climax will, of necessity, involve removing the mosques that currently stand on the Temple Mount, not necessarily by human agency, and the restoration of the Temple. Many of Gush Emunim's views have been held by Orthodox Jews who have no intention of lifting a hand against the mosques. Gush Emunim was different. According to one student of the movement, Gush Emunim's "uniqueness and novelty lies not in its 'political radicalism,' nor in its messianism as such, but rather in its transformation of the Jewish messianic vision into a radical and all-embracing programme to be fully implemented 'here and now.'"[9] *Of especial importance has been Gush Emunim's insistence that the settlement of Judea and Samaria, the so-called West Bank, is a divinely mandated religious obligation of the highest priority.* Gush Emunim regards Jews as partners with God in the ingathering of the exiles and in the wars that have finally brought the whole Land of Israel, Eretz Israel, under Jewish control. Gush Emunim further insists that this partnership must continue until the Temple is rebuilt and a messianic king reigns over Israel. Moreover, the messianic climax of history is believed to be imminent.

Convinced of its divine mandate, Gush Emunim is unwilling to seek any accommodation with the Palestinians involving trading territory for peace. To surrender any part of the land would, in their view, be to set Israel in opposition to God and to reject the redemption. Gush Emunim also believes that *the redemption of the entire world* depends upon the settlement of the "whole" Land of Israel and the restoration of the Temple by observant religious Jews. This view is largely shared by many American Dispensationalist Protestants, who see the return of the Jewish people to Eretz Israel as an indispensable sign of the completion of history and of Christ's Second Coming. Moreover, the Dispensationalists have been among Gush Emunim's strongest political and financial supporters.[10] Like the Zealots who disregarded the superior power of the Romans in the Judeo-Roman Wars of 66–70 and 132–35 C.E., articulate spokespersons for Gush Emunim express no fear of the final military conflict between Israel and her enemies, confident that God is on Israel's side.[11] Nor are they concerned that Israeli intransigence might alienate whatever support Israel enjoys in the United States and elsewhere, claiming that, by reason of the covenant, Israel is "a people that dwells alone and that shall not be reckoned among the nations" (Num. 23:9).

Thus, attachment to the sacred space of the Land of Israel has so preeminent a value to the followers of Gush Emunim that all other values and religious obligations are to be subordinated to it. Unlike traditional Orthodox Jews, who separated themselves institutionally and socially from religiously less compliant Jews, Gush Emunim encourages its Orthodox members to work with secular Jews, provided they share the same attachment to the Land and the same commitment to settling the "whole Land of Israel" regardless of human cost. Undoubtedly, Gush Emunim's radical messianists would reject the ancient attachment to the land by worshipers of the Canaanite El, Baal, Asherah, Astarte, and Anath as *avodah zara*, the worst kind of paganism and rebellion against God's commandments. Nevertheless, I believe the members of Gush Emunim have experienced and are prepared to fight for precisely the same kind of attachment, although their commitments are expressed in the language of covenant, election, and radical messianism.

According to Jewish tradition, the basis for Israel's claim to the Land is God's promise to Abraham, "To your descendants I give this land" (Gen. 15:18). However, as noted in chapter 7, "Covenant, Holocaust, and Intifada," it is very likely that the god who promised the land to Abraham was *not* the same God who revealed himself to Moses from the Burning Bush saying "I am Yahweh and I appeared unto Abraham, Isaac and Jacob as *El Shaddai*, but my name Yahweh I did not make known unto them" (Exod. 6:3). Retrospectively, Yahweh was identified with *El* or *El Shaddai*, but it was a Canaanite deity that promised the land to Abraham.[12] Moreover, as W. D. Davies points out, one of the most persistent ideas in Scripture and later Jewish sources is that of Israel as the *center of the earth* and the Holy Temple in Jerusalem as its center. Indeed, the *'eben shetiyyah*, the Foundation Stone, which in the Second Temple occupied the place of the Holy Ark, stands at the very center of all the earth. According to rabbinic tradition, the Foundation Stone was the first solid object ever created.[13] Thus, to go up to Mount Zion is to return to the *omphalos*, the navel of the earth, the place of origin of all things.[14] As Mircea Eliade has pointed out, we find very similar conceptions of sacred space throughout the religious experience of humanity.[15] For our purposes it is important to note that the images of the *omphalos*, the center of all things, and the related images of the place of origin of all things are essentially feminine and matriarchal, deriving from the earth-mother traditions of the great mother goddesses. I believe Gush Emunim and contemporary apocalyptic Jewish messianism must be understood as passionately but unconsciously responding to that awesome, perennial phenomenon.

Nowhere does that passion manifest itself more strongly than in the attachment of the more radical members of Gush Emunim to the project of rebuilding the Temple. From the founding of the State of Israel there has always been the danger that the Arab-Israeli conflict would degenerate into a holy war over sacred space. The stoning of Jewish worshipers at the Western Wall of Jerusalem's Temple Mount and the subsequent killing of seventeen Palestinians by Israeli police on October 8, 1990, could prove to be an important event on the road to such a war. Islamic fundamentalists have done and will continue to do all they can to turn the conflict between Israelis and Palestinians into a *jihad*. In addition, some Arab leaders, like Saddam Hussein, who is not a believer, have shown no hesitation about using the power of religious symbols to move the masses. Unfortunately, Israeli society is not without a small but determined number of extremists.

Violent conflict on Judaism's most sacred space, Jerusalem's Temple Mount, has often had enduring historical consequences. It was there that Jesus of Nazareth "cleansed the Temple." By his actions Jesus challenged the political and religious authority of Jerusalem's priestly aristocracy (John 2:14–17; Mark 11:15–17). More than anything else, that act caused the Roman and Jewish leadership groups to move against him in the sequence of events that ended with his crucifixion.

After the Romans destroyed the Temple in 70 c.e., Jews were able to pray for its restoration. They could also study the laws of the Temple sacrifices, but there was no possibility that they might rebuild the Temple until 1967. Unfortunately, the Temple Mount is also regarded as a preeminent sacred space by Islam. Hence, rebuilding the Temple entails the destruction of the Mount's mosques, al-Aksa, the holiest Islamic shrine after Mecca and Medina, and the Dome of the Rock, built on the very spot from which Muhammed is reported in Islamic tradition to have ascended to heaven.

As we have noted, most Jews have little interest in taking active steps to rebuild the Temple. Moreover, many Jews—certainly all liberal and most conservative Jews—view prayer and study rather than sacrifice as the preferable media of redemption. Nor were all members of Gush Emunim prepared to instigate radical action against the Temple Mount mosques. However, Jewish messianic extremists have made a number of aborted attempts to seize and even blow up the mosques. The plotters have included army officers with a competent knowledge of explosives. For example, between 1978 and 1982 one extremist group plotted unsuccessfully to destroy the mosques. The extremists were more successful in placing bombs in the cars of the mayors of Nablus and Ramallah in revenge for the killing by Arabs of six Jewish settlers in Hebron. When one of the plotters, Yehuda Etzion, was tried for his part in the car bombing and the plot to destroy the mosques, he defended his actions as "the purification of the Temple Mount . . . from the structure now located upon it, on the site of the holy of holies, the building known as the Dome of the Rock." He further declared: "We only come to return Israel to its true purpose and destiny of Torah and Holiness . . . we are looking for the complete renewal of the true official authority—the Sanhedrin and the anointed from the House of David."[16]

The plotters acted on their own, but they were not fringe people. On the contrary, they were respected figures close to the Gush Emunim leadership. They constitute a continuing nightmare for those who hope for at least minimal Israeli-Palestinian coexistence. Nevertheless, as we shall see, their position has a certain compelling logic for anyone who accepts the traditional theology of covenant and election and is deeply moved to return to and dwell in Israel's place of primal origin.

Perhaps the October 8, 1990. Temple Mount incident was the most serious to date. The Palestinians claim that they had gathered at the Temple Mount to defend their holy places and that events got out of hand. The report of the official Israeli commission of inquiry dismissed this explanation, claiming that the government, not the mob, is legally responsible for protecting the Muslim holy places. However, the official report ignored the history of extremist attempts to destroy the mosques and the sympathetic relationship between the Likud government and Gush Emunim. Under the circumstances, it is easy to see how Palestinians could conclude that they could not trust the government to protect the mosques.

Undoubtedly, the wholehearted identification of the Palestinians with the cause of Saddam Hussein, who had threatened to exterminate half of Israel with poison gas, intensified the anger of the Israeli police when Palestinians on the Temple Mount started to throw large rocks at Jews worshiping below at the Western Wall. Jews had been gassed before—by Adolf Hitler. Whatever sufferings the Palestinians may have undergone under Israeli occupation, many Israelis came to see them as mortal enemies intent on settling for nothing less than their total destruction. Iraq's brutal destruction of Kuwait gave Israelis a mild foretaste of what they might expect in defeat. If U.S. support of Israel ever weakens, Israel's sense of isolation will intensify, lending greater credibility to Gush Emunim and its messianic program. The worst case scenario could be one in which political rationality in Israel gives way to the politics of apocalyptic messianism, as in the ill-fated Bar Kochba rebellion. This time, however, the Israelis will not go quietly into the dust.

Nevertheless, as potentially dangerous as the ideology of Gush Emunim may be, it is rooted in an authentic, traditional religious reading of Jewish history. As we have seen, when the theology of covenant and election is affirmed, the Holocaust can quite legitimately be interpreted as God's punishment of sinful Israel. That is not, of course, the only way in which God's presence can be affirmed in Jewish history and at Auschwitz. Harold Fisch, formerly rector of Bar-Ilan University, Israel's only Orthodox university, and an intellectual leader of Gush Emunim, has argued that the Holocaust was "the commandment written in blood upon the soil of Europe" in which "a new truth had been revealed . . . that the Emancipation no longer held the key to the future. The great liberal hope first proclaimed at the time of the French Revolution had come to an end."[17] Faith in the emancipation and Enlightenment was replaced by Zionism.

According to Fisch, Zionism itself was the offspring of the Enlightenment, but there was another side to the movement which could not be repressed. Zionism was also the child of "Jewish prophetic history," a claim that even the most secular Zionist could not deny. Fisch points out that in every one of the covenants with the patriarchs, Abraham, Isaac, and Jacob, "the promise of the land is included." According to Fisch, "the Jew is driven by a force as old as history itself to reunite himself with his land. It is the Holy Land where the sanctuary is to be constructed. There and there alone can Israel perform its service as 'a kingdom of priests and a holy nation.' If the vocation of Israel is a mystery, then the vocation of the land is no less mysterious."[18]

For Fisch and for Gush Emunim, prophetic history is a divinely bestowed revelation that imposes upon the Jewish people the unconditional obligation to return to Eretz Israel and restore the broken covenant with the Lord of Israel. Put differently, Eretz Israel was not meant to be a place of refuge for human refuse wanted by no other nation. Nor was Eretz Israel regained solely by human agency. God restored Eretz Israel for the redemption of Israel and, through Israel, of all of mankind.

Moreover, the linking of the coming of the Messiah with the restoration of Zion in Gush Emunim ideology is consistent with Jewish tradition. No less an authority than Moses Maimonides has asserted: "King Messiah will arise and restore the kingdom of David to its former state and original sovereignty. He will rebuild the sanctuary and gather the dispersed of Israel. All the ancient laws will be reinstituted in his days.[19]

Gush Emunim's ideology is more consistent with traditional Jewish teaching and liturgy than are either the Reform or Conservative revisions. For almost two thousand years in prayer and ritual, Jews have expressed (*a*) the fact that they were exiles and sojourners in the places of their domicile and (*b*) their yearning that God would ultimately restore them to their ancestral place of origin. In Scripture Eretz Israel is the land *promised* to Israel. During the long centuries of exile, even under crowded ghetto conditions, Jews celebrated the three great pilgrim festivals of ancient Israel—Passover, Shavuot, and Sukkot—each of which had an agrarian component linked to the land and its seasons. Moreover, the many rabbinic traditions that depict Eretz Israel as the *center of the earth* carry with them the notion of Israel as the place of origin not only of the Jewish people but of the entire world. In Jewish mysticism the yearning to return to Eretz Israel assumed cosmic significance. It was so powerful that it was expressed by all religious Jews three times a day in a series of prayers known as the *Amidah*.[20] Originally consisting of eighteen prayers, the weekday *Amidah* now consists of nineteen. Of that number, the tenth to the fifteenth are explicitly concerned with communal redemption and bringing exile to an end.

The tenth benediction implores God to gather the exiles of Israel "from the four corners of the earth," a condition Gush Emunim holds is now being fulfilled:

> Sound the great shofar for our freedom; raise the ensign to gather our exiles, and gather us from the four corners of the earth. Blessed art Thou, O Lord, who gatherest the banished ones of thy people Israel.[21]

The eleventh prayer is a petition for the restoration of the ancient theocratic polity in Eretz Israel, especially the sovereign and independent courts as they existed before the Judeo-Roman Wars. It also expresses the hope that God Himself, the Heavenly King, will reign over Israel, clearly a theological-political reference to the hope that Israel will no longer be subject to kings of flesh and blood:

> Restore our judges as in former times, and our counsellors as at the beginning . . . reign Thou over us, O Lord, Thou alone.

The fourteenth prayer presupposes the rabbinic idea that with the exile of the Jewish people after the Roman wars, God's holy *Shekhinah*, his Divine Presence so to speak, also went into exile. The prayer asks for the rebuilding of Jerusalem, the return of the *Shekhinah*, and the restoration of the throne of David, clearly a messianic reference:

> And to Jerusalem, Thy city, return in mercy and dwell therein as Thou hast spoken; rebuild it soon in our days as an everlasting building; and speedily set up therein the throne of David. Blessed art Thou, O Lord, who rebuildest Jerusalem.

The fifteenth blessing refers to the reign of the messianic King over Israel:

Speedily cause the offspring of David, Thy servant, to flourish, and lift up his glory by Thy divine help.

Over the years, few, if any, prayers have been recited with greater ambivalence than the seventeenth, which appeals for the restoration of the Temple service in Jerusalem. As we have seen, after the Six-Day War it became possible to restore the Temple and its sacrifices, *provided one were willing to incur the unremitting enmity of the entire Muslim world.* In 1967 few Jews in Israel or elsewhere took seriously the small but growing number of Jews for whom the restoration of the Temple sacrifices was a primary objective. The latter read the following prayer as a challenge to action that could not be left to God alone. The prayer reads:

> Accept, O Lord our God, Thy people and their prayer; restore the sacrificial offerings (*Avodah*) to the inner sanctuary of Thy house; receive in love and favor both the fire offerings ('*ishê*) of Israel and their prayer; and may the sacrificial worship (*Avodat*) of Thy people Israel ever be acceptable to Thee.

When these prayers were uttered after the Fall of Jerusalem, the rabbis believed their distinctive institutions and traditions were *interim arrangements* that would last only until Israel's redemption from exile. Moreover, the rabbis had no doubt the restoration would entail the rebuilding of the Holy Temple and the coming of the Messianic King. *Redemption entailed the recovery of sacred space, and vice versa.* In that sense the project of religious Zionism has always been messianic. Nevertheless, from the end of the Bar Kochba rebellion of 132–35 C.E. until modern times, there was no active Jewish attempt to restore Jewish sovereignty in Eretz Israel. On the contrary, *until the twentieth century the rabbis were almost unanimous in their resolve to prevent such an effort.*

Because of the spread of Christianity with its belief in Jesus as the Messiah and in the redemptive power of his death and resurrection, Jewish faith in the *eventual* coming of the Messiah was coupled with considerable skepticism concerning *any* report of his imminent advent. According to historian Gerson D. Cohen, between the destruction of the Jerusalem Temple in 70 C.E. and the movement of the pseudo-messiah Sabbatai Zvi (1626–76), the rabbis were almost unanimously opposed to messianic movements.[22] Gershom Scholem, the preeminent twentieth-century authority on Jewish mysticism and messianism, notes that there were localized messianic outbreaks from time to time, but they were generally lay movements. Nevertheless, the "preservers of the traditional element . . . perceived in these acute messianic outbreaks an element of nonconformity which endangered the continuity of the authoritative tradition."[23] There was, as Scholem points out, a profound aversion to the "Forcers of the End," those who could not wait patiently for the coming of the Messiah but took it upon themselves to bring about the messianic fulfillment.

Ironically, it was the emancipation of the Jews during the French Revolution that initiated the process that finally resulted in the abandonment of Jewish political quietism and the beginning of active efforts to return to Eretz Israel and, in our time, the revival of a messianism passionately attached to the land. Emancipation promised the Jews more than it could possibly deliver while making Jewish rights and even the very presence of Jews a political issue for the first time. Although sharing a common human condition with their neighbors, the Jews did not share common memories, common rituals, a common religious calendar, or a common place of origin, a matter of considerable importance in nonmobile, predominantly agrarian societies. Apart from all difference of belief, Jewish religious tradition was the repository of memories replete with exile, defeat, and injury. Jews were by no means the only people with such memories, but Jewish memories were decisive in conditioning their manner of being in the world. Moreover, as we have seen, Judaism insisted on the uniqueness of the Jewish people and its covenantal relationship with God, which included very specific promises concerning Eretz Israel. Even if there had been no rise of anti-Semitism in the nineteenth and twentieth centuries, it would have been impossible for emancipation to have been an unqualified success in the nation-states of Europe.

A foretaste of the dilemmas inherent in emancipation could be discerned in the debate on that subject in the French National Assembly on December 23, 1789. According to Count Stanislas de Clermont-Tonnerre (1752–92), a member of the assembly and an advocate of Jewish rights:

> The Jews should be denied everything as a nation, but granted everything as individuals. They must be citizens. . . . *There cannot be one nation within another nation.* . . . It is intolerable that the Jews become a separate political formation or class in the country. Every one of them must individually become a citizen; if they do not want this, they must inform us and we shall be compelled to expel them (italics added).[24]

Speaking in opposition to emancipation, Anne-Lois Henri de la Fare, bishop of Nancy (1752–1829), declared:

> The Jews certainly have grievances which require redress. . . . It is necessary to grant them protection, security, liberty; *but must one admit into the family a tribe that is stranger to oneself,* that constantly turns its eyes toward [another] homeland? (Italics added.)[25]

For the count, citizenship was a legal status of individuals; for the bishop it was the inherited status of members of an extended family who shared common memories and culture as well as a common relation to ancestral land. However, the count joined the bishop in rejecting the idea of "one nation within another nation." Jews could be French citizens only if they transformed their religion into something it had never been, an individual affair from which all external territorial aspirations were expunged.

Had France been a multiethnic political community, it might have been possible to emancipate the Jews while permitting them some degree of ethnic distinctiveness and communal cohesiveness, but France conceived of itself as a nation-state that expected its Jews to transform themselves into worthy Frenchmen, whatever that meant.[26]

The Bishop of Nancy was by no means the only Roman Catholic prelate opposed to Jewish emancipation. Emancipation was fought by the Church as an institution and by royalist circles opposed to the passing of traditional society. After France's defeat in the Franco-Prussian War of 1870, anti-Semitic movements and publications proliferated. A similar growth of anti-Semitism took place throughout much of Europe and even the United States during this period. Nevertheless, it was neither France nor Germany but the czarist empire where the principal social and economic transformations took place which were to lead to both the rise of modern racial anti-Semitism and the birth of modern political Zionism. As unpopular as was Jewish emancipation in France and elsewhere in western Europe, emancipation was, as we have seen, a political consequence of the Enlightenment. However, both the Russian Orthodox Church and the czarist government emphatically rejected the ideas of the Enlightenment. Hence, there was no official interest in the political emancipation of the Jews without conversion to the established church.

"As noted above, 1881 appears to have been a turning point for the Jewish communities of eastern Europe. Many of the subterranean economic and social forces which ultimately rendered untenable the situation of the Jews of eastern Europe finally exploded with the assassination of Czar Alexander II." The larger impact of this social explosion was felt in both North America and what was to become the State of Israel.

The situation of the Jews of Russia had been deteriorating throughout the decades of the seventies. The reign of Czar Alexander II (1855–81) appeared to begin auspiciously. On the day of his coronation, August 26, 1856, juvenile conscription, one of the most degrading aspects of the *rekrutshchina* or conscription system introduced by Czar Nicholas I (1825–1855) in 1827, was abolished.[27] Thereafter many, but by no means all, of the disabilities affecting Jews were ameliorated.[28]

The new, more liberal policies toward the Jews initiated by the czar were part of a larger trend toward rationalization of Russia's economy and political structure.[29] The policies appeared to confirm the optimism of those Jews who favored secularization, modernization and some degree of Russification. It was the hope of both the Russifying and the Hebraic parties among the modernizers that internal Jewish reform would be met by political emancipation.[30]

In spite of the optimism of the modernizers, some troubling developments had already taken place. In 1871 a pogrom in Odessa anticipated the far bloodier pogroms of 1881 and after. Like Manchester, Odessa, founded on a site that until 1789 had been occupied by the Turkish fortress of Khadzhi-Bei, was a city without an indigenous feudal tradition. Hence, it was more hospitable to economic rationalization and capitalist development than older cities like Moscow and Kiev. As a free port and seat of the governors of Novorossia (New Russia) and Bessarabia, it was the most secularized and economically liberal city in eastern Europe. The Russian authorities were interested in developing this outpost. Unlike Moscow and St. Petersburg, where the right of domicile was accorded only exceptionally to a minuscule number of Jews, Jews were permitted to settle in Odessa. From the 1880s to the Russian Revolution, Odessa had the second largest Jewish population in the czarist empire, Warsaw having the largest.[31] As the most westernized city in the empire, Odessa was the leading intellectual and literary center of the Hebrew Enlightenment. Compared with the rest of Russia, Odessa was a relatively open and liberal city. Its non-Jewish population had a relatively higher level of education. Odessa represented everything that the Slavophiles found wanting in the "new" Russia.[32]

The 1871 pogrom foreshadowed things to come. Directed primarily against Jewish artisans and small merchants, it revealed that secularized Jews were as likely to be targets of overt anti-Semitic aggression as Orthodox Jews. It also revealed that modernization, secularization, and even professional status did not prevent Jews from being targeted. One of the nastier aspects of the Odessa pogrom, again foreshadowing things to come, was the tendency to blame the victims. Both revolutionaries and conservative political spokesmen were inclined to see the violence as a response of the "people" to Jewish exploitation.[33]

As noted, the full force of modern anti-Semitism became manifest in the czarist empire in the aftermath of the assassination of Czar Alexander II on March 13, 1881 (new calendar), by members of the revolutionary terrorist group Narodnaya Volya.[34] A massive, violent anti-Semitic reaction was triggered throughout the empire—pogroms and other acts of violence exploded in 160 cities and villages—when it became known that one of the plotters, Gessia Gelfman, was of Jewish origin. When the pogroms of 1881 were followed by the "May Laws" promulgated on May 13, 1882, it was apparent that the government intended to injure and insult the Jews so harshly that they would be driven either to convert or emigrate. Emigration was the state's preferred option.

The state had abrogated the social contract, the essence of which is the citizen's obedience to the sovereign's laws in exchange for the sovereign's protection against predatory lawlessness. In czarist Russia, however, the sovereign and his agents had become the chief perpetrators of injury by their overt sympathy with the rioters and their subsequent bureaucratic violence. Whatever legitimacy the regime had previously commanded in Jewish eyes was understandably a thing of the past, especially for the young.

The long-term historical significance of the pogroms has been stated succinctly by historian David Vital: "The pogroms of 1881–4 and the sea-change which came over Russian policy toward the Jews of the Empire precipitated what can now be recognized as the first extended, tragic, and still incomplete evacuation of the Jews from eastern Europe."[35]

But where were the Jews to go? As we know, for the vast majority, the answer was the United States. The beginning of the mass emigration of eastern European Jews was in this period. Nevertheless, there were voices that rejected the United States as the goal of Jewish emigration, one of which was Moshe Leib Lilienblum (1843–1910), who had settled in Odessa in 1869. Even before the 1881 pogroms, he had become pessimistic about the possibility of the secular integration of the Jews into the empire. The May 1881 pogrom in Odessa caused him to reconsider his views concerning the viability of a continued Jewish presence in Russia. Lilienblum became convinced that the rise of anti-Semitism throughout modern Europe was not a passing phenomenon. According to Lilienblum, anti-Semitism was an expression of the universal attitude toward the stranger.[36] When the stranger competes successfully with the hungry native for sustenance, conflict is unavoidable and the stranger seldom is the victor. Before the French Revolution, the problem was mitigated by limiting Jews to those fields in which the natives had no interest or were forbidden. If, however, the native decided to enter the so-called Jewish fields, Jews were either compelled to abandon these fields or were expelled altogether. Put differently, before the Enlightenment, the caste system worked.

Lilienblum rejected both assimilation and emigration to America. Emigration to the United States would, he maintained, change nothing because the Jews would still be strangers in their new place of domicile. There was only one solution—*return to Zion*. It is important to note, however, that Lilienblum's belief in the urgency of the return was an essentially *secular, national* response to the direct experience of violent, modern anti-Semitism.

Lilienblum offered no practical solution to the problem of implementing the return. His contribution rests largely on his influence on his readers, one of whom was Leon (Yehuda Leib) Pinsker (1821–91). Born in Tomaszow, Poland, Pinsker was taken by his family to Odessa at an early age. Shaken by the 1871 pogroms in Odessa, he nevertheless remained a secular Jew committed to the assimilation of Russia's Jews to the Russian language and culture until the pogroms of 1881. The pogroms and the subsequent behavior of the czarist government convinced Pinsker that the promise of liberalism and the Enlightenment were delusions and that emigration to a Jewish national center was imperative. He formulated his ideas in one of the most important classics of the Zionist movement, *Autoemancipation: An Appeal to His People by a Russian Jew*.[37] He agreed with Lilienblum that anti-Semitism was rooted in the fact that Jews were everywhere strangers. He added, however, that most other strangers had a home somewhere, whereas the Jews led a ghostlike existence of universal alienation. He rejected the political quietism of Orthodoxy, which held that the exile must continue until the coming of the Messiah. Pinsker called for the "autoemancipation" of the Jewish people, *"their emancipation as a nation among nations* by the acquisition of a home of their own."[38] Like Theodor Herzl (1860–1904) after him, Pinsker was more interested in finding a territorial center for the Jewish people than in establishing Eretz Israel. Pinsker's Zionism was thus secular and national, arising out of his perception of the desperate situation of the Jews after 1881. It ignored the territorial dimension of Judaism and the millennial Jewish yearning to return to the place of origin.

Both Pinsker and Herzl agreed that emancipation had failed.[39] Herzl, an assimilated Jew unfamiliar with Russian-Jewish life and literature, is even reported to have said that, had he known of Pinsker's *Autoemancipation*, he might never have written the *Judenstaat*, the most important classic of modern political Zionism.[40] Pinsker was unable to create the kind of mass movement needed to organize the second great Exodus of all Jewish history, not the Exodus from Egypt but the Exodus from the charnel house of Europe. *Like Pinsker, Herzl still sought to achieve what the emancipation had promised, the normalization and secularization of Jewish life,* not by the political integration of the Jews into the nations of Europe but by the creation of an independent, secular Jewish state. Thus, early Zionism did not envision the kind of activist religious Zionism that has risen to prominence in recent decades.

In the years that separated publication of the *Judenstaat* from *Autoemancipation* the condition of eastern European Jews became ever more desperate and the need for a solution ever more urgent. Herzl was prepared to entertain *any* proposal that would give the Jews some assurance of a normal existence somewhere in the world. His resolve was further strengthened by the Kishinev pogrom of April 6–7, 1903, in which forty-five Jews were killed and more than fifteen hundred Jewish homes and shops were destroyed.[41] The pogrom was more than the spontaneous outburst of an angry mob. There were between two hundred and three hundred active rioters and twelve thousand government troops in Kishinev at the time. Nevertheless, the government did nothing to stop the violence and the slaughter until the damage had been done.[42] It was soon learned that Vyacheslav K. Plehve, Minister of the Interior, and Konstantin Pobedonostsev, Procurator of the Holy Synod, were directly implicated. Plehve and Pobedonostsev were encouraged by Czar Nicholas II.

Two weeks after the Kishinev pogroms Joseph Chamberlain (1836–1914), England's Secretary of State for the Colonies, suggested to Herzl the possibility of establishing a self-governing Jewish settlement in Uganda, East Africa.[43] The government's readiness to grant, in principle, "certain territorial" concessions was confirmed on August 14 by Sir Clement Hill, Superintendent of African Protectorates. Herzl was inclined to accept because *he saw his first priority as saving Jews, not bringing about the return of the Jewish people to Zion.* In 1903, as a result of opposition by Turkey, the power in control of Palestine, mass settlement was not a credible option. While Herzl had little enthusiasm for Uganda, he saw it as at least a way station for those eager to escape further czarist pogroms. Herzl was also concerned that Joseph Chamberlain was too important a politician to antagonize by a rejection.[44]

At the Sixth Zionist Congress in Basel, August 22, 1903, the delegates were shocked to see a map of East Africa hung on the wall behind the dais instead of the map of Palestine which had hung there at each of the previous conferences. More than words could convey, the new map was graphic, emotionally compelling evidence that the movement's predominantly secular leadership had subordinated the territorial dimension of Judaism to the work of rescue. Clearly, sacred space had little meaning for Herzl, the assimilated Jew. At the congress Herzl proposed that a committee be appointed to study the Uganda proposal. Debate on appointing a committee quickly turned into an impassioned debate on the

Uganda proposal itself. The issue was crystal clear: *Was the Zionist movement an historic movement of return to Zion, Israel's sacred space, in fulfillment of Judaism's millennial longings, or was it a purely secular movement seeking any territorial base, preferably though not necessarily in Zion, in order to normalize the Jewish condition?* Put differently, was the Zionist movement to be imbued by the spirit of God's covenant, a covenant whose earliest expression included the promise of sacred space, in which case the Jewish people could never lead a "normal" existence, or was it to be a purely secular, nationalist movement? As Harold Fisch has observed, that issue has not been resolved to this day.[45]

Herzl won a technical victory. The congress voted to appoint a committee by a vote of 295 to 177, with 100 abstentions, but the "victory" threatened to destroy the Zionist movement. The crisis was averted because English colonists in British East Africa made known their unconditional opposition to the mass immigration of Russian Jews. Chamberlain gave the project the *coup de grâce* by suggesting that the area was probably too small for Jewish settlement.[46]

Herzl died on July 4, 1904. After his death, the Seventh Zionist Congress in Basel in 1905 passed a resolution thanking the British government for "its offer of a territory in East Africa" and reaffirming its commitment to "the establishment of a legally-secure, publicly recognised home for the Jewish people." It also rejected "either as an end or as a means all colonising activity outside Palestine and its adjacent lands."[47]

Attachment to Zion, to Israel's sacred space, was too deeply rooted in the hearts of both secularist and religious Jews for any other place to be acceptable. Judaism, with its territorial dimension, had shaped the identities and culture of secular as well as religious Jews. But, the conflicting interpretations of Zionism and of the ultimate character of the State of Israel continued.

The idea of Judaism as the national, *cultural* inheritance of the Jewish people is implicit in the Proclamation of the State of Israel, Israel's Declaration of Independence, dated "the eve of the Sabbath, 5th Iyar, 5708, 14th May 1948."[48] The proclamation began:

> The Land of Israel was the birthplace of the Jewish people. Here their spiritual, religious and national identity was formed. Here they achieved independence and created a culture of national and universal significance. Here *they wrote* and gave the Bible to the world.
> Exiled from Palestine, the Jewish people remained faithful to it in all the lands of their dispersion (italics added).

This is not a statement written by traditionally religious Jews. In the Proclamation, it is the Jewish people who wrote the Bible; for Orthodox Jews, it is God who *revealed* to Moses and the prophets the contents of the Bible with its record of God's covenant with Israel and its promise of the land. Nevertheless, the Proclamation begins with an assertion of the centrality of the Land of Israel in Jewish history and Jewish experience.

The Proclamation also states:

> It is, moreover, the self-evident right of the Jewish people to be a nation, like all other nations, in its own sovereign state.

Here we discern the fundamental theme of secular Zionism, *"a nation like all other nations."* No Orthodox Jew could possibly accept this objective as valid.

As Orthodox Judaism began to recover from the unprecedented trauma of the Holocaust, it had no alternative but to affirm God's direct involvement in the Holocaust and to interpret *both* the Holocaust and the establishment of the State of Israel as decisive moments in Israel's divinely ordained redemptive history. After the German obliteration of all of the centers of Orthodox Jewish life in eastern Europe, Orthodox opposition to emigration was no longer possible. Before the war Agudat Israel was the most influential Orthodox organization opposed to emigration.[49] In 1946 Agudat Israel saw Eretz Israel as the only acceptable place of Jewish settlement. It promised its followers that it would create a life there "in the true Jewish spirit." Now God was understood as having given religious Jews a life-or-death decision, death in Europe or a life of Torah in Zion.[50] Although formulated at a later date, Harold Fisch's interpretation of the Holocaust as a sign from God not to attempt to renew Jewish life in postwar Europe but to emigrate to Eretz Israel expresses the same spirit.

An important Jewish strategy for finding meaning in a catastrophic event such as the Holocaust has been to interpret it as the imminent prelude to redemption. According to Gershom Scholem, the advent of the Messiah was not thought of as the consequence of humanity's incremental progress in history but as the reversal "of all that had produced *Galut*" (exile).[51] In early rabbinic times, R. Johanan ben Nappaha (180–279 C.E.) taught that the Messiah "will come only in a generation that is either altogether righteous or altogether wicked."[52] One could cite many such texts. As we have seen, the rabbis normally tended to play down the messianic-apocalyptic elements in Judaism, but in the aftermath of the Holocaust the messianic-apocalyptic interpretation of Jewish history took on heightened plausibility for Orthodox Jews. Gershon Greenberg, a leading authority on the Orthodox response to the Holocaust, has observed that Orthodox thinkers continued to pray for the Messiah, but the Holocaust and the return to Eretz Israel "narrowed the distance between prayer and anticipated fulfillment."[53]

In addition to the radical rethinking of religious ideology by Orthodox Jewish thinkers, other factors contributed to the growing influence of Orthodox Zionism. One factor was Israel's two state-financed school systems, a state-run secular system and an autonomous religious system. Gush Emunim's membership was largely drawn from the latter system. Another factor of great importance was the failure of secular Zionism to offer a credible system of values to replace the values of traditional Judaism.

Nonreligious Zionism was able to postpone the crisis of secularization as long as it was preoccupied with rescuing Jews from European anti-Semitism and working toward the creation of a viable Jewish settlement in Eretz Israel. Those projects gave meaning to the movement. However, the problems arising from secularism appeared long before the Six-Day War. Harold Fisch points to the 1961 trial of Adolf Eichmann in Jerusalem as an important turning point.[54] Before the Eichmann trial, there was a strong tendency, encouraged by Prime Minister David Ben Gurion and his secular Labor-Zionist government, to stress the difference between Israelis and those Diaspora Jews who went to their death without resistance. Israelis identified with the few examples of heroic resistance during the Holocaust, such as the Warsaw Ghetto uprising in April and May of 1943. As the Israeli public listened day in and day out to the testimony of survivors at the Eichmann trial and as the survivors' terrible experiences were linked with the determination of the Arab states to destroy the State of Israel, every Israeli came to identify with the Jewish people who perished in the Holocaust.

The Jewish identity of the Israelis was intensified by the Six-Day War. Immediately before the war, the Arab states boasted of their intention to drive the Israelis into the sea, and Jews throughout the world were fearful that a second Holocaust was imminent a generation after Auschwitz. As stated above, when Jews came to the Western Wall of the Temple immediately after the war, they were surprised not only by the depth of their feelings in this encounter with sacred space, but also by their sense of identification and continuity with the entire sweep of Jewish history. When I stood at the wall on Tishe B'Ab in 1967 for the first time, I thought of the countless generations of my ancestors who were consoled for the indignities they had to endure by praying that the Temple, one of the most potent and enduring symbols of Judaism, might be rebuilt "speedily and in our days." The Temple was not restored in 1967, but its site and all of Jerusalem were once again in Jewish hands.

Following the Six-Day War, many Israelis hoped to develop their country into a small nation on the model of the Western industrialized countries. The Yom Kippur War of 1973 changed this attitude, and the period between this war and the accession to power of Menachem Begin in 1977 was one of political and spiritual reorientation for much of Israel's population. Unlike the 1967 war, the Yom Kippur War of 1973 was not an unqualified Israeli success. The government was unprepared for the attack by Egypt and Syria and found itself dependent upon the U.S. airlift of weapons for Israel's survival. Israel also incurred proportionally heavier losses than in its previous wars.[55] In addition, there was a serious loss of public confidence in the Labor government as a result of revelations of economic corruption and greed among some government leaders, heads of state-owned banks, corporations, and the Histradut labor federation.[56] In the Israel of the post–Yom Kippur War period, one of the worst aspects of secular life—the tendency for communal values to deteriorate and to be replaced by the pursuit of private gain—was plainly apparent. Moreover, by attacking Israel on its holiest day, Egypt and Syria were perceived as expressing the deepest possible enmity and contempt for Judaism as well as the secular State of Israel. No Jew—secular or religious—could remain indifferent to the symbolism inherent in the attack.

In spite of the negative aspects of the Yom Kippur War, Israel retained the territorial gains of the Six-Day War, a victory which made possible a renewal of one of the most important aspects of the pioneer period of Zionism, resettlement of the whole land of Israel. As noted, the pioneering spirit had given meaning to secular Zionism in the first decades of settlement. By 1967 that spirit had lost much of its force. Tel Aviv, Israel's largest city, had become a sprawling urban metropolis with many of the problems of most large modern cities. New immigrants who found an apartment in Tel Aviv did not experience the same pioneering spirit as had the early settlers in the *kibbutzim* and *moshavim*. Moreover, it is difficult, if not impossible, to think of Tel Aviv as sacred space, as one thinks of Jerusalem.

On the other hand, the pioneering spirit and a sense of working for a meaningful communal objective were experienced by those who settled in newly conquered Judea and Samaria. Large-scale settlement was discouraged by the Labor party, but Labor was defeated in the 1977 elections by a coalition of the right-wing Likud party and smaller Orthodox parties. The new government pursued an active policy of encouraging West Bank settlement. The government offered the settlers tax and other financial inducements. The new policy was the result of an alliance between right-wing secular nationalists and Orthodox activists, especially Gush Emunim. The nationalists regarded large-scale West Bank settlement as indispensable to Israel's military security. They were also committed to the view that Israel has an undisputed right to "the whole Land of Israel."[57] Orthodox activists agreed with the secular nationalists, but they added a theological legitimation for the settlement policy: settlement of *all* of Eretz Israel rests ultimately on the covenant with Abraham, in which God promises the patriarch: "And I will give you and your seed after you the land in which you do now sojourn, all the land of Canaan for an everlasting possession; and I will be unto them their God" (Gen. 17:8).

Clearly, a new Zionist ideology, authentically grounded in the historical and religious continuity of Jewish life and tradition, was needed to give meaning and purpose to Jewish experience. Gush Emunim and Orthodox Jewish intellectuals were by far the most influential in meeting that profound need. By interpreting the twentieth-century experience of the Jews in terms of God's election of Israel and His promise of imminent messianic redemption, Orthodox Jewish thinkers made it possible to discern a coherent system of meaning in the tragedies and triumphs of Jewry in modern times. Neither the liberal optimism of Reform and Reconstructionist Judaism nor the secular nationalism of the early Zionists could match the coherence of Orthodox thought. Gush Emunim also infused the lives of its members with an idealism no secular or liberal religious reading of Jewish experience could possibly match. Gush Emunim was part of a worldwide reaction against the absence of meaning in secularism and the failure of this-worldly ideologies to supply an alternative to religion. The same forces that had brought about an enormous growth of religious fundamentalism in Christianity and Islam were at work in the rise of activist, redemptionist messianic Orthodoxy.

Nevertheless, in spite of the gain in meaning and authenticity, there are awesome dangers in the growth of the political influence of both Gush Emunim and Israeli Orthodoxy. In accordance with the teachings of Rabbi Abraham Isaac Kook, Gush Emunim recruits secular, nationalist Jews as well as Orthodox Jews for its projects. There is, however, the clear expectation that the secular Jews will see the light as redemption unfolds. Moreover, by using its power to make and break government coalitions in Israel to reject the legitimacy of all forms of non-Orthodox Judaism, Orthodoxy threatens an irreparable schism between Orthodox and all other Jews. This tendency will be exacerbated should the greater birth rate of Orthodox Jews yield a majority in Israel committed to a state governed exclusively by *Halakha* and its authoritative rabbinic interpreters. Such a state would be consistent with the redemptionist program of Gush Emunim, but it would under no circumstances resemble a state in which the minority rights of its non-Orthodox Jewish citizens, not to mention its non-Jewish citizens, would be respected.

When we turn from domestic to external considerations, the program of contemporary messianic-apocalyptic Judaism could lead to an abandonment of rational politics and a catastrophe even more terrible than that which was consequent upon the Bar Kokhba rebellion. One wonders what kind of Judaism, if any, could follow such a denouement. We have already discussed the efforts of radical messianists to blow up the mosques on the Temple Mount. One Israeli journalist, Doron Rosenblum, has expressed the fear that the destruction of the mosques is "only a matter of time."[58] Ian Lustick quotes Yoel Ben-Porat, an Israel Defense Forces reserve general, who has written:

> I personally know of fighters from elite [army] units, graduates of the finest yeshivas in Jerusalem and Judea, who are imbued with messianic fervor: "May the Temple be rebuilt speedily in our own days." These irresponsible people could get hold of a ton of explosives, and, under cover of a foggy dawn, approach the Temple Mount in a couple of armored personnel carriers . . . and plant the explosives at the Dome of the Rock. If they managed to plant a few hundred kilos, they could bring the dome crashing onto the rock, thereby visiting disaster on themselves and on us.[59]

To repeat, by no means do all members of Gush Emunim have any such intentions. Still, destruction of the mosques is the aim of some of its more radical members. Nor for those who see settlement as an unconditional divine imperative is there any possibility of serious negotiations concerning the future of the Palestinians. The identification of the Palestinians with the cause of Saddam Hussein and their well-nigh unanimous delight at Iraq's missile attacks against Israeli civilian targets makes any kind of peace settlement difficult to imagine. Nevertheless, there is a fundamental difference between negotiations aimed at arriving at a peace agreement that does not compromise national security and rigid adherence to a program of messianic redemption no matter what the consequences. The prospect of realistic negotiations aimed at some sort of a *modus vivendi* has been threatened by the rising power of Islamic fundamentalists and their goal of eliminating the State of Israel, but matters are not improved when uncompromising fundamentalists on one side confront equally uncompromising fundamentalists on the other.

Those committed to messianic politics have made it clear that they will be deterred neither by the threat of war nor by Israel's total isolation from the nations of the world, including the United States. Their understanding of covenant theology assumes both isolation and the entire world's unremitting hostility. Anti-Semitism, the Holocaust, Israel's experience with the United Nations, especially the U.N.'s Zionism-is-racism resolution, and the claims to exclusive truth set forth in a literalist reading of each of the three great monotheistic religions have rendered this dark interpretation of Israel's situation plausible to believers. Having interpreted the worst Jewish catastrophe of all time as an episode in Israel's redemptive history, the radical messianists have no reason to regard total war as anything other than the climax of Israel's final redemption.[60] Twice in Jewish history—in the wars of 66–70 and 132–35 C.E.—the Jewish people were led into war by men who were convinced that they were acting in accordance with the divine imperative and that divine assistance would assure the victory of their cause. Both wars ended in disaster. Even worse disaster awaits Israel should the views of contemporary Jewish messianists prevail.

About the time the first edition of *After Auschwitz* was published, Raphael Patai, a distinguished Jewish scholar, speculated concerning the prospects of the revival of the old earth deities, especially the great maternal deity, in the "old-new land" of Israel:

> Is the Hebrew goddess dead, or does she merely slumber, soon to awaken rejuvenated by her rest and reclaim the hearts of her sons and lovers? No one can say. But should she manage to revive, we can expect this to take place only in the Land of Israel. It was there that she first clasped to her bosom the wild Hebrew warriors who irrupted from the desert. It was there that most of her life-history, including her amazing metamorphoses took place. . . . It will be there, therefore, if at all that she will re-emerge, in who knows what surprising old-new image.[61]

As stated at the beginning of this chapter, I believe that the old earth goddess has reappeared in Eretz Israel and that her principal, though by no means only, worshipers are to be found among those religious Jews for whom settlement of the land is the overriding religious obligation, regardless of practical consequences. In 1966 I looked favorably upon the possible revival of paganism in the land of Israel. Today, I have become ambivalent about it. Admittedly, to come into contact with earth is to come in contact with the primal maternal source to which everyone is ultimately drawn. It is from her that we have come, and it is to her that we must inevitably return.

Nevertheless, it is only by *leaving home and mother*, taking upon oneself the promise and the perils of adult life, that life's fullness can truly be known. Some measure of exile—if only that of intellectual distance and critical rationality—is the price we must pay for adult existence. We know our earthly mothers most intimately when we are babes and dependent children. We know the Earth Mother as our original and final resting place, where the cycle of womb and tomb are joined. That is why an overly passionate attachment to the Land and its divinities can be so dangerous. Auschwitz taught us the worst perils of exile, but there are other perils. We must not permit a passionate yearning to return to our place of origin so to cloud our vision that we lose all perspective concerning everyday life. There is profound wisdom in the rabbinic injunction warning Israel not to "force the End." If the Messiah is to come, let it be in God's own time, not ours, lest the one we take to be the Messiah prove to be the Angel of Death.

CHAPTER 12

The Meaning of Torah in Contemporary Jewish Theology

In the nineteenth and twentieth centuries, the scholarly disciplines have achieved an ever greater measure of precision in determining the history of Judaism. This heightened sophistication has added an important element of religious difficulty to the cataclysmic social and political changes that occurred within the Jewish world between the French Revolution and the wars of the State of Israel. In a period of such vast social instability, it is hardly surprising that the theological foundations of Judaism have exhibited a concomitant instability.

Biblical scholarship has had an especially important impact on modern Jewish thought. At least one result of this scholarship seems beyond refutation: The Torah is not a document written by a single author. It is the fruit of a long period of historical development. Normative Judaism has always claimed that, save for a few verses at the end of Deuteronomy describing the death of Moses, the entire Torah is a unitary work communicated directly by God to Moses. As long as this view retained credibility, it had enormous consequences in the life of the individual Jew. If, when properly interpreted, the Torah was the perfect revelation of God's will, then none of its injunctions, no matter how opaque to common sense, could be ignored. To ignore them was to rebel against the will of the Creator.

Unlike their traditional forebears, who enjoyed a cognitive monopoly within the Jewish community, modern non-Orthodox Jews lack the security of knowing that their religious acts are meaningfully related to God's will. Whether they fulfill all of the Torah's commandments or none of them, they enter a spiritual wager not unlike that made by believing Christians who make a decision concerning the centrality of Christ in their personal life. As Kierkegaard has suggested, religious life hovers over a sea of doubt seventy thousand fathoms deep.[1]

When doubts have lain fallow for many centuries, as they have in normative Judaism, and then become the object of concerted attention, one must look beyond thought alone to comprehend the full scope of the crisis. The theological foundations of normative Judaism were most keenly disrupted in a period when Jews were entering the secular society of contract and commerce which developed in the Western world following the Industrial Revolution in England and the political revolution of 1789 in France. Full participation in the economic opportunities of the new society demanded a radical curtailment of the ritual aspects of Jewish life. These had included distinctive modes of dress, religious behavior, eating, and measurement of sacred and profane time, which had been ordained by or derived from the Torah. The decision to "reform" Judaism was as rooted in economic and social reality as it was in any purely religious need for change.[2] In a highly competitive bourgeois-capitalist society, most Jewish business and professional people in western Europe and the United States assigned a low priority to those aspects of religious life which were rooted in the priestly or the sacrificial. The well-known tendency of all branches of nineteenth-century Judaism, but especially of Reform, to emphasize the moral and the rational aspects of the Torah at the expense of the sacerdotal served a dual need: it addressed Jews most practically in their economic activities, and it sought to guide them against misuse of these activities at a time when Western Jews wanted to minimize the differences separating them from their neighbors. Moreover, the new stress on the moral aspects of the Torah provided an unconsciously formulated defense against the Judas image of the Jew which an increasingly secular society not only failed to repress but actually magnified. Psychological and economic pressures alike forced a new attitude toward the Torah by Western Jews in the nineteenth century. Just as the continuing differences between Jew and gentile were glossed over by surface similarities of dress and appearance, so too the rational and the conscious in religion were emphasized over the unconscious and the mythic. It is no accident that those Jews who tended toward greatest success in economic enterprise were usually least impeded by the priestly and sacerdotal aspects of their religion. By and large, adherence to Deuteronomy made for better and more successful capitalists than diligent attention to Leviticus, which has, in any event, been the most embarrassing book of the Torah for "enlightened," "modern" Jews.

A similar shift from the sacerdotal to the moral, from ritual to creed, in Christianity had analogous results in the rise of capitalism, as Troeltsch, Weber, and other Protestant sociologists of religion have demonstrated.[3]

But the new freedom to question and reformulate Judaism, which figured so prominently in the nineteenth century, was not expended solely in economic activities. The time was one of the most exciting in all areas of intellectual and artistic creativity. Business and professional people usually found it easier to retain a measure of loyalty to the reformulated Judaism than did creative artists and intellectuals. With an intuitive feeling for authenticity in all domains of the human spirit, the creative artist could hardly regard bourgeois, moralistic Judaism as an "advance" over the older and more traditional forms. Though the great themes of religion—sacrifice, atonement, confession, and human brokenness—which had nourished so much of the art and music of the Western world were largely of biblical inspiration, the new Judaism was as barren of artistic creativity as it was of emotional depth. This contrasts, for example, with the continuing vitality of Hasidic themes in the art of Marc Chagall and the thought of Martin Buber. The estrangement from the Torah and the life of the synagogue of those possessed of artistic creativity has remained a problem throughout modern times.

As in military strategy a good general, when faced by an apparently successful attack, withdraws and regroups, nineteenth-century Jewish thinkers, leading their ill-starred community in the land of Clausewitz and Von Moltke, employed a similar tactic. In the face of a many-pronged intellectual, spiritual, economic, and social attack against normative Judaism, they employed a withdrawing and regrouping strategy. Seeking to assert the priority of those elements of the Torah which seemed to remain relevant and defensible in their own times, they tended to distinguish between the spirit of Torah and its frequently embarrassing letter by emphasizing the abiding relevance of the moral elements of the Torah.[4] The Torah's intent, they contended, was to call people to a life of holiness, which they usually equated with the moral relations between one person and another.[5] *Imitatio dei* was reduced to fulfillment of the ethical deed. This tendency is explicit in such representative German Jewish thinkers of another day as Abraham Geiger and Leo Baeck.[6] Little was said of religious and moral failure or of the tragic inevitability that so frequently destines men and women to incur guilt in the very act of existing. Judaism, whose power had ever been enhanced by intimate contact with the tragic and the ironic, turned its back on the destined fatalities of humanity. Those aspects of the Torah which could not be translated into moral or ethical categories were discarded. The old sacrificial order and *kashruth* (the dietary laws), the continuing embodiment of the sacrificial order in everyday life, were rejected. The opaque, the irrational, and the mystical were equated with the "primitive," and a pseudoevolutionary mythology was employed to obscure their often continuing relevance. Whatever in the Torah dealt with the dilemmas of bodily existence and sought to root Jews in the vicissitudes of earth and human biology became an acute embarrassment. The ancient longing of Judaism for an existence in its own territorial domain was rejected as inconsistent with the "higher," "spiritual" forms toward which Judaism had "evolved." What remained was a desiccated, unimaginative moralism with little symbolic or mythic power.

Nevertheless, in spite of all attempts to divide the Torah into "higher" and "lower" spheres, the liturgical preeminence of the Torah has remained unchanged in Jewish life. In all three branches of Judaism, the Torah continues to be read on an annual or on a triennial basis. No distinction is made in its recitation or in preaching between the sacrificial and the moral portions of Scripture. All alike have the same preeminent status. In spite of the theological, social, and critical objections, the Torah remains the decisive center of Jewish religious life, though there is no longer any assurance that all, or even an identifiable part, expresses God's will explicitly and unambiguously. At the heart of Jewish life today is an ineradicable tension between fixed form (the Torah) and personal subjectivity, which all must endure. Long ago the rabbis asserted the primacy of the religious act over its interpretation in normative Judaism.[7] Their insight has a perennial relevance. What Jews do is often a greater indication of what they truly think than what they sometimes express verbally. To this day the central religious act at every synagogue service for the Sabbath, Festivals, and Holy Days is the reading from the Torah. One of the tasks of contemporary Jewish theology is to understand why the Torah remains the decisive center of Jewish religious life.

In order to understand the centrality of the Torah for contemporary Judaism, it is necessary to comprehend why the secular alternatives are problematic for the Jewish community. The most radical alternatives are extreme atheism and secular humanism. These positions have the virtue of unambiguous clarity. For those who accept secular humanism, the problem of Judaism ceases to exist. I reject secular humanism, not because I have a less tragic view of ultimate human destiny, but because secular humanism is unmindful of the full determinants of the personal aspects of existence, which root each individual irrevocably in a definite situation involving the shared vicissitudes of history, culture, values, and psychological perspective. Affirmation of secular humanism involves a dilution of the facticities of each person's distinctive situation. The secular humanist is most cognizant of abstract universal values that are shared with all other human beings. For religious Jews, the historical experiences of twentieth-century Jewish life are too much a part of the fiber of our beings to regard as meaningful any philosophy that ignores the actualities of present-day Jewish fate and destiny. One must be a particular kind of person with a limited, concrete life situation to be a person at all. The conception of humanity in general is a meaningless and tragic abstraction. As Hannah Arendt has shown, the process whereby Jews were turned into human beings in general, lacking all concrete legal, political, and national status, was the final preparatory step to turning them into superfluous people whose extermination was of no consequence to any existing political community.[8] Those European Jews who achieved the longed-for goal of the secular humanists, that of being merely human rather than rooted in the actualities and limitations of a historically determined community, found that this was no messianic blessing but the final preparation for annihilation.

Another alternative available to contemporary Jews is atheism combined with some form of Jewish nationalism. This is the choice of many Israelis. Atheists committed to some form of Jewish identity recognize and share with other Jews the essential particularity and "thrownness" (*Geworfenheit*) of the Jewish situation. This is the special strength of nonreligious Jewish nationalism. Nevertheless, Jewish atheism offers no way of actively participating with other Jews in the wisdom, the aspirations, the remembrances, and the insights of earlier generations. In the severity of its honesty, Jewish atheism knows the living Jewish present but little more than the surface manifestations of the Jewish past. Only he or she who can also experience or empathize with the agonies and the yearnings of past Jewish generations in their awesome confrontation with the God of Israel can truly partake of the fullness of Jewish experience.

The atheist frequently forgets that process is as important as result. Even the most pious Jews, in their innermost selves, are likely to have moments in which they regard human existence as a tragic and gratuitous absurdity, entirely without meaning save for the meanings and the projects we ourselves actualize, a life bracketed in its "thrownness" between two oblivions. In those undefended moments, the religiously compliant Jew can expect neither future boon nor salvation. Nevertheless, it is the atheist who may fail to see that *it is precisely the ultimate hopelessness and gratuity of our human predicament which calls forth our strongest need for religious community.* Even the old religious promises of redemption and resurrection have decisive meaning for those who are nevertheless undeceived concerning man's fate. Such promises still define the domain of a religious community in modern times. Only within the religious community can people share their aspirations, hopes, defeats, tragedies, and guilt. Even if we cannot unite with previous generations in a community of faith, we are the more strongly united with them in a community of shared predicament and ultimate concern. Nor could we, at this late date, invent a better medium than the Torah to unite us with our own and past generations.

The situation of the contemporary Jew is thus absurd, tragic, and free. Paradoxically, the recognition of this situation allows us to recapture for the first time in the modern period the *entire* Torah as our decisive religious text. Jewish religion is inseparable from Jewish identity. In turn, identity is inseparable from the facticity of the Jewish situation, a facticity that is historically determined.[9] Jews are not simply abstract people devoid of the defining limitations of a very special history, psychology, and culture. They are what they are as a result of the entire range of Jewish history. Part of that history involves the fact that the Jewish community is what it is because it has accepted the Torah as its decisive religious text. This is the community's concrete mode of being-in-the-world. It has had awesome and, at times, terrifying consequences in the lives and deaths of millions of Jews over thousands of years. In its dialogue with Christianity, the Synagogue insisted that its religious life required neither additions nor subtractions from the form in which the Torah had been received. The canonicity of the Torah made Christianity's way impossible for Judaism. Jews are heirs both to that text and to the historical conflicts it engendered. Nor is it likely that any amount of critical skepticism would diminish the fervor with which we take our stand. If we are no longer entirely convinced that God is revealed in and through the Torah, we are nevertheless grateful that it remains the inheritance of the house of Jacob, becoming a part of the very fabric of what we are. To deny the Torah would be to deny a supremely important element in ourselves.

The conviction that the Torah is our decisive religious text, rooted in Jewish identity if not Jewish belief, has in no sense diminished the religious insecurity in which we find ourselves. We can no longer avoid our freedom. At times we experience it, as does Sartre, as a condemnation. We hold the Torah to be holy, yet we cannot and will not eliminate the subjectivism, the voluntarism, and the consequent anxiety that in fact, if not in theory, have triumphed in all non-Orthodox, and even in some Orthodox, Jewish groups.[10] No two decisions concerning religious commitment will be identical. No modernist division of the Torah into "essential" and "inessential" elements will offer an altogether convincing rationale for a new security in religious life. There is, and there will continue to be, a recognizably anarchic element in contemporary Jewish life. This anarchy coexists with the affirmation of the Torah as supreme in Israel. The anarchy can be ended only by bringing an end to freedom. We will not pay that price.

Some of the contents of the Torah will be an embarrassment to every age, though what puzzles or embarrasses Jews in one period will not necessarily embarrass those in another. For the Reform Jews of nineteenth-century Germany and America, imbued with a fervor for moral perfection and rationality in human affairs, the sacrificial aspects of the Torah were, as noted, an acute embarrassment. I have attempted to learn from their partial vision. I propose that, as contemporary Jews, we use our freedom to ignore or reject what we find embarrassing in the Torah for ourselves alone and not, in our arrogance, to decide that our embarrassments will be shared by future generations. In this sense I reject the path of liberal Judaism, though my alternative is by no means Orthodox. The old religious dichotomies have become as theologically meaningless in Judaism as they have in Christianity.

Elsewhere, I have argued for the meaningful character of the atonement and sacrificial aspects of the Torah for contemporary Judaism.[11] At the heart of the sacrificial system lay the unspoken conviction that human beings are more likely to repeat their characteristic failings from one generation to the next than they are to improve upon them, as the nineteenth-century religious moralists had hoped. By means of the sacrificial system people were able to express their aggressive impulses in ways that enhanced communal solidarity and caused least harm to others instead of being threatened by the possibility of irrational and uncontrolled outbursts of violence, as we have witnessed in our own times. Nineteenth-century liberal Jews were so convinced that the "primitive" character of the sacrificial tradition would be shared by their successors that they expunged all reference to it from the Scripture reading of our holiest of days, Yom Kippur. True to their own preferences, they substituted a Deuteronomic exhortation to moral choice.[12] Whether they were ultimately correct in their embarrassment with sacrifice in Judaism, or we in our renewed appreciation of what they rejected, is less important than that we understand the subjective nature of freedom in religious matters. Those who claim it must do so for themselves alone. Jews are free to accept or reject all or part of the Torah as individuals. Nevertheless, such freedom carries with it the responsibility that each generation, in making its own commitments, leave the inherited corpus of tradition intact for subsequent generations to make their own choices. Here again we encounter the perennial tension between form and subjectivity in Judaism.

Many Jews today regard some provisions of the Torah as cruel, if not bordering on the barbaric. We have, for example, radically different ways of handling sexual deviance today than the violent methods enjoined in the Torah, even allowing for their humane limitation in rabbinic interpretation. Here again a measure of restraint is advisable before turning our personal values into a community evaluation. The *lex talionis* has been the object of much misunderstanding and no small measure of malice. Yet the law of an "eye for an eye" introduced an element of equity into punishment where previously retaliatory violence knew few limits. Before the imposition of the limitations of the *lex talionis*, the norm was more like that expressed in Lamech's address to his wives: "If Cain shall be avenged sevenfold, truly Lamech seventy and sevenfold" (Gen. 4:24). Moreover, few of the seeming cruelties found in the Torah have the gratuitous barbarity that is utterly rampant in modern life.

While the Torah's harsher injunctions obviously no longer obtain, as they have not for centuries, there is little in the Torah to compare with the rationalized cruelties of the twentieth century. We will never contrast unfavorably the "primitive" character of even a single verse of the Torah with the "advanced" character of contemporary civilization. Only by asserting the unity of the Torah can the essential continuity of Jewish religious and historical identity be maintained. We can rid ourselves of the Torah only by being quit of our Jewishness.

The sacrificial system undoubtedly had its origins in pre-Judaic paganism. Tradition and history alike have emphasized the pagan character of the religion of our earliest ancestors. Having learned at far too great a cost the difference between modern nihilism and paganism, today we possess increasing respect for and a sense of community with our pagan, pre-Torah origins as well as those rooted in the Torah itself. With the return of the Jewish people to their ancestral earth, it is hardly surprising that there has been a renewed interest in, if not contact with, the old gods of that land.

Place has a renewed importance for all contemporary Jews, and it is the Torah that has given all Jews the sense that the land of Israel is their holy land. Few incidents demonstrate this fact more dramatically than the Zionist response to the British offer of Uganda as a place of Jewish settlement. As noted in the preceding chapter, in April 1903 Joseph Chamberlain, then the British Foreign Secretary, suggested the possibility to Theodor Herzl. With the outbreak of the Kishinev pogroms one month later and Turkish hostility to further Jewish settlements in Palestine, Herzl was desperate to find a haven for endangered eastern European Jews. He proposed to the Sixth Zionist Congress in August 1903 that a commission be sent to East Africa to investigate its feasibility as a Jewish colony. The vast majority of both religious and secular Zionists, especially in eastern Europe, vehemently opposed the project, which was quickly abandoned.[13] No matter how desperate the situation had become in eastern Europe, Palestine alone had an emotional hold on Jewish hearts, and the source of that hold was the Torah. Modern Israel may be a secular state but its spiritual foundations for believer and nonbeliever alike rest on God's promises, recorded in the Torah, to the people of Israel concerning their possession and settlement of the land of Israel.

While Judaism has wisely asserted the ultimate unity of the God of Nature and the God of History, our times are peculiarly suited to a rediscovery and a reaffirmation of the primordial powers of earth and fatality that have on occasion bedecked themselves in the guise of the God of History. The reformers of the nineteenth century were quick to note the underlying paganism of much of the priestly tradition in the Torah; they were embarrassed and they sought to expunge this phoenix.[14] For some, it sufficed to identify a source as containing pagan relics to reject it. Understandably, those who most bitterly opposed the continuing viability of the priestly traditions were those who were most vehement in their opposition to the never-suppressed longing of the children of Israel for the earth of Israel. The earth of Israel and its gods were part of the same reality, as the liberals understood all too well.

The rediscovery of the earth of Israel, with its earthly gods, is not nearly as disturbing to us as it was to the nineteenth-century reformers. Whereas their evolutionary mythology cast the primal and the archaic into disrepute and gave to modernity a specious respectability that rested on no greater credential than temporal sequence, we have acquired a renewed respect for the primal and the archaic. While yet a student at Tübingen, Hegel bitterly complained that, in accepting Christianity, the Teutons had alienated themselves, not merely from their own past and history, but from their innermost beings.[15] According to the young Hegel, acceptance of Christianity created a radical split in the German soul which had yet to be healed in his time.[16] More than one hundred fifty years ago, Heinrich Heine warned that the rejected gods of the Teutons slumbered but had not died. Heine predicted that when Thor awoke with his mighty hammer, *there would be played out on the European scene a catastrophe which would make the French Revolution seem like child's play.*[17] We have lived through that catastrophe. For those who took it seriously, the grandeur of the Torah is that it never permitted a comparable split between archaic inheritance and contemporary identity to occur in the Jewish psyche. The priests of ancient Israel wisely never suffered Yahweh entirely to win his war with Baal, Astarte, and Anath. That is why religious Jews were never cut off from their inner life and the powers of earth which engendered it. In Judaism paganism was transformed but never entirely done away with. In the ceremony of the redemption of the firstborn son (*pidyon ha-ben*), for example, the murderous quality of paganism was deflected, but its essential insight into the need to overcome intergenerational hostility was retained.[18] Canaanite agrarian festivals were transformed into celebrations of Israel's sacred time, but their inner connection with nature's fertility was never lost. Even Jewish folkways shared in this wisdom. Whenever possible, Jews did not make their inevitable journey of return to the earth in entirely strange soil. A token of the sacred earth of the land of Israel accompanied them. Few, if any, elements, pagan or monotheistic, in the formation of the Jewish religious consciousness were ever entirely repressed in the Torah. In our era we have learned much concerning the futility of repression in personal matters. The Torah instinctively and intuitively understood this futility long ago in religious matters. Nothing within the domain of human experience escaped its attention. It understood the paradoxical truth that one can best overcome atavisms and primitivisms, in so far as they are destructive, by acknowledging their potency and attractiveness and channeling their expression to eliminate their harm. *Sublimation has been a perennial Jewish strategy.*

The Torah is also the record of Israel's continuing confrontation with the holiness of God. Religious liberalism and rationalism fail before this primordial and ultimate reality. Liberal Judaism wants a good and moral God because it lacks the courage of the absurd. Religious liberalism cannot abide the tragic limitations of the cosmos indifferent to human aspiration in which we are enclosed without hope of exit. It envisages a world in which people, like corporation returns, can get better and better in every way, ignoring the fated destiny that so frequently turns human encounter into tragic conflict. One does not have to join Sartre in his reiteration of Hegel's idea that consciousness desires the death of the other to know how deeply tragic human encounter can be.[19] Where the holiness of God is real, the tragic element inherent in existence and even in Divinity can never be ignored. One has only to read the many accounts in Scripture concerning the fatal consequences of an improper or an unprepared approach before the Holy to understand that God in His holiness is more than a moral force. He who makes alive is also He who slays by His very presence. This teaching of Scripture made liberals uncomfortable. Had they paid attention to this teaching, rather than relegated it to the domain of outlived antiquities, they would have had a fuller appreciation of human existence before God.

Earth is a nurturing mother, but Earth is also a cannibal mother. Sooner or later she consumes what she gives birth to. Before the opaque facticity of Earth we can ask with Schelling, but never answer, the question: Why is there something rather than nothing? Out of this unanswerable question comes our sense of the mystery and the absurdity of existence. Before this Abyss, we come to intuit something of the holiness of God. When we speak of that holiness we dimly point to the realm of God's utter singularity, uniqueness, and incommensurability with all categories of measurement, logic, or relation. He who intuits, no matter how dimly, the holiness of God, need construct no "God above the God of theism," as does Paul Tillich, to provide a mental hint of that which dwells in its own groundlessness.[20] *God in His holiness is beyond both the masculinity of the Judeo-Christian tradition and the femininity of the pagan mother goddesses.* The old distinction of patriarchal and matriarchal religions evaporates in this final reality. Rabbinic mythology loved to dwell on kingly metaphors for God's relation to Israel. This, too, was a limitation and an anesthetizing of the awe and mystery felt before the cannibal powers of Earth. Both the Jews and the Greeks attributed masculine traits to God in order to dull the sense of terror and wonder people feel before Earth's mystery.[21] Sky and thunder gods were invented to be superior to Earth and its engendering goddess, but to no avail. In its awesome awareness of the holiness of God, Biblical monotheism is at one with the old Earth paganisms. The commanding Father God, the King who lovingly guided His regal son, and the thunder god dwelling in his heavenly abode are all manifold aspects of the same unknowable Abyss.

The tragic truth of earthly existence was never lost in the Torah and came out of disguise when least expected. In the sacrificial offerings of the temple service as well as in *kashruth,* Israelites were enjoined to return the blood of the slaughtered animal to the earth before consuming the rest of the animal. Is this not one of the oldest offerings to thank and appease their cannibal Earth Mother? By offering Earth the blood, in which the soul was found, it was hoped that the rest of the animal would be permitted for human consumption. To this day, this symbolic recognition of the power of Earth continues in *kashruth* to play an important role in Jewish religious life.

Another example of how deeply rooted the Torah is in the dilemmas of personal existence is to be found in Scripture's demand that the firstborn of men and cattle be devoted to God: "The first born of your sons you shall give to me. You shall do likewise with your oxen and your sheep; seven days will it be with its dam; on the eighth day you shall give it to me" (Exod. 22:28–29). This commandment hearkens back to an archaic, pre-Judaic time when all firstborn may actually have been sacrificed. Psychoanalysts have tended to see this demand as an example of the acting out of the Oedipal conflict.[22] This perspective has the virtue of recognizing how deeply rooted the Torah is in the actual dilemmas of personal existence. Nevertheless, in formulating its insights in terms of the Oedipal metaphor, the psychoanalytic school seems to have lost sight of a deeper reality. It is not only human firstborn that must be redeemed or devoted, but "the first born of every beast which thou hast" (Exod. 13:11–16) stands in a special relation to the Holy Abyss. Is this not another attempt to appease the Earth Mother with the first portion in the hope that men and women will be allowed safely to retain the remainder? The holiness of God knows neither masculinity nor femininity; it knows only life, fecundity, death, mystery, and wonder.

Whether Moses received any or all of the Torah on Sinai hardly matters. The Torah is the record of Israel's encounter with God in His terrible holiness. I have stressed some strange and atavistic elements rather deliberately, not because destructiveness is all that Earth offers, but because *this aspect of divinity has hardly received the attention in recent Jewish thought which recent Jewish experience suggests it deserves.* A further reason for this stress is to emphasize the extent to which no element in Torah, no matter how seemingly cruel, primitive, or atavistic, is without a potentiality of relevance and significance in our own times.

The tension between the historically determined form of the Torah and our own free subjectivity cannot be ended easily. We are free to accept or reject any or all of the Torah. Nevertheless, *all of the Torah is holy;* all of it confronts us, as it has confronted Israel and the world for millennia, with the holiness of God. As God's holiness can never be contained in fixed immutable form, our response will be what we choose to make it. No two responses will be the same. Some may be unable to endure more than a measure of the confrontation; others may find elements that are trite and commonplace. But the inner connection between our freedom and the mysterious awe with which our ancestors experienced His presence remains.

The final paradox is that the Torah, which is a book of words, points to a reality before which words are utterly impotent. Confronting the holiness of God touches a domain in which art and music safely carry us a little further into the Being's Holy Abyss than words. Art and music communicate much that is hidden beneath the surface. In the *Kedushah* of the Jewish liturgy, as well as in the *gloria,* the *sanctus,* and the *rex tre-mendae* of the Mass, musicians of all ages have expressed, better than words can utter, their sense of wonder and mystery before the Source of all existence. In the chant of the Hasidic Rebbe, in the songs of the ascending Levites in Jerusalem's Holy Temple, and in the soaring elevations of the great cantorial masters of eastern Europe, Jews have confronted the holiness of God in the fullness of their beings. Perhaps the most terrible thing that could be said of the liberal Judaism of the nineteenth century is that it was incapable of authentic art and song before God's mysterious holiness.

In the twentieth century the Jewish phoenix has known both death and rebirth: in Germany and eastern Europe, we Jews have endured the bitterest and the most degrading of deaths. Yet death was not the last word. It was followed by rebirth in our ancestral home, where we experienced a new freedom. Having lost everything, we had nothing further to lose and no further fear of loss. Our existence had become a being-unto-death. We had passed beyond all hope and illusion. In the crisis we learned that we were totally and nakedly alone, that we could expect neither support nor succor from God or from our fellow creatures. No people has known as deeply as have we how truly God in His holiness slays those to whom He gives life. For the survivors at least this was a liberating knowledge, and after Auschwitz all Jews regarded themselves as survivors wherever they were domiciled. Having lost all faith and hope, we had also lost all possibility of disappointment. Having come to expect absolutely nothing from God or the nations of the world, we rejoiced in whatever we received. No people has come to know, as have we, the insubstantial nothingness of human beings before the awesome and terrible majesty of the Lord. We affirm our nothingness—nay, we even rejoice in it—for in finding our nothingness we have found both ourselves and the God who alone is true substance. We did not ask to be born; we did not ask for our absurd existence in the world; nor did we ask for the terrible destiny that has hung about us as Jews. Yet we would neither exchange nor deny it, for when nothing is asked for, nothing is hoped for, nothing is expected; all that we receive is truly grace.

CHAPTER 13

Death-of-God Theology
and Judaism

The number of men and women in America who self-consciously regard themselves as theologians is relatively small. During the past decade [1955–65] a few of us have been writing and working on radical themes that have caused us much discomfort. It is not easy to part company with what one has been taught, but we were forced to rethink our positions in part because of the teaching of Paul Johannes Tillich.

Tillich is, as Thomas J. J. Altizer has suggested, the father of contemporary radical theology. Every one of today's radical theologians either was Tillich's student or was profoundly influenced by his writing. In my case, of all the courses I took during my graduate studies at Harvard, Tillich's course on classical German philosophy was the most memorable and the most influential.[1] Although he rejected the ideas of Altizer and of William Hamilton shortly before his death, Tillich, more than any other theologian at work in the fifties, made it inevitable that the generation of thinkers that followed him would include some for whom the *transcendent God of biblical monotheism* was "dead." It was Tillich himself who dared to follow the logic of his position to its radical conclusion when he wrote:

> The God of theological theism . . . is a being, not being-itself. As such he is bound to the subject-object structure of reality, he is an object for us as subjects. At the same time we are objects for him as a subject. And this is the decisive reason for transcending theological theism. For God as a subject makes me into an object which is nothing more than an object. He deprives me of my subjectivity because he is all-powerful and

247

all-knowing. I revolt and try to make *him* into an object, but the revolt
fails and becomes desperate. God appears as the invincible tyrant, the
being in contrast with whom all other beings are without freedom and
subjectivity. He is equated with the recent tyrants who with the help
of terror try to transform everything into . . . a cog in the machine
they control. . . . This is the God Nietzsche said had to be killed because nobody can tolerate being made into a mere object of absolute
knowledge.[2]

Writing in 1952 Tillich equated the all-powerful God of theological theism
with "the recent tyrants," a shocking reference to the totalitarian dicta-
tors Hitler and Stalin. He sought to depict the Old Testament God as the
harsh, merciless, unforgiving Lawgiver in contrast to the gracious, self-
sacrificing Christ, who, as the union of existential and essential being,
offers himself as a perfect sacrifice for the forgiveness of humanity's sins.
It is easy to see that Altizer's idea that God the Father dies so that humanity might be free is logically implied in Tillich's paraphrase of
Nietzsche that the "God of theological theism" had to be killed because
nobody can tolerate being an object of absolute knowledge. For Tillich
and Altizer, human freedom is the issue that compels humanity to will
the death of the theistic God; for me the problem of human freedom was
far less important than the problem of divine justice or theodicy. Moreover, I never "willed" the death of the theistic God; I sadly found the
idea of such a God lacking in credibility in the face of the Holocaust.

For several years, Altizer, Hamilton, and I thought we were working
alone on themes that departed radically from the normative traditions of
our communities. All of us had experienced the condescending disap-
proval of our denominational establishments. There were also frequent
crises of self-doubt. In my case, there were times when I hoped for a way
back to acceptance by my religious establishment. It was not easy to pursue this work.

A nursery rhyme helped me to continue my writing and research.
Whenever I yearned to write and say the "right thing," I would recite:

Humpty-Dumpty sat on the wall
Humpty-Dumpty had a big fall
All the king's horses and all the king's men
Couldn't put Humpty together again.

A breach had been made between the mood and the theological perspectives of our times and those of our predecessors, even so radical a
predecessor as Tillich. There was simply no way to escape the fact that
the second half of the twentieth century was radically different. Our theology would have to be an expression of the way we, rather than those

who preceded us, asked ultimate questions. It was impossible to renounce this work.

In 1963, I first became aware of the fact that other theologians were equally concerned with the radical profanity and secularity of our times. I received a postcard from Rabbi Abraham Karp of Rochester, New York, telling me of a professor of theology at Colgate-Rochester Divinity School, William Hamilton, who had been reading my theological articles and felt there were some similarities in our insights. Subsequently learning of the work of Professor Thomas J. J. Altizer of Emory University, I began to read whatever these men had written.

In the spring of 1965, I experienced something of a crisis upon reading William Hamilton's article, "The Death of God Theologies Today," in the *Christian Scholar*.[3] To my surprise, I learned that Hamilton regarded my writing as an example of death-of-God theology. My first reaction was one of acute embarrassment. *God simply doesn't die in Judaism.* The symbolism upon which the metaphor of the death of God rests is of obvious Christian origin. Although the divinity of the Christ is not supposed to have expired on the cross, the age-old, anti-Jewish deicide accusation bears witness to the fact that the crucifixion was often regarded as the occasion of the death of God. In Christianity Christ, the incarnate Savior, is both God and man in perfect union. There are also references in Luther and Hegel to the death of God.[4] Of course, it has always been possible for Christians, in asserting the death of God, to look beyond death to a new epiphany of the divine. Although we live in the time of the death of God, the Christian death-of-God theologians do not rule out the possibility of a reappearance of the resurrected God.

Because of our alienation from the symbolism of the cross, it is impossible for Jews to use the words, "God is dead." Nevertheless, I believe we must use these words of alien origin and connotation. American Jews share the same cultural universe as contemporary Christian thinkers; we experience the radical secularity of our times as they do. We have been deeply influenced by Freud, Sartre, Hegel, Dostoevski, Melville, and Kierkegaard. Above all, we have been moved by Nietzsche.

If I were asked to cite the text *par excellence* from which I derive the verbal origins of the radical mood, I would unhesitatingly follow William Hamilton and point to the chapter in Nietzsche's *Gay Science* entitled "The Madman."[5] In it the Madman proclaims his search for God, asserts that we have murdered Him, and becomes affrighted at the terrible event that has already happened but is yet too distant for us to comprehend. The Madman rhetorically asks the question, also crucial to Thomas Altizer's apocalyptic theology: "Shall we not ourselves have to become gods merely to be worthy of it?" The Madman then enters a church, which he has declared to be a sepulcher of God, and there sings his *Requiem aeternam deo.*⁶ After Nietzsche, it is impossible to avoid using his language to express the total absence of God from our experience. Martin Buber felt deeply the profanity of our times. He attempted to soften its harshness by speaking of an "eclipse of God."⁷ Buber's formulation would, however, seem to be a compromise. No words are entirely adequate to characterize a historical epoch. Nevertheless, I believe the most adequate theological description of our times is to be found in the assertion that *we live in the time of the death of God.*⁸ The vitality of death-of-God theology is rooted in the fact that it has faced more openly than any other contemporary theological movement the truth of the divine-human encounter in our times. In truth, the divine-human encounter is totally nonexistent. Those theologies that attempt to find the reality of God's presence in the contemporary world manifest a deep insensitivity to the art, literature, and technology of our times. Whatever may be its shortcomings, death-of-God theology is very much aware of the cultural universe of which it is a significant expression. Radical theology is no fad. It will not be replaced by some other theological novelty in the foreseeable future. Too many tendencies in classical theology, philosophy, and literature have intersected in this movement for it to disappear as rapidly as it has gained attention.

Nevertheless, *I believe that radical theology errs in its assertion that God is dead.* Such an assertion exceeds human knowledge. The statement, "God is dead," is only significant in what it reveals about those who make it. It imparts information concerning what the speaker believes about God; it reveals nothing about God. I should like to suggest that, since this information has strictly phenomenological import, *we ought to formulate it from the viewpoint of the observer.* It is more precise to assert that *we live in the time of the death of God* than to declare "God is dead." *The death of God is a cultural fact. We shall never know whether it is more than that.*

The ultimate relevance of theology is anthropological. Though theology purports to make statements about God, its significance rests on what it reveals about the theologian as well as the theologian's community and culture. All theologies have a subjective component. They are statements about the way the theologian experiences the world.

The theologian is really closer to the poet or the creative artist than to the physical scientist. The value of artistic creation lies in the fact that someone with a highly sensitive subjectivity is able to communicate something of a personal experience which others recognize as clarifying and enriching their own experience. Theologians, no matter how religiously committed they may seem to be, in reality communicate an inner world they believe others may share. The term "God" is very much like the unstructured inkblot used in the Rorschach test. Its very lack of concrete content invites us to express our fears, aspirations, and yearnings concerning our origin, our destiny, and our end. From a technical point of view, theological statements would seem to be most precise when they are enunciated in a phenomenological context. There are some indications that Professors Altizer and Hamilton accept this methodological limitation on theological assertion. Nevertheless, it is not clear whether they speak of what they have experienced or whether they believe God has literally perished.

Although my first reaction to Professor Hamilton's identification of my writing as death of God theology was embarrassment, I am grateful to him for causing me to reconsider my theological moorings. I have concluded that, alien and non-Jewish as the terminology may be, Christian death-of-God theology is closer than any other movement in Christian theology to my own theological writing. We are at least agreed upon our analysis of the radical secularity of contemporary culture as a starting point for theological speculation. We concur that ours is the time of the death of God. We are, each in our own way, convinced that both the methods and the conclusions of contemporary theology will reflect the radical hiatus between our world and the traditional communities out of which we have come.

Nevertheless, *in the time of the death of God the Jewish radical theologian remains profoundly Jewish, as the Christian radical remains profoundly Christian.* The old Law-Gospel controversy, which has separated Jew and Christian from the inception of Christianity, continues to separate Jew and Christian in our time. Christian death-of-God theologians may have lost God, but, as Professor Hamilton has suggested, they have by no means lost the Messiah. Radical Christian theology is profoundly Christocentric; for all Jews, Jesus is simply another Jew of no abiding religious significance. Nothing in contemporary radical Jewish theology would elevate Jesus to a higher status than he has had for Jews for two millennia.

I became aware of the differences between contemporary Jewish and Christian radical theology as a result of first reading, then meeting, Professor Thomas J. J. Altizer of Emory University. I was invited to respond to his paper, "Theology and the Contemporary Sensibility," at the Conference on America and the Future of Theology at Emory in November 1965.[9] I was fascinated by Altizer's writings, as I had been with Hamilton's. At a certain level I had the feeling that we were concerned with the same issues and that there were similarities in our theological methods. In spite of very great differences, I have enormous respect for him as a thinker and as a co-worker in a common task of contemporary theological exploration. Altizer and Hamilton are investigating the meaning of the time of the death of God for Christianity. I believe I am attempting to understand its meaning for Judaism. Professor Altizer speaks of the death of God, but he reveals the profound connection between his theology and the classical heritage of Christian theology and mysticism. Although the Father God has died for him, Christ has become, if anything, more meaningful. His thought is deeply rooted in both dialectical mysticism and its product, Hegelian philosophy. Professor Altizer views creation as the result of God's kenotic self-emptying out of His own substance. The view is not unlike that of Lurianic Kabbalism, which I find theologically attractive. The Lurianic view of creation suggests that God, who was originally all-in-all, created the world by an act of self-division and self-diminution. Through this act, the world came into being out of the divine *Urgrund* or in the language of the Kabbalah, the *Ayn Sof*. Since the divine *Urgrund* lacked all inner division or predication, it was no-thing. Creation in the Lurianic scheme was a *creatio ex nihilo*, a creation by God out of His own no-thing-ness. In both the Kabbalistic view and Professor Altizer's theology, creation is an act of self-diminution of the divine ground.

The thrust of Altizer's view is ultimately dependent upon his *either-God-or-man-but-not-both* approach. Altizer is convinced that the slightest trace of the divine is sufficient to impede and thwart the full development of mankind's potentialities. During my recent visit to Poland [1965], a Catholic theologian in Warsaw expressed a scholastic formula somewhat similar in mood to Altizer's basic approach: *"Si Deus est, Petrus non est; si Petrus est, Deus non est."*[10] Altizer suggests that God's greatest love for mankind is to be found in an act of divine self-riddance. He believes that in the crucifixion God voluntarily *empties* Himself out of His own being. Humanity rather than divinity is resurrected on Easter Sunday. The real meaning of the cross is the total liberation of mankind as a concomitant of the death of God the Father. It is for this reason that Altizer joyously proclaims the Gospel—the good tidings—of Christian atheism. In the final analysis, for Altizer the Christian message is mankind's liberation from God the Father.

The profoundly Christian inspiration of this radical speculation is obvious. This is a Christian theology, albeit one of high daring and originality. The Christian character of Altizer's thought is also evident in his identification of the God of the Old Testament as the tyrannical lawgiver who enslaves mankind with His rigid, sin-inducing Law. This interpretation of the Law has a very respectable Christian theological lineage. Nevertheless, no Jew, having experienced the Law, could accept it. In Pauline theology, the sacrificial death of the Christ is an atonement capable of liberating humanity from its bondage to sin and the Law. The atonement of the Christ, the Second Adam, suffices for all who are "in Christ." In Altizer's thought, it is the Father, source and author of the Law, who sacrifices Himself through the Son, thereby dissolving the Law and liberating humanity from sin and repression alike. Altizer sees the time of the death of God in apocalyptic terms. The death of God is the true meaning of the Christ's sacrifice. The promise of the Christ is the promise of radical human freedom.

There are dialectic affinities between Altizer's theology and the psychosexual hopefulness that pervades Herbert Marcuse's conclusions in *Eros and Civilization* and Norman O. Brown's in *Life against Death*.[11] All three envisage the dialectic promise of our time as an end to repression and the potentiality of absolute human liberty. There are strong overtones of Nietzsche's most thoroughly Dionysian mood in Altizer. Altizer would in all likelihood assent to Nietzsche's Madman's request that we become gods in place of the dead God. The freedom envisaged by Altizer is certainly godlike. Altizer would also agree with Ivan Karamazov's observation: "If there is no God, all things are permissible." Unless I misread him, Altizer concurs that, in the time of the death of God, all things are permissible.

There is, however, an enormous difference between Dostoevsky and Altizer. Dostoevsky examined with prophetic insight the meaning of the death of God almost a century ago. What he saw gave him no comfort. Smerdyakov, Ivan's bastard half-brother and *Doppelgänger*, carries Ivan's logic to its extreme: if all things are permissible, parricide is permissible. Ivan is the thinker; the thinker's ideas provide motivation for men of action. Thinkers are not always happy when men of action such as Smerdyakov translate apparently impotent ideas into real deeds. The freedom Ivan intuits as the fruit of the death of God ultimately drives him insane. Unlike Orestes in Jean-Paul Sartre's play, *The Flies*, Ivan is not capable of living in the wasteland. I fear Professor Altizer rejoices too soon. The time of the death of God must ultimately become a time of mourning, as it was for the Karamazovs. We shall learn bitterly to regret our loss of the Divine.

Altizer's sensitivity to his cultural milieu is especially evident in his self-conscious avowal that America has a theological mission. He is drawn to William Blake's mystical vision of America as the place where the apocalyptic freedom of the Christian will finally be realized. For both

Altizer and Blake, America's mission is to reject the past and create a world in which totally free, autonomous men and women may flourish for the first time. According to Altizer, America is the land of the future in which the promise of the Gospel will ultimately be achieved. There are obvious similarities of perspective between Altizer's interpretation of America and Harvey Cox's assertion in *The Secular City* that "technopolis" is the self-realizing kingdom of God.[12] Cox contrasts "legalistic" tribal and village forms of social organization with the "gospel-like" freedom of the anonymous, highly mobile inhabitants of the secular city; Altizer sees America, cut off from the past and tradition and looking forward only to the future, as a realization of the true meaning of the Gospel. There is a pervasive note of optimism in the work of Altizer, Hamilton, and Cox which reflects the characteristics of American popular culture. All three thinkers exhibit a typically American rejection of history and tradition.[13] Altizer and Cox are especially future oriented. All three reject tragedy and the tragic sense. For Altizer, the death of God means the end to tragedy. Hamilton has echoed this mood in his assertion that, as Americans, we are future oriented. Deeply sensitive to the various aspects of popular culture, he wisely intuited an element of seriousness in the Beatles' motion picture, *A Hard Day's Night*. He interprets the final scene of the film, in which the Beatles sing, dance, and then depart by rising helicopter from the overly complex world of the television studio, as a symbol of a new mood of optimism which floats above the despair and alienation of our times. "The death of tragedy," Professor Hamilton claims, "is due to the death of the Christian God."[14]

Altizer's optimism is also rooted in his very exciting attempt to interpret the meaning of the "sacred" in Christian and non-Christian religions. Relying heavily on the insights of his teacher, Mircea Eliade, Altizer points out that the oriental mystic follows a path of *anamnesis*, that is, of remembrance and recollection. His goal is the restoration of a lost, paradisaical Beginning. His effort is to return ultimately to the primordial totality out of which he has come.[15] In contrast to the non-Christian's attempt to make of history a circle restoring the primordial harmony of all things in the nothingness of the *Urgrund*, Altizer sees Christianity as making of the historical process an ascending spiral. For the Christian the posture of faith cannot be the attempt to retrieve an irretrievable past; the Christian must turn his back upon the past, thereby allowing the future dawning of the Kingdom to break in upon the present and penetrate its structures. Altizer is committed to a forward-moving dynamism. He will not commit the error of Lot's wife. The Word came into the world to negate the past; it has become fully flesh; it remains in the world only as long as it abjures nostalgia and continues to negate the past in its movement toward the realization of the Kingdom. Although Altizer believes that the self-negating, self-transcending movement of the Word-become-flesh is developed fully only in Christianity, he does see anticipations of this forward movement in the prophets of ancient Israel and their negation of Israelite priestly religion.

Altizer is radically antipriestly. He has no doctrine of the Church. He is not especially concerned with its ritual and liturgy. He shares this anticultic bias with Harvey Cox. The tension between the Word and fixed ritual, so necessary for the celebration of the crises of life, has always been more of a problem for Protestantism than for Judaism or Roman Catholicism. Altizer interprets Jewish and Christian priestly religious forms as attempts at *recollection* or a *concrete renewal* of a sacred time in the past.

I would agree with this analysis, though I would prefer to formulate in it psychoanalytic terminology. The rituals of priestly religion are in part akin to *regressions in the service of the ego*. Their purpose is in part to bring us into contact with those sources of *basic trust*, rooted in our earliest childhood, which are indispensable to our meeting the profane, secular world with confidence. That is why the language of parent and child is so necessary in religious rituals, which are significant precisely because they are indispensable attempts at recollection.

Altizer will have none of this *recherche du temps perdu* (remembrance of things past). For dialectic, Christian, and American reasons he will face only toward the future. Such a dynamic posture means a perpetual negation of what lies at hand. Ultimately the Kingdom will be won by the negation of every link to primordial Beginnings, including God. The Christian, according to Altizer, must not regret the loss of God in our time. He must reject this perilous nostalgia and joyously will His death.

As I read Altizer, I am aware of how radically different our theologies are. I am both amazed and fascinated that I can both comprehend and communicate with him. I suspect it is because we both understand that only a limited number of theological options are available when one deals with the problems of eschatology. I cannot share his rejection of the past, either on existential or on psychoanalytic grounds. *How could a Jew ignore history?* The basic terms of our encounters with our Christian neighbors were spelled out almost two thousand years ago. The very spectacle of the most august assemblage of Christian leaders of our times, Vatican II, discussing the responsibility of the current generation of Jews for a crime that happened almost two thousand years ago is an indication of how deeply Jews are still affected by history. How could Jews follow Professor

Altizer's lead and look only to the future? To do so would be to denude our attempts to deal with any degree of competence with our present. All Jews (and Christians, though it is less obvious with them) are at least two thousand years old the day they are born.

Cox, Altizer, and Hamilton all assert that it is American to negate the past and look primarily toward the future, an assertion that anyone who has visited the small towns and villages of New England, the Middle Atlantic states, and the South knows is not entirely valid. To the extent that it is true, one must ask whether there is something adolescent about this denial of roots. Europeans probably distrust Americans more for our failure to understand the abiding impact of history than for any other aspect of our culture. Altizer believes that it is the destiny of America to lead the world away from its past. In all likelihood, America's real destiny is to become Europeanized as it comes to experience the defeats and the limitations of power which sooner or later history visits upon all nations without exception. We already see anticipatory signs in the Far East. Until the Korean War, we had never lost a foreign war. The Korean War ended in a stalemate; no one can predict how the Vietnam War will end. Nor can any person rest certain that America is destined to be victorious against every potential adversary or combination of adversaries in the centuries that lie ahead. Invincibility is simply not an attribute of men or nations.

The optimism of Altizer, Hamilton, and Cox is rooted in the American success story to date [1966]. The real test of America will come only when the going gets rough, when we experience, as has every other nation in history, the bitterness of defeat. It will come; it may not come in our lifetime, but it will assuredly come. Will we have the tragic dignity, the stoicism, and the inner courage to meet the challenge of national disaster?

The American South has produced more than its share of first-rate literature. Perhaps the reason is to be found in the fact that the South is the only part of America that has had defeat engraved on its psyche. William Hamilton denies that the tragic sense of life is possible in our time. If Hamilton is correct, it is not because the death of God means the death of tragedy, as he asserts, but because we no longer regard human loss as significant. As Aristotle understood, the tragic vision is possible only when something perishes which is of worth and dignity. Everything human must perish. Every life lost is in some sense tragic, provided we regard every life as unique and irreplaceable. If we have lost the tragic sense, it is because an era of mass death has sterilized the impact of death and translated it into a nonhuman statistic devoid of emotional impact.

When we regard human beings as replaceable ciphers whose role is to keep the machinery of technopolis functioning, the tragic sense is lost. That loss does not lead to a new optimism but to the depersonalization and dehumanization of life and death alike.

Is it true that if God is dead all things are permissible? I suspect Altizer, following Ivan Karamazov, has taken the myth of God as lawgiver much too literally. Although Altizer is acutely aware of such prophets of the death of God in the nineteenth and twentieth centuries as Nietzsche, Dostoevsky, Melville, and, in his own way, Kierkegaard, there is one prophet whom he all but ignores, Sigmund Freud. This is especially significant because Freud's myth of the origin of religion begins with a parricide that is almost immediately interpreted as if it had been a deicide. For our purposes, Freud's etiological myth is not significant as a mode of explaining religious origins; it is important insofar as it lends insight into the indispensability of law and discipline for the social process. As we have noted, in both *Totem and Taboo* and *Moses and Monotheism*, Freud sees God as the first object of human criminality, the Primal Father cannibalistically murdered by the envious band of brothers, his male offspring, who sought to take possession of his women, their mothers and sisters.[16]

According to Freud, the victory over the father proved empty and ironic. Having murdered the father, the sons quickly realized that some instrumentality had to be devised whereby sexual need would not disrupt social structure. Freud hypothesizes that the law of exogamy was instituted in order to prevent the group from descending to the level of *bellum omnes contra omnes*, the war of all against all. Freud's myth is important because he understood that *reality rather than the father is the author of repression*. In the end, the sons impose upon themselves the very restrictions the father had imposed upon them.

When the authority of the Father God is overcome, Altizer rejoices in the ensuing freedom. However, I do not understand what Altizer means by freedom in the time of the death of God. Does he mean sexual freedom? If he believes that there will be no giving and taking in marriage, it is unlikely that even our sexually permissive society will ever tolerate an absolute absence of law in sexual matters. In reality, human freedom is limited the moment the nursing infant is compelled to refrain from using its milk teeth to bite the breast of its mother. The radical limitation inflicted by toilet training leaves a further repressive mark upon us for life. Furthermore, even if men had free access to the women of their choice as adults, the women would remain substitute sources of gratification, hardly capable of compensating for the loss of the first and most precious object of love, the mother, unless the men were to come to terms with their archaic yearnings.

As Freud understood in *Civilization and Its Discontents*, civilization is purchased at the price of an enormous, perhaps an insupportable, degree of repression.[17] Contemporary apocalyptic visions of an end to repression, such as those of Marcuse, Norman O. Brown, and Altizer, provide no means of altering in adult life those archaic instrumentalities of repression which become operative long before the child is aware of them. Psychoanalysis is nonrepressive only insofar as it liberates the individual from neurotic elements of repression which are irrelevant to his adult realities. There is, however, a renunciatory side to psychoanalysis; it arises less out of ideology than from a need for realism in meeting the demands of the social process. Psychoanalysis leads to the acceptance of the realistic limitation of infantile yearnings as much as to the rejection of neurotic repression. Altizer must do more than interpret freedom as a dialectic entailment consequent upon the death of the Lawgiver. He must spell out what he means by freedom as well as how it becomes operative. At least Cox sees freedom as a potential consequence of the anonymity and mobility of the urban metropolis. However, even Cox refers primarily to adult, conscious freedom of choice. He says little concerning the framework of repression which is built into the human being almost from the moment of birth and which is indispensable in view of the long period of dependence required for human nurture and growth. It is simply not true that if God is dead all things are permissible. The structure of human reality is itself inherently limiting and frustrating. If there is to be any kind of society, it will have to be a somewhat renunciatory society. One cannot ignore Freud in searching out the meaning of the death of God.

Can one speak of freedom and the death of God, yet ignore Sartre and Camus? The whole thrust of Sartre's ethical and psychological concern rests upon his exploration of the meaning of freedom after the death of God. Sartre agrees that if God is dead all is possible, but he does not rejoice in the freedom consequent upon the death of God. He asserts, through one of the characters in his novels, that we are *condemned* to be free.[18] He sees anxiety as a direct consequence of our freedom. If there is no God, then we and we alone are responsible for our actions. Like Dostoevski's Grand Inquisitor, Sartre is deeply skeptical concerning humanity's ability to accept that responsibility. If there is a characteristic human flaw according to Sartre, it is *mauvaise foi*, bad faith, our incapacity to accept responsibility for the deeds we freely perform.[19] For Sartre, the time of the death of God is one of overwhelming irony.

Perhaps no contemporary author has explored the meaning of the freedom of the flesh more insightfully or more beautifully than Albert Camus in his small but important essay, "Summer in Algiers." Camus's handsome young men and women who delight in the sea, the sun, and the flesh on the beaches of Algiers are "gods of this earth." For them as well as for Camus, there is neither afterlife nor personal God; we die and our only kingdom "is of this earth." Camus celebrates his compatriots, a race of men "without a past, without tradition," over whom "no delusive divinity traces the signs of hope or redemption." For the first time in two thousand years the nude body has appeared upon the shores of the Mediterranean. These men and women know only the pleasures of the flesh; nothing is banished by this pagan race.[20]

These "gods of the earth" are joyous—when they are twenty—but, Camus continues, "I know of no more hideous spot than the cemetery on Boulevard Bru, opposite one of the most beautiful landscapes in the world. . . . This race, wholly cast into its present, lives without myths, without solace. It has put all of its possessions on this earth and therefore remains without defense against death."[21]

The world of the death of God is a world devoid of hope and illusion. People grow old, decline, and die. It is relatively simple to celebrate apocalyptic liberation in one's youth, but what of the later years? The death of God does not cancel death. It heightens our sad knowledge that no power, human or divine, can ultimately withstand the dissolving onslaughts of omnipotent Nothingness, the true Lord of all creation. If one penetrates beneath the surface of the joys of the flesh, one finds sadness even in our most precious moments of liberation and gratification. Love and death have been inseparable themes throughout the history of literature. The celebration of the joys of the body carries with it the certain knowledge that this vessel of delight must disappear as if it had never been.

The island of Ibiza in the Balearic Islands was a favorite of Camus. It is one of the most beautiful places I have ever visited. Everywhere one turns, one is struck by the richness and beauty of the sea, the sun, the beaches, and human youthfulness. If human beings have found a place where the joys of the flesh can be celebrated most fully, it is beautiful Ibiza. Yet, underneath Ibiza's abiding beauty, one meets a tragic sadness, perhaps one might better say the other side of her beauty. On the hill overlooking the harbor, there is an ancient cathedral sacred to the Virgin. In the museum next door is a statue of the Carthaginian goddess Taanith, who was the Holy Mother of this island long before the advent of Christianity. Religions have come and gone, but the adoration of the Mother has never ceased in this place—and with good reason, for She who gives birth announces the hour of death in that very moment. The wise pagans of the ancient Mediterranean unconsciously bequeathed their wisdom to their contemporary descendants. Neither Judaism nor Christianity could entirely suppress the awesome knowledge that Earth is a Mother, a cannibal Mother who gives forth Her own children only that She may consume the fruit of Her own womb. Almighty Necessity has never ceased Her omnipotent reign. We are born but to perish. We are more than the fools of the gods; we are their food. I do not understand Altizer's optimism. The Kingdom lies ahead of us, but it is not the new reality as he supposes. It is the Nothingness out of which we have come and to which we are inescapably destined to return.

As Christians, Altizer, Hamilton, and Cox cannot reject hope. I would agree that we have much reason to hope when we contemplate the possibility of fulfillment in the here and now; there are, however, absolutely no grounds for eschatological hope. Let me again quote Camus's essay. Referring to his Algerian men and women, he writes:

> Gods of summer they were at twenty by their enthusiasm for life, and they still are, deprived of all hope. I have seen two of them die. They were full of horror, but silent. It is better thus. *From Pandora's box, where all the ills of humanity swarmed, the Greeks drew out hope after all the others as the most dreadful of all. I know of no more stirring symbol; for contrary to the general belief, hope equals resignation. And to live is not to resign oneself* (italics added).[22]

In the time of the death of God, some form of pagan sanity may better accord with the deepest instincts of mankind than does an atheistic Christian apocalypticism. I believe that paganism has in reality triumphed in the hearts of men. Paganism, such as that of the ancient Mediterranean world, was not a vulgar appeal to what is base in men; it was a wise intuition of man's place in the order of things. In spite of Altizer's hostility to priestly religion, priestly religion has won the day in both Judaism and Christianity simply by appropriating their inherited rituals and symbols as instrumentalities whereby the decisive crises of life can be celebrated and shared. What remains of Judaism and Christianity in contemporary America is largely pagan. This phenomenon is by no means an unmitigated disaster. People's instincts are often better than their ideologies. Life has its way of imposing religious demands upon us. Birth, adolescence, marriage, and death demand religious celebration. At such times we are far less interested in prophetic proclamation than in cultic acts. The cultic approach has always had obvious shortcomings; let us not exaggerate them. At least pagan cultic religion is deeply rooted in the realities of human biology and psychology.

Altizer's proclamation of apocalyptic freedom is dependent upon Christianity's conviction that the Gospel liberates man from the Law. As I confront Altizer, and incidentally Harvey Cox, I get the feeling that the ancient debate between the Pharisees and the Christians has not ceased. A the time of the birth of Christianity, Christians asserted that something decisively new had occurred which had the power to transform the human condition. The Pharisees, my spiritual predecessors, hoped for such a transformation as earnestly as did the Christians. They looked both within and around themselves. They sadly concluded that no such transformation had occurred and there was no alternative but to remain faithful to the Law. It was and remains a difficult instrument, but it seemed to be the only means by which their society could avoid disintegration and moral chaos. Two thousand years and the time of the death of God have done little to alter that judgment in Jewish eyes. If we must live without God, religious law is more necessary for us than ever. Our temptation to anarchic omnipotence and the total indifference of the cosmos to our deeds call forth the need for a set of guidelines to enable us to apprehend the limits of appropriate behavior. Without God, we need law, tradition, and structure far more than ever before. I grant that these guidelines will not easily be found because of the breach between our culture and its antecedents. Little wisdom is now transferred from generation to generation. We prefer to let people discover their limits through trial and error. At present, I see no way of altering this preference. Nevertheless, I question whether we can in the long run afford to pay the cumulative cost of the inevitable errors that people must make in discovering their limits. In the long run, the trial-and-error method is a costly detour to the acquisition of behavioral norms not unlike those perennially suggested within the religious traditions of mankind.

In the time of the death of God, Judaism and Christianity remain as decisively separated on the issue of the Messiah as they were at the founding of the Church. For Altizer, ours is the messianic age. Mankind has now been liberated from sin and Law through the death of God in the Christ. I would like to suggest as an alternative a contemporary Jewish doctrine of the Messiah which seems far more descriptive of the human condition than Altizer's apocalyptic enthusiasm. The doctrine derives from an insight on the part of the contemporary Jewish novelist Isaac Bashevis Singer. It is a horrible doctrine. Nevertheless, I believe it is a credible messianic doctrine. At the end of his epic novel, *The Family Muskat*, Singer portrays the family meeting for the last time as the Germans are at the gates of Warsaw in September 1939. One member of the family makes the assertion that he believes the Messiah will come speedily. The others are astonished at this pronouncement. Hertz Yanovar explains: "Death is the Messiah."[23] The insight is irrefutable. The Messiah traditionally promises an end to the inescapable infirmities and limitations of the human condition. But there is only one way out of the ironies and the dilemmas of existence—that exit is death. The oriental religions understood this in their quest for Nirvana. I have no desire to hasten the end. I would rather pay the price for the continuation of my existence, but I know that payment involves an acceptance of finitude, imperfection, and all of the problematics of the human condition. I cannot accept Altizer's apocalypse because for me, the Messiah's kingdom is truly not of this world. This world will forever remain a place of pain, suffering, alienation, and ultimate defeat. Much in this world occasions rejoicing, but true rejoicing is possible only if one remains mindful of the price we must ultimately pay for having entered this world of finitude, temporality, and mortality. This is the only world we shall ever know. Our pleasures must be precious in our sight, for we purchase them with our lives. The Messiah will come. He tarrieth not. We need not welcome Him. The world is not large enough for both humanity and its Redeemer.

Altizer does welcome the coming of the Kingdom. He bids the Christian, especially the American Christian, to take upon himself the joyous task of willing the death of God. God must be overcome that the Kingdom may break in upon us. The Promethean element in this task draws Altizer to the figure of Captain Ahab in Melville's *Moby Dick*. Ahab hates God and sees the great white whale, "be the white whale agent or be the white whale principal," as the ultimate symbol of that malignant creator-divinity whom he must destroy in order to liberate himself as a man. Altizer and Ahab concur in their judgment: either God or man but not both. In his paper "Theology and the Contemporary Sensibility," Altizer bids us join Ahab in his attempt to bring about the death of God. Ahab is for Altizer the prototype of the new American become "madness maddened" with whom we must move through "this rebirth of the primordial chaos to the dawn of a new and glorious Jerusalem."[24]

I earnestly hope that Ahab is not the prototype of the new American. As Maurice Friedman has observed, Ahab is the best example in literature of Kierkegaard's "demonic shut-inness."[25] He forsakes human sanity in a mad quest whose real goal is totally beyond his conscious knowledge. When, toward the end of the book, Starbuck attempts to bring Ahab back to sanity, the captain tells his mate that he has been on the sea for forty years and that he married only after he was fifty. The woman was more widow than wife. Hardly had he dented the marital pillow before he returned to sea. Undeterred by wife or the normal comforts other men cherish, he would not now be deterred from his quest of the great white whale.

Melville, a master of symbolism, was by no means unfamiliar with biblical imagery. His use of forty years as the duration of Ahab's sojourn upon the sea was not accidental. The forty years upon the sea were Ahab's sojourn in the wilderness. *The great whale is the Captain's promised land.* As much as he hates the whale, he yearns unknowingly to be consumed by it. It is not the whale or even God that enrages Ahab. Ahab is maddened by a reality that has frustrated him from the moment he left the womb. Altizer has said that all non-Christian religions seek a way back to primordial beginnings. Ahab assuredly seeks a way back to his blissful origins in the womb. The captain yearns to return to his source, thereby ending the problematics and the agonies of the human condition. Nevertheless, I believe that the whale is less a symbol of the malignant father god than of the all-consuming, cannibal mother goddess and that there is more to that slight dent upon the marital bed than meets the eye. Ahab's inability to enter into a real I-Thou relationship, accepting thereby the frustrations and the promise of adult encounter, does not rest upon his insane passion for the whale. His search for the whale is his ultimate confession of his failure to leave the rages of infancy, accept the limitations, but also the opportunities, of adult responsibility, and prove himself a man. Freud saw the mature person as having the capacity to *work* and to *love—arbeiten und lieben*. Ahab has neither capacity. He remains a petulant infant, wholly incapable of accepting reality and made all the more terrifying by the power he wields over other men.

Instead of regarding Ahab as an anticipation of the new American, as does Altizer, I believe he is more accurately seen as a prototype of Adolf Hitler. The same petulant rage at a limiting reality combined with overwhelming power enabled Hitler to carry his ship of state to almost total ruin. When Hitler could no longer bend reality to his anarchic will, he did what he had wanted to do from the very beginning: he put an end through suicide to the frustrations of finitude, which had enraged him even in those moments when he had more power than any human being before or since. What troubles Ahab is precisely the fact that we live in a universe he regards as malign, in which human existence is filled with anxiety and despair. There is only one escape. It is certainly not the New Jerusalem, and *Moby Dick* does not end with the New Jerusalem; it ends when Ahab returns to the nothingness out of which he has come. What he hates and fears, he also yearns for most deeply.

If, as Altizer suggests, Ahab is the prototypical new American, we will lack the tolerance for the ambiguity, irony, hopelessness, and inevitable meaninglessness of the time of the death of God. Lacking this tolerance, we will choose self-destruction rather than learn to accept an incomplete and not altogether satisfying life. Unlike Altizer, I cannot rejoice in the death of God. If I am a death-of-God theologian, it is with a cry of agony.

What then is the function of religion in the time of the death of God? It is the way we share and celebrate, both consciously and unconsciously, through the inherited myths, rituals, and traditions of our communities, the dilemmas and the crises of life and death, good and evil. Religion is the way we share our predicament; it is never the way we overcome our condition.

I find myself both united with and separated from the Christian believer and his Savior. I look behind the Savior and see in this figure the Christian's yearning to overcome guilt and the broken condition of human finitude. I understand that yearning, although I do not believe that Christ or any power can truly redeem men. When I participate in Jewish worship, I am sadly aware of the pathetic yearnings of my fellow Jews to make a meaningless life meaningful. This in large measure is the significance of the religious community, both Jewish and Christian, to me—the absurd, pathetic attempt, for which there can be no substitute, to make a meaningless life meaningful.[26] The attempt is futile but sociologically and psychologically indispensable.

In conclusion I would like to relate a conversation I had with a Thomistic theologian at the Catholic University of Lublin, Poland, in October 1965. I had just completed a lecture on American theology which reflected many of the same perspectives I have described in this essay. Three days before, I had visited Auschwitz. The Polish theologian asked me, "Do you love God?"

I replied, "I should. We are enjoined to love God 'with all thy heart, with all thy soul and with all thy might,' but I cannot. I am aware of His holiness. I am struck with wonder and terror before His Nothingness, but I cannot love Him. I am affrighted before Him. Perhaps, in the end, all I have is silence."

"He said, "You know, we Catholics believe that God Himself gives us the grace with which we are able to love Him."

"You're really saying the same thing I am," I replied. "It is only because you believe God Himself has enabled you to love Him that you speak as you do. If you didn't believe you have that grace, you couldn't love Him either. On your own, you could not love Him any more than I do."

Here again is the difference between Christian and Jew. The Gospel ends beyond tragedy, on a note of hope. Resurrection is the final word. I wish it were so. But I believe my Pharisee progenitors were essentially correct two thousand years ago when they sadly concluded that the promise of radical novelty in the human condition was a pathetic, though altogether understandable, illusion; that the old world goes on today as it did yesterday and as it will tomorrow. Against my deepest yearnings, I am compelled to end with their tragic acceptance rather than the eschatological hope that still infuses my Christian brother after the death of God.

CHAPTER 14

Jews, Israel, and
Liberation Theology

No contemporary movement in Christian theology has aroused as much interest as liberation theology. Given the tendency of major theological movements within Christianity to influence Jewish thinkers, it was almost inevitable that some Jewish thinkers would explore the relevance of liberation theology for Jewish theology. A beginning has now been made by Marc H. Ellis and Rabbi Dan Cohn-Sherbok.[1] Of the two efforts, Ellis's contribution has had the greater impact partly because Ellis is a member of the faculty of the Maryknoll School of Theology, the intellectual and spiritual center of liberation theology in North America, but also because he adopts far more radical positions than Cohn-Sherbok. In this essay, I am primarily, though not exclusively, concerned with Ellis's contribution and discuss his attitude toward the Jewish community, Holocaust theology, Israel, and the Palestinians.

Ellis's first book on the subject, *Toward a Jewish Theology of Liberation*, appeared in 1987. It sold well and a second, enlarged edition with a new concluding chapter entitled, "The Palestinian Uprising and the Future of the Jewish People," was published in March 1989. He has since enlarged upon his views in two books, *Beyond Innocence and Redemption* and *Beyond Occupation: American Jewish, Christian, and Palestinian Voices for Peace.*[2]

Ellis describes himself as "a student of contemporary religious thought rather than a trained theologian." As indicated by the word *toward* in the title of his book, he has not written a Jewish liberation theology but has attempted to spell out the spiritual, intellectual, and political preconditions that "might give birth" to such a theology.

Although Ellis describes himself as a practicing Jew, most of his work and study have been with what he describes as "progressive Roman Catholic groups and institutions." He received his Ph.D. from Marquette University and has written an extremely interesting book entitled, *A Year of the Catholic Worker*, describing his experiences in that institution.[3] Ellis writes that his affiliations might evoke "fear or wonder" in members of the Jewish community. They aroused neither in me. I have known and admired Ellis since he was an undergraduate student in religious studies at Florida State University.

Admiration and respect do not imply agreement. Ellis has presented a theological and political critique of both Israel and the American Jewish community which is far harsher and, I believe, far less realistic than anything suggested even by the vast majority of those Jewish intellectuals and laymen on the Left who are more actively involved in the Jewish community.

According to Ellis, the "dialectic of slavery and liberation" is at the heart of Jewish life. That dialectic is derived from the experience of the Exodus. While acknowledging that there has been some "fidelity to covenantal values" in contemporary Jewish life, Ellis complains that "the Jewish community's struggle to be faithful to those values has been shadowed by the reality of *betrayal*, for in advance of our own interests we have been slave merchants and masters, supported corrupt kings and governments, and even at times oppressed one another" (italics added).[4]

The theme of Jewish betrayal of Judaism's ideals runs through Ellis's exposition. Some may regard Ellis's accusation of betrayal as a contemporary expression of the prophets' denunciation of Israel's want of faithfulness to its divinely bestowed covenant. Others, myself included, see it as extraordinarily insensitive to Jewish feelings and a misreading of history in which Ellis tends to offer a more charitable interpretation of Israel's enemies than he does of Israel itself. According to *Webster's New Collegiate Dictionary,* the primary meaning of *betray* is "to deliver to an enemy *by treachery or fraud,* in violation of trust" as would be the case when a military leader betrays his native city. A second meaning is "to be a traitor; to prove faithless or treacherous to, as to a trust or one who trusts; to fail or desert in a moment of need." Ellis's use of the term is indicative of why *Toward a Jewish Theology of Liberation* is not likely to be the beginning of a dialogue on a new Jewish theology. Aside from any shortcomings the Jewish community may have, it is not likely to give a serious hearing to any theological writing that repeats, albeit unintentionally, the kind of anti-Jewish defamations that in the past have led to the casting of the Jews wholly outside of any shared universe of moral obligation with their neighbors.[5] That Jews, like most other peoples, have often fallen short of their highest ideals and that some have from time to time been rebellious and disobedient are beyond dispute. Such failures place them within the range of normal human behavior. Regrettably, the *betrayal* accusation carries with it altogether different associations. The ascription to Jews of betrayal and treason as fundamental characteristics has its roots in the image of Judas Iscariot betraying his Master for money with a kiss, which I discuss elsewhere in this work. Implied in that image is the not so subliminal message that, as Judas used a loving act to betray Jesus for money, so the Jews are not to be trusted even when they give the appearance of fidelity. The image of the Jew as betrayer has done almost as much as the Christ-killer accusation to cast the Jew wholly outside of any conceivable universe of moral obligation with Christians, especially in times of stress.[6]

Ellis would under no circumstances intentionally lend support to the anti-Semitic defamation of the Jewish people. Unfortunately, his thesis does not completely avoid this possibility. Some words have a long and bitter history and often elicit associations that far outrun the intentions of those who employ them. *Betrayal* is such a word. Lest there be the slightest misunderstanding, I do not accuse Ellis of anti-Semitism, intentional or unintentional. His writings involve a different problem: he is largely indebted to the Christian liberation theologians for his theological framework. Unfortunately, their views of Jews and Judaism are almost uniformly shaped by the Church's supersessionist theological claims over the Synagogue, as Ellis himself points out and protests.

Christian influence is also prominent in Cohn-Sherbok's book, although its expression differs markedly from Ellis's analysis. According to Cohn-Sherbok, liberation theology offers Jews a "new orientation to Jesus" in which the primary emphasis falls on the "flesh and blood Jesus of history" rather than on the incarnate Lord of traditional theology.[7] As an example of this "new" perspective, Cohn-Sherbok writes: "The ancient prophets condemned the leaders of the nation; Jesus attacked the Scribes and the Pharisees for their iniquity." Cohn-Sherbok then proceeds to list the "iniquities" of the Pharisees. They include "mockery of God's law," fostering of "moribund religious practices," and indifference to hunger so long as the Sabbath rituals were formally observed. Cohn-Sherbok quotes Juan L. Segundo on Jesus and the Pharisees: "The ultimate criterion in Jesus' theology is the remedy brought to some sort of human suffering."[8] Commenting on Segundo, Cohn-Sherbok writes, "The Pharisees did not share his concern; they were in Jesus' words, a 'brood of vipers.' 'How can you speak good,' he asks, 'when you are evil?'"[9] Cohn-Sherbok also depicts Jesus as confronting the Pharisees "who were described in Luke as 'lovers of money'" and condemning them for preferring to serve mammon rather than God.[10]

That the authors of the Gospel narratives depict Jesus as having hostile and polemic attitudes toward the Pharisees is not in dispute. Nevertheless, the consensus of modern critical scholarship, both Jewish and Christian, is that the Gospels can no longer be regarded as literal, eye-witness accounts of the events they depict. Instead, each of the Gospels is seen has having been written and edited in the spirit of one of the Christian communities that arose in the aftermath of the Judeo-Roman War of 66–70 C.E. Each of these communities was in some sense a religious rival of the Pharisees, who were in turn divided among themselves. Jesus' encounters with the Pharisees, as depicted in the Gospels, must be read in the light of these conflicts. Put differently, the Gospels cannot be taken uncritically as historical documents; they must be seen, at least by theologians and historians of religion, in the light of the religious and political imperatives of the communities in which they arose.

An enormous amount of critical scholarship, both Christian and Jewish, has given us a more accurate and complete picture of the Pharisees than is to be found in either the Gospel accounts or the uncritical repetition of those accounts by the Christian liberation theologians.[11] As is obvious from a reading of their works, the more prominent liberation theologians are far more at home in contemporary European social thought than they are with recent critical studies of first-century Christianity and Judaism. The presence of theological bias and the absence of critical, historical examination of the sources of first-century Judaism on the part of the liberation theologians are especially evident in their treatment of the encounters between Jesus and the Pharisees.

It is difficult to tell whether the views described concerning the Pharisees are those of Rabbi Cohn-Sherbok or of the liberation theologians. I was so astonished by the uncritical depiction of Jesus and the Pharisees in Cohn-Sherbok's book that I asked him whether he concurs in the views of the Pharisees offered in his book. He told me that they were the views of the liberation theologians.

While the liberation theologians hold Moses and the prophets in high esteem, their view of the founders of the Jewish religious mainstream is based upon the traditional, negative stereotypes of the Pharisees and of rabbinic Judaism which predominated in the Christian world before the era of interreligious dialogue and unbiased critical scholarship. Moreover, as Ellis points out, the liberation theologians have no place in their writings for contemporary Jews. At the very least, fruitful theological dialogue between religious Jews and liberation theologians requires that the latter at least acquaint themselves with Christian critical scholarship on first-century Judaism and Christianity.

Ellis recognizes something of the anti-Jewish theological bias in the writings of the liberation theologians. Nevertheless, the negative bias in those writings appears to have had a greater influence on his interpretations of the contemporary Jewish situation than he recognizes. This is especially evident in his treatment of the encounters between Jews and such groups as the Palestinians and the American Black community. Where others are inclined to see tragic conflict, Ellis is prepared to see Jewish "betrayal" of Jewish ideals.

Many important issues divide Jewish conservatives and the mainstream Black leadership in the United States. These include conservative distrust of affirmative action programs, the generally pro-Arab position of Black leadership, and the place of honor and influence accorded by Black activists to the author of the most overt public praise of Hitler's extermination program uttered by any American religious leader since World War II, Louis Farrakhan.

Affirmative action is one issue on which Blacks and many, though not all, Jewish conservatives are strongly at odds. Nevertheless, there is nothing distinctively Jewish about middle-class white opposition to affirmative action. Those middle-class whites, both Jewish and Christian, who prefer strict adherence to the merit system in employment and school admissions, see affirmative action as giving Blacks a government-sponsored unfair advantage. They do not see why they should be penalized for previous generations' exploitation of Blacks. By contrast, Blacks see themselves as having been disadvantaged by a social structure from which *all* whites have derived benefit. They regard affirmative action as indispensable to creating the beginnings of genuine equality in America. Values and interests are honestly in conflict on this issue. Regrettably, Ellis turns an honest conflict of interests into an expression of moral failing by one of the parties to the conflict, insisting that "justice" is on the side of the Blacks and that Jewish views constitute a "betrayal" of Jewish ideals. As in the other conflicts he examines, the side he almost always faults is Jewish.

Another complaint Ellis raises against the mainstream of the Jewish community both in Israel and in North America is that its "policies and alliances . . . increasingly resemble those historically used to oppress our own people." These are said to include "continued subjugation of the West Bank and Gaza Palestinians," Israel's sale of sophisticated weaponry to and cooperation in developing military hardware with South Africa, and its alleged military assistance to "the murderous governments" of Guatemala and El Salvador. Ellis also sees "betrayal" in American Jewish neoconservatism. He traces the alleged turn to political conservatism on the part of the leadership of the American Jewish community to the Holocaust, the "formative event" for contemporary Judaism. He cites the feeling of isolation and abandonment which the Jews of the world experienced at the time of the Holocaust. In my opinion, the feeling of abandonment stems from the passive complicity of the overwhelming majority of the peoples of Europe in the extermination project. This was almost as hard to bear as the outright acts of the avowed enemy. As we have seen, those survivors foolish enough to try to return to their old homes after the war were often subject to the harshest harassment, and, in some parts of Poland, to outright murder. Under the circumstances, it was hardly surprising that most of the Holocaust survivors wanted nothing so much as the chance to leave that continent forever.

Ellis sees Rabbi Yitzchak Greenberg's theological and religious response to the Holocaust as representative of the Jewish mainstream, albeit highly problematic. Greenberg insists that in the post-Holocaust era the survival of the Jewish people, without which there can be no Judaism, has become the fundamental value of the Jewish community.[12] This is a view Ellis cannot accept. As Ellis points out, Greenberg sees the Holocaust as symbolizing radical alienation from God and "immersion in nihilism." However, this negative experience is dialectically linked to the positive experience of the recovery of Jerusalem and the Western Wall, the site of the ancient Jerusalem Temple. Jerusalem thus symbolizes "the presence of God and the continuation of the people." After the experience of extermination and utter abandonment at Auschwitz, Greenberg holds that it is absolutely imperative that the Jews of Israel cease to be victims and do whatever they must to ensure their survival. Thus, Greenberg elevates to a sacred principle the need to achieve sufficient power to guarantee the survival of the State of Israel, insofar as such a guarantee is humanly possible. In the post-Holocaust period, endangering that power becomes the closest thing to an unpardonable sin for Judaism. As Ellis points out, the Holocaust theologians, among whom he includes Emil L. Fackenheim and myself, are nearly unanimous on this point.

Ellis argues that Greenberg's elevation of power to a sacred principle is highly problematic, as Greenberg himself would acknowledge. Greenberg's position is not unlike the realism of Reinhold Neibuhr and seems to be derived from Max Weber's contrast of an "ethic of responsibility" and an "ethic of ultimate ends."[13] According to Greenberg, Israel's present exercise of power can no longer be judged in the light of the absolute standards of the ancient prophets. When Israel commits herself to action in the political sphere, guilt and imperfect responses are inevitable. Only the utterly powerless can judge political action in terms of absolute standards of good and evil. Following Nietzsche, I would add that the use of such standards by the powerless is an important psychological weapon in their own struggle for power. In place of an absolute standard of good and evil, Greenberg offers a pragmatism new to Jewish experience. Admittedly, such a pragmatism inevitably leads to the "occasional use of immoral strategies to achieve moral ends." To guard against abuse, Greenberg insists that the exercise of power must not be divorced from self-criticism and a sense of obligation and empathy toward the Palestinians. Nevertheless, under no circumstances can Israel grant any degree of empowerment to the Palestinians which would endanger the existence and security of the Jewish people.[14] According to Greenberg, to do so is to collaborate with attempted genocide, albeit unintentionally.

Ellis disagrees most emphatically with Greenberg and the Holocaust theologians on this point. For him, the Holocaust theologians represent the regnant ideology of the mainstream American Jewish community. Ellis maintains that the Jewish community, having opted for power in place of powerlessness, is paying a prohibitive price for that choice. Among the negative expressions of "empowerment" Ellis includes "the rise of the neoconservative movement in North America" and "the ascendancy to power in Israel of religious and secular expansionists, exemplified by Rabbi Meir Kahane . . . and Ariel Sharon." Ellis further argues that the Jewish community, presumably the Israeli community, has exchanged the misery of the victim for the role of "conqueror." He accuses the Jewish community of having forgotten its own oppression and having opened "the possibility of becoming an oppressor."

In addition to these accusations, Ellis cites approvingly the harsh judgments leveled at Jewish neoconservatives by Earl Shorris and Roberta Strauss Feuerlicht. Shorris contends that Jewish neoconservatives oppose helping Blacks or other minorities because the Blacks are anti-Semitic and, they believe, the others will become so. Shorris also argues that the neoconservatives hold that the State of Israel can do no wrong, the Palestinians have no right to a state, and the killing of an Israeli civilian by a Palestinian is an act of terror whereas the killing of a Palestinian civilian by an Israeli is an act of self-defense. Moreover, Shorris assigns to the Jews the view that the poor in America are an underclass without dignity that can best be served by neglect because only through the goad of necessity will they ever achieve a dignified place in American life.[15] Regrettably, Shorris offers a malicious caricature of responsible conservative opinion. No responsible conservative holds that the State of Israel can do no wrong. Nor do conservatives take issue with Black leadership simply because of Blacks alleged anti-Semitism but because of honest differences on issues, some of which are discussed above. That terrorism has been practiced by both sides in the Arab-Israeli conflict cannot be denied. Nor is there any doubt that innocent Palestinians have been killed both before and during the Intifada. Nevertheless, Shorris's equation of the Arab terrorists' cold-blooded killing of the innocent of all ages, both Jewish and non-Jewish, on land, sea, and in the air with the behavior of the Israeli army and even hard-line Israeli settlers toward the Palestinians is contemptible, as is his statement that Jewish conservatives regard the poor as an underclass without dignity. It would be best for both the Israelis and the Palestinians were it possible for the Palestinians to have their own state *without endangering Israel's existence.* However, a state is a "human community that (successfully) claims a monopoly on the legitimate use of physical force within a given territory."[16] Unless the Israelis have credible assurance that the guns of a newly established Palestinian state and its allies in Jordan, Iraq, and elsewhere in the Arab world will not be used against them, it would be suicidal for Israel to consent to such a transfer of power. It is regrettable that Ellis has chosen to take Shorris seriously.

Ellis also approves of Roberta Strauss Feuerlicht's views. She argues that all Jews are bound together not by statehood but by "the burden they placed upon themselves and posterity when they internalized morality and gave the world the ethical imperative."[17] Having defined the bond allegedly uniting Jewry, Feuerlicht proceeds to accuse the Jews of violating their own ethical imperatives. She condemns them for having been "slave owners, slave traders and slave auctioneers" out of all proportion to their numbers in the antebellum South. This is a rather curious accusation, and one wonders what Feuerlicht's motives were for making it. The ancestors of the vast majority of American Jews did not arrive in the United States until long after the Civil War. Moreover, in the antebellum period the majority of American Jews did not live in the South. Yet, Feuerlicht feels compelled to impute to "the Jews" the guilt of slavery as an institution. Clearly, Feuerlicht is more interested in establishing the so-called guilt of contemporary Jews vis-à-vis the Blacks than in establishing a genuine past grievance. Although Feuerlicht concedes that many Jews participated in the civil rights movement of the sixties, she characterizes the current position of the Jewish community toward the Blacks as bordering on arrogance.

Feuerlicht sees the State of Israel as founded upon a policy of expropriation and denial of the rights of Palestinians. Although she condemns the State of Israel as an example of colonialism rather than national liberation, she concedes that it must continue to exist because the alternative would be another Holocaust.

Concluding his discussion of Shorris and Feuerlicht, Ellis suggests that they have assumed the role of latter-day prophets who critique Israel's policies, such as the sale of arms to right-wing Central American governments, "continuing contributions to the scientific, military, and economic interests of South Africa," and "wholesale expropriation of Palestinian land on the West Bank and in Gaza." He sees Shorris and Feuerlicht as naming the "new forms of idolatry" embraced by the Jewish community: "capitalism; nationalism; survival at any cost."

In spite of what he considers the failings of the Israeli and American Jewish mainstreams, Ellis is somewhat encouraged by "movements of Jewish renewal," mostly movements on the left. They include the New Jewish Agenda in the United States; the *Oz VeShalom* movement in Israel, which strongly opposes continued Israeli occupation of the West Bank and Gaza; and the Jewish peace movement.

Ellis is especially encouraged by the action of Todd Kaplan, who was part of a group that entered the Martin Marietta plant in Orlando, Florida, in April 1984 and used hammers to damage several of the army's Pershing II intermediate-range ballistic missiles that were being fabricated at the plant. The group also poured blood on the installation. While this was going on, Kaplan blew a shofar as a symbolic call to repentance. Kaplan characterized the event as the "Plowshares action." He was subsequently sentenced to a three-year term in the minimal security Federal Prison in Danbury, Connecticut.

Ellis characterizes Kaplan's behavior as an "act for justice." He cites with approval Kaplan's defense of the "Plowshares action": "I believe that the elimination of nuclear arms is a goal we Jews should embrace. . . . We should take the idea of holocaust prevention both seriously and personally."[18]

Ellis's use of Kaplan's "Plowshares action" highlights the striking difference between his political theology and a conservative political theology. In supporting Kaplan's dramatic plea for unilateral disarmament, Ellis demonstrates his own naiveté. Nowhere in his book does Ellis consider the voluminous literature on the subject of arms control, disarmament, and deterrence which has developed since 1945. Kaplan's theatrical behavior is utterly unrelated to the real world of nuclear weapons. The United States and the Soviet Union have avoided the ultimate horror of nuclear warfare for over forty years. As is well known, in those years

when the Soviet Union possessed superiority in conventional armaments, its military capabilities were balanced by the nuclear arsenal possessed by the United States, Britain, and France. When a realistic
opportunity arose for both sides to reduce nuclear weapons, the conservative, anticommunist administration of Ronald Reagan took the necessary first steps.

Ellis faults the Holocaust theologians for having "virtually nothing
to say about the ethics of a Jewish state possessing nuclear weapons."
For Ellis mere possession of such weapons is an evil. Although the Israelis have never admitted that they posses a nuclear arsenal, arms control experts widely agree that Israel does in fact possess such weapons.
Israel's policy has been characterized as that of a "bomb in the base-
ment," meaning that the Israelis have the bomb but find it prudent to
refrain from going public.[19]

Nowhere does Ellis discuss Israel's reasons for believing that her survival depends upon her nuclear arsenal. For at least a decade Saddam Hussein's Iraq—a country that has repeatedly and unambiguously pledged
itself to the *total* destruction of Israel—has attempted to acquire the capability to produce nuclear weapons. Iraq today possesses intermediate-range
ballistic missiles with chemical warheads and may still be working to acquire
nuclear warheads. At the time of his mysterious murder, renegade Canadian scientist Gerald Bull, the world's greatest artillery expert, was actively
working with Iraq to produce a high-tech "supergun" capable of launching
a 1,200-pound, rocket-propelled projectile to a target as much as three thousand miles away.[20] Nor was Saddam Hussein reticent about his intentions,
having threatened to destroy "half of Israel" by poison gas. In the aftermath
of the Holocaust, no threat could have been more inflammatory to any Israeli. With a population many times that of Israel, and with a battle-hard-
ened army of one million at the end of Iraq's war with Iran, only Israel's
nuclear capability may have served to deter Hussein's desire utterly to destroy the State of Israel and its Jewish population. Even after the Gulf War,
without nuclear weapons Israel has no credible means of overcoming the
enormous advantage the Arab states enjoy in population, wealth, and conventional weapons.

Similarly, in discussing Israel's occupation of the West Bank and
Gaza, Ellis is more concerned with the harm done to Palestinians than
with the reasons why most Israelis believe they have no choice but to
hold on to the occupied territories, in spite of the injury to both the Palestinians and Israeli society. Ellis complains that Holocaust theology is
unable to articulate a path of solidarity with the Palestinian people. He
further asserts that an essential task of Jewish theology must be to "de-

absolutize" the State of Israel. Regrettably, Ellis has little to say concerning the refusal of the Arab states, save Egypt, to make peace with Israel after more than forty years, their persistent attempts to delegitimize Israel by the obscene U.N. resolution declaring that Zionism is racism, and their oft-repeated statements, uttered more often in Arabic than in English, that their ultimate goal is the total destruction of the State of Israel.

Nor when discussing the Israeli occupation does Ellis mention the fact that the West Bank was occupied because King Hussein of Jordan went to war against Israel in 1967 in spite of entreaties by the Israeli government that he keep his country out of the conflict. Although Jordan was soundly defeated, it never sought to make peace with Israel. It is one thing for Israel to give up territory to an enemy who is willing to enter into a credible peace treaty. It is an altogether different matter to give up a territorial buffer to enemies bent on Israel's ultimate destruction.

Few Jews like to see Israeli soldiers beating up Palestinians or blowing up their houses. Moreover, Israeli policy toward the Palestinians has had its share of errors, misperceptions, and miscalculations. Nevertheless, the real problem is that, unlike Ellis, neither the Palestinians nor the Israelis see the Palestinians of the West Bank and Gaza as powerless or Israel as powerful. In spite of Ellis's constant references to the heavy moral price the Jews are paying for "empowerment," the Palestinians see themselves as part of the larger Arab world that will someday overwhelm and destroy the Israelis as an earlier generation of Arabs destroyed the Crusader kingdoms. Both sides understand that the Arabs can sustain innumerable defeats without having any incentive to make peace. The Arabs are convinced that sooner or later they will win the final war.

In spite of Ellis's insistence that the lessons of the Holocaust are largely irrelevant to Israel's current situation of what he strangely calls "empowerment" and his contention that Holocaust theology is irrelevant to the situation in contemporary Israel, *the Holocaust is precisely the operative model the Israelis must consider as their worst possible case scenario.* The Holocaust cannot be used as a model for day-to-day relations between Jews and non-Jews, either in the Diaspora or even in the encounter between Israeli and Palestinian. Nevertheless, few military analysts have any doubt that a decisive defeat of Israel by the Arab states would be followed by a merciless slaughter that would assure the Arabs of the "Final Solution" of their Jewish problem. Robert Harkavy has succinctly stated the reasons why the Arabs will be satisfied with nothing less than total vengeance: "The Middle East conflict is not fundamentally one of territorial irredentism or self-determination, nor is it simply a zero-sum clash of rival nationalisms over control of Palestine. These are contributing factors. A more fundamental reason that a permanent peace is virtually impossible is the overwhelming, deep-seated humiliation felt by all Arabs over having been defeated six times in wars by Israel."[21]

The Holocaust itself and the consistently antagonistic positions taken against Israel in the United Nations provide a realistic basis for assessing the kind of help Israel might expect if it were ever threatened with imminent extermination. Instead of helping, it is much more likely that many foreign offices even in the Western world, especially in Europe, would regard the likely Arab action as a convenient exercise in problem solving.

Ellis argues that "at the center of the struggle to be faithful as a Jew today is the suffering and liberation of the Palestinian people." Furthermore, he contends that the situation requires "a fundamental confession and repentance of past and present transgressions" on the part of the Jews. Thus, for Ellis the weight of solving the conflict is thrust upon the Israelis with little or no consideration of the persistent Palestinian refusal to offer their own *credible* scenario for Israeli-Palestinian coexistence. In contrast to Israeli fundamentalists, who see Israel's claim to the whole of Palestine and even Jordan as divinely mandated, I believe that the optimal solution to the Arab-Israeli conflict would be one in which the national aspirations of both communities are reasonably satisfied. Regrettably, the PLO made a promise to the Jews which, after Hitler, can neither be forgotten nor explained away—the promise to drive the Jews out of the land and into the sea. Since that promise was made, the Palestinian position has altered course a number of times. For a while Yassir Arafat moderated his position with an ambiguous revision of the original Palestinian intent, the revision having a different meaning depending on whether it was expressed in English or in Arabic. In retrospect, Arafat's "moderation" seems to have been aimed primarily at establishing dialogue with the United States in order to weaken America's support of Israel. However, even the Bush administration, before the Iraq crisis the most overtly pro-Arab administration since World War II, could not continue the so-called dialogue when Arafat refused to disown the blatantly terrorist activities of constituent groups of the PLO. Nevertheless, once having been uttered, the promise to destroy Israel is one that, after Auschwitz, no Jew can dismiss. It was Elie Wiesel who wrote, in *Night*, that only Hitler kept his promises to the Jews. In the aftermath of Hitler, Jews are no longer disposed to ignore such promises. Moreover, the overt support the PLO and the vast majority of the Palestinians have given to Saddam Hussein during the Gulf war is an important indication of their ultimate intentions. Those Jews who, like Ellis, believe the fundamental problem is Israeli denial of Palestinian human rights are likely to argue that Israeli intransigence drove the Palestinians to Saddam Hussein. In reality, the PLO was never prepared to accept anything less than the total destruction of Israel. Their "recognition" of Israel's "right to exist" was never more than a strategic move toward that end. When the Israelis look at the Intifada, they do not see a Palestinian population prepared to create a peaceful national existence alongside of them. They see a population determined to take the necessary steps in conjunction with their Arab brethren eventually to destroy them.

Ellis raises the problem of justice for the Palestinians. However, justice is not an abstract concept but one rooted in the realities of communal living. *One owes very little, if anything, to those who are determined to destroy one's community.* Words about Israeli-Palestinian solidarity come easily, but there can be no solidarity when both sides have reason to believe, as many do, that they are locked in long-term mortal combat. As Ellis recognizes, the Holocaust made the creation of the State of Israel absolutely imperative. The historic eastern European Jewish community was finished. With the birth of the State of Israel, the Jews were brutally expelled from Arab lands, a population "solution" only the most extremist Israelis propose to reciprocate for the Palestinians. There was no longer any place in the Islamic world for Jews. *The ingathering of the exiles was neither an act of colonialism/imperialism nor a felicitous act of voluntary homecoming but the desperate act of people for whom the world offered no other place.* With the collapse of communism and the revival of Russian anti-Semitism, Israel is currently in the process of receiving more than one million Russian Jews. Were it not for Israel's determination to absorb this new immigration, Russian Jews would have found themselves despised strangers in the confused, embittered, and disoriented land of their birth with no place to which to escape.

Surrounded on all sides by enemies who regard her as a wholly alien presence destined sooner or later to be destroyed as were the Crusader kingdoms, founded in the aftermath of the extermination of Europe's Jews, the State of Israel has created a nuclear arsenal as a deterrent against its own destruction. *Israel's basic nuclear strategy consists in radically escalating the cost of exterminating its citizens.* This strategy is largely a consequence of the destruction of Europe's Jews during World War II. It is also a consequence of the expulsion of the Jews from Moslem lands. The Israelis know that, at its most merciful, an Arab victory over Israel would result in yet another total expulsion. Saddam Hussein's brutal occupation of Kuwait and his treatment of the Kurds offer the Israelis a foretaste of what they can expect. In all likelihood, Arab treatment of defeated Israelis would be infinitely more vicious. In Nazi Europe Jewish victims lacked all means of self-defense and were incapable of inflicting significant damage on their enemies. There was little, if any, economic cost to the Germans in the extermination project, when the value of confiscated Jewish property and the use of Jewish institutions to facilitate the destruction is factored in. An Israeli resort to nuclear weapons would, of course, be utterly suicidal. Nevertheless, after the Germans succeeded in slaughtering millions of Jews with impunity and after the Arabs promised to do the same to the Israelis, it is highly unlikely that the Israelis would go silently into the dust. Israel's deterrent strategy can be seen as a variation on the MAD strategy, mutually assured destruction.

Methodologically, Ellis is entirely consistent in seeking to diminish the relevance of Holocaust theology and of the Holocaust itself for the contemporary Jewish situation. Instead of garnering the exceedingly modest resources of the post-Holocaust Jewish community to assure its own survival, Ellis demands that Jews adopt the utopian program of moving "beyond empowerment to a liberation encompassing *all those struggling for justice,* including those we *once* knew as enemy" (italics added). There is more than a little irony in these words after the Palestinians' enthusiastic embrace of Saddam Hussein. Apart from the fact that few, if any, of the larger and more powerful peoples of the world have adopted a program of justice for all people, save as pious rhetoric, it does not seem to have occurred to Ellis that in a world of conflicting peoples with conflicting rights, it is utterly impossible to render justice to all. That is why theologians, both Christian and Jewish, cannot entirely ignore the doctrine of the Fall. Moreover, Ellis's call for a deabsolutizing Israel seems to anticipate Israel's eventual demise. Ellis argues that it might be possible for Israel to avoid defeat and annihilation by making "peace when you are powerful." Here again, Ellis *prefers the utopian to the actual.* Apart from the fact that Israel is not powerful in any realistic, long-term sense, Ellis's proposal that Israel make peace only makes sense if there were someone with whom to make peace. To expect that the Palestinians would be satisfied with a rump state on the West Bank and in Gaza is contrary to all we know about their national aspirations and their sense of national dignity. Even that much would seriously threaten Israel at a time when Arab wealth, numbers, and technological sophistication continue to increase.

Ellis recognizes that military defeat may someday come to Israel. Here again, he is compelled to devalue the Holocaust as a model for the outcome of such a defeat. He argues: "But if military defeat does come and if the civilian population is attacked, the result, though tragic, will not by any meaningful definition be another Holocaust. And it would not by any means signal the end of the Jewish people, as many Holocaust theologians continue to speculate."[22]

It is impossible to predict the future. Ellis may be correct in his optimism concerning a military defeat, but no responsible Jewish leader dare risk a situation in which the lives of Israel's Jews depend upon the tender mercies of the Palestinians or their fellow Arabs. Nor would the mortal threat be faced solely by the Israelis. As Robert Harkavy has argued, "Levels of anti-Semitism would rise rather than fall if Israel were destroyed and its people massacred," for "there has been a historical psychological connection between Jewish defeat . . . and sadistic anti-Semitism."[23]

Ellis's theological views are important because they are an authentic expression of what a Jewish version of Christian liberation theology would be like. They are also important because of the widespread hearing Ellis has received, especially in colleges, universities, and theological seminaries. A genuinely Jewish liberation theology would take greater account of recent and current Jewish history than does Ellis. In particular, a Jewish liberation theology would understand as tragic conflict that which Ellis so readily denounces as oppression and betrayal. As with a nonutopian Christian theology, it would work for the realistic amelioration of the inhuman condition of the marginalized. It would do so by soundly based economic and political measures that take full account of the modernizing economic and technological forces that have fostered mass marginalization since the beginnings of the Industrial Revolution.[24] It would under no circumstances seek a revolutionary overturning of the current economic and political order, which would inevitably end in tyranny, mass repression, and mass murder by regimes far more inhumane than present bourgeois or right-wing governments, as the history of both the Soviet Union and the Peoples Republic of China demonstrate. Above all, such a theology would insist that the Holocaust has lost none of its relevance for Jewish faith and experience. On the contrary, in spite of fantasies of Jewish empowerment, the Holocaust gains further relevance with the Intifada and the Iraqi behavior toward Kuwait and the Kurds as ever-present reminders of the fate that awaits Israel should its defenses falter.

CHAPTER 15

Muslims, Jews, and the Western World

A JEWISH VIEW

W&I: Could you speak on the Jewish-Islamic issue from the point of view of a Jewish scholar?

R: I don't think there is a *specific* Jewish-Islamic issue. Even though Islam arises after Judaism and Christianity, it regards itself as the original true religion, whose fundamental meaning was revealed by the Prophet Mohammed. Islam regards both Judaism and Christianity as distorted views of the original true religion. Islam thus has a supersessionary interpretation of both Judaism and Christianity that neither can accept. Moreover, in its history, Christianity has been confronted by three potential and two actual major challenges. One was Judaism. The second was Islam, and third atheistic communism. After Christianity became the official religion of the Roman Empire, Judaism was no longer a serious challenge, because in the Diaspora Jews were not culturally influential or numerous enough for Judaism to be an effective religious alternative. On the other hand, Islam has been the most powerful of all challenges to Christianity. In 711 Islamic forces occupied almost all of the Iberian peninsula. At one time or another, large parts of Christian Europe were dominated by Islamic forces, including Bulgaria, Romania, the Balkans, southern Italy, and much of southern Russia. Almost from its inception, Islam has constituted the major challenge to Christianity.

In the last two centuries, however, Islam has experienced a series of cultural shocks. Islam was unable to do what the Japanese have done, namely, successfully meet the challenge of Western modernization. When Islam first entered Europe in the eighth century, it was the superior civilization. It had a level of sophistication and culture that was far higher than that of northern Europe. For several centuries, the victories of Islam were of such a magnitude that they were taken as signs of the truth and superiority of the Muslim religion. The shock was therefore all the greater when, starting in the eighteenth century, European Christian countries began to modernize effectively. They had gone through the Renaissance, the Reformation, and the Enlightenment and had the capacity to develop skills and to advance learning in a way that left the Islamic world behind, especially in the area of military power.

What the Islamic world did have, and has to this day, is the *Shari'a*, the Islamic way of life as found in the laws derived from the Koran. To this day, the Islamic world looks down on the civilization that came out of the European Enlightenment as lacking the genuine morality and social discipline possessed by traditional Muslim society.

W&I: In the Middle Ages the Islamic world was ahead scientifically and culturally, but then they fell behind. Why?

R: The Islamic world fell behind scientifically and culturally because Muslims were so convinced of the superiority of their religiously legitimated civilization that they saw no reason to adapt to modernization. By contrast, the European Christian nations were able to modernize. For two centuries, the Islamic world experienced a kind of inner dislocation because Muslims thought of themselves as possessing the true religion and the superior civilization, yet the "infidels" were everywhere victorious. The British took over Egypt as well as the Indian subcontinent at a time when it was dominated by Muslim rulers; the Dutch took over predominantly Muslim Indonesia; the French controlled Algeria, Morocco, and Syria; the Italians controlled Libya.

Finding themselves unexpectedly under Christian domination, the Muslim nations then tried to overcome the situation of defeat. They tried secularization, modernization, and westernization. Unlike the Japanese, who successfully modernized in a way that permitted them to preserve their cultural integrity, the Islamic world was unable to create a comparable cultural synthesis without imperiling their own religion and culture. One of the worst shocks experienced by the Islamic world was the capture by the Israelis in the Six-Day War of 1967 of all of Jerusalem, known to Muslims as *al-Quds*.

When Arabs argue that Saddam Hussein's occupation of Kuwait was no different than the Israeli occupation of the West Bank and Gaza, it is important to remember how the 1967 war started. Beginning in 1965 a series of intensifying border crises erupted between Syria and Israel and escalated into artillery duels and aerial combat. Syria encouraged the radical Palestinian al-Fatah group to carry out raids aginst both civilian and military targets inside Israel. Protected by Syrian artillery, Fatah inflicted many Israeli casualties. On April 7, 1967, Israel struck back, downing six Syrian MiGs. The Russians then began to warn the Israelis not to take further action against their client, Syria. The Russians also mischievously accused the Israelis of preparing a massive attack against Syria and passed on false "information" concerning Israeli intentions to Egypt.

On May 15 Gamal Abd al-Nasser, the Egyptian leader, ordered most of his army into the Sinai peninsula. On May 17 he ordered the United Nations forces out of Sinai. U Thant, the U.N. Secretary General, complied without protest, and the Egyptian army moved into Gaza, only a few miles from Tel Aviv. On May 21 Nasser declared a blockade against Israeli shipping through the Strait of Tiran. The blockade was an unprovoked act of war. When the Western powers refused to take action, Israel had no choice but to prepare to defend its interest alone. King Hussein of Jordan then flew to Cairo to place his army under Egyptian command. As the Arab masses demonstrated for *jihad*, holy war, the troops of Egypt, Syria, Iraq, and Jordan were mobilized against Israel. They outnumbered Israeli forces by three to one. The Israelis pleaded with the Jordanians to stay out of the war everyone knew was imminent, but King Hussein refused. When the Jordanians entered the war, the Israelis, in order to defend themselves against the threat to their very existence, expelled the Jordanian army from East Jerusalem and the West Bank and took the whole territory of Palestine for the first time in almost two thousand years. The whole of Jerusalem, the holy city of Judaism and the third most holy city in the Muslim world, fell to the Jews.

Not only had the Islamic world experienced defeats at the hands of the Christians, whose power was obvious, but now a small group of Jews had unexpectedly defeated them in 1948 and again in 1967. The Jews were able to fight a modern war. Like the Christians, the Jews had learned how to adapt to modernization. Had the Islamic world successfully modernized, the Israelis could not have won any of their wars.

W&I: Islamic scholars and religious leaders claim that there is no impediment in Islam to rapprochement between Islam and Judaism, that this is purely a political problem.

R: It is not correct that there is no religious impediment or religious tension between Islam and Judaism, that this is purely a political problem. I respect Islam as a culture highly, but there are real religious differences between Judaism and Christianity on the one hand, and Islam on the other. As I have said, Islam claims that it alone is the original true religion of God and that both Judaism and Christianity are distortions of the true religion. Islam divides the world into the *Dar al-Islam* and the *Dar al-Harb*. The *Dar al-Islam* is that part of the world under Islamic control and governed, at least in theory, by traditional Islamic law. The *Dar al-Harb* is in the hands of infidels. From the Islamic point of view, since Islam is the true religion, its ultimate aim is to make sure that the whole world eventually falls under the sway of Islamic law and becomes part of *Dar al-Islam*. For any part of *Dar al-Islam* to fall back into infidel hands constitutes a real defeat. And, from a Muslim perspective, that is exactly what took place when the State of Israel was established. Hence, the conflict between the Palestinians and Israelis is not just political; it is also religious.

Moreover, I doubt that most Americans realize just how much religious significance the oil boom of 1973 has had for the Islamic world. The boom was perceived by Muslims as a sign that a tremendous power reversal was taking place. The greatest amount of oil is found in those countries that have been most loyal to the most traditional reading of Islam, namely Libya, Saudi Arabia, and some of the emirates. It is not surprising that Islamic thinkers saw the oil wealth of these countries as divine confirmation of the preeminent status of Islam. Significantly, many found a direct correlation between faithfulness and fidelity to traditional Islam and the new oil prosperity. They also interpreted the 1973 war of Israel against Egypt and Syria as a victory for the Islamic world, although the war actually ended in a stalemate.

After the oil boom started, the former colonial powers treated the leaders of oil-rich Arab countries with respect and deference. The modern economies of the West were largely dependent on Arab oil for survival. The Saudis, for example, were able to tell the British, "You can't show the film *The Death of a Princess* on your television." The film showed an unpleasant side of life in Saudi Arabia, and the English acquiesced. The British, the U.S. government, the French, and the Italians all saw the tremendous increase of Islamic wealth and began to behave toward Islam with a new respect. Oil gave Muslim countries greatly increased wealth, much of which was spent to strengthen Islam and, implicitly, to discredit Judaism and Christianity. Because of the advanced weapons systems oil money could buy, oil gave countries like Iraq greatly enhanced military power. At the same time, there was a disenchantment with Western ways, not only in Iran but among the masses throughout the Islamic world, and a turn back to the fundamentals of Islam.

In 1973, after OPEC quadrupled the price of oil and instituted the oil boycott against countries suspected of aiding Israel, one of the Arab ministers said to Western reporters, "This is our revenge for Poitiers." (Poitiers [or Tours] was the battle in 732 C.E. at which Christian forces, under Charles Martel, finally stopped the Muslims, who had invaded almost all of Spain and had succeeded in invading southern France.) Muslims are people with very long historical memories who now see that, with oil, they have the possibility of once again becoming a dominant world force.

As far as the Jews are concerned, I doubt that the Muslims are going to rest content with a Palestinian state on the West Bank and in Gaza. They will take it if that is all they can get for the time being, but they will then start making new demands, perhaps for the predominantly Arab sections of Israel around Nazareth as a starter. Such a rump Israeli state will only be the prelude to the next move, and eventually the Muslims will want to make all of Palestine once again part of *Dar al-Islam*, that is, a territory governed by Islamic law, which it had been for centuries. To achieve this goal, they must either expel or kill off all the Israelis.

I am also very concerned about the long-term situation in which the United States finds itself in the Middle East. If one reads Saddam Hussein's speeches, such as the one of August 9, 1990, we see a leader who called for *jihad*, a holy war, against the United States. In response to the American military buildup in Saudi Arabia, he appealed to Muslims to expel the infidels so that they would not pollute the holy cities of Mecca and Medina. Just as the oil boom of the 1970s was seen as confirmation of God's grace toward Islam, Saddam Hussein, a secular leader, used the language of faith to see whether he could find a way to lead a revived Islam to dominate the Christian West with oil and the high-tech weapons oil can buy.

Moreover, the question of whether or not Saddam Hussein is a believer is like the question a taxi driver was recently asked at a checkpoint between Muslim and Christian Beirut: "Are you a Christian or Muslim?" He replied, "No I am an atheist." He was then asked, "What kind of an atheist, Christian or Muslim?" It really makes no difference whether Saddam Hussein is a believer. If not, he is a Muslim nonbeliever who resorted to age-old aspects of militant Islam in an attempt to make the West dependent upon what he hoped would be his control of almost half of the world's energy supply. For Saddam Hussein, the continuing conflict was ultimately religious, a continuation of a fight that goes back to Poitiers. His repeated attempts to obstruct U.N. inspection of his nuclear and chemical warfare facilities demonstrates that he believes he can outlast George Bush and the allied coalition and eventually resume the fight on his own terms. If he were ever to succeed, and as long as he remains in power he will never give up, it would be a final reversal of the fortunes of Islam after centuries of humiliation.

I don't see the conflict as essentially Jewish-Islamic. On the contrary, I see it in larger terms. One of its more disturbing aspects is the destructive potential of Saddam Hussein's armaments, which have been drastically underestimated by Western intelligence agencies, especially Iraq's nuclear weapons program. According to *Scientific American* (September 1990), the long-range, high-tech cannon invented by the Canadian renegade genius Gerald Bull—the cannon that was manufactured in separate parts and that the British finally discovered just as the parts were about to be shipped to Iraq—has a range of three thousand miles. This is clear evidence that, in addition to trying to build intermediate-range nuclear missiles, Saddam Hussein attempted to acquire intercontinental ballistic missiles.

Why did he want these weapons? Why, after the Gulf War, does he still want them? Perhaps he hopes someday to tell the United States, "We will control the price of oil and, if we control the world's energy, you cannot touch us because we can defend ourselves with our nuclear weapons and our intercontinental missile delivery systems. We will become dominant in the world as Allah intended." He cannot achieve such an objective, but he could do horrendous damage in the attempt. If nothing else, that would satisfy his thirst for vengeance.

His appeal was for a religious war, for a holy war. He put conservative Arab leaders, like President Mubarak of Egypt and the Saudi royal family, in a difficult bind. He spoke the language of traditional Islam. He portrayed America's Muslim allies as traitors to Islam. He called upon the masses in Egypt and the ordinary people in Saudi Arabia to disobey their rulers and to join his fight in the name of the ancient Muslim rivalry with Christianity and Judaism.

I am concerned that, even in defeat, Saddam Hussein will leave behind a legacy of hatred that will last for decades, if not longer, and carry with it the seeds of future wars. *The wars of the twenty-first century may prove to be wars of religion.*

W&I: Islamic scholars and religious leaders say that Islamic fundamentalism is a distortion of real Islam and that it is being used for political purposes. That's one point. Second point: All of the Muslims we have spoken to express a certain bitterness at what they see as the lack of evenhandedness in the West. They claim that America, for example, supposedly stands up for the principle of human rights and the rule of law but that it applies them selectively. It is not applied, for example, to Israeli behavior in Palestine, whereas it is applied to the Iraqi invasion of Kuwait.

R: Here again they are not seeing things straight. As I have tried to show, the Israelis took over the West Bank and Gaza as an act of self-defense in a war in which the joint military forces of Egypt, Syria, Jordan, and Iraq sought to annihilate them. Moreover, whether or not Israeli behavior toward the Palestinians is justified—and it certainly is far less harsh than the behavior of Saddam Hussein and Hafez El Assad toward their domestic opponents—that behavior will not result in a hostile country controlling half of the world's oil supply, whereas if Saddam Hussein's conquest of Kuwait had succeeded, he could have become a worldwide menace. The issue was never oil alone; for Saddam Hussein it was the military power oil wealth could purchase. The real issue for the United States in opposing Iraq's invasion of Kuwait was whether America was going to remain passive while Saddam Hussein gained control of half of the world's oil supply, thereby controlling America's economic destiny. The Israelis never had any interest in doing this; not so Saddam Hussein.

As far as the Arab-Israeli conflict is concerned, I do not believe the Israelis owe the Palestinians much. If the Palestinians had the power to do so, they would drive the Israelis into the sea, no matter what their "moderates" say, and no one would lift a finger to stop them. The Israelis have no such murderous objectives for the Palestinians. Any people who threaten to drive the Israelis into the sea and who, after the Nazi Holocaust, are in alliance with Saddam Hussein, who promised to gas Jews and turn Tel Aviv into a crematorium, must be seen as a mortal enemy.

W&I: Is it fair to invoke the Nazi Holocaust in this dispute?

R: The Nazi Holocaust was invoked by Saddam Hussein when he promised to gas half of Israel and turned to German corporations that were all too willing to build the poison gas plants to do the job. It didn't take much imagination to determine who Saddam's targets were. Hitler killed millions of Jews with gas, and then Saddam Hussein came along with his German-made gas equipment made available to him by German export permits and said, "I've got the weapons and I can gas half of Israel out of existence." That is very, very provocative language, and it was precisely the threat that was bound to create the greatest possible anger and distrust on the part of the Jews everywhere.

W&I: And you interpret his language as deliberately chosen?

R: Absolutely. That man has proven that, if he has a weapon, he will use it if he can. If he is ever in a position to use the gas weapon, he will.

The one thing that gave the Israelis any kind of security during the Gulf War was that they knew Saddam Hussein understood that the cost of using gas against Israel would have been so great in terms of the damage the Israelis could have inflicted on his country that he must have had second and third thoughts about using gas. Threats of this kind are not made lightly. Elie Wiesel once observed that Hitler was the only one who kept his promises to the Jews. He promised to kill them and he did. After Hitler, anyone who promises to kill Jews is going to be taken seriously.

I was in Israel in the summer of 1989. I was also in Israel three weeks after the end of the 1967 Six-Day War. In 1967 when I learned that all of the hotels on the Jewish side were filled, a friend suggested that I try an Arab hotel in East Jerusalem. My wife, Dr. Betty Rubenstein, and I stayed at an Arab hotel. We were treated with exquisite courtesy. Naturally, the management was ambivalent because there had been no Jews in East Jerusalem before the war. All of a sudden, the hotels had to take in Jewish guests or be empty. The food and the service were good. We liked the hotel enough so that we went back for several years.

In 1989, however, nothing could make me go to a hotel in East Jerusalem. While I was in Jerusalem, Professor Menachem Stern, a famous scholar on the faculty of the Hebrew University, was stabbed to death as he walked from his office at the university to his home. Relations between Jews and Palestinians had so deteriorated that I could not risk staying at that East Jerusalem hotel. Nor could I let down my guard with any young Palestinian. When people are that divided, with absolutely no trust between them, when the Palestinians perceive the Israelis as dominating and exploiting them, when the Israelis perceive the Palestinians as potential murderers, then you have a witches' brew.

W&I: When we speak to the two sides, each blames the other wholly for the conflict.

R: I don't blame the Arabs. If I were a Palestinian, I would see the Israelis as alien occupiers who have come back to a country they left centuries ago. But, I am not a Palestinian. I liken the conflict to that between Antigone and Creon in Sophocles' tragedy, *Antigone*. Antigone must be loyal to the law of the family, which says she must bury her brother, no matter what the personal cost. Creon, the king, must be obedient to the law of the polis, which stipulates that the rebel against the polis must not be given an honorable burial. There is an "ethical collision" between two partial rights in a conflict neither side can avoid. That is how I see the situation.

W&I: You used the term witches' brew a minute ago, and now again you come back to language that suggests hopelessness.

R: I honestly don't see any solution to this problem. I have long believed that the Israelis will survive only as long as they can escalate the cost of killing Jews beyond what the Arabs are willing to pay. That is what the morality between enemy nations has been reduced to.

W&I: So we end there with this hopeless view?

R: I would only regard it as hopeless if the Israelis were, like the victims of the Holocaust, without weapons to defend themselves. The situation in the Middle East is not unlike that which used to exist between the United States and the Soviet Union during the Cold War. It is an unstable peace based on a credible nuclear threat. As long as the Israelis have a credible second-strike nuclear capability, they have a chance to survive. The Israelis must convince the Arabs that, even after they are attacked, they will have the will and the capability to unleash so many nuclear missiles that it would not be worthwhile for the Arabs to try to destroy them. I regret that this is what the situation comes down to. There's simply no other way to adjudicate this conflict. Under the circumstances, I cannot see the Israelis giving up an inch of territory, although they might give the Palestinians a greater measure of unarmed autonomy in a partial settlement.

I have no problem coming to an interreligious conference and having cordial conversations with Islamic scholars; I enjoy talking to them. The problem is that, if there is to be a solution to the Israeli-Palestinian conflict, it must be one in which both sides see the situation as other than a zero-sum game. Right now, both sides see the conflict as a zero-sum game. It may be want of imagination on my part, but I don't see any alternatives.

W&I: Is there any metalevel context that the two sides can go to?

R: If I meet an Islamic scholar who also lives in the United States, both of us have the metalevel context of American democracy. We are both free to pursue our religious life and to enter into dialogue with each other. Each of us is likely to have a home. If we do, the government will protect our property rights. We do not threaten each other's turf. Moreover, he is not going to impose the *Shari'a* on me, nor am I going to impose my religious views on him. In Israel the metalevel context simply doesn't exist. Two communities are in conflict, and there is no mediator both sides trust. In the United States, it doesn't bother me when a Muslim or a Christian makes supersessionary claims vis-à-vis Judaism, as long as there is a context in which we can freely exchange ideas and insights without negative political consequences. However, when supersessionary claims give religious legitimation to political conflicts and no trustworthy metalevel context exists, there can be real trouble. Certainly, the United Nations with its viciously defamatory Zionism-is-racism resolution, its Kurt Waldheim legacy, and its large number of Arab and pro-Arab member states offers no metalevel context. The United Nations has been consistently pro-Arab almost from the very beginning. No Israeli trusts the United Nations, and with good reason. Nor are the great powers, even the United States, able to offer a metalevel context. Though nations use the rhetoric of international morality and some of their leaders profess to believe in it, they nevertheless see their own nation's interests as having a prior moral claim to all others. No third-party nation can be trusted to act as an impartial mediator, disregarding its own national interests. Perhaps some religious group could provide the metalevel, but I doubt it. Religious groups also have their own interests. Witness the steadfast refusal of the Vatican to enter into diplomatic relations with the State of Israel, although it had no difficulty entering into diplomatic relations with Nazi Germany and with some very brutal, atheistic communist regimes. I am afraid the Arab-Israeli conflict is going to be one of the most difficult to resolve.

W&I: You speak like an advocate for the Israeli-Jewish side.

R: Of course, I am. As a Jew and a Holocaust theologian, I cannot be indifferent when Jews are threatened with gas after Auschwitz. Nevertheless, I haven't closed the door to a peaceful solution. I would like to see a solution. I would even favor the surrender of territory in Gaza and the West Bank if—and it is a very big if—Israel's security were not thereby seriously compromised. As I have said, I don't see a way out. Nevertheless, there is an enormous difference between not seeing a way out and wanting things to be the way they are. I feel these things very strongly, not as an advocate for one side, but because I have spent much of my life studying Jewish history and the place of Judaism in the modern world.

If you ask me about the conflict with Iraq as distinct from the Palestinian conflict, I must say I am disturbed. To repeat, I see the continuing possibility of a holy war. Saddam Hussein is apparently convinced that, having lost the initial round, he can still win the long-term religio-political conflict, even if he himself has departed from the scene.

I shall never forget an encounter my wife and I had shortly after we checked into that Arab hotel in East Jerusalem at the end of the Six-Day War. We had never been to the Old City. Before the war, Jews couldn't go into East Jerusalem or the Old City. We decided to walk through the Old City, entering by the Damascus Gate. As we entered, a thin, young Palestinian, maybe about twenty years old, came up to me and asked, "Would you like a guide?" I decided that it would be prudent to have one for the first visit. And, for the next two hours, I heard the most bitter rage and resentment against Israel I have ever heard in my life. The guide assumed that we were Christian because of Betty's blonde hair and blue eyes and because we entered from East Jerusalem. As we listened to him, both of us decided that it was much more important to hear what he had to say than to argue with him. So for two hours I listened attentively. He assured us that the day would come when the Palestinians would drive the Jews into the sea and wipe them out. It was, he said, just a question of time. At the end of the two hours, I paid him the amount we had agreed upon and thanked him, but felt I had to say something in response.

"There is one thing I think you ought to know," I said, "we're not Christian; we're Jewish."

He replied, "Oh, you're Jewish. You Jews have long memories. You remember the destruction of the Temple by the Romans."

"Yes, we do, and now we have Jerusalem back again."

"Well, we are your cousins. What makes you think that we have shorter memories? We remember the Crusades."

"I know you have long memories. That's why there can't be peace between us."

W&I: Maybe you should learn to forget.

R: A person can only forget a danger when the danger is no longer there. If it is only a fantasy danger, then it is possible, and even desirable, to forget. But when the danger is real, and this one is, then forgetfulness is the height of folly. Don't you understand that for years Saddam Hussein thought in terms of the Crusades and that he did everything he could to get the masses in all Arab countries to think in terms of the Crusades? Listen to his rhetoric. Read his speeches. You can take this man at his word when he promises *jihad*. Keep in mind Elie Wiesel's comment that "Hitler kept his promises to the Jews." These are people who have promised to drive the Israelis into the sea, and they still talk like that when they are broadcasting in Arabic even though they have moderated their rhetoric in English. These are promises I simply must take seriously.

W&I: The Islamic religious leaders and scholars tend to say that this is a kind of popular hysteria whipped up for political reasons by unscrupulous politicians and that it is not the real voice of Islam that you are hearing.

R: If you are talking about people like Sheik Zaki Badawi, who lives in London and is a very learned and cultivated man, I would say he is undoubtedly sincere about this. But there are many Islamic scholars in places like Iraq, Iran, Jordan, and even the West Bank who are quite sincere about a less peaceful synthesis of politics and religion. Their point of view is deeply rooted in Muslim history. The Muslims did not conquer faraway lands for the sake of material advantage. They conquered because they were convinced that they alone had the true faith, that they were giving people the true faith. And very few people whom they conquered and converted ever apostasized from their new religion. Islamic political moves always had a religious foundation, and I believe that is still true today.

CHAPTER 16

God after the Death of God

When I reflect on the question of God after the death of God, I recall a crucial conversation with the late Swami Muktananda of Ganeshpuri which took place at a major turning point in my spiritual life. One of my academic colleagues, Dr. Gulshan Khaki, a disciple of the guru, invited Dr. Betty Rubenstein and me to spend a weekend at his American ashram when he was in attendance. At the time I met Swami Muktananda, I was experiencing something akin to the "dark night of the soul" concerning which mystics in all of the great traditions have testified. Although happily married and grateful that I had found appropriate academic employment, I was bitterly pessimistic about almost every aspect of the human condition. I was especially intolerant of the men and women within my own religious tradition who could not or would not understand the difficulties involved in affirming the traditional God of covenant and election after Auschwitz.

The very first thing the guru said to me was: "You mustn't believe in your own religion; I don't believe in mine. Religions are like the fences that hold young saplings erect. Without the fence the sapling could fall over. When it takes firm root and becomes a tree, the fence is no longer needed. However, most people never lose their need for the fence."

I have never forgotten the guru's counsel. Although he had never met me before, he knew instinctively what I needed to be told. Here was a profoundly religious man telling me that he was not a believer. I understood his real meaning, that there is an esoteric as well as an exoteric tradition in all of the major religions. He helped me to see that my "death-

of-God" theology, with its radical questioning of tradition, was not negative rebellion but contained the seeds of affirmation of the esoteric tradition. The guru's counsel caused me to recall the esoteric character of
Jewish mysticism, before Sabbatianism and the rise of Hasidism, when
Kabbalah was taught as secret knowledge and confined to a small elite
and their disciples.[1] He also helped me to achieve a measure of empathy
with traditional believers, both Jewish and Christian.

The guru reminded me that there are levels of religious sophistication in every tradition. Nowhere is that insight more relevant than when
reflecting on the meaning of the death of God. *It must be stressed at the
outset of this essay that the death of God is not something that has happened to
God.* It is a *cultural* event experienced by men and women, many of whom
remain faithful members of their religious communities. No longer able
to believe in a transcendent God who is sovereign over human history
and who rewards and punishes men and women according to their de-
serts, they nevertheless render homage to that God in the rituals and
liturgy of the community of their inheritance. They instinctively intuit
that the "fence" of traditional meanings is indispensable to their sense
of religious identity. As we have seen, belief in the sovereign God of covenant and election requires interpreting events such as the extermination
of European Jewry and the bitter strife of our times as God's providential
way of leading humanity to its final redemption. Many thoughtful men
and women find this idea too great a strain on their credulity. Their experience of the death of God rests upon their loss of faith in the transcendent God of History, but not necessarily upon the loss of the sense
of the sacred.

Faith in the transcendent God is also rendered problematic by the
promise of redemption itself. What indeed does redemption mean? In
the biblical religions, the God of History is depicted as promising that
the sorrows of the present era will ultimately be overcome by the establishment of a "kingdom of heaven," perhaps here on earth. This belief
entails the conviction that history has a meaning, a purpose, and a cli-
mactic goal. The belief has become so pervasive in the world of Judeo-
Christian inheritance that hope for the coming of the "kingdom" is no
longer necessarily dependent upon faith in the existence of God. Marxism, for example, has its own secular version of the coming of the
kingdom.

Judeo-Christian faith in the transcendent God stands in contrast to
Buddhist religious sensibility. In Buddhism redemption is understood to
involve the cessation of all craving for, and attachment to, the ephemeral
states of existence to which humanity mistakenly ascribes permanence

and stability. As we know, attainment of such peace and enlightenment is called *nirvana*. In contrast to biblical religion, Buddhism holds that no transcendent deity can bestow enlightenment upon human beings. On the contrary, the way to enlightenment is through knowledge of the Four Noble Truths, namely: existence is permeated by suffering and unhappiness; the origin of unhappiness lies in craving or desire; an end to suffering is possible through the cessation of craving; and craving can be terminated by following the Eightfold Path, consisting of right understanding, right purpose (aspiration), right speech, right conduct, right livelihood, right effort, right mindfulness, and right contemplation (concentration).

Although firmly rooted in the Jewish tradition, I was struck by the fact that the difficulties arising from theistic belief do not constitute a problem for Buddhism. Moreover, the Buddhist view would appear to be more in harmony with the facts of human biology and psychology than the Western view. Every human being is a perpetually changing process from the beginning to the end of life. At no moment in the ongoing transformation can one discern an underlying substantial, essential, unchangeable self. Every human action attempts to gratify some felt need. But, needs are experienced as disturbances we seek to overcome. That is as true of eating, breathing, and love-making as it is of spiritual activities such as prayer. Were all needs perfectly and permanently gratified, the individual bodily organism as we know it would not persevere. In reality, suffering and need can only be overcome in death or through the immersion of the self in the seamless ocean of being in which individual identity is dissolved. Redemption thus involves the dissolution of the self or, from a Buddhist perspective, of the illusion of the self. Such redemption may bear a greater resemblance to Buddhist *nirvana* than to the Western conception of the coming of God's "kingdom," insofar as the latter is thought of as endowing the self with a measure of discrete, enduring identity.

In place of a biblical image of a transcendent Creator God, an understanding of God which gives priority to the indwelling immanence of the Divine may be more credible in our era. Where God is thought of as predominantly immanent in the cosmos, the cosmos in all of its temporal and spatial multiplicity is understood as the manifestation of the single unified and unifying, self-unfolding, self-realizing Divine Source, Ground, Spirit, or Absolute. The names proliferate because we are attempting to speak of that which cannot be spoken of or even named, as mystics in every age have understood. Moreover, the cosmos itself is understood to be capable of vitality, feeling, thought, and reflection, at least in its human manifestation. As the Ground of Being and of all beings, Divinity can be understood as the ground of feeling, thought, and reflection. Human thought and feeling are thus expressions of divine thought and feeling, albeit in a dialectical form.

In the West emphasis on Divine immanence has been expressed in mysticism and nature paganism. If one finds the transcendent God of covenant and election lacking in credibility, some form of mysticism can become a meaningful religious path. Another alternative would be some form of Buddhist enlightenment. The Buddhist view reminds us that religion and theism are not necessarily identical.

To choose immanence, mysticism, nature paganism, or the quest for Buddhist enlightenment is to choose a synthesizing *system of continuity* over a dichotomizing *system of gaps*, such as faith in the radically transcendent Creator God of biblical religion, who bestows a covenant upon Israel for His own utterly inscrutable reasons. Deutero-Isaiah expressed the unbridgeable gap between God and humanity in biblical religion when, speaking on God's behalf, he declared: "For my thoughts are not your thoughts, neither are your ways my ways, saith the Lord. For as the heavens are higher than the earth, so are my ways higher than your ways, and my thoughts than your thoughts" (Isa. 55:8,9). The inherent logic of the gap between the radically transcendent biblical God and humanity finally comes to full expression in Calvinism's doctrine of double predestination, which holds that, at the very first instant of creation, the sovereign, omnipotent Creator predestined all of humanity to either election or damnation and that no human institution, action, or petition can have the slightest effect on a person's eternal destiny. Cut off completely from any influence upon the Creator, men and women can only glorify from afar the one who may be the Author of their eternal damnation.

In philosophy and philosophical theology, choice of a system of continuity reflects a preference for Hegel over Kant, Buber, Kierkegaard, and Barth, who stress the infinite qualitative difference between God and humanity. Among the systems of continuity we find mystical and pantheistic traditions that affirm the ultimate, though not necessarily the immediate, unity of God, humanity, and the cosmos.

To understand the preference for a system of continuities over a system of gaps, it is helpful to recall Hegel's reformulation of Kant's distinction of *Verstand* (understanding) and *Vernunft* (Reason).[2] Hegel defined the activity of *Verstand* as the analytic definition, organization, and fixation of seemingly discrete phenomena—the hard, concrete, matter-of-fact events and the existents of the empirical world. He characterized *Verstand* as "isolated reflection," insisting that it could only apprehend a partial, limited aspect of reality. *Verstand* can analyze discrete phenomena; it cannot understand the ultimate interconnectedness of all things. For Hegel, the finite, empirical existence apprehended by *Verstand* is not what it appears to be; it is actually the self-manifestation of the single, universal, infinite Ground and Source. Were this not so, reality would be divided into mutually repellent sectors that are incomprehensible to and incommunicable with each other. Beyond the empirical world of dichotomous oppositions and discrete, isolated entities, there is, according to Hegel, a unified totality that can be rationally and conceptually grasped. Thus, belief in the transcendent God of History, who relates to the empirical world as subject to object, is an expression of the partial and incomplete perspectives of *Verstand*. Although not false, the finite perspectives of *Verstand* are partial. They constitute developmental stages within the all-encompassing activity of speculative Reason or *Vernunft*, which is the Absolute or *Geist* for philosophy and Divinity for religious mysticism. It is, however, important to note that Hegel does not deny the reality of concrete entities. He holds that the Absolute exists only in and through its finite constituents: *"Ohne Welt ist Gott nicht Gott."* (Without the world God is not God.)[3]

Stressing the indispensable nature of each and every finite entity and event in the world as an expression of the underlying Absolute, Hegel attempted to comprehend all of nature and history as expressions of the self-positing, self-unfolding rational totality. Instead of seeing God, man, and nature as separate and distinct, which would be the perspective of *Verstand* without *Vernunft*, Hegel insisted upon the "identity of identity and nonidentity" of phenomena. He sought to demonstrate that humanity in its historical development and nature in its evolution are expressions of the same ultimate Reality. I would add, absent the unifying comprehension of *Vernunft*, *Verstand* is the mode of comprehension appropriate to a system of gaps; *Vernunft* is the mode appropriate to a system of continuities. Above all, *in a system of continuities there are no mystifying leaps of faith.*

Among Hegel's successors, the Hegelian left denied the divinity of the Absolute.[4] However, in a theological reading of Hegel, the divinity of the Absolute or *Geist* is affirmed. According to Hegel, religion can only anticipate the reconciliation and ultimate union in the Absolute of nature, humanity, and Divinity in the *subjectivity of faith and feeling.* Like the guru, Hegel regarded religion as the fence for the young tree yet to take deep roots. For Hegel, philosophy alone can attain the reconciliation in its comprehensiveness through the activity of *Vernunft*. Indeed, for Hegel true philosophy is nothing less than the Absolute's fully rational, self-trans-parent knowledge, so to speak, of Himself *in se ipsum*. Hegel's thought expresses a perennial human aspiration, namely, humanity's desire to understand its place in the order of things with lucidity and without self-deception or bad faith. That same aspiration can be seen in dialectical mysticism and Buddhism. For me, however, true self-knowledge and the insights of dialectical mysticism attain the reconciliation.

Although deeply indebted to Hegel, I believe that his quest for a system of continuity can best be achieved by turning to another name for the Unnameable. I also believe there is a conception of God which does not falsify or mystify reality, as a system of gaps must inevitably do, and which remains meaningful after the death of the transcendent God of History. It is a very old conception of God with deep roots in both Western and oriental mysticism. In this conception, God is spoken of as the Holy Nothingness, *das Heilige Nichts*, and, in Kabbalah, as the *En-Sof*, that which is without limit or end.[5] God, thus designated, is regarded as the Ground and Source of all existence. To speak, admittedly in inadequate language, of God as the "Nothingness" is not to suggest that God is a void; on the contrary, the Holy Nothingness is a *plenum* so rich that all existence derives therefrom. God as the "Nothing" is not absence of being, but a superfluity of being.

Use of the term *Nothingness* to point to the divine reality rests in part on an ancient observation that all definition of finite phenomena involves negation. In order to know something, we must know what it is not. The infinite God, the Ground of all that is finite, cannot be defined, for there is nothing outside of God, so to speak. In no sense is God a definite thing or a being bearing any resemblance to the finite beings of the empirical world. *The infinite God is not a thing; the infinite God is no-thing.* At times, the mystics spoke of God in similar terms as the *Urgrund*, the primordial ground, the dark unnameable Abyss out of which the empirical world has come.

At first glance, these ideas may appear to be little more than word play. Nevertheless, thinkers in all of the major religious traditions express themselves in almost identical images when they attempt to communicate their conception of God. Those who believe that God is the Source or Ground of Being usually believe that discrete human identity is co-terminous with the life of the physical organism. Death may be entrance into eternal life, the perfect life of God, and it may also end pain, craving, and suffering, but it involves the dissolution of individual identity. Thus, in speaking of God, we also formulate a judgment concerning the nature and limitations of human existence.

Perhaps the best available metaphor for the conception of God as the

Holy Nothingness is that God is the ocean and we the waves. Each wave has its moment when it is identifiable as a somewhat separate entity. Nevertheless, no wave is entirely distinct from the ocean, which is its substantial ground. Furthermore, because the waves are surface manifestations of the ocean, our knowledge of the ocean is largely dependent upon the way the ocean manifests itself in the waves.

The waves are caught in contradictory tendencies. They are the resultants of forces that allow them their moment of separate existence. At the same time, they are wholly within the grasp of greater tendencies that merge them into the oceanic ground from which they are momentarily distinguished without ever really separating from it. Similarly, all living beings seek to maintain their individual identities, yet there is absolutely nothing in them which does not derive from their originating ground. This is especially evident in the most intimate of all human activities, sexual love. Nothing could be more private or personally involving. Nevertheless, at no time is the individual more in the grip of universal forces than in the act of love. Only to the extent that we are capable of letting these overwhelming forces flow through us of their own accord is the act of love complete and fulfilling. Only those who have the capacity to lose themselves totally in love can achieve this fulfillment.

The same reality is evident in the life cycle. Because our bodies are the most deeply personal aspects of our beings, identity begins as body identity and the earliest development of the ego is as body ego. Our fundamental projects are related to the care and nurture of our bodies. Yet, nothing is more universal and impersonal than the shape, demands, and sexual character of our bodies. We do not choose to be born; we do not choose our gender; we do not choose the course of our life from its beginnings in cellular existence through physical maturity, old age, and finally, death. We simply repeat, each in our own way, a destiny common to billions of other human beings. Admittedly, we possess a measure of freedom to work out our distinctive path in the world. Nevertheless, both the individual and the race are the consequence of vast, nonpersonal forces that transcend yet permeate their every activity and project.

Questions about the relation between discrete phenomena and universals are not new. In the Middle Ages there was an important controversy in the field of logic and metaphysics concerning the nature of universals. One group of thinkers, the nominalists, regarded the universal as the *name* given to a class of objects that resemble each other. Another, the realists, argued that the universal has an extra-mental *reality* of its own which is exemplified in each of its particulars. We call their system realism. The controversy has been one of the most abiding and complicated in the history of philosophy.[6] Since the time of Luther, there has been a tendency, especially in countries strongly influenced by Protestantism, to regard individuals as real and universals as merely names, although Hegel obviously regarded the Absolute, the Universal *par excellence*, as the one and only true reality. The social and cultural expression of the triumph of nominalism is reflected in the growth of individualism and the stress on private rather than corporate experience. In the political order nominalism was paralleled by the rise of the middle class and its preference for free, unregulated competition and commerce.

Although realism has largely gone out of fashion, its insight into the extent to which our personal and social lives are pervaded by universal, nonpersonal forces suggests that the doctrine contains important insights. In addition to human biology, the interdependent character of the human world renders questionable the idea that individuals are the primary reality and universals but a name. Apart from the complex processes of production in a high-technology civilization, within the privacy of the home each family participates in the contemporary revival of corporate experience. Through the communications media, especially satellite TV, we share identical sensory experiences and even thought contents. When the war with Iraq commenced, even Secretary of Defense Dick Cheney and General Colin Powell admitted that they got much of their initial information from watching the same media source as the general public, CNN. Marshall McLuhan has suggested that one effect of the communications revolution has been to bring about the return of tribalized man, whose experiences are more corporate, sensuous, involving, and universal than those of the inner-directed, isolated individualist described by David Reisman in *The Lonely Crowd*.[7] Like archaic men and women, their contemporary descendants tend largely to share common media images and thought with their peers. In the age of the global village, it is more apparent than ever that we are not isolated, private individuals, but exemplification of the all-embracing, universal totality we name as God.

Although we can press the metaphor of the ocean and the waves too far, it is very useful and very old. The Sumerians saw all things, even the gods, arising out of the divine oceanic substratum of existence, which they called Nammu. Nammu was the archaic sea goddess in Sumerian mythology.[8] She was not the goddess of the sea, but the *goddess who is the sea*. Hegel used a similar metaphor at the conclusion of the *Phenomenology* when, after describing the full scope of human activity and passion in the course of history, he concluded that all of the apparent diversity of both natural existence and the drama of history was the self-positing expression of one underlying, ever-changing, and yet ever-constant divine Spirit or *Geist*. He adapted a line from the poet Schiller to summarize this paradox of divine unity and diversity:

> nur
> aus dem Kelche dieses Geisterreiches
> schäumt ihm seine Unendlichkeit.

> Only
> The chalice of this realm of spirits
> Foams forth to God His own Infinitude.[9]

When God is imaged as the Holy Nothingness, the divine Ground of Being is thought of as beyond all finite categories. It may be the source and precondition of the empirical world, but it is not identical with that world. There is an inescapable tension between God's essential unity and his process of self-manifestation in the multiplicity of the empirical world. Hegel caught something of the tension between God as ground, on the one hand, and the natural and historical world as epiphenomenal manifestation of the divine Reality, on the other. This is reflected in the preface to the *Phenomenology*:

> *Per se* the divine life is no doubt undisturbed identity and oneness with itself, which finds no serious obstacle in otherness and estrangement. . . . But this "per se" is abstract generality. . . . The truth is whole. The whole, however, is merely the essential nature reaching its completeness through the process of its own development.[10]

> Spirit alone is reality. It is the inner being of the world, that which essentially is, and is *per se*; it assumes objective, determinate form and enters into relations with itself—it is externality (otherness) and exists for self; yet, in this determinateness, and in its otherness, it is still one with itself—it is self-contained and self-complete, in itself and for itself at once.[11]

Hegel used a very complicated philosophical language to express the idea of the fundamental identity of God as unchanging unity and of the world as the divine means of expressing itself in diversity. I prefer the more graphic metaphor of the ocean and waves, but the fundamental conception underlying both images is much the same.

Hegel called the divine Ground *Geist* or Spirit; Paul Tillich used the term "Ground of Being." There is nothing original about my use of Holy Nothingness. All three designations reflect a preference for metaphors rooted in maternity rather than paternity. Words like "ground," "source," and "abyss" have maternal overtones. This is also true of the image of God as the oceanic substratum. In the symbolism of both religion and dreams, ocean often represents womb. In the evolution of the species, the womb is a surrogate ocean providing mammals with a replica of their original aquatic habitat through which they can reproduce in an encompassing fluid and recapitulate the evolution of the race in their own ontogenesis.

Terms like "ground" and "source" stand in contrast to the terms used for the biblical God of History. The biblical God is known as a supreme king, a father, a creator, a judge, a maker. When He creates the world, He does so as do males, producing something external to Himself. He remains essentially outside of and judges the creative processes He has initiated. As ground and source, God creates as does a mother, in and through her own very substance. As ground of being, God participates in all the joys and sorrows of the drama of creation, which is, at the same time, the deepest expression of the divine life. God's unchanging unitary life and that of the cosmos's ever-changing, dynamic multiplicity ultimately reflect a single unitary reality.

Although I have cited Hegel and Tillich, I could have cited a long list of Eastern and Western mystics who have had similar conceptions of God. J. N. Findlay, an authoritative commentator on Hegel, has observed that Hegel's conception of God as the Spirit underlying nature and history "has an obvious parentage in the glorious mysticism of mediaeval and renaissance Germany."[12] Findlay finds echoes of Hegel in Meister Eckhart, Angelus Silesius, and Jakob Boehme. He comments:

> In all these systems there is that approximation of the finite to the infinite Spirit which fits in with Hegel's notions: there is also that profound, theologically heretical stress on the necessity to the infinite Spirit of a world of Nature and created Spirit, which by enabling him to exercise his creative energies and redemptive love, also enable him to know and be himself. Hegel quotes with approval the following statement of Meister Eckhart: "The eye with which God sees me, is the eye with which I see Him, my eye and his eye are one. In the meting out of justice I am weighed in God and He in me. *If God were not, I should not be, and if I were not, He too would not be* (italics added).[13]

This conception of God also implies a judgment on the overly individualistic conception of the self which has predominated in the Western world.

In spite of the resemblance between the term Nothingness as a designation for the divine substratum and Hegel's use of the term Spirit to point to the same reality, there is an absolutely crucial difference between them. Hegel saw the self-positing of Spirit as a process leading to a final goal in which Spirit would come to know itself as Spirit. For Hegel the ultimate goal of all existence is the fully self-realized knowledge of God. God will come fully to know Himself as God only when He finally recognizes every event in natural evolution and human history as the very road He has had to traverse in order to become and know Himself as self-conscious Spirit. Everything that has ever happened would then be seen as an indispensable moment in the life of God.

According to Hegel, had Spirit not gone through the infinite pain of the negative, of human history, its self-knowledge and its very nature would have been empty, a void. In order to be God, Spirit had to suffer the tortuous path we call history. Without it, God would not have had a self, so to speak, to know. The image here is not unlike human self-knowledge. The newborn infant has no possibility of self-recognition or self-knowledge. Such insight is only possible when the self has a memory of events, conflicts, victories, and defeats. True self-knowledge involves recognition and acceptance of the fact that the unique path taken was indispensable to the formation of the person who he or she has become. For Hegel the goal of history will be attained when God recognizes that all the diversity of existence is but His own unique life history.[14] The one true Substance would then become the one true Subject.

Biblical and Cosmological Images of God

By attributing a goal to history Hegel reflected the influence on his thought of biblical teleology, an influence that is understandably shared by many other Western thinkers. Pierre Teilhard de Chardin, for example, interpreted the whole of the cosmic process as having a goal he identified as the "Omega-point." Taking the incarnation of God and humanity in Christ as his starting point, Teilhard looked forward to the moment when the cosmic Christ would be "All-in-everything." All of matter and spirit would then express fully and completely the perfect unity already made manifest in Christ incarnate according to the Christian tradition.[15] Biblical religion expresses itself in redemptive hope. To the extent that Hegel, Teilhard, and Karl Marx saw history as a process with a goal, they were influenced by biblical religion.

An alternative vision may be more plausible: If creation is understood as the self-unfolding of God's life, so to speak, then the process itself may be a vast cosmic detour originating in the Nothingness of God and ultimately returning to God's Nothingness. This would appear to be the viewpoint of the Kabbalah of Rabbi Isaac Luria. In Lurianic Kabbalism the Fall is regarded as the catastrophic moment at which God's Holy *Shekhinah*, his Divine Presence, was exiled from the primordial Divine

Ground, the *En-Sof*.[16] Thus, "a part of God Himself was exiled from God."[17] The goal of all existence is regarded as the overcoming of the cosmic *galut* or exile and the restoration of the cosmos to its seamless unity with primordial source, the aboriginal *Urgrund*. Thus, the final reversal of Adam's Fall, depicted in Jewish mysticism as both an anthropological and a cosmic event, would ultimately entail the restoration of God to God. Insofar as God is experienced as a Thou by a human I in the present eon, it is only because God Himself, so to speak, is separated from His true nature as primordial *Urgrund* and, in the final analysis, Holy Nothingness or *En-Sof*. God restored to Himself as *En-Sof* would truly be "all in all." In the language of Buddhism, the goal of all existence is none other than the attainment of primordial nirvana and the restoration of all things to the originating Womb of existence.

Not surprisingly, a similar vision is to be found in the thought of Paul of Tarsus, whom Gershom Scholem called a "revolutionary Jewish mystic" and who was, after all, trained by the Pharisees.[18] In Paul's vision of the final consummation of redemptive history, Christ, the Messiah, utterly destroys "every rule and every authority and power" and does away with the "last enemy," death. Christ then submits himself "to the one who made the universe subject to him, *so that God may be all in all*" (1 Cor. 15:20–28).[19] Elsewhere I have attempted to show that Paul's meaning is that, at the end of all things, the distinction between the transcendent God, the I-and-Thou God, as subject and the cosmos as object is overcome and God entire, so to speak, becomes "all in all."[20] Put differently, at the end of all things God and the world return to the originating Sacred Womb out of which both have come. The logic of such a restoration is expressed in the idea, *Endzeit ist Urzeit* (the end time is the original time), which signifies that the end of all things recapitulates their primordial beginning.

A somewhat similar vision is to be found in the later writings of Sigmund Freud. In *Beyond the Pleasure Principle*, Freud depicted organic existence as primordially inclined to seek to return to the inanimate condition out of which it had arisen. According to Freud, both the animate and inanimate realms are ultimately linked by the common tendency of all things in the universe to return to the simplest equilibrium of the cosmic system with itself. For Freud, as for so many of his scientific contemporaries, this meant that the universe would ultimately "run down," resulting in a universal cosmic death.[21] Nevertheless, as Norman O. Brown and others have observed, Freud's ideas on this subject have deep affinities with the great mystical systems in which the goal of all existence is return to the Divine Ground out of which it has arisen.[22]

I have often expressed my deepest religious feelings by saying that *omnipotent Nothingness is Lord of all creation*. This affirmation of mystical faith seems to offer a concise way of synthesizing mystical, dialectical, psychoanalytic, and archaic insights concerning God as the ground, content, and final destiny of all things. It also has obvious affinities to the Buddhist doctrine of *Sunyata* or emptiness, although Buddhist thinkers would not use poetic images such as "Lord of all creation." According to Masao Abe,

> The ultimate reality for Buddhism is neither Being nor God, but Sunyata. Sunyata literally means "emptiness" or "voidness" and can imply "absolute nothingness." This is because Sunyata is entirely unobjectifiable, unconceptualizable, and unattainable by reason or will. Accordingly, if Sunyata is conceived as *somewhere outside of* or *beyond* one's self-existence, it is not true Sunyata, for Sunyata thus conceived . . . turns into *something* which one represents and calls "Sunyata" (italics author's).[23]

The affirmation of "Omnipotent Nothingness" is *ipso facto* the affirmation of God as *Urgrund*, source and final goal. It also implies that the only eternal life is the life, so to speak, of God. There cannot, however, be a separated eternal life for the individual, for that would be eternal separation and estrangement from God.

An analogous vision can be expressed in cosmological images. For those who hold that the universe originated in a cosmic "big bang," there are two general hypotheses concerning its ultimate fate. Some could argue that all of the exploding matter of the universe has been rushing away from its originating point in all directions and will continue to do so, world without end. Others reason that, if space is curved, the matter of the cosmos will eventually implode and return in unimaginable density to its cosmic starting point. Whatever the evidence of the scientists, the second hypothesis is more consistent with dialectical mysticism and with an appropriate theological vision after the death of the transcendent biblical God of History, the God of I-and-Thou. Perhaps the vast cosmic implosion, by its very force, might be followed by yet another "big bang." If so, the universe might be a vast exploding-imploding domain that completes its cosmic cycle in about eighty-four billion years. This vision would resemble that of the ancient pagans, who believed that time is cyclical, ultimately returning to its starting point, rather than a straight line proceeding to a future fulfillment.

Writing in the *Christian Century* shortly after the publication of the first edition of *After Auschwitz*, Ronald Goetz argued that to regard God as the Holy Nothingness is to regard Him as death. He based his comment on my argument that we have no ultimate hope save return to the

Nothingness of God.[24] I believe Goetz was arguing for the religion of the young sapling and its indispensable fence rather than for the religion of the tree that has taken deep roots. Admittedly, a rejection of the popular notion of the Judeo-Christian hope for the eternal life of the *individual* presents difficulties for men and women brought up in a culture fundamentally nourished by the biblical tradition. Nevertheless, as we have seen, even within the Judeo-Christian tradition the idea of redemption as *return to the Source* and the ultimate dissolution of the individual self is to be found in the mystical conception of redemption as the return of the exiled *Shekhinah* to union with the *En-Sof*, as well as in Paul's vision of God as "all in all."

God is not death; He, so to speak, is the source of both life and death. Death is the final price we pay for life and love, but death is not all there is. Life has its deep, abiding, and profound moments of joy and fulfillment. Were there no death of the individual, there would be no biological need for love in the order of things. Moreover, every act of love truly consummated is to some degree a joyful dying to the self. It is a distortion to see God solely as love, for love and death are inseparable. God creates, so to speak, out of his own substance; He nurtures, but He also sets a term to individual existence, which in its individuality is no less indivisibly an epiphenomenal manifestation of the divine substance. The creative process is a totality. It is impossible to affirm the loving and the creative aspects of God's activity without also affirming that creation and destruction are part of an indivisible process. Each wave in the ocean of God's Nothingness has its moment, but it must inevitably give way to other waves. We are not, like Job, destined to receive back everything twofold.

The world of the death of the biblical God need not be a place of gloom or despair. One need not live forever for life to be worth living. Creation, however impermanent, is full of promise. Those who affirm the inseparability of the creative and the destructive in the divine activity thereby affirm their understanding of the necessity to pay in full measure with their own return to the Holy Nothingness for the gift of life.

Notes

Preface

1. The chapters not included are: "Reconstructionism and the Problem of Evil," "Atonement and Sacrifice in Contemporary Jewish Liturgy," "Symposium on Jewish Belief," "The Protestant Establishment and the Jews," "The 'Supernatural' Jew," "Judaism and 'The Secular City'," "The Making of a Rabbi," "The Symbols of Judaism and the Death of God," and "Dialogue on the New Theology and the New Morality."

2. *The Flow of World Civilization and Japan's Role in the Twenty-first Century: A Dialogue between Prime Minister Yasuhiro Nakasone and Professor Takeshi Umehara* (Tokyo: Prime Minister's Office, April 1986).

3. For a preliminary statement, see Richard L. Rubenstein, "Religion and the Rise of Capitalism: The Case of Japan," *World and I*, February 1987.

Chapter 1
The Dean and the Chosen People

1. Martin Luther, *Dictata Super Psalterium*, in James S. Preus, *From Shadow to Promise* (Cambridge, Mass.: Harvard University Press, 1969), p. 305. I am indebted to Professor Walter Moore of Florida State University for this reference.

2. Erich Fromm, *Escape from Freedom* (New York: Rinehart and Co., 1941), pp. 163–201.

3. See ch. 4, "The Auschwitz Convent Controversy."

4. See ch. 8, "Covenant and Divinity."

Chapter 2
Person and Myth in the Judeo-Christian Encounter

The original version of this essay was delivered in German—my first lecture in that language—at the Fifteenth Annual Conference on Church and Judaism held in Recklinghausen in February 1963. The Recklinghausen lectures were my first in Germany. The earlier English version of this essay appeared in the Winter 1963 issue of the *Christian Scholar*. At the time, I was not aware of the affinities between my own theological perspectives and those of Protestant radical theologians. Thus, I was surprised to read William Hamilton's article, "The Death of God Theologies Today," in the *Christian Scholar*, Spring 1965, in which he cited this essay as an example of death-of-God theology.

Nevertheless, while there were affinities between us, there were also profound differences. In 1963 I was more inclined to stress the affinities than I am today, especially the affinities between Thomas J. J. Altizer and myself. We had both read Hegel and Nietzsche. We had both been instructed by the lectures of Paul Johannes Tillich. We could no longer affirm faith in the transcendent God of biblical theism. Nevertheless, Altizer's death-of-God theology was firmly grounded in his radical Christology. Altizer saw the demise of the transcendent God as the consequence of that same Divinity's kenosis, the voluntary self-emptying of God so that humanity might be free of the tyranny of divine Lordship. In my case, faith in the biblical Lord of covenant and election had been lost at Auschwitz. Where Altizer proclaimed a message of fulfillment and victory, the shadow of Auschwitz fell across everything I wrote.

As I reread the essay twenty-seven years later, I realize that I was partly in error concerning the probable course of religious developments in Israel. In the 1960s Israel's cultural and political life was dominated by the largely secular Labor party and secular Zionists. Orthodox Jews were politically quiescent, waiting passively for redemption and leaving the restoration of the Holy Temple in God's hands. Then as now I was convinced that a pure secularism was untenable. I had written that religion is the way we share the crises of life in accordance with our inherited traditions. I reasoned that secular Israelis would turn to the nature religion aspects of Judaism during those seasons, such as the New Year, Succoth, and Passover, as well as on those occasions, such as circumcision, bar mitzvah, marriage, and death, when meaningful ritual was emotionally indispensable for the vast majority. I was convinced that faith in the God of Nature would replace faith in the biblical God of History for most Israelis.

Today, faith in the God of History is stronger than ever among Israelis. Israeli Orthodoxy is no longer apolitical. The religious situation changed drastically when a radical, messianic-apocalyptic Orthodox movement, Gush Emunim, "the bloc of the faithful," came into being after the Yom Kippur War. Ironically, faith in earth religion, albeit expressed in traditional rabbinic language, is strongest among the radical messianists. According to Gush Emunim, the Holocaust, the creation of the State of Israel, and the occupation and settlement of all of the land of Israel, including Gaza, the West Bank, and Jordan, are divinely ordained, indispensable preludes to the final messianic climax of Jewish history, which, they believe, is in the process of unfolding. That climax would, of necessity, involve the destruction of the al Aksa Mosque and the Dome of the Rock on the Temple Mount and the restoration of the Holy Temple, and, above all, the "whole land of Israel" to the Jewish people. Radical messianism is the legitimating ideology of a highly influential, politically active, right-wing movement among Israel's Orthodox Jews, providing the theological rationale for the uncompromising refusal on the part of many Orthodox Jews to consider limiting Israeli settlement on the West Bank.

Nevertheless, I do not regret my own affirmation of the God of nature. On the contrary, should politically active, right-wing Orthodox parties, with their faith in the covenant and election of Israel, increase their hold on Israeli policy, it does not require much imagination to foresee disaster for that unhappy nation. Let us remember that in the year 66 C.E. the Zealots went to war against Rome secure in the knowledge that the biblical God of covenant and election looked with favor on their cause.

1. See Max Weber, *Ancient Judaism*, trans. Hans H. Gerth and Don Martindale (Glencoe, Ill.: Free Press, 1952), pp. 336–55.

2. Oscar Cullman, *Christ and Time: The Primitive Christian Conception of Time and History*, trans. Floyd V. Filson (Philadelphia: Westminster Press, 1950).

3. Hans Joachim Schoeps, *Paul: The Theology of the Apostle in the Light of Jewish History*, trans. Harold J. Knight (Philadelphia: Westminster Press, 1961), p. 192.

4. See Jacob Neusner, *First Century Judaism in Crisis: Yohanan ben Zakkai and the Renaissance of Torah* (Nashville: Abingdon Press, 1975), pp. 165–68.

5. Justin Martyr, *Dialogue with Trypho*, in *The Ante-Nicene Fathers*, ed. Alexander Roberts and James Donaldson (Grand Rapids, Mich.: Eerdmans, 1950), col. 1, p. 202.

6. See chap. 1, "The Dean and the Chosen People."

7. See *B. Hagigah* 14bff. for the principal rabbinic source on Elisha b. Abuyah.

8. Although the first person plural is used in the statement of belief that follows, most religious Jews in both Israel and the Diaspora would not concur. I remain committed to the views expressed here.

9. See introductory note, this chapter.

10. This statement holds true of even the apocalyptic messianism of Gush Emunim. See chap. 11, "War, Zionism, and Sacred Space."

11. This statement was valid only as long as the founding of the State of Israel was seen as a purely secular enterprise, as it was in 1948 even by most Orthodox Jews.

12. Although this statement was true when the first edition of *After Auschwitz* was published, almost all Jewish theology has become Holocaust theology since then.

13. This must be read as a personal statement. Most religious Jews continue to affirm traditional faith.

14. Unfortunately, such praise is today uttered in Israel and elsewhere by the extreme Orthodox.

15. Again, this must be read as a personal statement.

16. A similar process is now going on in Russia where right-wing Russian nationalists are blaming that country's Jews for seventy years of Bolshevism. See Alexander Yanov, *The Russian Challenge and the Year 2000*, trans. Iden J. Rosenthal (Oxford: Basil Blackwell, 1987), pp. 142–48.

17. I no longer believe this to be the case, nor do I believe that homogeneous populations are necessarily indicators of "regression." The rise of nationalism in eastern Europe and the former Soviet Union is evidence that pluralism is by no means irreversible. Moreover, the Japanese constitute a highly successful homogeneous population, but they can hardly be considered regressive or primitive. Nevertheless, there is a sense in which pluralism is irreversible. As a result of instantaneous global communications, no society or tradition is wholly insulated from exogenous influences.

18. The text read "in his myth" in the first edition.
19. The text read "just another Jew" in the first edition.

Chapter 3
Religion and the Origins of the Death Camps

My first visit to Germany took place in August 1960 during a vacation in Wijk aan Zee on Holland's North Sea coast. Most of the other vacationers were Germans. Because of the then recent Jewish catastrophe, I was both enormously hostile and curious concerning the Germans. Every time I passed a German adult male, I wondered what he had been doing during the war. Undoubtedly, some of my fellow vacationers had been involved in murdering Jews. They were now well-behaved, courteous tourists whose children sometimes played ball with my children. I had not planned to visit Germany, but my curiosity finally overcame me. I visited Düsseldorf, Cologne, and Bonn. Quite by accident, I was invited to attend briefings that were being held for American-Jewish leaders in Bonn under the auspices of the Bundespresseamt, the Press and Information Office of the Federal Republic. I accepted the invitation and had my first contact with Germans as human beings. The contact was brief but important.

On returning home, I pondered the question of how the Germans, who seemed as normal as any other people, could have perpetrated such crimes. This essay was my first attempt at comprehension. As my earliest effort to comprehend and demystify the phenomenon of genocide, it focused on the religious origins of the Holocaust and makes much use of psychoanalytic explanation. In my later writings I have also attempted to deal with the economic, sociological, and demographic origins; in them, psychoanalysis recedes in importance without being entirely abandoned.

This essay may seem extreme at times; it is hardly as extreme as the phenomenon it seeks to explain. In 1966 I could write that there were still men and women in Germany and Austria whose watchword was "Long live Auschwitz!" Even today (1990) there are men and women who regard Auschwitz as having at least partially solved Europe's most urgent religious, social, and cultural problem.

Many of the themes that are elaborated in my later theological and political writings are already present in this paper: the dangers of apocalyptic enthusiasm, the meaning of the death of God, the political and social consequences of the modernization process, and the problematics of the Judeo-Cbristian encounter.

1. There are several reports of Eichmann's alleged statement. One comes from Dieter Wisliceny, Eichmann's associate. See Jochen von Lang, ed., *Eichmann Interrogated: Transcripts from the Archives of the Israeli Police*, trans. Ralph Manheim (New York: Farrar, Straus, and Giroux, 1983), p. 164.
2. I am indebted for this insight to Jean-Paul Sartre, *Baudelaire*, trans. H. Martin Turnell (Norfolk, Conn.: New Directions Books, 1950), pp. 71ff.
3. Paul's fateful discussion of the place of Israel in the Christian dispensation is to be found in Romans 9–11.
4. For a fuller development of Paul's attitude to his former coreligionists, see Richard L. Rubenstein, *My Brother Paul* (New York: Harper and Row, 1975), pp. 114–43.

5. See S. G. F. Brandon, *The Fall of Jerusalem and the Christian Church: A Study of the Effects of the Jewish Overthrow of* A.D. *70 on Christianity* (London: SPCK, 1968), pp. 206–207; 212, 227ff.

6. Justin Martyr, *Dialogue with Trypho*, in *The Ante-Nicene Fathers*, ed. Alexander Roberts and James Donaldson (Grand Rapids, Mich.: Eerdmans, 1950), vol. 1, p. 202.

7. For a discussion of the importance of the conflict between Teuton and Latin for the growth of German anti-Semitism, see Erik H. Erikson, *Childhood and Society* (New York: W. W. Norton, 1963), pp. 347ff.

8. Hermann Rauschning, *Hitler Speaks: A Series of Political Conversations with Adolf Hitler on His Real Aims* (London: T. Butterworth, 1939), p. 57. For this citation I am indebted to J. S. Conway, *The Nazi Persecution of the Churches: 1933–1945* (New York: Basic Books, 1968), p. 15.

9. G. W. F. Hegel, *Early Theological Writings*, trans. T. M. Knox and Richard Kroner (Chicago: University of Chicago Press, 1948), pp. 145ff. For an informed discussion of Hegel and anti-Semitism, see Shlomo Avineri, *Hegel's Theory of the Modern State* (Cambridge: Cambridge University Press, 1972), pp. 119–20, 170–71.

10. When Clemens August Cardinal von Galen, Bishop of Münster, effectively brought the "euthanasia" project to a halt, the possibility of arresting him was discussed at a meeting in Himmler's office on October 27, 1941 attended by representatives of the Ministries of Justice, Propaganda, and Churches. It was unanimously agreed that he should be arrested, but the final decision was left to Hitler. Hitler replied that he wanted to avoid controversy with the Catholic Church during the war, but would settle accounts with the bishop when victory was won. See Gitta Sereny, *Into That Darkness: An Examination of Conscience* (New York: Vintage Books, 1983), pp. 295–96.

11. Sigmund Freud, *Moses and Monotheism*, trans. Katherine Jones (New York: Vintage Books, 1967), p. 116.

12. This idea is more fully developed in connection with the theory of cognitive dissonance and the idea of *the Jew as the disconfirming other* for Christianity and vice versa. Richard L. Rubenstein, *The Age of Triage* (Boston: Beacon Press, 1983), pp. 131–32, and Richard L. Rubenstein and John K. Roth, *Approaches to Auschwitz* (Atlanta: John Knox Press, 1986), pp. 42–43.

13. See Norman Cohn, "The Myth of Jewish World-Conspiracy," *Commentary,* June 1966, and *Warrant for Genocide: The Myth of the Jewish World-Conspiracy and the Protocols of the Elders of Zion* (New York: Harper and Row, 1967). The parallel between the Jew and the witches of the Middle Ages is also important. Bruno Bettelheim has suggested that an irrational fear of the Jews' capacity to do great harm provided the SS with the inner justification necessary to do their work in the camps. See *The Informed Heart* (Glencoe, Ill.: Free Press, 1960), pp. 221ff.

14. Alexander Yanov, *The Russian Challenge and the Year 2000* (Oxford: Basil Blackwell, 1987), p. 253.

15. André Schwarz-Bart, *The Last of the Just*, trans. Stephen Becker (New York: Bantam Books, 1976).

16. See Richard L. Rubenstein, "Psychoanalysis and the Origins of Judaism," *Reconstructionist*, December 2, 1960. This theme is further elaborated in Richard L. Rubenstein, *The Religious Imagination* (Indianapolis: Bobbs-Merrill, 1968), pp. 43–57, and *My Brother Paul* (New York: Harper and Row, 1972), pp. 78–86.

17. This idea is later developed as an example of the Jews having been cast wholly outside of any shared *universe of moral obligation* with Christians. See Helen Fein, *Accounting for Genocide: National Responses and Jewish Victimization during the Holocaust* (New York: Free Press, 1979), pp. 4, 8–9.

18. Justin Martyr, *Dialogue with Trypho*, p. 203.

19. Joshua Trachtenberg has gathered an impressive catalogue of such identifications of the Jew with the demonic in *The Devil and the Jews* (New Haven: Yale University Press, 1943). pp. 11–52.

20. See ibid., pp. 33–42.

21. As an exile from Nazi Germany in 1936, Klaus Mann, the son of Thomas Mann, wrote a novel, *Mephisto* (trans. Robin Smyth [New York: Random House, 1977]), concerning the career of Gründgens, his former brother-in-law. Gründgens had been a Communist, but switched sides and became a favorite of Hermann Goering, who appointed him director of the state theater after seeing the actor play Mephistopheles in *Faust*. The novel was subsequently made into a motion picture in 1981 in Hungary. Published in France, Austria, Switzerland, Yugoslavia, and the United States, the novel was banned in the Federal Republic of Germany after a ten-year law suit brought by Gründgens's adopted son.

22. See James George Frazer, *The New Golden Bough*, ed. Theodore H. Gaster (New York: Criterion Books, 1959), pp. 305ff. However, see Gaster's note on p. 314 that Frazer fails to distinguish between the scapegoat, which is a means of "cleansing" a community, and the surrogate, which is a substitute for a person or persons.

23. For the later development of this theme, see Rubenstein, *My Brother Paul*, p. 107.

24. See Martin P. Nilsson, *Greek Piety* (London: Oxford University Press, 1948), pp. 52–59.

25. Herman Melville, *Moby Dick or The White Whale* (Philadelphia: John C. Winston Co., 1931), p. 29.

26. This analysis has affinities with Albert Camus's comments on Christianity in his essay, "Helen's Exile," in *The Myth of Sisyphus*, trans. Justin O'Brien (New York: Vintage Books, 1955), pp. 134ff. I am indebted to Camus for many of the insights in this chapter.

27. Referring to Adolf Eichmann at the time of his trial in Jerusalem in 1961, "I like Eich" was a word play on the election slogan of the Eisenhower years, "I like Ike."

28. For a recent study of the Vienna of Freud, Hitler, and Theodore Herzl, see Carl E. Schorske, *Fin de Siècle Vienna: Politics and Culture* (New York: Alfred A. Knopf, 1980).

29. See George Schöpflin, "The Political Traditions of Eastern Europe," *Daedalus*, Winter 1990, pp. 83–85.

30. This point is stressed by Harvey Cox in *The Secular City* (New York: Macmillan, 1965).

31. The conflict between urban pluralism and folk culture was reflected in the conflict between cosmopolitans and right-wing nationalists in Germany. See Erik H. Erikson, *Childhood and Society* (New York: W. W. Norton, 1947), pp. 349ff.

32. Sigmund Freud, *Group Psychology and the Analysis of the Ego*, trans. James Strachey (London: Hogarth Press, 1921).

33. Eberhard Busch, *Karl Barth: His Life from Letters and Autobiographical Texts,* trans. John Bowden (Philadelphia: Fortress Press, 1976), pp. 255–56.

34. The OKH, *Oberkommando des Heeres,* not the OKW, the *Oberkommando der Wehrmacht,* which was little more than a rubber stamp for Hitler's whims.

35. Peter J. Haas has recently (1990) argued that the success of the Nazis in organizing the German people for the extermination of the Jews was due to the fact that the "Nazi ethic" was so able to redefine right and wrong that extermination of the Jews came to be considered a moral necessity by the perpetrators of the Final Solution. By "ethic" Haas means "a complete and coherent system of convictions, values, and ideas that provide a grid within which some sorts of actions can be classified as evil, and so to be avoided, while other sorts of actions can be classified as good, and so to be tolerated and even to be pursued." According to Haas, for the Germans between 1933 and 1945, and for much of the rest of the world, elimination of the Jews was considered a good. See Peter J. Haas, *Morality after Auschwitz: The Radical Challenge of the Nazi Ethic* (Philadelphia: Fortress Press, 1988), pp. 1–9.

36. See Ferdinand Tönnies, *Community and Society,* trans. and ed. Charles P. Loomis (East Lansing: Michigan State University Press, 1957).

37. See Maurice Friedman, *Martin Buber: The Life of Dialogue* (Chicago: University of Chicago Press, 1955), pp. 45ff.

38. For an elaboration of this theme see Schorske, *Fin de Siècle Vienna.*

39. Peter Viereck, *Meta-Politics: The Roots of the Nazi Mind* (New York: Capricorn Books, 1961), pp. 126ff.

40. Cited in Nicholas Halasz, *Captain Dreyfus: The Story of A Mass Hysteria* (New York: Simon and Schuster, 1955), pp. 20–21. See Rubenstein and Roth, *Approaches to Auschwitz,* pp. 69–89.

41. Cited in Halasz, *Captain Dreyfus,* p. 57.

42. An alternative theory has been suggested by Norman Cohn, who stresses the role of the Jews as the castrating father in the paranoid fantasies of the anti-Semite. There is merit to Cohn's hypothesis, which does not necessarily contradict the point of view expressed here. I concur in Cohn's view that anti-Semites are often afflicted with the paranoid delusion that the Jew can inflict great harm upon them. However, I have stressed the irrational fear of the omnipotent, demonic magic betrayer largely because of Germany's history after 1918. In a delusional system this fear can easily coexist with the fear of the castrating father stressed by Cohn. Nevertheless, I do not believe that Cohn takes the Judas tradition or the deicide accusation seriously enough. In my opinion the age-old Christian accusation that the Jews have murdered God is far more decisive than the fear of the Jew as the castrating father. In the final analysis, the anti-Semite sees the Jew as the demonic, all-powerful sibling. See Norman Cohn, "The Myth of the Jewish World Conspiracy," *Commentary,* June 1966. For a balanced evaluation of the attempt to understand anti-Semitism primarily in terms of castration anxiety, see Erikson, *Childhood and Society,* p. 354.

43. Norman O. Brown, *Life against Death: The Psychoanalytic Interpretation of History* (Middletown, Conn.: Wesleyan University Press, 1959).

44. Trachtenberg, *The Devil and the Jews,* pp. 47–50.

45. *Commandant of Auschwitz: The Autobiography of Rudolph Hoess,* trans. Constantine Fitzgibbon (Cleveland: World Publishing Co., 1959), p. 171.

46. Adolph Leschnitzer, *The Magic Background of Anti-Semitism* (New York: International Universities Press, 1956).

47. Adolf Hitler, *Mein Kampf*, trans. Ralph Mannheim (Boston: Houghton Mifflin, 1971), p. 679.

48. In a letter dated September 16, 1919 Hitler outlined the difference between "rational anti-Semitism," whose final objective would be the "total elimination (*Entfernung*) of all Jews from our midst," and "anti-Semitism on purely emotional grounds." In *The Age of Triage* (p. 160), I came to the conclusion that Hitler had decided upon "rational anti-Semitism" no later than the date of the 1919 letter. For the text of the letter, see Werner Maser, ed., *Hitler's Letters and Notes* (New York: Harper and Row, 1974), p. 211.

49. Miklós Nyiszli, *Auschwitz: A Doctor's Eyewitness Account*, trans. Tibere Kremer and Richard Seaver (New York: Frederick Fell, 1960), p. 46.

50. See the chapter, "Excremental Assault," in Terrence Des Pres, *The Survivor: An Anatomy of Life in the Death Camps* (New York: Oxford University Press, 1976), pp. 51–72.

51. Gisella Perl, *I Was a Doctor in Auschwitz* (New York: International Universities Press, 1948), pp. 32–33.

52. See Pelagia Lewinska, *Twenty Months at Auschwitz*, trans. Albert Teichner (New York: Lyle Stuart, 1968), pp. 41–42 (cited by Des Pres, *The Survivor*, pp. 62–63.

53. For an informed account of the Euthanasia project, see Robert J. Lifton, *The Nazi Doctors: Medical Killing and the Psychology of Genocide* (New York: Basic Books, 1986).

54. Brown, *Life against Death*, pp. 202–33.

55. Robert G. L. Waite, *The Psychopathic God: Adolf Hitler* (New York: Basic books, 1977), pp. 177–78. For money as a substitute for feces, see Otto Fenichel, *The Psychoanalytic Theory of Neurosis* (New York: Basic Books, 1945), pp. 281f.

56. Percy Schramm, ed., *Hitlers Tischespräche im Führerhauptquartier, 1941–1942*, 2d ed. (Stuttgart: Seewald, 1965), p. 171. See Robert G. L. Waite, *Psychopathic God*, pp. 178, 311. See also Albert Speer, *Spandau, The Secret Diaries*, trans. Richard and Clara Winston (New York: Macmillan, 1976), p. 346.

57. On the subject of anal character traits, see Sigmund Freud, "Character and Anal Eroticism" (1908), *Collected Papers*, trans. Joan Riviere (London: The Hogarth Press and the Institute of Psycho-Analysis, 1957), vol. 2, pp. 45ff.

58. Dr. Edward Bloch, "My Patient Hitler," *Collier's Magazine* , March 15, 1941, p. 36. For this reference I am indebted to Robert G. L. Waite, *Psychopathic God*, pp. 292, 168.

59. Robert G. L. Waite, *Psychopathic God*, p. 291.

60. Freud, "Anal Eroticism," p. 45.

61. See Erikson, *Childhood and Society*, p. 341. For a discussion of rebelliousness and submission in German identity, see ibid., pp. 326–58.

62. Otto Fenichel, *The Psychoanalytic Theory of Neurosis* (New York: W. W. Norton, 1945), pp. 280–84.

63. Ibid.

64. See David Bakan, *The Duality of Human Existence* (Boston: Beacon Press, 1966), pp. 83ff.

65. My disagreement with Thomas J. J. Altizer is most complete on this issue,

although we both start our theological reflection from the sense of the total absence of the transcendent God of biblical religion.

66. John W. Wheeler-Bennett, *The Nemesis of Power* (London: Macmillan, 1961), p. 31.

67. See especially the chapter, "Totalitarianism in Power," Hannah Arendt, *The Origins of Totalitarianism* (New York: Harcourt, Brace, 1951), pp. 389–459.

68. Sebastian Hafner, *The Meaning of Hitler* (Cambridge, Mass.: Harvard University Press, 1983), pp. 151–65.

69. See H. R. Trevor-Roper, *The Last Days of Adolf Hitler* (London: Macmillan, 1950), p. 51.

70. See Joachim Fest, *Hitler*, trans. Richard and Clara Winston (New York: Harcourt Brace Jovanovich, 1974), pp. 737–38.

71. Albert Speer, *Inside the Third Reich* (New York: Macmillan, 1970), p. 440.

72. William L. Shirer, *The Rise and Fall of the Third Reich* (New York: Simon and Schuster, 1960).

73. Heinrich Himmler's address to SS leaders at Posen, October 4, 1943. Text is to be found in Joachim Remak, ed., *The Nazi Years* (Englewood Cliffs, N.J.: Prentice Hall, 1969), p. 159.

Chapter 4
The Auschwitz Convent Controversy

In the fall of 1989 my friend and co-author of *Approaches to Auschwitz*, Professor John K. Roth of Claremont-McKenna College, and Sister Carol Rittner of the Elie Wiesel Foundation invited me to contribute to a multiauthored book, *Memory Offended* (New York: Praeger, 1991) they were planning on the controversy over the location of the Carmelite convent at Auschwitz.

I had been following the controversy closely and welcomed the opportunity to share my thoughts with a wider audience of Jews and Christians. Shortly thereafter, I was invited to lecture in Poland and Czechoslovakia during the period between December 9 and 16, 1989. It was a heady time to visit eastern Europe. The Berlin Wall had come down on November 9, 1989, the anniversary of Kristallnacht, and there was considerable euphoria over the end of communist rule. The full extent of the economic, social, and ethnic problems besetting the region had yet to become manifest. Nevertheless, wherever I went, I encountered Poles who were concerned about the convent controversy. I describe some of the more important encounters in this chapter.

My 1989 Kraków lectures were given almost exactly twenty-four years after my first and only previous lectures in that city. The earlier lectures had been made possible by Mr. Charles E. Merrill, Jr., then Headmaster of Boston's Commonwealth School. Although a Protestant, Mr. Merrill was hopeful that constructive dialogue between Poles and Jews might be possible in the aftermath of the Holocaust. He had excellent Polish contacts and arranged for me to make the trip. Unfortunately, in spite of the courtesy and hospitality with which I was received in Poland, the legacy of the past proved too difficult to overcome at the time, especially after the revival of official anti-Semitism by the communist government in the aftermath of the Six-Day War. Hopefully, with the end of communist rule and the presence of only a minuscule Jewish minority in Poland, it may be possible for genuine dialogue now to take place. It is my hope that this chapter is a contribution to that dialogue.

During my 1965 visit to Kraków, I visited the nearby Auschwitz camp complex. When I left for Poland, the completed text of my first book was being made ready for publication, but I had yet to decide on a title for it. Upon returning home, I knew that only one title was appropriate, *After Auschwitz*.

1. For an elaboration of this problem from the perspective of the theory of cognitive dissonance in social psychology, see chap. 5, "The Unmastered Trauma."

2. Abraham Brumberg, "Silence on Anti-Semitism," Letter to the Editor, *New York Times Book Review*, January 27, 1985, p. 37. See also Brumberg, "A Parting for Solidarity and the Church?" *New York Times*, September 1, 1989.

3. See Richard M. Watt, *Bitter Glory: Poland and Its Fate 1918 to 1939* (New York: Simon and Schuster, 1982), pp. 40–41.

4. Roman Dmowski, *Upadek mysli konserwatywnej w Polsce* (Warsaw: A. Sadzewicz et al., 1914), pp. 134–35; cited by Edward D. Wynot, Jr., "'A Necessary Cruelty': The Emergence of Official Anti-Semitism in Poland, 1936–39," *American Historical Review*, vol. 76 (October 1971), p. 1036.

5. Stephen Bonsal, *Suitors and Suppliants: The Little Nations at Versailles* (New York: Prentice-Hall, 1946), p. 124; cited in Watt, *Bitter Glory*, p. 75.

6. See Celia S. Heller, *On the Edge of Destruction: Jews of Poland Between the Two World Wars* (New York: Columbia University Press, 1977), pp. 53–57.

7. Max Weber, *The Religion of India: The Sociology of Hinduism and Buddhism*, trans. Hans H. Gerth and Don Martindale (New York: Free Press, 1958), p. 39.

8. Heller, *On the Edge of Destruction*, p. 58.

9. Ibid., p. 57.

10. Watt, *Bitter Glory*, p. 360.

11. See "Pilsudski, Józef," *Encyclopaedia Judaica*, vol. 13, p. 528.

12. "Poland," *Encyclopaedia Judaica*, vol. 13, pp. 739–49.

13. *Gazeta Polska*, June 5, 1937; cited by Wynot, "A Necessary Cruelty," p. 1038.

14. Emil Lengyel, "Europe's Anti-Semitic Twins: Poland," *Current History*, vol. 48 (1938), p. 45.

15. *Gazeta Polska*, January 12, 1937; cited by Wynot, "A Necessary Cruelty," p. 1039.

16. OZON was established by leaders of the government party on February 21, 1937.

17. Wynot, "A Necessary Cruelty," p. 1048. The theses and Miedzinski's commentaries were published in the official *Gazeta Polska* on May 22, 25, 26, 27, June 4, 9, 12, 1938.

18. *Gazeta Polska*, July 23, 1939; cited by Wynot, ibid., p. 1057.

19. August Cardinal Hlond, *Listy Pasterskie* (Poznan, 1936), pp. 192–93. The pastoral letter is dated February 29, 1936. Cited by Celia S. Heller, *On the Edge of Destruction*, p. 113.

20. For an account of Bartoszewski's experiences, see Wladyslaw Bartoszewski, *The Warsaw Ghetto: A Christian's Testimony* (Boston: Beacon Press, 1987).

21. Heller, *On the Edge of Destructiveness*, p. 295. See also "Poland," *Encyclopaedia Judaica*, vol. 13, p. 783.

22. The full text of Cardinal Glemp's homily is to be found in *Origins*, October 5, 1989, vol. 19 (no. 18), pp. 291–94. For a discussion of the homily, see pp. 113–17.

23. Brumberg, "A Parting for Solidarity and the Church."

24. Anna Husarska, "Malice or Misunderstanding over Auschwitz?" *Washington Post*, August 17, 1989.

25. "John Paul Cites Suffering of Jews," *New York Times*, June 26, 1988, p. 6.

26. See the response to the pope by Alfred Lipson and Samuel Lipson, "A Reply to the Pope's Request," *New York Times*, July 16, 1988. The Lipsons are Holocaust survivors.

27. This subject is discussed by Gitta Sereny, *Into That Darkness: From Mercy Killing to Mass Murder* (London: Andre Deutsch, 1974), pp. 289–333. Sereny is a Roman Catholic.

28. The Solidarity-led Polish government is sensitive both to these problems and to the fact that its Communist predecessors had refused to permit any acknowledgment at the site that the vast majority of the millions murdered there were Jews. It has established a State Commission on the Future of Auschwitz to deal with the issues. On May 6–8, 1990, the chairperson of the commission, Mme. Krystyna Marszalek-Mlynczyk, Vice Minister of Culture and Art, and Stefan Wilanowicz, secretary of the commission, met at Oxford with Jewish intellectual leaders from Israel, Europe, and the United States to seek counsel concerning Jewish views on (*a*) establishing an interfaith center at Auschwitz and (*b*) making the site an appropriate memorial for all who perished there.

29. See Avraham Weiss, "We Did Not Go to Auschwitz to Be Beaten," Letter to the Editor, *New York Times*, September 12, 1989.

30. John Tagliabue, "Polish Prelate Assails Protests by Jews at Auschwitz Convent," *New York Times*, August 11, 1989.

31. Religious News Service, August 11, 1989.

32. Alan Riding, "Jewish Group Protests Remarks Made by Pope," *New York Times*, August 13, 1989.

33. See *Origins*, October 5, 1989 (vol. 19, no. 18), pp. 291–94.

34. There is a difference between the translation offered in *Origins* and the *Times* translation (August 29, 1989). The *New York Times* uses "do not dictate" where *Origins* translates "do not set conditions."

35. John Tagliabue, "Polish Cardinal Terms Agreement on Auschwitz 'Offensive,'" *New York Times*, September 3, 1989.

36. John Tagliabue, "Polish Primate Criticizes Jews in Dispute on Auschwitz Convent," *New York Times*, August 29, 1989.

37. Ari L. Goldman, "O'Connor Assails Remarks by Glemp," *New York Times*, August 30, 1989.

38. Youssef M. Ibrahim, "Three Cardinals Defend Convent Pact against Attack by Polish Primate," *New York Times*, September 4, 1989.

39. *Origins*, p. 291.

40. Patrick Buchanan, "Hardball Is a Game That Two Can Play," *Washington Times*, September 25, 1989.

Chapter 5
The Unmastered Trauma: Interpreting the Holocaust

Chapter 5 has gone through a number of changes. It appeared originally in *Humanities and Society,* vol. 2, no. 4, Fall 1979. A revised version was published as chapter 7 in *The Age of Triage* (1983). Considerable new material has been added to the present, enlarged version, which is a comprehensive revision of the original essay.

1. Raul Hilberg, *The Destruction of the European Jews* (Chicago: Quadrangle Books, 1967).

2. George Kren and Leon Rappoport, *The Holocaust and the Crisis of Human Behavior* (New York: Holmes and Meier, 1979), p. 128.

3. I am indebted for this insight to Peter J. Haas, *Morality after Auschwitz: The Radical Challenge of the Nazi Ethic* (Philadelphia: Fortress Press, 1988), p. 58.

4. Kren and Rappoport, *The Holocaust,* pp. 133–34.

5. Among the more important works in which the theory of cognitive dissonance is discussed are: Leon Festinger, Henry W. Riecken, and Stanley Schachter, *When Prophecy Fails* (Minneapolis: University of Minnesota Press, 1956); Festinger, *A Theory of Cognitive Dissonance* (Evanston: Row, Peterson, 1957); Festinger, *Conflict, Decision, and Dissonance* (Stanford: Stanford University Press, 1964); Robert Abelson, ed., *Theories of Cognitive Consistency: A Source Book* (Chicago: Rand McNally, 1968); Elliot Aronson and Gardner Lindzey, eds., *The Handbook of Social Psychology* (New York: Random House, 1985); Aronson, *The Social Animal,* 5th ed. (New York: W. H. Freeman, 1988); Aronson, "The Rationalizing Animal," *Psychology Today,* May 1973; Anthony Greenwald and David L. Ronis, "Twenty Years of Cognitive Dissonance: Case Study of the Evolution of a Theory," *Psychology Review* 85, January 1978.

6. Festinger, "Cognitive Dissonance," *Scientific American,* 207, (October 1962), p. 93.

7. Ibid., p. 93.

8. Festinger, *When Prophecy Fails,* pp. 3ff.

9. The most authoritative work on Sabbatai Zvi is Gershom Scholem, *Sabbatai Sevi: The Mystical Messiah, 1626–1676* (Princeton: Princeton University Press, 1973).

10. The dissonance reduction role of the theologian is especially evident in the career of Nathan of Gaza, the theologian of the Sabbatian movement. Nathan argued that Sabbatai Zvi's conversion to Islam was indispensable to his role as Messiah. See Scholem, *Sabbatai Sevi,* pp. 197–326. It is my conviction that Paul of Tarsus was also engaging in dissonance reduction in passages such as the following: "But we proclaim Christ—yes, Christ nailed to the cross; and though this is a stumbling-block to Jews and folly to the Greeks, yet to those who have heard his call, Jews and Greeks alike, he is the power of God and the wisdom of God" (I Cor. 1:23–24). For a somewhat similar interpretation of the role of the theologian, see Peter Berger, *The Sacred Canopy* (Garden City, N.J.: Doubleday, 1966), pp. 53–80.

11. See, for example, Malcolm Hay, *Europe and the Jews: The Pressure of Christendom on the People of Israel for 1900 Years* (Boston: Beacon Press, 1961); Jules Isaac, *The Teaching of Contempt* (New York: Holt, Rinehart and Winston, 1965);

Leon Poliakov, *The History of Anti-Semitism*, trans. Richard Howard (New York: Schocken Books, 1974).

12. Hilberg, *The Destruction of the European Jews*, p. 12.

13. See Alan T. Davies, *Anti-Semitism and the Christian Mind: The Crisis of Conscience after Auschwitz* (New York: Herder and Herder, 1969); Rosemary Ruether, *Faith and Fratricide: The Theological Roots of Anti-Semitism* (New York: Seabury, 1974); Richard L. Rubenstein, *After Auschwitz: Radical Theology and Contemporary Judaism*, 1st ed. (Indianapolis: Bobbs-Merrill, 1966), pp. 1–21; Franklin H. Littell, *The Crucifixion of the Jews* (New York: Harper and Row, 1975), pp. 24–43.

14. Hilberg, *The Destruction of the European Jews*; Lucy Dawidowicz, *The War against the Jews: 1933–1945* (New York: Bantam Books, 1975); Nora Levin, *The Holocaust: The Destruction of European Jewry, 1933–1945* (New York: Schocken Books, 1973).

15. Hilberg, *The Destruction of the European Jews*, pp. 3–4.

16. Dawidowicz, *The War against the Jews*, p. 28.

17. Ibid., p. 29.

18. Ibid., p. 30.

19. Ibid., pp. 61–62.

20. See chap. 3, "Religion and the Origins of the Death Camps: A Psychoanalytic Interpretation."

21. See Richard L. Rubenstein, "Response to the Issue on Judaism and Psycho-History of the *Journal of Psycho-History*," *Journal of Psycho-History*, Spring 1979.

22. A characteristic example of this approach is to be found in Lucy Dawidowicz, *The War against the Jews*, p. 221, where post–World War I, German anti-Semitism is characterized as a "delusional disorder" involving "pathological fantasies about the Jews." Dawidowicz also describes anti-Semitism as "the mass psychosis" that "deranged a whole people." Earlier examples are found in N. Ackerman and M. Jahoda, *Anti-Semitism and Emotional Disorder* (New York: Harper and Brothers, 1950); E. Simmel, ed., *Anti-Semitism: A Social Disease* (New York: Harper and Brothers, 1946); T. W. Adorno, Else Frenkel-Brunswick, Daniel J. Levinson, and R. Nevitt Sanford, *The Authoritarian Personality* (New York: Harper and Brothers, 1950); Otto Fenichel, "The Psycho-analysis of Anti-Semitism," *American Imago* 1 (1940), 24–39.

23. See Roy Schafer, *Psychoanalytic Interpretation in Rorschach Testing* (New York: Grune and Stratton, 1954), pp. 74ff.

24. Dawidowicz, *The War against the Jews*, pp. 191ff.

25. For a modern Jewish work of classical authority that sees Christianity as endangered by the presence of elements of both paganism and idolatry, see Franz Rosenzweig, *The Star of Redemption*, trans. William W. Hallo (New York: Holt, Rhinehart and Winston, 1970), pp. 399ff.

26. See Moshe Leshem, *Israel Alone* (New York: Touchstone, 1989), p. 277. This book was originally published as *Baalam's Curse: How the Jewish State Lost Its Way and How It Can Find It Again* (New York: Simon and Schuster, 1989).

27. Patrick Girard, "Historical Foundations of Antisemitism," in Joel Dinsdale, ed., *Survivors, Victims, and Perpetrators: Essays on the Nazi Holocaust* (Washington: Hemisphere Publishing Company, 1980), p. 71. For this reference, I am indebted to Zygmunt Bauman, *Modernity and the Holocaust* (Ithaca: Cornell University Press, 1989), p. 58.

28. For a more detailed discussion of Luther's virulent anti-Semitism, see Richard L. Rubenstein and John K. Roth, *Approaches to Auschwitz: The Holocaust and Its Legacy* (Atlanta: John Knox Press, 1987), pp. 52–55.

29. I am indebted to Celia S. Heller for this succinct characterization of the transformation of the Jewish economic situation in modern times. See Celia S. Heller, *On the Edge of Destruction: Jews of Poland between the Two World Wars* (New York: Columbia University Press, 1977), p. 16.

30. On the conception of "elite" minorities, see Harold D. Lasswell, Daniel Lerner, and C. E. Rothwell, *The Comparative Study of Elites: An Introduction and Bibliography*, Hoover Institute Studies (Stanford: Stanford University Press, 1952). On the idea of a "middleman minority," see Walter P. Zenner, "Middleman Minorities and Genocide," in *Genocide and the Modern Age: Etiology and Case Study of Mass Death*, ed. Isidor Walliman and Michael N. Dobkowski (Westport, Conn.: Greenwood, 1987), pp. 253–81.

31. Hannah Arendt, *The Origins of Totalitarianism* (New York: Harcourt, Brace, 1951), p. 52.

32. See E. Digby Baltzell, *The Protestant Establishment: Caste and Class in America* (New Haven: Yale University Press, 1987), pp. 336ff.; Dan A. Oren, *Joining the Club: A History of Jews and Yale* (New Haven: Yale University Press, 1985), pp. 112–35.

33. See Max Weber, *Economy and Society*, ed. Guenther Roth and Claus Wittich (New York: Bedminster Press, 1968), vol. 2, p. 613.

34. For a neglected but important interpretation of Jewish economic history, see Abram Leon, *The Jewish Question: A Marxist Interpretation* (New York: Pathfinder Press, 1970). For critical reviews of Leon's thesis, see Oscar Handlin, "Does Economics Explain Racism?" *Commentary*, vol. 6, no. 1 (July 1948), pp. 79–85; Werner J. Cahnman, "Socio-Economic Causes of Antisemitism," *Social Problems*, vol 5, no. 1 (July 1957). On the economic history of the Jews, see also "Economic History," *Encyclopaedia Judaica*, vol. 13, pp. 1295–1325.

35. "Population," *Encyclopaedia Judaica*, vol. 13, pp. 889–92.

36. See Stephen Kieniewicz, *The Emancipation of the Polish Peasantry* (Chicago: University of Chicago Press, 1969), pp. 140–90.

37. See Edward Crankshaw, *The Shadow of the Winter Palace: The Drift to Revolution, 1825–1917* (Harmondsworth, U.K.: Penguin Books, 1978), pp. 197ff; David Vital, *The Origins of Zionism* (Oxford: Oxford University Press, 1975), p. 49.

38. The statistics tell the story. In 1862, 72 percent of the Jewish population of Warsaw was engaged in commerce; in 1897, the percentage had dropped to 62. "Poland," *Encyclopedia Judaica*, vol. 13, pp. 735–40. In 1914, 72 percent of the stores in Polish villages were owned by Jews; in 1935, only 35 percent were in Jewish hands. Leon, *The Jewish Question*, p. 228.

39. Leon, *The Jewish Question*, p. 228.

40. In 1781 the Jewish population of Warsaw was 3,532, or 4.5 percent of the total; in 1882 it was 127,917, or 33.4 percent of the total; in 1897 it was 219,141, or 33.9 percent of the total. In Lodz, an important manufacturing center, there were 2,775 Jews in 1856, or 12.2 percent of the total; in 1910 Lodz had 166,628 Jews, or 40.7 percent of the total. "Poland," *Encyclopedia Judaica*.

41. Ibid.

42. Leon, *The Jewish Question*, p. 206.

43. Ibid., p. 207.

44. See Vital, *The Origins of Zionism*, p. 52; S. Ettinger, "Anti-Semitism as Official Government Policy in Eastern Europe," in *A History of the Jewish People*, ed. H. H. Ben Sasson (Cambridge, Mass.: Harvard University Press, 1976), pp. 881–90; Howard M. Sachar, *The Course of Modern Jewish History* (New York: Delta Books, 1970), pp. 240–46. For an older, but still useful, account of the events of 1881 and their aftermath, see Louis Greenberg, *The Jews in Russia* (New York: Schocken Books, 1976), vol. 2, pp. 1–75.

45. See Stephen M. Berk, *Year of Crisis, Year of Hope: Russian Jewry and the Pogroms of 1881–1882* (Westport, Conn.: Greenwood Press, 1985), pp. 36–55, for a succinct discussion and analysis of the pogroms. See also Louis Greenberg, *The Jews in Russia*, 2d ed. (New York: Schocken Books, 1976), pp. 1–75; "Pogroms," *Encyclopaedia Judaica*, vol. 13, pp. 695–98; and David Vital, *The Origins of Zionism*, p. 52.

46. Berk, *Year of Crisis*, p. 42.

47. Ibid., p. 39.

48. Ibid.

49. Vital, *The Origins of Zionism*, p. 70.

50. Berk, *Year of Crisis*, p. 41.

51. See Stephen M. Berk, "The Russian Revolutionary Movement and the Pogroms of 1881–1882," *Soviet Jewish Affairs*, vol. 7, no. 2 (1977), pp. 22–39; "Pogroms," *Encyclopaedia Judaica*, vol. 13, pp. 695–98; Vital, *The Origins of Zionism*, p. 56.

52. See Crankshaw, *The Shadow of the Winter Palace*, pp. 333–41.

53. Statistics on Jewish emigration are to be found in Mark Wischnitzer, *To Dwell in Safety: The Story of Jewish Migration Since 1800* (Philadelphia: Jewish Publication Society, 1948), p. 289; Leon, *The Jewish Question*, p. 200; Sachar, *Modern Jewish History*, p. 306. For an overall view of the great European immigration to the United States, see Oscar Handlin, *The Uprooted*, 2d ed. (Boston: Atlantic, Little Brown, 1973).

54. Vital, *The Origins of Zionism*, p. 59.

55. Alexander III, "The May Laws (May 2, 1882)" in *The Jew in the Modern World: A Documentary History*, ed. Paul Mendes-Flohr and Jehuda Reinharz (New York: Oxford University Press, 1980), p. 309; Sachar, *Modern Jewish History*, pp. 244–45.

56. "May Laws," *Encyclopaedia Judaica*, vol. 11, pp. 1147–48.

57. Sachar, *Modern Jewish History*, p. 245.

58. Crankshaw, *The Shadow of the Winter Palace*, p. 331. For a biography of Pobedonostsev, see R. F. Byrnes, *Pobedonostsev* (Bloomington: Indiana University Press, 1968).

59. See Manuel Sarkisyanz, *A Modern History of Transcaucasian Armenia*, privately printed by author (Nagpur: Udyama Commercial Press, 1975), p. 142 (distributed by E. J. Brill, Leiden).

60. See Richard L. Rubenstein, *The Age of Triage* (Boston: Beacon Press, 1983), pp. 12–19.

61. James Billington, *The Icon and the Axe: An Interpretive History of Russian Culture* (New York: Vintage Books, 1970), p. 441.

62. "Pobedonostsev," *Encyclopaedia Judaica*, vol. 13, p. 663; Sachar, *Modern Jewish History*, p. 246.

Notes to Pages 106–111

63. See Carl Schorske, *Fin de Siècle Vienna: Politics and Culture* (New York: Alfred A. Knopf, 1980), p. 128. On the impact of industrial capitalism on the lower middle class, see Theodore S. Hamerow, *Restoration, Revolution, Reaction: Economics and Politics in Germany, 1815–1871* (Princeton: Princeton University Press, 1958), pp. 3–91; Hamerow, *The Social Foundations of German Unification, 1858–1871* (Princeton: Princeton University Press, 1972), pp. 49–97.

64. Hans Rosenberg, "Political and Social Consequences of the Great Depression of 1873–1896 in Central Europe," in *Imperial Germany*, ed. James Sheehan (New York: New Viewpoints, 1972), p. 45. See also Martin Kitchen, *The Political Economy of Germany: 1815–1914* (London: Croon Helm, 1978), pp. 161–79; Ismar Schorsch, *Jewish Reactions to German Anti-Semitism, 1870–1914* (New York: Columbia University Press, 1972), pp. 361ff.

65. Adolf Stöcker's first anti-Semitic speech, delivered at the Christian Social Workers party on September 19, 1879, is reprinted in Paul Massing, *Rehearsal for Destruction: A Study of Political Anti-Semitism in Imperial Germany* (New York: Harper and Brothers, 1949), pp. 278–87. Ernst Nolte, "Germany," in *The European Right: A Historical Profile*, ed. Hans Rogger and Eugen Weber, (Berkeley: University of California Press, 1966), pp. 287ff.

66. Heinrich von Treitschke, "A Word about Our Jewry," in *The Jews in the Modern World*, pp. 280–84.

67. Andrew Whiteside, "Austria," in *The European Right*, p. 318. For a brief but illuminating study of Schönerer, see Schorske, *Fin de Siècle Vienna*, pp. 120–33.

68. Whiteside, "Austria," p. 314.

69. See Ernst Pawel, *The Labyrinth of Exile: A Life of Theodore Herzl* (New York: Farrar, Straus and Giroux, 1989), pp. 69–70.

70. See Celia S. Heller, *On the Edge of Destruction: Jews of Poland between Two World Wars* (New York: Columbia University Press, 1977), pp. 118–24; Geoffrey Pridham, *Hitler's Rise to Power: The Nazi Movement in Bavaria, 1923–1933* (New York: Harper and Row, 1974), pp. 209–15.

71. "Vienna," *Encyclopaedia Judaica*, vol. 16, p. 1247; see Leon, *The Jewish Question*, p. 215.

72. "Berlin," *Encyclopaedia Judaica*, vol. 4, p. 64.

73. Schorske, *Fin de Siècle Vienna*, p. 129.

74. Rogger and Weber, *The European Right*, pp. 312–14.

75. For a comprehensive study of German emigration during the nineteenth century, see Mack Walker, *Germany and the Emigration, 1816–1885* (Cambridge: Harvard University Press, 1965). On the character of the emigration during the period, see ibid., pp. 175–94.

76. Ibid.

77. See George L. Mosse, *Toward the Final Solution: A History of European Racism* (New York: Harper and Row, 1978), pp. 177ff.

78. G. W. F. Hegel, *Philosophy of Right*, trans. T. M. Knox (Oxford: Oxford University Press, 1942), addition to par. 182.

79. Ibid., par. 187.

80. A. J. Ryder, *Twentieth-Century Germany: From Bismarck to Brandt* (New York: Columbia University Press, 1972), p. 40.

81. Handlin, "Does Economics Explain Racism?" p. 32.

82. A. M. Carr-Sanders, *World Population* (Oxford: Oxford University Press, 1936), pp. 49ff.

83. Robert G. L. Waite, *Adolf Hitler: The Psychopathic God* (New York: New American Library, 1978), p. 73.

84. Adolf Hitler, *Mein Kampf*, trans. Ralph Mannheim (Boston: Houghton, Mifflin, 1943), pp. 649ff.

85. Waite, *Adolf Hitler*, p. 11.

86. Karl Dietrich Bracher, *The German Dictatorship* (New York: Praeger, 1973), pp. 272–86.

87. See Allan Mitchell, *Revolution in Bavaria* (Princeton: Princeton University Press, 1965), and Richard Grunberger, *Red Rising in Bavaria* (New York: St. Martin's Press, 1973).

88. See Robert Pois, "Introduction to Alfred Rosenberg," in *Race and Race History*, ed. Robert Pois (New York: Harper and Row, 1974).

89. On the wartime attitudes of Pope Pius XII to National Socialist Germany, see Saul Friedlander, *Pius XII and the Third Reich: A Documentation*, trans. Charles Fullman (New York: Alfred A. Knopf, 1966), pp. 174–76.

90. Hitler, *Mein Kampf*, pp. 622–24.

91. Treitschke, "A Word about Our Jewry," p. 281. On the impact of Jewish immigration, see also Arthur J. May, *The Hapsburg Monarchy* (Cambridge: Harvard University Press, 1951), pp. 178–80.

92. Hannah Arendt, *The Origins of Totalitarianism*, pp. 275ff. Richard L. Rubenstein, *The Cunning of History* (New York: Harper and Row, 1957), pp. 141ff.

93. Ryder, *Twentieth-Century Germany*, p. 345.

94. U.S. Congress, Committee on Immigration, *Temporary Suspension of Immigration*, 65th Cong., 3d sess., 1920, H. Rept. 1109.

95. Sachar, *Modern Jewish History*, pp. 313–14.

96. Heller, *On the Edge of Destruction*, pp. 101–107.

97. "Poland," *Encyclopaedia Judaica*, vol. 13, pp. 739–49.

98. Heller, *On the Edge of Destruction*, p. 113.

99. Ibid., pp. 136–39.

100. See, for example, Edward D. Wynot, Jr., "A Necessary Cruelty: The Emergence of Official Anti-Semitism in Poland, 1936–39," *The American Historical Review*, vol. 76, no. 4 (October 1971), p. 1057.

101. Heller, *On the Edge of Destruction*, p. 295.

102. Adolf Hitler, Letter to Staff-Captain Karl Mayr, September 16, 1919, in *Hitler's Letters and Notes*, ed. Werner Maser (New York: Harper and Row, 1974), p. 211.

103. Waite, *Adolf Hitler*, p. 373.

104. Gil Eliot, *The Twentieth Century Book of the Dead* (New York: Charles Scribner's Sons, 1972), p. 23.

105. Waite, *Adolf Hitler*, p. 373.

106. For a scholarly survey of Marxist views on Jews and Judaism, see Julius Carlebach, *Karl Marx and the Radical Critique of Judaism* (London: Routledge and Kegan Paul, 1978).

Chapter 6
Modernization and the Politics of Extermination:
Genocide in Historical Context

Chapter 6 originally appeared in Michael Berenbaum, ed., *A Mosaic of Victims: Non-Jews Persecuted and Murdered by the Nazis* (New York: New York University Press, 1990).

1. For an important book on the subject, see Isidor Walliman and Michael N. Dobkowski, eds., *Genocide and the Modern Age: Etiology and Case Study of Mass Death* (Westport, Conn.: Greenwood Press, 1987). See also Leo Kuper, *Genocide: Its Political Use in the Twentieth Century* (New Haven: Yale University Press, 1987), and Irving Louis Horowitz, *Genocide: State Power and Mass Murder* (New Brunswick, N.J.: Transaction Books, 1980).

2. Zygmunt Bauman, *Modernity and the Holocaust* (Ithaca: Cornell University Press, 1989), pp. 1–30. Bauman is Professor of Sociology at the University of Leeds.

3. The Holocaust was characterized as an atypical "episode" by General Vernon Walters, American Ambassador to the Federal Republic of Germany, during a special *Firing Line* debate, chaired by William F. Buckley Jr., entitled, "United Germany: Anything to Worry?" on June 26, 1990. General Walters had previously served as Deputy Director of the C.I.A. and American Ambassador to the United Nations.

4. This is a generalization of my fundamental thesis concerning the Holocaust as expressed in *The Cunning of History* (New York: Harper and Row, 1975), p. 6.

5. Tony Barta, "Relations of Genocide: Land and Lives in the Colonization of Australia," in Wallimann and Dobkowski, *Genocide and the Modern Age*, pp. 237–52.

6. For another account of the impact of English colonizing on the aborigines, see Alan Moorhead, *The Fatal Impact: An Account of the Invasion of the South Pacific* (New York: Harper and Row, 1966), pp. 119–33, 168–76.

7. This thesis is spelled out in Richard L. Rubenstein, *The Age of Triage: Fear and Hope in an Overcrowded World* (Boston: Beacon Press, 1983), pp. 34–59.

8. See Helen Fein, *Accounting for Genocide: National Responses and Jewish Victimization during the Holocaust* (New York: Free Press, 1979), p. 4.

9. See J. Thomas Kelly, *Thorn on the Tudor Rose: Monks, Rogues, Vagabonds, and Sturdy Beggars* (Jackson: University Press of Mississippi, 1977), pp. 83ff.

10. See Robert Hughes, *The Fatal Shore: The Epic of Australia's Founding* (New York: Alfred A. Knopf, 1987), pp. 1–42.

11. For a study of the fate of the Indians of North America, see Bernard W. Sheehan, *Seeds of Extinction: Jeffersonian Philanthropy and the American Indian* (Chapel Hill: University of North Carolina Press, 1973).

12. Christopher Hill, *God's Englishman: Oliver Cromwell and the English Revolution* (New York: Harper Torchbooks, 1972), p. 113.

13. R. P. Stearns, *Hugh Peter: The Strenuous Puritan, 1598–1660* (Champagne: University of Illinois Press, 1954), p. 356; cited by Hill, *God's Englishman*, p. 117.

14. Cecil Woodham-Smith, *The Great Hunger: Ireland, 1845–1849* (New York: E. P. Dutton, 1980), pp. 411–12.

15. See Rubenstein, *Age of Triage*, pp. 120–27.

16. "Effects of Emigration on Production and Consumption," *Economist*, February 12, 1853, pp. 168–69. See my comments in *Age of Triage*, p. 122.

17. See "The Irish Priesthood and the Irish Laity," *Economist*, June 19, 1852.

18. See Rubenstein, *Age of Triage*, pp. 165–94.

19. See chap. 3, "Religion and the Origins of the Death Camps."

20. See Walter P. Zenner, "Middleman Minorities and Genocide," in Wallimann and Dobkowski, *Genocide and the Modern Age*, pp. 253–81; Zenner, *Middleman Minority Theories and the Jews: A Historical Assessment* (New York: YIVO Working Papers in Yiddish and East European Jewish Studies Series, No. 31, 1978); Edna Bonacich and J. Modell, *The Economic Basis of Ethnic Solidarity: The Case of Japanese-Americans* (Berkeley: University of California Press, 1981).

21. For a discussion of the elimination of the ethnic Chinese from Vietnam, see Rubenstein, *Age of Triage*, pp. 165–94.

22. See Benjamin Nelson, *The Idea of Usury: From Tribal Brotherhood to Universal Otherhood*, 2d ed. (Chicago: University of Chicago Press, 1969).

23. See George Schöpflin, "The Political Traditions of Central Europe," *Daedalus*, Winter 1990, pp. 830–85.

24. Rubenstein, *The Age of Triage*, pp. 128–64.

25. See chap. 5, "The Unmastered Trauma."

26. See Irving Louis Horowitz, "Genocide and the Reconstruction of Social Theory: Observations on the Exclusivity of Social Death," in Wallimann and Dobkowski, *Genocide and the Modern Age*, pp. 61–80.

27. See chap. 3, "Religion and the Origins of the Death Camps."

28. In chap. 3, "Religion and the Origins of the Death Camps," originally written early in 1961, I argued that the Holocaust was largely an irrational affair whose *roots* are to be found in magical thinking and the Christian identification of the Jews with Satan and Judas. I now hold that these were necessary but not sufficient conditions for genocide to become an overt instrument of public policy. In addition to the religious and psychological roots, I now believe we must add the monumental destabilization of the economy and society of the nations of Europe which accompanied the process of modernization.

29. See Roger Smith, "Human Destructiveness and Politics: The Twentieth Century as an Age of Genocide," in Wallimann and Dobkowski, *Genocide and the Modern Age*, pp. 21–40. See also Baumann, *Modernity and the Holocaust*, pp. 31–82.

30. Max Weber, *Economy and Society: An Outline of Interpretive Sociology*, ed. Guenther Roth and Claus Wittich (New York: Bedminster Press, 1968), vol. 1, pp. 24–26.

31. Ronald Aronson, *The Dialectics of Disaster* (London: Verso, 1983).

32. See George E. Mendenhall, *The Tenth Generation: The Origins of the Biblical Tradition* (Baltimore: Johns Hopkins University Press, 1973), pp. 19ff.; see also Rubenstein, *The Age of Triage*, pp. 229–40.

33. Richard L. Rubenstein, *The Cunning of History* (New York: Harper and Row, 1975), p. 90.

Chapter 7
Covenant, Holocaust, and Intifada

Faith in the covenant between God and Israel has been absolutely fundamental to both biblical and rabbinic Judaism. Hence, my rejection of covenant and election in the first edition of *After Auschwitz* and subsequent writings was the most radical theological step I could have taken as a Jewish thinker.

Over the years, however, I have reflected upon the obvious fact that wise and learned men and women in both Judaism and Christianity have believed in and found profound meaning in the idea of a covenant between God and His people. I had too much respect for these men and women to dismiss their faith. I therefore attempted to find meaning in it. As I had once found meaning in religious ritual by inquiring into its social or psychological function, I began to find meaning in the idea of covenant and election by attempting to understand its function in the life of the religious community.

Initially, I stressed the idea of covenant and election as psychic compensation for political impotence. This is especially evident in *The Religious Imagination* (1968). At present, I believe that the idea did serve that function but that there was far more to the story. My current views are spelled out in chapter 7. It should be noted that I have not rejected my earlier theological and sociological views. I have, however, added to and considerably modified them.

1. The idea of a community of moral obligation is based upon Helen Fein's concept of a "universe of moral obligation." See Helen Fein, *Accounting for Genocide: National Responses and Jewish Victimization during the Holocaust* (New York: Free Press, 1979), p. 4.

2. See George Mendenhall, *Law and Covenant in Israel and the Ancient Near East* (Pittsburgh: Biblical Colloquium, 1955); 'Covenant,' in G. A. Buttrick, ed., *The Interpreter's Dictionary of the Bible* (Nashville: Abingdon, 1962), vol. 1; Dennis J. McCarthy, S.J., *Old Testament Covenant* (Richmond: John Knox Press, 1972); "Covenant," *Encyclopedia Judaica*, vol. 5, pp. 1012–22.

3. See George Mendenhall, *The Tenth Generation: The Origins of the Biblical Tradition* (Baltimore: Johns Hopkins University Press, 1973), pp. 19ff.

4. Mendenhall, "Covenant Forms in Israelite Tradition," pp. 29ff.

5. Ibid., pp. 35ff.

6. Mendenhall, *The Tenth Generation*, p. 30.

7. The relationship between Israel's fidelity to her obligations under the covenant and her fate are spelled out in many places in Scripture. See, for example, Leviticus 26:3–45; Amos 4:6–11; Jeremiah 44:1–4.

8. See Richard L. Rubenstein, *The Religious Imagination* (Indianapolis: Bobbs-Merrill, 1968), pp. 127ff.

9. This point is implied in the discussion of the secularization process in Peter Berger, *The Sacred Canopy* (Garden City: Doubleday, 1966), pp. 106ff.

10. "Science as a Vocation," in *From Max Weber: Essays in Sociology*, ed. H. H. Gerth and C. Wright Mills (New York: Oxford University Press, 1946), p. 139.

11. See Montgomery Watt, *Muhammed at Mecca* (Oxford: Oxford University Press, 1953), pp. 151–53.

12. See Bernard Wysocki, Jr., "Christian Missions Convert Few in Japan," in *Asian Wall Street Journal*, July 16, 1986.

13. See Robert N. Bellah, *The Broken Covenant: American Civil Religion in Time of Trial* (New York: Seabury Press, 1975), pp. 87–112.

14. Thucydides, *The Peloponnesian War*, trans. Rex Warner (Harmondsworth, U.K.: Penguin Books, 1980), p. 408.

15. There is debate concerning the degree to which the inhabitants of Ca-

naanite cities were actually put to death. There were, apparently, some instances in which the injunction was put into practice in defense of Israel's religiocultural world. See Johannes Pedersen, *Israel: Its Life and Culture* (London: Geoffrey Cumberlege, 1940), vol. 3, pp. 24–25.

16. Robert K. Massie, *Peter the Great: His Life and World* (New York: Ballantine Books, 1988), p. 743.

17. H. G. Nichols, ed., *Washington Dispatches, 1941–1945: Weekly Political Reports from the British Embassy* (Chicago: University of Chicago Press, 1981), p. 558. Most of the dispatches were written by Sir Isaiah Berlin.

18. This cartoon is reproduced in John W. Dower, *War without Mercy: Race and Power in the Pacific War* (New York: Pantheon Books, 1986), p. 185.

19. Ibid., pp. 29, 36–37, 52–57, 70–73, 81–83, 90–92, 184–85, 196–97, 232–33, 247–49.

20. Ibid., p. 54.

21. Jared Taylor, *Shadows of the Rising Sun: A Critical View of the Japanese Miracle* (New York: William Morrow, 1983), p. 91.

22. Isaiah Ben-Dasan, *The Japanese and the Jews*, trans. Richard L. Gage (Tokyo: Weatherhill, 1985), pp. 134ff.

23. See Taylor, *Shadows of the Rising Sun*, pp. 28–39.

24. See, for example, Anton Shammas, "A Stone's Throw," *New York Review of Books*, March 31, 1988.

25. For a reliable account of the Vanunu affair and its relationship to Israel's nuclear arsenal, see Louis Toscano, *Triple Cross: Israel, the Atomic Bomb, and the Man Who Spilled the Secrets* (Secaucus, N.J.: Carol Publishing Group, 1990).

Chapter 8
Covenant and Divinity: The Holocaust and the Problematics of Religious Faith, Part 1

Chapters 8 and 9 constitute a record of my ongoing dialogue with my theological contemporaries in Judaism. A number of earlier essays form the basis of these chapters. One of the earliest is "The Radical Monotheism of Emil Fackenheim," *Soundings*, Summer 1974. At the time, both Fackenheim and I were more inclined to stress our differences than our common vocation. The differences are still there, but, on my part and I have reason to believe on his, there has been growing respect and appreciation.

Mutual respect and appreciation also characterized my dialogue with the late Arthur Cohen. In the first edition of *After Auschwitz*, I discussed his *The Natural and the Supernatural Jew* (1962) in a chapter entitled "The 'Supernatural' Jew." *The Natural and the Supernatural Jew* was the first major theological work by an American Jewish thinker of my generation. It is difficult to think of two books so fundamentally different in perspective than *The Natural and the Supernatural Jew* and the first edition of *After Auschwitz*, in which I was very critical of Cohen's initial theological effort. As Cohen himself acknowledges in *The Tremendum* (1981), he was completely silent concerning the Holocaust in his earlier work. In *The Tremendum* he finally turned to the problem of Holocaust theology. I responded in "Naming the Unnameable; Thinking the Unthinkable: A Review

Essay on Arthur Cohen's *The Tremendum*," *Journal of Reform Judaism* 31 (Spring 1984). That essay forms the basis of the discussion of Cohen in chapter 9.

When John K. Roth and I decided to write *Approaches to Auschwitz* (1987), we agreed that I would do the section on Jewish theological responses to the Holocaust in chapter 10, "The Silence of God: Philosophical and Religious Reflection on the Holocaust." That material, revised and updated, forms the basis of chapters 8 and 9 of the current volume.

1. Isaiah 45:7 is thought to be such a rejection: "I form the light, and create darkness: I make peace and create evil: I the Lord do all these things."

2. G. W. F. Hegel, "Introduction: Reason in History," in *Lectures on the Philosophy of World History*, ed. Johannes Hoffmeister, trans. H. B. Nisbet (Cambridge: Cambridge University Press, 1975), p. 43.

3. Theodore Adorno, *Negative Dialects*, trans. E. B. Ashton (New York: Seabury Press, 1973), pp. 361–62.

4. James H. Markham, "Over Philosophy's Temple, Shadow of a Swastika," *New York Times*, February 4, 1988.

5. Heidegger's letter to Marcuse, dated January 28, 1948, is found in the Marcuse archives in Frankfurt. See Thomas Sheehan, "Heidegger and the Nazis," *New York Review of Books*, June 16, 1988, p. 42.

6. Richard L. Rubenstein, *The Age of Triage* (Boston: Beacon Press, 1983), p. 132.

7. The phrase is from Irving Greenberg, "Cloud of Smoke, Pillar of Fire: Judaism, Christianity, and Modernity after the Holocaust," in *Auschwitz: Beginning of a New Era?* ed. Eva Fleischner (New York: Ktav, 1977), pp. 9–13.

8. Elchonon Wassermann, *Ma'amar Ikvossoh Demeshicho Vema'mamar Al Ha'emunah* (Treatise on the Footsteps of the Messiah and on Faith) (New York: 1939, in Yiddish), cited by Gershon Greenberg, "Orthodox Theological Responses to Kristallnacht: Chayyim Ozer Grodzensky ("Achiezer") and Elchonon Wassermann," paper presented at the Eighteenth Annual Scholars Conference on the Church Struggle and the Holocaust, Washington, D.C., 1988. I am indebted to Professor Greenberg for having made this paper available to me, as well as several others dealing with Orthodox responses to the Holocaust.

9. Ibid., p. 40.

10. Efraim Oshry, *Churban Litta* (New York: 1951, in Yiddish), pp. 48–50, cited and translated by Gershon Greenberg, "Orthodox Theological Responses to Kristallnacht."

11. Joseph Isaac Schneersohn, "Redemption Now," *Netzach Yisroel* III (1948) 6–7 [Hebrew], cited by Gershon Greenberg, "Reflections upon the Holocaust within American Orthodoxy, 1945–1948," unpublished paper, 1988.

12. Joseph H. Hertz, ed., *The Authorised Daily Prayer Book* (New York, 1948), pp. 820–21. See also Richard L. Rubenstein, *The Religious Imagination* (Indianapolis: Bobbs-Merrill, 1968), pp. 127–30.

13. For an overview of this development, see Ian Lustick, *For the Land and the Lord: Jewish Fundamentalism in Israel* (New York: Council on Foreign Relations, 1988); see also Michael Berenbaum, *After Tragedy and Triumph: Modern Jewish Thought and the American Experience* (Cambridge: Cambridge University Press, 1990), pp. 134–55.

14. I have dealt with the elements of continuity and singularity of the Holocaust as a state-sponsored program of population elimination in *The Age of Triage*.

15. Martin Luther, "On the Jews and Their Lies," trans. Martin Bertram, in *Luther's Works*, ed. Franklin T. Sherman and Helmut T. Lehman (Philadelphia: Fortress Press, 1971), vol. 47, p. 139.

16. In a well-known tradition, Yohanan is depicted as having seen a famine-stricken Jewish girl on the road to Emmaus after the Fall of Jerusalem in 70 C.E. Out of desperation for something to eat, the girl extracted undigested barleycorn from the excrement dropped by an Arab's horse. Yohanan commented to his disciples on what he had seen, citing Deuteronomy 28:47–48: "Because you did not serve the Lord your God when you had plenty, therefore you shall serve your enemy in hunger and thirst. Because you did not serve the Lord . . . by reason of the abundance of all things, therefore you shall serve your enemy in want of all things." "Mekhilta Bahodesh," in Jacob Z. Lauterbach, ed. and trans., *Mekhilta de Rabbi Ishmael* (Philadelphia: Jewish Publication Society, 1948), vol. 2, pp. 193–94.

17. To this day the classical rabbinic response to the Fall of Jerusalem determines the character of the traditional liturgy. For example, the Musaf service for the Holy Days and Festivals includes the following prayer: "Thou has chosen us from among all peoples; thou hast loved us and taken pleasure in us, and hast exalted us above all tongues; thou has allowed us by thy commandments, and brought us near unto thy service, O our King, and thou has called us by thy great and holy Name. . . . *But on account of our sins we were exiled from our land and removed far from our country*" (italics added). Hertz, *Daily Prayer Book*, pp. 820–21. See also Rubenstein, *Religious Imagination*, pp. 127–30.

18. Ignaz Maybaum, *The Face of God after Auschwitz* (Amsterdam: Polak and Van Gennep, 1965); Richard L. Rubenstein, *After Auschwitz: Radical Theology and Contemporary Judaism*, (Indianapolis: Bobbs-Merrill, 1966).

19. Maybaum, *Face of God*, p. 36.

20. It should be noted that not all Jews or Christians regard the displacement of sacrificial forms of worship as progress. To this day, Orthodox Jews pray for the restoration of the Jerusalem Temple and its biblically ordained sacrifices. Roman Catholics participate in sacrificial worship whenever the Mass is celebrated, and all Christians regard Jesus as the supreme sacrifice. Maybaum's conception of religious "progress" thus appeared to be dependent upon an unexamined affirmation of the values of nineteenth-century Reform Judaism, which are by no means universally accepted in the late twentieth century. See Rubenstein, *After Auschwitz*, 1st ed., pp. 93–112, where the idea that prayer is a higher mode of religious life than sacrifice is rejected.

21. In Christianity Adam's sin is sometimes regarded as a *felix culpa*, a fortunate fall. "*O felix culpa, quae talem ac tantum meruit habere Redemptorum!*" (O happy fault, that merited such a redeemer), *The English Latin Sacramentary* (Roman Missal) (New York: Benziger, 1966), p. 124. I am indebted to Professor Maureen Tilley of Florida State University for this citation.

22. Maybaum, *Face of God*, p. 67.

23. For an overview of Polish Jewry in the between-the-wars period, see Celia S. Heller, *On the Edge of Destruction: Jews of Poland between the Two World Wars* (New York: Columbia University Press, 1977).

24. Maybaum, *Face of God*, p. 63. I am indebted to Steven Katz, *Post-Holocaust Dialogues* (New York: New York University Press, 1983), p. 162, for this citation.

25. See ch. 10, "The Rebirth of Israel in Contemporary Jewish Theology."

26. Maybaum, *Face of God*, p. 67.

27. Ibid.

28. See Peter Berger, *The Sacred Canopy: Elements of a Sociological Theory of Religion* (Garden City: Anchor Books, 1966), pp. 23–26.

29. This thesis is set forth in Richard L. Rubenstein, *The Cunning of History* (New York: Harper and Row, 1975), and Richard L. Rubenstein and John K. Roth, *Approaches to Auschwitz: The Holocaust and Its Legacy* (Atlanta: John Knox Press, 1987).

30. See ch. 1, "The Dean and the Chosen People."

31. "Ein Wort zur Judenfrage, der Reichsbruderrat der Evangelischen Kirche in Deutschland," April 8, 1949, in *Der Ungekundigte Bund: Neue Bewegung von Juden und Christlicher,* ed. Dietrich Goldschmidt and Hans-Joachim Kraus (Stuttgart: Gemeinde Kreuz-Verlag, 1962), pp. 251–54.

32. See ch. 10, "The Rebirth of Israel in Contemporary Jewish Theology."

33. Rubenstein, *Religious Imagination.*

34. "The State of Jewish Belief: A Symposium," *Commentary,* August 1966; reprinted in *After Auschwitz,* 1st ed., p. 153.

35. Rubenstein, *After Auschwitz,* 1st ed., pp. 151–52.

36. On the Armenian genocide as cultural and psychic inheritance, see Michael Arlen, *Passage to Ararat* (New York: Farrar, Straus and Giroux, 1975).

37. See ch. 16, "God after the Death of God."

38. Among the typical prayers of this genre, we find:

> Sound the great shofar for our freedom; raise the ensign to gather our exiles, and gather us from the four corners of the earth. Blessed art thou, O Lord, who gatherest the dispersed of thy people. . . .
>
> And to Jerusalem, thy city, return in mercy, and dwell therein as thou has spoken; rebuild it soon in our days as an everlasting building, and speedily set up therein the throne of David. Blessed art thou, O Lord, who rebuildest Jerusalem.

(Hertz, *Daily Prayer Book,* pp. 146–47).

Chapter 9
Covenant and Divinity: The Holocaust and the Problematics of Religious Faith, Part 2

1. Emil L. Fackenheim, *Encounters between Judaism and Modern Philosophy* (New York: Basic Books, 1973), p. 21.

2. Emil L. Fackenheim, *Christian Century,* May 6, 1970.

3. Fackenheim, *To Mend the World: Foundations of Future Jewish Though* (New York: Schocken Books, 1982), p. 13.

4. Irving Greenberg, "Cloud of Smoke, Pillar of Fire: Judaism, Christianity, and Modernity after the Holocaust," in *Auschwitz: Beginning of a New Era?* ed. Eva Fleischner (New York: KTAV, 1977), pp. 9–11. See Fackenheim, *To Mend the World,* p. 11.

5. See ch. 8, "Covenant and Divinity, Part 1."

6. Emil Fackenheim, "Can There Be Judaism without Revelation?" in *Quest for Past and Future: Essays in Jewish Theology* (Indianapolis: Indiana University Press, 1968), pp. 80–81; reprinted from *Commentary,* December 1951.

7. Fackenheim, *God's Presence in History* (New York: Harper and Row, 1972), p. 11.

8. In traditional Judaism the number of commandments given by God to Israel in Scripture is said to be 613.

9. Fackenheim, "Transcendence in Contemporary Culture: Philosophical Reflections and a Jewish Theology," in *Transcendence*, ed. Herbert W. Richardson and Donald R. Cutler (Boston: Beacon Press, 1969), p. 150.

10. Ibid.

11. Fackenheim, *The Jewish Return to History: Reflections in the Age of Auschwitz and the New Jerusalem* (New York: Schocken Books, 1978), p. 31.

12. Fackenheim, *To Mend the World*, p. 10.

13. George M. Kren and Leon Rappoport, *The Holocaust and the Crisis of Human Behavior* (New York: Holmes and Meir, 1980), p. 13.

14. This view is elaborated in Peter J. Haas, *Morality after Auschwitz: The Radical Challenge of the Nazi Ethic* (Philadelphia: Fortress Press, 1988). On the aid given to the perpetrators after the war, see Gitta Sereny, *Into That Darkness* (New York: Vintage, 1983), pp. 276–328.

15. Fackenheim, *To Mend the World*, p. 13.

16. Terence Des Pres, *The Survivor: An Anatomy of Life in the Death Camps* (New York: Oxford University Press, 1976), pp. 51–72. See ch. 3, "Religion and the Origins of the Death Camps," n. 50.

17. Primo Levi, *Survival in Auschwitz*, trans. Stuart Woolf (New York: Collier Books, 1976, p. 82.

18. G. W. F. Hegel, *Phenomenology of the Mind*, trans. J. B. Baillie (London: George Allen and Unwin, 1949), p. 676.

19. See Richard L. Rubenstein and John K. Roth, *Approaches to Auschwitz: The Holocaust and Its Legacy* (Atlanta: John Knox Press, 1986), p. 324. See also Zygmunt Bauman, *Modernity and the Holocaust* (Ithaca: Cornell University Press, 1989).

20. Fackenheim, *To Mend the World*, p. 248.

21. Pelagia Lewinska, *Twenty Months at Auschwitz* (New York: Lyle Stuart, 1986), pp. 141ff., 150.

22. Fackenheim, *To Mend the World*, p. 250.

23. Ibid., p. 304.

24. Ibid.

25. Arthur A. Cohen, *The Natural and the Supernatural Jew* (New York: Pantheon, 1962).

26. Arthur A. Cohen, *The Tremendum* (New York: Crossroad, 1981), p. 34.

27. Rubenstein, "The Supernatural Jew," *After Auschwitz*, 1st ed., pp. 177–90.

28. Cohen, *Tremendum*, p. 36.

29. Ibid., pp. 18–19.

30. Ibid., p. 19.

31. Ibid.

32. See Rubenstein, *The Cunning of History* (New York: Harper & Row, 1975); Rubenstein, *The Age of Triage* (Boston: Beacon Press, 1983); Rubenstein and Roth, *Approaches to Auschwitz*. See also in this volume, ch. 3, "Religion and the Origins of the Death Camps," and ch. 5, "The Unmastered Trauma."

33. Cohen, *Tremendum*, p. 97.
34. Ibid., pp. 97–98.
35. See Eliezer Berkovits, *Faith after the Holocaust* (New York: Ktav, 1973); *Crisis and Faith* (New York: Sanhedrin Press, 1976); *With God in Hell* (New York: Sanhedrin Press, 1979).
36. Berkovits, *Faith after the Holocaust*, p. 107. I am indebted to Steven Katz, *Post-Holocaust Dialogues* (New York: New York University Press, 1983), p. 271, for this citation.
37. Cohen, *Tremendum*, p. 11.
38. Ibid., p. 101.
39. Ibid.
40. Ibid., p. 108.
41. See Rubenstein, "Naming the Unnameable; Thinking the Unthinkable (A Review Essay on Arthur Cohen's *The Tremendum*)," *Journal of Reform Judaism*, Spring 1984, pp. 43–54.
42. For the New Testament source of these ideas, see Romans 9–11.

Chapter 10
The Rebirth of Israel in
Contemporary Jewish Theology

The most significant events in twentieth-century Jewish history have been the European catastrophe and the rebirth of Israel. Both events have decisive significance for contemporary Jewish theology. In the first edition of *After Auschwitz*, I argued that the Holocaust marks the death of the God of History and that the founding of the State of Israel marks the rebirth of the long-forgotten Earth divinities within Jewish experience.

My ideas concerning the rebirth of Israel and the Earth divinities were originally expressed in this essay, first published in a slightly different form in the *Reconstructionist*, April 29, 1960, long before the Six-Day War of 1967, the Yom Kippur War of 1973, the Palestinian Intifada, and Iraqi missile attacks on Israel. Today I am considerably less enthusiastic about the messianic aspects of both Zionism and the rebirth of Israel, although messianic Zionism has become a stronger force by far in contemporary Israel than when this essay was written. When I wrote the essay, I saw Israel's rebirth as *athalta de geulah*, "the beginning of redemption." I no longer so regard it. I now see existence itself as coterminous with exile and the grave as the real locus of "redemption." What I retain of this paper's perspectives is a fundamental conviction that an insightful mystical paganism, using the forms of traditional Jewish religion, is the most meaningful religious option for Jews after Auschwitz and the rebirth of Israel. For further indications of how my current opinions differ from those expressed in this essay, see the notes to this chapter.

1. See G. W. F. Hegel, "The Spirit of Christianity and Its Fate," in *Early Theological Writings*, trans. T. M. Knox and Richard Kroner (Chicago: University of Chicago Press, 1948), pp. 182–205

2. I no longer hold that "we are prisoners of the past only as long as we permit ourselves to be" or that the "chain of sin and punishment" was self-

imposed. On the contrary, I believe that we are all, willy-nilly, heirs of the past and its conflicts. I further believe that by blaming itself for its troubles, the Jewish people used its spiritual resources in a harsh but ultimately constructive way to cope with a tragic and imperiled existence. Only by blaming itself could it finally muster the necessary resources to extricate itself from the Second Egypt, the continent of Europe, and create a new life for itself in Israel.

3. Clearly, I was mistaken but by no means alone in prematurely proclaiming the "end of history." Israel's existence has hardly been "posthistorical" since 1960, when this essay was first written.

4. This would, of course, be true if Israel were to attain "the goal of Jewish history." That prospect now seems a long way off.

5. Today, I believe that, insofar as Israel's survival is based on high-technology weapons perpetually made obsolescent by advances in software, solid-state physics, and mathematics, faith in the transcendent God of History—the God who rules the universe through His own immaterial software—is likely to be affirmed by those who focus on the technological imperatives of Israel's survival; insofar as emphasis is placed on settlement of the *whole* land of Israel, the old earth divinities are likely to reassert their power. See chap. 11, "War, Zionism, and Sacred Space."

6. Herbert Marcuse, *Eros and Civilization* (Boston: Beacon Press, 1948), pp. 112ff.

7. G. W. F. Hegel, *Phenomenology of Mind*, trans. A. V. Miller (Oxford: Oxford University Press, 1977), p. 27.

8. The distinction between "existing beings" and "Being Itself" rests upon Martin Heidegger's distinction between *Seienden* and *Sein*. See Martin Heidegger, *Identity and Difference*, trans. Joan Stambaugh (New York: Harper & Row, 1969), p. 65.

9. The words "bourgeois existence" in the first edition of *After Auschwitz* have been replaced by "membership in a middleman minority."

10. These observations were offered before the Six-Day War. There was in reality no break with middle-class aspirations and values. According to Howard M. Sachar, "By the 1970s and 1980s, the dream of Israeli families for their children tended to mirror that of Diaspora families, for white-collar business and professional careers." Sachar, *A History of Israel: From the Aftermath of the Yom Kippur War* (New York: Oxford University Press, 1987), vol. 2, p. 226. Moreover, Israel began to use Palestinians in large numbers as a low-pay working class in factories, the construction industry, and service industries. Their employment was not unlike the use of *Gastarbeiter*, "guest workers," by Germany, Austria, and Switzerland.

11. See Paul Tillich, *The Courage to Be* (New Haven: Yale University Press, 1952), pp. 182–85.

12. The words "inanimate and dead" in the first edition of *After Auschwitz* have been replaced by "devoid of the divine."

13. The words "as it does" in the first edition of *After Auschwitz* have been replaced by "as it will."

14. The words "has finished" in the first edition of *After Auschwitz* have been replaced by "are in the process of completing."

Chapter 11
War, Zionism, and Sacred Space

This chapter was written shortly after the violent Temple Mount incident between Israeli police and Palestinian demonstrators which took place on October 8, 1990. The essay constitutes my response to the rise of radical messianism within contemporary Israeli Orthodox Judaism.

1. Richard L. Rubenstein, *After Auschwitz: Radical Theology and Contemporary Judaism*, 1st ed. (Indianapolis: Bobbs-Merrill, 1966), p. 106.

2. See Baruch Kurzweil, "The New Canaanites," *Judaism*, vol. 2 (January 1953), pp. 3–15.

3. See "The Works of Creation" and "Souls of Chaos," in *Abraham Isaac Kook: The Lights of Penitence, Lights of Holiness, The Moral Principles, Essays, Letters, and Poems*, ed. and trans. Ben Zion Bokser (New York: Paulist Press, 1978), pp. 259–60 ,356–58. See also Ian Lustick, *For the Land and the Lord: Jewish Fundamentalism in Israel* (New York: Council on Foreign Relations, 1988), pp. 31–32.

4. Elizer Don-Yehiya, "Jewish Messianism, Religious Zionism, and Israeli Politics: The Impact and Origins of Gush Emunim," *Middle Eastern Studies*, vol. 23, no. 2 (April 1987), p. 227.

5. Notes to the address of Tzvi Yehudah Kook, "This Is the State of Which the Prophets Dreamed," *Nekuda*, no. 86 (April 26, 1985), pp. 6–7. For this citation, I am indebted to Lustick, *For the Land and the Lord*, p. 37.

6. Ibid.

7. E. Offenbacher, "Prayer on the Temple Mount," *Jerusalem Quarterly*, no. 36 (Summer 1985), p. 134.

8. Lustick, *For the Land and the Lord*, p. 45.

9. Elizer Don-Yehiya, "Jewish Messianism, Religious Zionism, and Israeli Politics," p. 225.

10. This subject is dealt with by Grace Halsell, *Prophecy and Politics: The Secret Alliance between Israel and the U.S. Christian Right* (Chicago: Lawrence Hill Books, 1986), pp. 95–116. Halsell is strongly biased against Israel. Nevertheless, her facts on right-wing Christian support for Gush Emunim are essentially correct.

11. Yehoshafat Harkabi has made a parallel between contemporary religious nationalists and the Zealots who were responsible for starting the ill-fated Judeo-Roman War of 66–70 C.E. and the Bar Kochba rebellion. See *Israel's Fateful Hour* (New York: Harper and Row, 1988), pp. 194–95. See also Harkabi, *The Bar Kochba Syndrome: Risk and Realism in International Politics*, trans. Max D. Ticktin, ed. David Altschuler (Chappaqua, N.Y.: Rossel Books, 1983).

12. For a succinct, authoritative discussion of the place of the Land in biblical Judaism, see W. D. Davies, *The Territorial Dimension of Judaism* (Berkeley: University of California Press, 1982), pp. 6–28.

13. See ibid., pp. 2–3; Raphael Patai, *Man and Temple* (London: Thomas Nelson, 1947), pp. 85, 95.

14. Jub. 8:12; B. Sanhedrin 37a. For other sources, see Davies, *The Territorial Dimension of Judaism*, p. 2.

15. Mircea Eliade, *The Sacred and the Profane: The Nature of Religion* (New York: Harcourt, Brace and World, 1959), pp. 20–67.

16. Etzion's remarks are quoted in Lustick, *For the Land the Lord*, pp. 97–98.

17. Harold Fisch, *The Zionist Revolution: A New Perspective* (London: Weidenfeld and Nicholson, 1978), pp. 85–86.

18. Ibid., p. 20.

19. Moses Maimonides, *Mishneh Torah*. English translation, *The Code of Maimonides: The Book of Judges*, trans. Abraham M. Hershman (New Haven: Yale University Press, 1949), chap. 11, p. 238.

20. They were so named because of the requirement that they be recited while standing.

21. The text of the *Shemoneh Esreh* is to be found in Joseph H. Hertz, ed., *The Authorized Daily Prayer Book*, rev. ed. (New York: Bloch Publishing Company, 1948). However, caution must be exercised in using Hertz's translation and commentary, both of which have a tendency to play down the national and territorial elements in the received text. For an important discussion of the place of Eretz Israel in Judaism, see Davies, *The Territorial Dimension of Judaism*.

22. See Gerson D. Cohen, *Messianic Postures of Ashkenazim and Sephardim (Prior to Sabbatai Zevi)*, Leo Baeck Memorial Lecture IX (New York: Leo Baeck Institute, 1967).

23. Gershom Scholem, *The Messianic Idea in Judaism and Other Essays on Jewish Spirituality* (New York: Schocken Books, 1971), p. 56.

24. "The French National Assembly: Debate on the Eligibility of the Jews for Citizenship," in *The Jew in the Modern World: A Documentary History*, ed. Paul Mendes-Flohr and Jehuda Reinharz (New York: Oxford University Press, 1980), p. 104.

25. Ibid.

26. See Arthur Hertzberg, *The French Enlightenment and the Jews* (New York: Columbia University Press, 1968), pp. 314–68.

27. An abbreviated version of Nicholas I's "Statutes Regarding the Military Service of Jews" (August 26, 1827) is found in Mendes-Flohr and Reinharz, *The Jews in the Modern World*, pp. 305–306.

28. See Stephen M. Berk, *Year of Crisis, Year of Hope: Russian Jewry and the Pogroms of 1881–1882* (Westport, Conn.: Greenwood Press, 1985), pp. 8–9.

29. See James H. Billington, *The Icon and the Axe: An Interpretive History of Russian Culture* (New York: Vintage Books, 1970), pp. 163–203.

30. The modernizing mood was perhaps expressed most characteristically in the celebrated poem of Yehudah Leib Gordon, *Hakiza Ammi* ("Awake My People," 1866), which reads in part:
Awake, my people! How long will you slumber?
The night has passed, the sun shines bright. . . .
This land of Eden [Russia] now opens its gates to you,
Her sons now call you "brother"!
How long will you dwell among them as a guest,
And why do you now affront them?
Already they have removed the weight of suffering from your shoulder,
They have lifted off the yoke from your neck
They have erased from their hearts gratuitous hatred and folly,
They give you their hand, they greet you with peace . . .
Open your heart to wisdom and knowledge
Become an enlightened people, and speak their language.

See Judah Leib Gordon, "Awake My People," in Mendes-Flohr and Reinharz, *The Jews in the Modern World,* pp. 312–13.

31. In 1855 the Jews of Odessa numbered 17,000 or 21.7 percent of the population; in 1895, 139,984 or 34.65 percent. See "Odessa," *Encyclopaedia Judaica,* vol. 12, pp. 1319–25.

32. On the Slavophiles, see Hans Rogger, "Russia," in *The European Right,* ed. Hans Rogger and Eugen Weber (Berkeley: University of California Press, 1966), pp. 443–99.

33. Berk, *Year of Crisis,* p. 71.

34. See chap. 5, "The Unmastered Trauma: Interpreting the Holocaust."

35. David Vital, *The Origins of Zionism* (Oxford: Oxford University Press, 1975), p. 109.

36. For a brief overview of Lilienblum's contribution to the evolution of modern Zionism, see ibid., pp. 116–22.

37. The bulk of the text of Pinsker's *Autoemancipation* is included in *The Zionist Idea: A Historical Analysis and Reader,* ed. Arthur Hertzberg (New York: Atheneum, 1970), pp. 181–95.

38. Ibid.

39. For an excellent biography of Herzl, see Ernst Pawel, *The Labyrinth of Exile: A Life of Theodore Herzl* (New York: Farrar, Straus and Giroux, 1989).

40. Ibid., pp. 214f. *Der Judenstaat* has been translated as *The Jewish State* (New York: Dover Publications, 1988), trans. Sylvia d'Avigdor, 1st ed. 1896.

41. The numbers differ slightly in different sources. I have used Howard M. Sachar, *A History of Israel: From the Rise of Zionism to Our Own Time* (New York: Alfred A. Knopf, 1979), p. 59.

42. "The Massacre of Jews at Kishinev," in Mendes-Flohr and Reinharz, *The Jew in the Modern World,* p. 330.

43. The actual territory was located in what is now Kenya.

44. Pawel, *Labyrinth of Exile,* p. 493.

45. Fisch, *The Zionist Revolution,* p. 79.

46. Sachar, *History of Israel,* pp. 62–63.

47. Seventh Zionist Congress, "Anti-Uganda Resolution," in Mendes-Flohr and Reinharz, *The Jew in the Modern World,* p. 437.

48. The text of the proclamation was printed in the *Palestine Post,* May 16, 1948; reprinted in Mendes-Flohr and Reinharz, *op. cit.,* pp. 477–79.

49. The Founding Program of Agudat Israel is in Mendes-Flohr and Reinharz, *The Jew in the Modern World,* pp. 446–47.

50. Gershon Greenberg, "From *Hurban* to Redemption: Orthodox Jewish Thought in the Munich Area, 1945–1948" in *Simon Wiesenthal Center Annual 1989* (New York: Philosophical Library, 1989), pp. 99–103.

51. Scholem, *The Messianic Idea,* p. 37.

52. B. Sanhedrin 98a.

53. Greenberg, "Orthodox Theological Responses to Kristallnacht," p. 1030.

54. Fisch, *The Zionist Revolution,* pp. 109–11.

55. See Sachar, *History of Israel,* p. 3. See also Michael Berenbaum, *After Tragedy and Triumph: Modern Jewish Thought and the American Experience* (Cambridge: Cambridge University Press, 1990), p. 150.

56. See Sachar, *History of Israel,* pp. 18–20.

57. See Howard M. Sachar, *A History of Israel.* Volume 2: *From the Aftermath of the Yom Kippur War* (New York: Oxford University Press, 1987), pp. 92–95.

58. Lustick, *For the Land and the Lord,* pp. 172–73.

59. Yoel Ben-Porat, "The Messiah Brigades Must Be Stopped," *Maariv,* May 10, 1987; English translation, *Israel Press Briefs,* no. 53 (May–June 1987), p. 14; cited by Lustick, *For the Land and the Lord,* p. 173.

60. Rabbi Eleazar Waldman, a Gush Emunim leader and member of Kenesset, has taught that wars are a natural part of the redemptive process and that "it is impossible to complete the Redemption by any other means." Eleazar Waldman, "Struggle on the Road to Peace," *Arzi,* vol. 2 (1982), p. 20; cited by Lustick, *For the Land and the Lord,* p. 82.

61. Raphael Patai, *The Hebrew Goddess,* 3d ed. (Detroit: Wayne State University Press, 1990), p. 33.

Chapter 12
The Meaning of Torah in Contemporary Jewish Theology

This essay was first delivered in German at the Fifteenth Annual Conference on Church and Judaism at Recklinghausen, Germany, in February 1963. It is an attempt to answer the question: What can the modern Jew retain of the Torah as the authoritative source of Jewish religious inspiration? My turning away from prophetic religion and the God of History to priestly religion and the God of Nature is evident in this effort.

The current version of the essay has been modified in style and tone, though not in basic content.

1. Søren Aabye Kierkegaard, *Concluding Unscientific Postscript,* trans. David F. Swenson (Princeton: Princeton University Press, 1941), p. 188.

2. For an overview of Reform Judaism as a "response to modernity," see Michael A. Meyer, *Response to Modernity: A History of the Reform Movement in Judaism* (New York: Oxford University Press, 1988).

3. Ernst Troeltsch, *The Social Teachings of the Christian Churches,* trans. Olive Wyon (London: Allen and Unwin, 1931), pp. 640ff; Max Weber, *The Protestant Ethic and the Spirit of Capitalism* (New York: Charles Scribner's Sons, 1958), pp. 98ff.

4. "The idea that pure religious faith is essentially moral rapidly became the theoretical basis and the practical operative principle of the Reform movement," Meyer, *Response to Modernity,* p. 65.

5. An influential expression of this tendency was Moritz Lazarus, *Die Ethik des Judenthums* (1898) (New York: Arno Press, 1980), 2 vols.; English translation, *The Ethics of Judaism,* trans. Henrietta Szold (Philadelphia: Jewish Publication Society of America, 1900–1901) (in four parts, parts 1 and 2 of which were published).

6. Abraham Geiger, *Judaism and Its History,* trans. Charles Neuburgh (New York: Bloch Publishing Co., 1911), pp. 61ff.; Max Wiener, *Abraham Geiger and Liberal Judaism: The Challenge of the Nineteenth Century,* compiled with a biographical introduction by Max Wiener, trans. Ernst J. Schlochauer (Philadelphia: Jewish Publication Society of America, 1962); Leo Baeck, *The Essence of Judaism,* trans. Irving Howe (New York: Schocken Books, 1948), p. 130.

7. *Mishnah Aboth,* I:14: "Simeon [the Son of Rabban Gamaliel] said . . . not learning but doing is the chief thing." The "doing" is, of course, preeminently the religious deed.

8. Hannah Arendt, *The Origins of Totalitarianism* (New York: Harcourt Brace, 1951), pp. 277ff.

9. By "facticity," I mean the irreducible givenness of the Jewish situation.

10. In the first edition, the text read "in all contemporary Jewish groups."

11. See "Atonement and Sacrifice in Contemporary Jewish Liturgy," *After Auschwitz*, 1st ed., pp. 93–112.

12. The traditional reading from Scripture for Yom Kippur is Lev. 16:1–34; the Reform substitution is Deut. 29:9–14; 30:11–20.

13. More of Kenya than Uganda was included in the proposed colony. For a brief discussion of the incident, see Howard M. Sachar, *A History of Israel: From the Rise of Zionism to Our Time* (New York: Alfred A. Knopf, 1979), pp. 53, 59–63.

14. Geiger, *Judaism and Its History*, pp. 76ff.

15. G. W. F. Hegel, *Early Theological Writings*, trans. T. M. Knox and Richard Kroner (Chicago: University of Chicago Press, 1948), pp. 145ff.

16. Ibid., p. 147: "Thus we are without any religious imagery which is home-grown or linked with our history, and we are without any political imagery whatever; all that we have is the remains of an imagery of our own, lurking amid the common people under the name of superstition."

17. Heinrich Heine, *Religion and Philosophy in Germany*, trans. John Snodgrass (Boston: Beacon Press, 1951), pp. 158ff. This is a paperback reprint of the edition of 1882.

18. Thirty days after the birth of a firstborn male child, it is incumbent upon the traditional Jewish father to offer a *cohen* or Jewish priest the equivalent of five silver shekels to "redeem" his son. The ceremony goes back to the archaic practice of offering a surrogate for the firstborn male child, who otherwise would have been a sacrificial offering, as indeed the first son was among the Canaanites and the Semitic Carthaginians. For the text of the ritual, see J. H. Hertz, ed., *The Authorised Daily Prayer Book* (New York: Bloch Publishing Co., 1957), pp. 1034ff. I discuss both the ritual and my own reaction to participating in it when my firstborn son was thirty days old in Richard L. Rubenstein, *Power Struggle: An Autobiographical Confession* (New York: Charles Scribner's Sons, 1974), pp. 112–14.

19. Jean-Paul Sartre, *Being and Nothingness*, trans. Hazel Barnes (New York: Philosophical Library, 1956), p. 237. The phrase, "each seeks the death of the other," appears in the dialectic of the Master and the Slave in G. W. F. Hegel, *The Phenomenology of the Mind*, trans. A. V. Miller (New York: Oxford University Press, 1979), p. 113. In German: "*Insofern es Tun des andern ist, geht also jeder auf den Tod des andern.*" Hegel, *Phänomenologie des Geistes* (Hamburg: Felix Meiner, 1952), p. 144.

20. Paul Tillich, *The Courage to Be* (New Haven: Yale University Press, 1952), pp. 186–90.

21. One of the principal conclusions of my research on rabbinic legend and homily was that the stress on the masculine aspects of divinity was at bottom a *defense* against the far greater anxiety and terror the ancient mother goddesses were capable of engendering. See Rubenstein, *The Religious Imagination: A Study in Psychoanalysis and Jewish Theology* (Indianapolis: Bobbs-Merrill, 1968), pp. 93–100.

22. Theodore Reik, *Ritual* (London: Hogarth Press, 1931), p. 71. See also Erich Wellisch, *Isaac and Oedipus* (London: Routledge and Kegan Paul, 1954).

Chapter 13
Death-of-God Theology and Judaism

The original version of this essay was the result of encounters with the leading American death-of-God theologians, Thomas J. J. Altizer, then a professor at Emory University in Atlanta, and William Hamilton, at the time a professor at Colgate-Rochester Theological Seminary in Rochester, N.Y. In November 1965 I was invited to respond to Altizer at the Conference on America and the Future of Theology held at Emory University. In May 1966 Hamilton and I were jointly invited to give the Gilkey Lecture at the University of Chicago. We were asked to discuss death of God theology from Jewish and Christian perspectives. These encounters enabled me to formulate explicitly my response to Christian radical theology. That response was embodied in the original version of this essay. The changes made in the present version are primarily matters of style and enhanced documentation. It is also important to note that Altizer's theology has developed and deepened since 1965.

1. For a discussion of Tillich's influence on my intellectual development, see Richard L. Rubenstein, *Power Struggle: An Autobiographical Confession* (New York: Charles Scribner's Sons, 1975), pp. 154–65.

2. Paul Johannes Tillich, *The Courage to Be* (New Haven: Yale University Press, 1952), pp. 184–85.

3. William Hamilton, "The Death of God Theologies," *Christian Scholar* (Spring 1965).

4. "Er ist das schmerzliche Gefühl des unglücklichen Bewusstseins, *dass Gott selbst gestorben ist.*" (Death is the bitterness of feeling of the 'unhappy consciousness,' when it feels that God is dead.) Georg Wilhelm Friedrich Hegel, *Phänomenologie des Geistes* (Hamburg: Felix Meiner, 1952), p. 546.

5. See Hamilton, "Death of God Theologies."

6. Friedrich Nietzsche, *The Gay Science*, in Walter Kaufmann, ed., *The Portable Nietzsche* (New York: Viking Press, 1954), pp. 95–96.

7. Martin Buber, *Eclipse of God: Studies in the Relation between Philosophy and Religion* (New York: Harper & Row, 1952).

8. In spite of the worldwide growth of religious belief and institutions, this is a position I still maintain in 1990.

9. Richard L. Rubenstein, "Thomas Altizer's Apocalypse," in *America and the Future of Theology*, ed. William Beardslee (Philadelphia: Westminster Press, 1966); revised and enlarged version in *The Theology of Thomas Altizer: Critique and Response*, ed. John Cobb (Philadelphia: Westminster Press, 1970).

10. The visit to Poland took place in October 1965.

11. Herbert Marcuse, *Eros and Civilization: A Philosophical Inquiry into Freud* (New York: Vintage Books, 1955); Norman O. Brown, *Life against Death: The Psychoanalytical Meaning of History* (Middletown, Conn.: Wesleyan University Press, 1959).

12. Harvey Cox, *The Secular City* (New York: Macmillan, 1965), pp. 115–23.

13. This essay was written before Vietnam, Watergate, the excesses of the

1980s, and the disenchantment of many Americans with politicians and the political process.

14. William Hamilton, "The New Optimism—from Prufrock to Ringo," in *Radical Theology and the Death of God,* ed. William Hamilton and Thomas J. J. Altizer (New York: Bobbs-Merrill, 1966), pp. 164–68.

15. See Thomas J. J. Altizer, *The Gospel of Christian Atheism* (Philadelphia: Westminster Press, 1966), pp. 33ff., and "Word and History," in Hamilton and Altizer, *Radical Theology,* pp. 121ff.

16. Sigmund Freud, *Totem and Taboo,* trans. James Strachey (New York: W. W. Norton, 1962) (1913), and *Moses and Monotheism,* trans. Katherine Jones (New York: Vintage Books, 1955) (1939).

17. Sigmund Freud, *Civilization and Its Discontents,* trans. Joan Riviere (London: The Hogarth Press and the Institute of Psychoanalysis, 1957) (1930).

18. For a discussion of Sartre's understanding of freedom, see Joseph S. Catalano, *A Commentary on Jean-Paul Sartre's Being and Nothingness* (New York: Harper and Row, 1974), pp. 196–213.

19. On bad faith or *mauvaise foi,* see Jean-Paul Sartre, *Being and Nothingness: An Essay on Phenomenological Ontology,* trans. Hazel Barnes (New York: Philosophical Library, 1956), pp. 47–72.

20. See Germain Brée, *Camus* (New York: Harbinger Books, 1964), pp. 8off.

21. Albert Camus, "Summer in Algiers," in *The Myth of Sisyphus,* trans. Justin O'Brien (New York: Vintage Books, 1961), p. 113.

22. Ibid., p. 113.

23. Isaac Bashevis Singer, *The Family Muskat,* trans. A. H. Gross (New York: Alfred A. Knopf, 1950), p. 611.

24. Thomas J. J. Altizer, "Theology and the Contemporary Sensibility," in William Beardslee, ed., *America and the Future of Theology* (Philadelphia: Westminster Press, 1967), p. 25.

25. Maurice Friedman, *Problematic Rebel: An Image of Modern Man* (New York: Random House, 1963), p. 206.

26. A similar idea was expressed by sociologist Peter Berger: "Religion implies the farthest reach of man's self-externalization, of *his infusion of reality with his own meanings.* Religion implies that the human order is projected into the totality of being. Put differently, religion is the audacious attempt to conceive of the entire universe as being humanly significant" (italics added). Peter Berger, *The Sacred Canopy: Elements of a Sociological Theory of Religion* (Garden City, N.Y.: Anchor Books, 1969), p. 28.

Chapter 14
Jews, Israel, and Liberation Theology

1. Marc H. Ellis, *Toward a Jewish Theology of Liberation,* 2d ed. (Maryknoll, N.Y.: Orbis Books, 1989); Dan Cohn-Sherbok, *On Earth As It Is In Heaven: Jews, Christians, and Liberation Theology* (Maryknoll, N.Y.: Orbis Books, 1987).

2. Marc H. Ellis, *Beyond Innocence and Redemption: Confronting the Holocaust and Israeli Power: Creating a Moral Future for the Jewish People* (San Francisco: Harper and Row, 1990); Rosemary Radford Ruether and Marc H. Ellis, eds., *Beyond Occupation: American Jewish, Christian, and Palestinian Voices for Peace* (Boston: Beacon Press, 1990). Ellis is also the co-editor of Marc H. Ellis and Otto Maduro,

The Future of Liberation Theology: Essays in Honor of Gustavo Gutierrez (Maryknoll, N.Y.: Orbis Books, 1989).

3. Marc H. Ellis, *A Year at the Catholic Worker* (New York: Paulist Press, 1978).

4. Ellis, *Toward a Jewish Theology of Liberation*, p. 2.

5. I am indebted to Helen Fein, *Accounting for Genocide* (New York: Free Press, 1979) for this concept.

6. See ch. 3, "Religion and the Origins of the Death Camps."

7. Cohn-Sherbok, *On Earth As It Is in Heaven*, p. 35.

8. Juan L. Segundo, *The Liberation of Theology*, trans. John Drury (Maryknoll, N.Y.: Orbis Books, 1976), p. 79.

9. Cohn-Sherbok, *On Earth As It Is in Heaven*, p. 43.

10. Ibid., pp. 45–46.

11. A good place to begin is Jacob Neusner, *From Politics to Piety: The Emergence of Pharisaic Judaism* (Englewood Cliffs, N.J.: Prentice-Hall, 1973).

12. See Irving (Yitzchak) Greenberg, "The Third Great Cycle in Jewish History," in *Perspectives* (New York: National Jewish Resource Center, 1981), p. 18.

13. This distinction is discussed in Max Weber, "Politics as a Vocation," in *From Max Weber: Essays in Sociology*, ed. H. H. Gerth and C. Wright Mills (New York: Oxford University Press, 1946), pp. 120ff.

14. Greenberg, "Third Great Cycle," pp. 25–26.

15. These views are expressed in Robert Shorris, *Jews without Mercy: A Lament* (Garden City: Doubleday, 1982).

16. Max Weber, "Politics as a Vocation," p. 79.

17. Roberta Strauss Feuerlicht, *The Fate of the Jews: A People Torn between Israeli Power and Jewish Ethics* (New York: Times Books, 1983), p. 31.

18. Kaplan is cited in Ellis, *Toward a Jewish Theology of Liberation*, p. 59.

19. On the subject of Israel's ambiguous statements concerning the possibility that it possesses nuclear weapons, see Alan Dowty, "Going Public with the Bomb," in *Transaction: Social Science and Modern Society*, pp. 52–58.

20. See Kevin Tools, "The Man behind Iraq's Supergun," *New York Times Magazine*, August 26, 1990.

21. Robert Harkavy, "Survival Imperatives," *Transaction: Social Science and Modern Society*, January/February 1986, p. 63. Harkavy's article contains an excellent discussion of the reasons why Israel's survival requires a nuclear deterrent.

22. Ellis, *Toward a Jewish Theology of Liberation*, p. 134.

23. Harkavy, "Survival Imperatives," p. 64.

24. I have addressed that issue in detail in Richard L. Rubenstein, *The Age of Triage* (Boston: Beacon Press, 1983).

Chapter 15
Muslims, Jews, and the Western World: A Jewish View

About three weeks after Iraq's invasion of Kuwait on August 2, 1990, I was interviewed by Lloyd Eby of the *World & I* on Jewish-Muslim-Western relations for a special issue of the magazine on Islam (February 1991). Also interviewed by Dr. Eby were Sheik M. A. Zaki Badawi, Principal of the Muslim College of London, and Sheik Ahmad Kuftaro, Grand Mufti of Syria. At the time, I was attending a worldwide, interreligious conference, the Third Assembly of the

World's Religions, in San Francisco. I have edited the text of the interview for reasons of style and, in a few places, to clarify my position and take into account the Gulf War and its aftermath.

For my understanding of contemporary Islam, I am especially indebted to Daniel Pipes, *In the Path of God: Islam and Political Power* (New York: Basic Books, 1983).

Chapter 16
God after the Death of God

This is a revised version of an essay that first appeared in Richard L. Rubenstein, *Morality and Eros* (New York: McGraw-Hill, 1970), pp. 183–96. I have had a problem with the use of pronouns to designate God, who is beyond both masculinity and femininity. In the original version the pronoun "He" was used. I have let it stand, although I recognize fully its inadequacy.

1. Gershom Scholem, *Major Trends in Jewish Mysticism*, 2d ed. (New York: Schocken Books, 1946), p. 21.

2. See G. W. F. Hegel, "Vorrede," *Phänomenologie des Geistes*, ed. Johannes Hoffmeister (Hamburg: Felix Meiner, 1952), pp. 29ff.; English version, *Phenomenology of Spirit*, trans. A. V. Miller (Oxford: Oxford University Press, 1977), pp. 32ff. See also G. W. F. Hegel, *The Difference between Fichte's and Schelling's System of Philosophy*, trans. and ed. H. H. Harris and Walter Cerf (Albany: State University of New York Press, 1977), pp. 89–103. For an interpretation of Hegel's use of *Verstand* and *Vernunft*, see John Edward Toews, *Hegelianism: The Path to Dialectical Humanism, 1805–1841* (Cambridge: Cambridge University Press, 1985), pp. 51f.

3. G. W. F. Hegel, *Begriff der Religion* (Leipzig: Felix Meiner, 1928), p. 148.

4. "For Hegel, the real object of religious thought is Man himself: every theology is necessarily an anthropology." Alexandre Kojève, *Introduction to the Reading of Hegel*, trans. James H. Nichols, Jr., ed. Allen Bloom (New York: Basic Books, 1969), p. 71.

5. On the *En-Sof*, see Scholem, *Jewish Mysticism*, pp. 11ff.

6. For a brief overview see "Universals," *The Encyclopedia of Philosophy* (New York: Macmillan, 1967), vol. 8, pp. 194–206.

7. David Reisman, *The Lonely Crowd* (New Haven: Yale University Press, 1950). See also Marshall McLuhan, *The Medium Is the Message* (New York: Bantam Books, 1967).

8. See Samuel Noah Kramer, ed., *Mythologies of the Ancient World* (Garden City: Anchor Books, 1961), pp. 103–4.

9. Hegel, *Phänomenologie des Geistes*, p. 564 (*Phenomenology of Spirit*, trans. A. V. Miller, p. 493).

10. G. W. F. Hegel, *The Phenomenology of Mind*, trans. J. B. Baillie (London: George Allen and Unwin, 1931), p. 81. At times I prefer the Miller translation, at other times the older Baillie translation; hence the use of two translations of *The Phenomenology*.

11. Ibid., p. 86.

12. J. N. Findlay, *Hegel: A Reexamination* (London: George Allen and Unwin, 1958), p. 48.

13. Ibid., pp. 48–49.

14. Ibid., pp. 34–47.

15. Pierre Teilhard de Chardin, *The Divine Milieu* (New York: Harper and Row, 1965). For a sympathetic presentation of Teilhard's religious philosophy, see Henri de Lubac, *Teilhard de Chardin: The Man and His Meaning*, trans. René Hague (New York: Mentor-Omega Books, 1967).

16. See Scholem, *Jewish Mysticism*, pp. 244–86.

17. Gershom Scholem, *On the Kabbalah and Its Symbolism*, trans. Ralph Mannheim (New York: Schocken Books, 1965), p. 107.

18. Ibid., p. 14.

19. There is some minor disagreement concerning the Greek text translated as "all in all" in English, which we note but which need not detain us. I have accepted "all in all," the traditional translation and the one used by the Oxford New English Bible and the Jerusalem Bible.

20. See Richard L. Rubenstein, *My Brother Paul* (New York: Harper and Row, 1972), p. 170.

21. Sigmund Freud, *Beyond the Pleasure Principle*, trans. James Strachey (London: Hogarth Press, 1950).

22. Norman O. Brown, *Life Against Death* (New York: Vintage Books, 1959), p. 51.

23. Masao Abe, "Kenotic God and Dynamic Sunyata," in *The Emptying God: A Buddhist-Jewish-Christian Conversation*, ed. John B. Cobb, Jr., and Christopher Ives (Maryknoll, N.Y.: Orbis Books, 1990), p. 27.

24. Ronald Goetz, "God: Love or Death?" *Christian Century*, vol. 84 (1967), pp. 1487–90.

Acknowledgments

These chapters appeared in earlier versions elsewhere:
Chapter 1 in *The Reconstructionist*, 19 October 1962; Chapter 2 in *The Christian Scholar*, Winter 1963; Chapter 3 in *The Reconstructionist*, 5 and 19 May 1961; Chapter 4 in *The World and I*, July 1991, and in Carol Rittner and John K. Roth, eds., *Memory Offended: The Auschwitz Convent Controversy* (New York: Praeger, 1991); Chapter 5 in *Humanities and Society*, vol. 2, no. 4, Fall 1979, and in Richard L. Rubenstein, *The Age of Triage: Fear and Hope in an Overcrowded World* (Boston: Beacon Press, 1983); Chapter 6 in Michael Berenbaum, ed., *A Mosaic of Victims: Non-Jews Persecuted and Murdered by the Nazis* (New York: New York University Press, 1990); Chapters 8 and 9, originally "The Silence of God: Philosophical and Religious Reflection of the Holocaust," in Richard L. Rubenstein and John K. Roth, *Approaches to Auschwitz: The Holocaust and Its Legacy* (Atlanta: John Knox Press, 1987); Chapter 10, in *The Reconstructionist*, 29 April 1960; Chapter 12 in *The Journal of Bible and Religion* [now the *Journal of the American Academy of Religion*], vol. 32, no. 2, April 1964; Chapter 14 in Otto Maduro, ed., *Judaism, Christianity and Liberation: An Agenda for Dialogue* (Maryknoll, N.Y.: Orbis Books, 1991); Chapter 15 in *The World and I*, February 1991; Chapter 16 in Richard L. Rubenstein, *Morality and Eros* (New York: McGraw-Hill, 1970).

Index

AFTER AUSCHWITZ

Designed by Ann Walston

Composed by Brevis Press
in Palatino with Trajanus Italic display

Printed by Edwards Brothers, Inc.
on 50-lb. Glatfelter Natural